SIMON RATTLE

Nicholas Kenyon has been Director of the BBC Proms since 1996. He was a music critic for *The New Yorker*, *The Times* and the *Observer*, and was Cc͟ r ͟ ͟er, BBC Radio 3, from 1992 to 1998, responsible for the awar͟ ͟ ͟ng Radio 3 seasons 'Fairest Isle' and 'Sounding the Century'. He ͟s ar͟ ͟ ͟e history of the BBC Symphony Orchestra and edited the in͟ ne͟ ͟ ͟lume *Authenticity and Early Music*. He is now Controller, B͟ ar͟ ͟ Live Events and Television Classical Music, and was a ͟ ͟ ͟ ͟BE in 2001. He lives in London with his wife and four c͟ ͟ ͟ren.

SIMON RATTLE
From Birmingham to Berlin

NICHOLAS KENYON

faber and faber

First published in 1987
by Faber and Faber Limited
3 Queen Square London WC1N 3AU
This new edition first published in 2001
Published in the USA in 2001 by Faber and Faber, Inc.
This paperback edition first published in 2002

Photoset by RefineCatch Ltd, Bungay, Suffolk
Printed in England by Clays Ltd, St Ives plc

The right of Nicholas Kenyon to be identified as author
of this work has been asserted in accordance with
Section 77 of the Copyright, Designs and Patents Act 1988

A CIP record for this book
is available from the British Library
ISBN 0-571-21244-1

2 4 6 8 10 9 7 5 3 1

Contents

CONTENTS

Introduction

On 7 September 2002, Simon Rattle conducts his inaugural concert as music director of the Berlin Philharmonic Orchestra, at the beginning of a ten-year contract, and then takes the orchestra on a European tour. Typically, the Berlin programme is a bold declaration of intent: Thomas Adès's *Asyla* (premiered by Rattle and already a contemporary classic) and Mahler's Fifth Symphony (which will be recorded and released around the world within a month by EMI). So now it begins: the first act of a drama whose prologue began over three years before, on 23 June 1999, when the orchestra sensationally elected Rattle as its new music director in succession to Claudio Abbado.

That appointment was front-page news in papers across Britain and Germany. Even the *Sun* ran an editorial. (It later transpired that the editor had been at Rattle's CBSO Sibelius cycle when he was a student and had never forgotten it.) One of the world's most traditional musical institutions had elected a British conductor of forty-four as the heir to Furtwängler and Karajan. It was a massive leap of faith.

Natural elation at finding a world-beating young Brit – in any field, they seem to be rarer and rarer – masked something more important for music: the fact that this great orchestra had made a decisive choice in favour of the future, rather than attempting to recreate the past or pro-long the present. As this book makes clear, no one knows – even the orchestra itself does not know – what sort of continual revolution Rattle will bring to Berlin. He had major problems during 2001, ensuring that the conditions were right to sign his contract. But he finally signed in a ceremony in Berlin on 19 September 2001, the night after a triumphant performance of Schoenberg's *Gurrelieder* (recorded by EMI). His artistic renewal of the Berlin Philharmonic will be a process to watch, because it will be about creating a new model of an orchestra for the twenty-first century. Rattle is a musical force of nature, and he now has a world stage on which to operate. It cannot be anything but important for the future of music: risky, thrilling and probably a touch dangerous.

When I first wrote about Simon Rattle, fifteen years ago now, his was clearly a most stunning talent but no one could predict whether it would last or where it would lead him. It was his legendary – some would say stubborn – commitment to Birmingham that the first edition of this book explored. That commitment did not waver in the face of success around the world, and it was more than another decade later, an amazing eighteen years after he took on the job, that he bowed out of Birmingham.

In retrospect, three things that were vitally important for Rattle's musical future happened just as the book appeared in 1987. One was Rattle's long-delayed first appearance with the Berlin Philharmonic that autumn; the second was his début with the recently created period-instrument Orchestra of the Age of Enlightenment, and the third was the creation of the Birmingham Contemporary Music Group; together these can be seen as the central elements in Rattle's musical self-renewal in the decade that followed. In the book he was quoted as saying, 'My greatest danger is that I could become too lazy. It could all be too easy.' It didn't become too easy; he saw to that.

The first edition of this book aroused plenty of interest, and although it was a essentially a topical piece of journalism, it kept being used and referred to – at least, I took the many sentences from it that I found dotted around Rattle profiles over the following years to be the sincerest form of flattery. Rattle has always strictly rationed his public statements and interviews, so the book continued to be useful. A while after I joined the BBC in 1992 and stopped being a music critic, Jilly Cooper wrote nicely in *The Times* that she had been reading the book and how lucky young Simon Rattle had been to have had his biography written by the Controller of Radio 3. That wasn't how it was at all, but he and I did establish a different working relationship when I took over the BBC Proms in 1996, and one of the things that makes me cringe with embarrassment in retrospect is the first programme suggestion I sent him for a CBSO Prom. Happily, he ignored it completely and gave us something much better.

I had said I would not update the book. But promises are made to be broken, and Belinda Matthews at Faber persuaded me that the story should be brought up to date at the vital moment when he is poised to take over Berlin. It is still journalism, not history, still a totally open, unfinished story, and I'm sure Simon is still irritated that it has to be written at all. My thanks go especially to him and to Candace for their good-humoured patience, help and co-operation. At Faber, it was Donald Mitchell and Patrick Carnegy who originally suggested the book; I thank Belinda Matthews for all her work in making this new edition happen, especially for somehow convincing me that updating the book would be easy. It wasn't. In the end, only two chapters remain substantially as they were, because so much has changed in fifteen years.

This is still very much work in progress. Much of the story is told in the immediate, direct words of Simon Rattle and those who have worked with him. That retains the flavour of the present and highlights the fact that there are no final judgements here. (When the book originally appeared, it was suggested that I should have included my own considered appraisal of his work; that wasn't the purpose of the book, though some judgements by others were quoted. The same is true of this new edition.) I am most grateful to all Simon's friends and colleagues who made the time to speak openly and honestly about him and his work. As before, Martin Campbell-White and his colleagues at the Askonas Holt artists agency (who have managed Simon from the beginning of his career), Rona Eastwood, Clare Seddon and now Lisa Battersby, have been tirelessly helpful in unearthing material about Simon and in answering many questions. Beresford King-Smith has published his excellent seventy-fifth anniversary history of the CBSO, *Crescendo*, which is much fuller on the subject of the orchestra and its work than I could be; he has generously looked up material for me in the CBSO archives and read some of the new material. Jim Berrow managed to find the Central Television documentary about Rattle we made when the first edition of this book was published, and David Jackson of BBC Wales supplied a TV documentary made when Rattle left the CBSO.

The original interviews were transcribed by Jane Ruthven and Clare Ellis, and the new interviews for this book were transcribed by Yvette Pusey, who has also given invaluable administrative help and support. Above all, for Ghislaine and our family, having this happen again is probably like a recurring bad dream, but thanks to them for all the advice and encouragement.

For this paperback edition, some additions have been made to bring the story up to the time when Rattle takes over in Berlin. I have taken the opportunity to correct some errors and thank those who pointed them out, especially Elmar Weingarten, Andrew Clark, Ed Smith and the editors of the German edition which appears at the same time as this paperback. I have retained some small factual repetitions because of the interleaved chronological structure of the book. I have enlarged the discography to include all Rattle's recordings, not only those currently available from EMI.

NICHOLAS KENYON
The Red House, Aldeburgh
June 2002

CHAPTER ONE

'The stakes are just so high for everyone . . .'
Rattle 2000

Rehearsing in overdrive: Rattle with the players of the Berlin Philharmonic
(photo Reinhard Friedrich)

September 2000. In Berlin's dramatic, multi-angled Philharmonie, the music director designate of the Berlin Philharmonic Orchestra is rehearsing the orchestra, in overdrive, for a concert tonight in the Berlin Festival. The momentum of the rehearsal is unstoppable. There is a sense of shared energy, of shared exploration. You cannot imagine Herbert von Karajan behaving like this, wandering among the musicians while they are playing and having a look at the first flute's part in order to sort out a problem.

Janáček's music is not home territory for the Berlin Philharmonic any more than it was for Karajan. Rattle has performed Janáček's *Glagolitic Mass* with them once before, a decade ago, but *Taras Bulba* is entirely new to them, and quite awkward, with a lot of details to clarify. 'We need to hear the trills – can the wind just do that separately please?' Not long ago, the Berlin Philharmonic might have regarded it as an insult for a section to be asked to rehearse separately; now they are willing collaborators with Rattle's enquiring musical mind. 'I know it's impossible,' he admits to the first violins at one point during *Taras Bulba* as they struggle to be eloquent in an awkward high position. 'This would be a wonderful melody if only it was in another key.' As a concession to the Berliners, he gives them the bar numbers in German, but for everything else seems more comfortable talking English. At one point he urges them to 'keep it very relaxed to get those rhythms right'. And that is a feature of his conducting style now: far less brittle than in the early days, far more rounded, but with the famous incisiveness and drive undimmed.

The Philharmonie, Hans Scharoun's famous creation of the 1960s, is a rare example of an avant-garde building that still looks adventurous. Gold- (or perhaps mustard-)plated on the outside, intimate on the inside, it has proved an ideal example of a concert hall where the audience can feel drawn into the music but the music itself still has space to speak. I've been in it for a rehearsal only once before, when Bernard Haitink's massive account of Mahler's Eighth Symphony had just room enough to resonate in the empty hall – I didn't like to think what it would be like with an audience as well.

After the final rehearsal, Rattle is patience itself backstage, constantly available for queries about stage layout, chatting over a few points with the players. We retire to the dressing room with his agent, Martin Campbell-White, for a talk that turns into an off-the-record debate about his future plans ('and don't put that in the ****ing book'). We chat about the German language problem: 'They said to me, "Actually, Simon, until it's a bit better, what we find hard is if we get half a sentence in one and half in the other." There was a famous fortnight when I came and everything was apparently neuter. That will change. You want to be an adult when you communicate, and I'm still only six or seven.'

As we're leaving, he suddenly sees fellow conductor Kent Nagano – who is now an important colleague in Berlin – and abandons everyone to have an intense talk with him. Quite recently he said that Nagano's Salzburg performance of Messiaen's *Eclairs sur l'au-delà* was the finest he had heard: 'After twenty minutes I was simply overcome with tears. I sobbed through the rest of the piece.' It's clear that Rattle sees good relationships with Berlin musical colleagues, including Nagano, and Daniel Barenboim whom he defeated in the Philharmonic vote, as vital for the unity of the city's music-making in the future. But that unity was to be tested as Rattle and the Philharmonic made their bid in 2001 for more of Berlin's musical resources and for control of their hall.

The Berlin Festival's adventurous scenario for the end of the twentieth century is drawn in big, bold, single-composer concert programmes, reaching right across the symphonic repertory of the last hundred years and including some chamber music as well. The small hall of the Philharmonie hosts a beautiful little Dallapiccola concert and a Nono concert in the next few days. Rattle has claimed the all-Janáček concert and Nagano, rehearsing for the following day's concert with his Berlin Radio Symphony Orchestra, has an all-Berg programme; we don't speculate on who has drawn the short straw. As usual, Rattle has been clever at choosing repertory with which he feels totally at home, but where he will have something new to bring to the orchestra.

Back in the Philharmonie that evening, the sense of anticipation among the Berlin audience is palpable, the performance is staggering, and the blazing impact of the *Glagolitic Mass* in the hall is physical as well as musical. These two Janáček works are not necessarily crowd-pleasing pieces, but they have a huge effect in the Philharmonie, where everyone feels connected to the platform, drawn inwards as part of one group of people, the orchestra and choir indivisible from the audience. The reception is overwhelming in its enthusiasm; the Berlin audience has already clearly taken Rattle to its heart. Afterwards, it is strange to see him in Karajan's wood-panelled dressing room, full of imposed *gravitas*, so much quieter and more reserved than any backstage situation I've encountered him in before. And already there are passionate devotees: a lady audience member of uncertain years flourishes a camera the moment the dressing-room door opens, and Rattle begs for a minute's peace – 'please just let me get myself sorted out, and then you're fine' – before submitting to the obligatory snap. His first words are for colleagues from EMI: 'Ha, well, you know there's another version of the *Glagolitic* we haven't recorded yet!' And there are similarly pointed comments for everyone else in the room.

All this conceals a lot. Behind the scenes, the previous week has seen the biggest, most difficult revolution in the Berlin Philharmonic's recent history, and that, for this ego-scarred orchestra, is saying something. In taking on the Berlin job, even though he does not start until the autumn of 2002, Rattle has been already been plunged into a maelstrom, both political and musical. He is faced with the situation where the orchestra's intendant, Elmar Weingarten, has fallen out with Claudio Abbado and is about to leave, yet Abbado at that moment is ill and seems hardly likely to feature strongly in the orchestra's future plans. (In fact, against all the odds, Abbado conducted both a tour of Japan including *Tristan und Isolde* that autumn, and the anniversary Verdi *Requiem* in January 2001, both Herculean efforts carried out in great pain. Then, in improving health during 2001, he gave two superb and innovative Beethoven cycles in Rome and Vienna which players described as one of their best tours ever – with anyone.)

This week's revolution was not the appointment of Rattle, but the changes that followed in its wake. In an extremely tense series of meetings, Rattle and his new colleagues worked towards a new structure for the orchestra and it has just been accepted almost unanimously by the players, though a political struggle was to follow in the parliament. In particular, the existence of the virtually autonomous media committee, which had been running the orchestra's recording and video work and had dominated the planning of the orchestra to an alarming degree, was something that Rattle felt everyone had to agree to change if his music directorship was to work. In the past this media committee was all-powerful, and Rattle had come up against it very early in his relationship with Berlin (see chapter 2). The committee determined everything the orchestra recorded, irrespective of the concert programmes. This led to major conflicts: world-famous conductors would be elbowed out of the concert season and dates changed at the last minute if lucrative recording ventures presented themselves. Bernard Haitink had to make way for Nikolaus Harnoncourt; unsuitable dates with Lorin Maazel found their way into the diary because he brought a recording project with him. The media committee in fact controlled a separate orchestral company of its own, channelling all the income from records, videos, new recordings and Karajan's vast archive back to the orchestral players themselves.

The day after the Janáček concert, Rattle reflected on the events of the previous week:

SIMON RATTLE In every way at this point the stakes are just so high for everyone that psychologically it is very different for me from anything that has gone before. It's just as high stakes for the orchestra and the members as it is for me, and there really isn't any safety net under there. It was a serious possibility that after all this I would have to say no to them and not take up the post unless we changed things. It was a question of how they worked and what drove the artistic policy of the orchestra. Fortunately we have agreed, we've moved forward and it is the first breakthrough.

It was fascinating sitting last week with a group of ten of the leading lights of the orchestra and a violinist saying to me, 'Look, we have to ask you this: are we going to lose our repertory? Are you going to let us play our old favourites? Do you love what we have to offer as well?' And I said to him, 'The first thing you have to realize is that I have absolutely equal and opposite fears that you are not going to find me German enough; you are not going to find me steeped in your tradition. But if I didn't love this tradition, you can be dead sure I would not have stepped anywhere near it.' Now in fact there will probably be much less Mahler than they have been playing recently because they've got to get it out of their system a bit. Even Brahms: there basically hasn't been two years in the last twenty when they haven't toured all of Brahms's symphonies. The only difference has been which are paired together in the programmes! Of course they are wonderful and everyone wants to hear them play these pieces but actually they need some breathing space, just as in Birmingham we had to decide not to do the *Symphonie fantastique* for a few years.

It was a battle for me, an internal battle, knowing whether I should say, 'Yes, I'm prepared to be thought about as your conductor.' The question was: can I really do this? And is it fair to the orchestra; is it what they need? But there's a wonderful thing Karajan said (and not everything he said was wonderful by any means) about the orchestra's sound, which is that it's like one of those English lawns, which is not finished when you've bought the garden; you have to cut it once a week, and water it twice a day for years and years. That's really true, and the fact that I want different-coloured plants on the side of the lawn, or more colours, more variety in the types of plant, doesn't mean that the basic garden is changed. It just enables the same thing to be more flexible and do more different things. They are moving from being an orchestra that had one very, very distinct style, to which every composer had to fit, towards the idea that you do play differently for different composers, and that's a big psychological step.

Do you think they realized how much change would be necessary if you came?
In some ways no. I think a lot of them looked at what we had done and achieved in Birmingham and the things that I stood for, had fought for, and realized that this was what they needed. There was the feeling that they

were standing still, and they had the knowledge that, really, this cannot go on. They could easily become very isolated, carrying on with their music-making with the world changing around them. They desperately need to spread their wings. There is now a generation of musicians for whom Harnoncourt is not a provocation, he's a fact of life, part of the grammar of music-making today. There are styles of playing that may not be to everyone's tastes but that are absolutely now a part of what musicians need to know. I want to draw as many people into playing stylistically as possible so it's not a separate, specialist thing. That doesn't happen all at once.

So the structure you have persuaded them into is . . . ?
No, I'm sorry, I didn't. We all came into this together. On the other hand they did know it was necessary because otherwise there would be a problem. What's interesting is that the orchestra is actually now more democratic, the orchestra will now have more say than they used to, with the structure of [a committee consisting of] two players, intendant, and music director. It can work only with both a conductor and an intendant who have the confidence in their ability to get people together and agree. It's a time when everything is changing; the media is changing. Do you know how many records Karajan made a year?

I wouldn't be surprised if it was ten or twelve . . .
The average was twenty-four. He did only six programmes a year with them but made twenty-four records. You want to know why the CD market has flooded? They flooded it. But it was another world, and it's gone.

Autumn 2000. What makes Simon Rattle's music-making unique? One aspect that marks him out from even the greatest conductors of our age is his stylistic versatility. There is no one else in the world today – and, given the unprecedented breadth of the repertory these days, that means ever – who conducts such a wide range of music at such a high level. In the past, particularly the past of the Berlin Philharmonic, the symphonic conductor would take in the whole Germanic tradition from Bach and Handel onwards. Nowadays there has been a narrowing of the symphony orchestra repertory, a perhaps regrettable result of the period-instrument movement, which has made conductors at the moment nervous even to touch the baroque, and curiously reluctant to explore Haydn and Mozart. (The Bach anniversary year of 2000 brought some movement here, with András Schiff and Murray Perahia both encouraging conventional orchestras back to Bach, while period-instrument performances also became less dogmatic, more pragmatic.) But Rameau? Since I heard Andrew Davis with typical good-humoured flair try out a rearranged Rameau dance suite with the New York Philharmonic two decades ago, I can't think of any Rameau being programmed for modern orchestras, except by Rattle, for whom it has become a touchstone of an orchestra's flexibility and willingness to adapt.

Because Rattle has embraced the period-instrument movement in a way no other mainstream conductor has yet achieved, his range is now enormous. For example, in the 1999 BBC Proms, Rattle conducted Rameau's *Les boréades* with the Orchestra of the Age of Enlightenment, Bernstein's *Wonderful Town* with the Birmingham Contemporary Music Group, Mahler's Second Symphony and music by Kurtág, Beethoven and Ravel with the Vienna Philharmonic. Add to this range the extraordinary concert performance of Wagner's *Parsifal* in the 2000 BBC Proms and it becomes clear that no one else could do all this at such a stratospherically high level of achievement. That is why it is worth thinking of Simon Rattle as more than just another great conductor, but as *the* characteristic conductor of the twenty-first century.

For Rattle, the autumn of 2000 was a golden period of musical variety tantamount to stylistic promiscuity. He took full advantage of the freedom between ending his music directorship of the CBSO and committing himself to Berlin. Having started the autumn at the Berlin Festival, he leapt to Leeds, taking the opportunity to bring with him his mother Pauline and sister Susan who had travelled over from Liverpool. (His father Denis, who featured prominently in his musical upbringing, see chapter 3, had died of cancer in 1996.) In Yorkshire Simon paid a long-standing debt of loyalty to the Leeds International Pianoforte Competition and its founder Fanny Waterman by once again conducting the finals with the CBSO, following neophyte pianists around the tortuous corners of Brahms's First and Tchaikovsky's First Concertos. Then he went straight to New York with Candace Allen, his wife since 1996, to revive his Duke Ellington project, which was already an EMI recording and involved Candace's uncle, Ellington's long-time collaborator Luther Henderson, as arranger.

Then it was back to London for an intense Mahler Ninth Symphony with the LSO, then a huge Berlioz series and tour with the Orchestra of the Age of Enlightenment, the largest project they have undertaken, then off to the Vienna Philharmonic for Beethoven concerts, a recording and a tour, and to Amsterdam before Christmas to begin rehearsals with the Rotterdam Philharmonic for *Tristan und Isolde* (see chapter 12).

Apart from the jealous thought that no one should be allowed anything like this much fun, the 2000 autumn schedule demonstrates the breadth of Rattle's musical enthusiasms. But every conductor meets his stylistic Waterloo, and Rattle seemingly met it with Duke Ellington. He has conducted Gershwin and Bernstein with flair and success, and his performances of *Porgy and Bess* and *Wonderful Town* were unforgettable. But the jazz-meets-orchestra equation of the Ellington arrangements is another matter, and far trickier. This is a project to which he is enormously attached, and that audiences love, but which critics have decided to hate. It has been the most controversial area of Rattle's music-making in recent years.

In fact Rattle had originally planned to be in Birmingham during this period, giving the centenary performances of Elgar's *The Dream of Gerontius*. But these were now being conducted by the CBSO's music director Sakari Oramo, who had become anxious about the amount of work Rattle had been continuing to do with the orchestra and not surprisingly was concerned to put his own mark on the CBSO's major projects. So Rattle took the chance to withdraw from *Gerontius* and instead to revive the Ellington recording project that was so close to his heart. The Carnegie Hall date was made possible very late in the day thanks to the controversial director there, Franz Xaver Ohnesorg, who was shortly to jump ship and join Rattle in Berlin. He rehearsed with the Orchestra of St Luke's up in Riverside Church, the imposing building at the top of Riverside Drive where you can almost touch Harlem.

The critics of Rattle's Ellington recording have been unrelenting. Brian Hunt wrote of the recording in the *Daily Telegraph*: 'On behalf of the classical music world, I'd like to say sorry to anyone who plays, listens to or cares about jazz. For the past twenty years you have been subjected to attitudes from this highbrow side of the fence that range from the patronizing to the exploitative to something akin to a hostile takeover. The last straw must be *Classic Ellington*, this month's new release from Simon Rattle and the CBSO. Should we expect you to laugh or cry as the distinguished maestro and his virtuoso orchestra crash through Duke Ellington's tunes like a runaway bulldozer?'

Hunt criticized Rattle but praised 'the superb arranger Luther Henderson'. Which is ironic in view of how it all began.

SIMON RATTLE At the age of six I heard the Ellington band for the first time in Liverpool. I had not been taken to Lena Horne the previous year because I was too young. But if I had gone the man playing the piano would have been Luther Henderson, who was to be my future uncle! This music has always been in my system. My father was a jazz musician, it was all around me; it was a passion that was passed on to me and it has always been something I have been involved in. So when Candace Allen, who I had talked to about everything except music, and I got together, and I came into my new family, not only do I find Miles Davis had been one of her father's best friends, and her aunt Billie had been in the original cast of *On the Town*, but that Billie's husband was Luther Henderson who was working with Ellington from the early fifties!

The project came through Peter Alward at EMI, who said, 'You made a jazz album that really worked with the London Sinfonietta that people really liked. Why don't you do something with Ellington?' My immediate response was that it's very different doing Paul Whiteman arrangements where the improvising element is relatively minimal; the element of how it swings and walks is not so problematical. But until I sat down with Luther I had no idea that it had been such an idea of his and Ellington's to do this music with orchestras. They worked it out together. Now of course one's into authorship here and that's thought about completely differently in the jazz world. In fact the idea of a version that stayed the same would be nonsense to them. Ellington and Luther did 'Harlem' for orchestra but it would keep changing every time they played it. They'd go away on tour and it would come back unrecognizable, morphing before your eyes into a completely different piece.

Orchestras give a different sort of weight to this music. There's a long history of American 'pops' orchestras which are fantastically good, but in this music where there are types of calls and responses back and forth, the orchestra is not there just as a backing group. The way we did it, it had never been done quite like that before. It's a challenge for people on both sides of the spectrum and whichever side you are on you might find it irritating. No one's pretending that this is anything other than it is – it's not crossover, it's more the idea of two sides cross-pollinating, and the idea of how an orchestra reacts to that process is incredibly healthy. You have to try to come to terms with a new sense of rhythm. Luther had been really impressed when the CBSO came to New York and did the Rameau *Boréades* suite and he said, 'They can swing Rameau and so they can swing Ellington.'

At Carnegie Hall there was an audience full of musicians, full of every race and nationality. The critical response was mixed but mostly a little bit bewildered. In a way that's a shame but it doesn't make it any the less valid.

There was a room full of very happy people. For me it was a return to roots, and it was sad that only one of my parents was there to hear it . . . He would have enjoyed it so much.

Then it was quickly back to rehearsals in Birmingham and down to London's Barbican Hall for the first concert of a new tour by the Birmingham Contemporary Music Group, taking music by Pavel Haas, György Ligeti and Colin Matthews to some of the centres of European music-making. Rattle's commitment to contemporary music and British music is well known. He commissioned many new works in Birmingham and toured them around the world, and regards new work as an essential, natural part of being a conductor in a way matched by too few other conductors. The formation of the BCMG as part of the CBSO was a milestone in the history of the orchestra, and the young ensemble has gradually become more independent of its parent. Rattle's bringing together in 1998, for performances at Salzburg and the BBC Proms, of recent pieces by Thomas Adès, Oliver Knussen, Colin Matthews and Mark-Anthony Turnage not only showed what a bold track record BCMG had with new work but also prompted a violent disruption of the Prom concert by a disaffected composer who felt his work had been neglected by the musical establishment. Leaflets thrown into the hall claimed, alongside other more unpleasant things, that Rattle had only 'a modicum of competence', that 'if he had been a doctor, the world would be awash in corpses, killed while he gained experience' and that he 'represents the attempts by the UK apparatus of power, wealth and authority to recreate itself in the form of a great imperial figure'. Rattle as Queen Victoria was a new and puzzling image.

Even for a seasoned performer of new music, the programme is a special challenge: it includes *Continuum*, a forty-minute new work by Colin Matthews with soprano Cynthia Clarey. This is the third work of Matthews's the BCMG has been involved in originating; it was commissioned by Rattle and their artistic director, the long-serving CBSO cellist Simon Clugston, and was funded by the unique mechanism of the Sound Investment scheme, whose individual members provide small sums that add up to significant funds for new music.

SIMON RATTLE You heard the first concert; you should have heard the last! This is now such a brilliant group of musicians who can tackle anything on the very highest level. And the way it grew on the tour was amazing. I suppose the most remarkable thing was Cynthia, bless her, turning up by the end having learnt the whole piece and Colin saying, 'I don't think anyone has ever done anything like this for me before.' Simon Clugston has done such smart things with the group it will now take on a life of its own and just flourish.

The BCMG's success in taking contemporary music to new places and gaining good audiences for their programmes is now famous. They are as at home in a Shropshire village hall as they are in Vienna's Musikverein. They have sought funds from charitable and other bodies enabling them to take, during 2001, music by Judith Weir and David Sawer to the town hall in Wem or the leisure centre in Whitchurch. As well as developing the wholly original Sound Investment scheme they have raised funds to offer free tickets to their concerts: this is what developing and creating audiences for new music is all about.

COLIN MATTHEWS The thing I most remember was how good-natured the whole period was. I cannot remember a single cross word and that is rare in a project as tough as this with a schedule that was so intense. Simon was totally relaxed, but totally concentrated. It was a very intensive rehearsal period, and even after having worked a nine-hour day Simon was prepared to come along and talk to the BCMG Sound Investors about the piece. (About fifty people put their names to this piece and some of them followed it on the tour.)

I had originally thought the piece might be up to an hour long, and I devised a complicated scheme but in the end jettisoned two of the sections. Simon Clugston was very accommodating, and it became a bit of joke that if I rang him and asked for twenty alphorns he would book them right away. The gestation period was in the end very long, and the piece was finished only just in time, so that Simon [Rattle] did not have long to learn it. But Simon is brilliant at seeing problems before they arrive. We fixed a lot of details and we were still changing a few small things while the piece was on tour. I think there were things even towards the end of the tour in Vienna that hadn't been in before. I might have wanted to change more than I did after the first performance but he encouraged me that the thing had sort of got into gear and the performance just grew and grew. Then before the second-last performance Simon and I were sitting in the dressing room and Cynthia came in and just said, 'Tonight I'm flying.' She'd decided to do it without a score and the look on the faces of the players as she came on to the stage without her music was quite something.

One incident was so typical of Simon. We got stuck in Schiphol airport for a few hours on the way to Vienna, and all we could manage to buy was a game of Cluedo in Dutch. None of us could quite remember how to play, but there was a Dutch family sitting there with two kids who were also incredibly bored, and Simon caught the eye of the mother and asked her to explain all the Dutch instructions. It was all so completely natural and he had her eating out of the palm of his hand. We managed to struggle through the game, which Cynthia won (although I'm sure we were all cheating), and in the end we gave the Cluedo set to the Dutch family. And they were totally charmed. He just has an incredibly natural way with people.

When does your musical relationship with Simon go back to?
He had performed my brother David's music before he did mine. Then in 1987 he took up *Hidden Variables*, which Peter Donohoe had premièred with the BCMG, and then in 1994 . . . *through the glass*, which Simon premièred. We often saw each other at Aldeburgh, where Simon was involved at the period when there were a lot of artistic directors! I think there was a feeling among some people there that Simon just wanted to come in and do his own thing and his own things usually cost more than anyone else's. There was a very fine Britten *War Requiem*, Henze's *Barcarola* at Snape, Beethoven Nine, and I particularly remember the Schoenberg Brahms Quartet arrangement, after which Simon just said, 'After that goulash let's have some sorbet', and played the Fauré *Pavane* as an encore. Aldeburgh and Simon drifted apart, but the Festival is now rebuilding its relationship with the CBSO.

In 1998 I worked with him on an ill-fated film project, which turned out to be a pretty awful experience. It was the Hugh Hudson film *My Life So Far*, based on the Denis Forman memoirs, and I wrote and arranged a great deal of music, which Simon conducted. It took a good couple of months when I should have been writing *Continuum*. There were versions of bits of Beethoven, the storm from the Pastoral Symphony with harpsichord obbligato, and new material, and it was all recorded at great expense by the CBSO with Imogen Cooper and London Voices up at Abbey Road studios as a co-production with EMI. Then there was a lot of time spent on the editing, which I hadn't really wanted to be involved with, but the trail began to go a bit dead and no one from the film spoke to either of us. Eventually it became clear that the American producers did not want the music and had it all replaced. But the really ludicrous thing was that they would not tell me or even tell Simon what was happening. Then I saw an interview in a newspaper with Howard Blake saying he was writing the music for *My Life So Far*. The film eventually came out and played a few days in the West End. It seems to have sunk without trace. It was a huge wasted period but at least we all got paid. Simon took it in his stride, I think, and put it down to experience. We both felt we'd learned rather a lot.

After that Barbican première of the Matthews, there is an unusual occurrence for Rattle: not a sponsor's dinner or official reception to be escaped from as soon as possible, but a small party for Simon and Candace with friends back at the nearby home of his long-time teacher and supporter John Carewe and his wife Sally Cavender, where Carewe dispenses the pasta in his apron while a small clutch of composers and players discuss children, schools, holidays and all the things that forty-somethings worry about – plus music, of course. The evening is relaxed and totally unpretentious, far away from the incipient pressures of Berlin. This, you sense, is one family with whom Rattle feels very much at home.

October 2000. Later the same month, we are back in the Barbican Hall, but the atmosphere could scarcely be more different from that of the BCMG tour. This is the London Symphony Orchestra, felt by many to be now the UK's leading orchestra, currently on a roll in a year that has seen a spectacular Pierre Boulez series of twentieth-century and new music, and Colin Davis's wonderful (but wholly un-Age-of-Enlightenment) Berlioz series. Somehow they have managed to talk their way into Rattle's crowded diary and, after lavish concert performances of Strauss's *Ariadne auf Naxos*, he is now rehearsing the piece with which he conquered the Vienna Philharmonic, Mahler's Ninth Symphony (see p. 297). It is an unusual sight, because not only has Rattle ranged the first and second violins opposite each other at the front of the stage, a musical necessity in this piece, but he has also placed the double-basses across the very back of the Barbican stage, pushing the sound forward into the hall.

You don't often have an experience of such palpable intensity in a rehearsal as the last movement gradually evaporates. What is fascinating is Rattle's constant attention to string sound: 'If we can find a way of making a gentler, less pressurized sound, making the notes float . . . A more living sound, less into the string . . . The sound is gorgeous, but more air, less pressure.' The result of this is to keep the music floating aloft in the most gravity-defying way. 'The upbow, vibrate until the very end so the sound doesn't go dead on you.' Sometimes Rattle's gestures are just not quite enough to make it work: 'I'm causing chaos and dissension here. This has happened to me enough times that I know what I have to do.' At the end of the last movement there is an unearthly pause and then: 'I need to do three moments again, just for myself.'

In the rehearsal break, Rattle seems preoccupied by the uphill mountain they all have to climb:

> It is just so difficult, this piece. It's a very, very special sound you need, to do with getting a darker but not heavy sound, sustained but not relentless. Viennese blood is different. It really is easier to play that oboe solo at the end of the first movement with a Viennese oboe. The LSO is a marvellous orchestra right now, there are people here who I knew in the National Youth Orchestra, and I think they have a kind of racial memory going back from now to Claudio [Abbado] doing Mahler, with some fairly grisly experiences in between!

A while after the performance, Rattle was much more positive about the experience:

> I was so immensely impressed by what the orchestra did. I take my hats off to them because you can say anything to them. It was hard work finding a way to work with the acoustic and we really all achieved it together. The Barbican Hall is rather like a piano lid. I'm sure it wasn't designed like that, you wouldn't do it on purpose, but that is how it is in that tricky place.

> *You were doing a lot of work with the strings . . .*
> Strings, well, that's the weakness in British orchestras, as ensemble can be in other countries. You have so many virtues in British orchestras but you have to work to find that natural European depth of string sound. The LSO's ensemble and intonation is beyond belief now. I would always have the basses at the back now, even though it took getting used to for the players. The horns said it was wonderful having the bass line behind you to sit on! With the brass we discussed where the sound was coming from, the idea of a general area of sound rather than the concept of the laser, which was not the one we were looking for here.

Maybe, just maybe, if the Berlin Philharmonic had not worked out for Simon during 2000, and there was no other music directorship on offer to him, the LSO would have been well placed with these concerts to begin to persuade him that some time in the future they might be his orchestra for the twenty-first century. Whether that would have got past his rooted antipathy to London and its way of making music, which has surfaced so often in similar discussions in the past, is anyone's guess. Whether it would have got past the LSO's lack of ease in repertory that Rattle regards as crucial is another. In any case, because of Berlin the question now doesn't arise, and this is just a very satisfying one-night stand – or rather two as the concert is repeated.

At the concert I attended the achievement was huge, but I thought the electricity did not quite work. One thing happened, however, which shows that conducting isn't just magic, and that Rattle's skills are not illusory. Though he used the score to refer to in rehearsal, Rattle conducts the concert from memory and, in a very exposed section for wind, the bass clarinet comes in wrong. There is a momentary audible confusion before Rattle, with the tiniest of firm gestures, guides the player precisely back into place. Blink and you would have missed it; probably many people never heard it. But it takes an incredible mind, in the middle of the architecture of the hundreds of thousands of notes in Mahler's Ninth, to focus instantly on a few notes out of context, adjust and be able to put them back into shape. That moment – rather than the flamboyant activity that people usually recognize as 'conducting' – is what makes one think of conductors as superhuman.

Rattle's great mentor John Carewe, to whom you can always turn for a dispassionate but passionately involved view of Rattle's performances (see Interlude 1), also listened to some of the concerts of that autumn, and his view of the LSO concert is clear:

JOHN CAREWE I thought the Mahler 9 with the LSO was one of the very greatest performances I have ever heard and it was clear that the orchestra was gobsmacked too. The profile and the clarity and the character of the structure were so clear, and what I had never dreamt I would hear in Mahler 9 was a performance where it was all so clear and yet not at all desiccated. I've heard people give a magisterial, structural performance of the piece that remains totally distant and unemotional. Simon got it all. The thought I had when he was conducting the LSO after all these years was, 'This boy has earned it, really earned the right to stand in front of this orchestra and do this with them, to them, for them.'

I didn't think the Mahler 9 with Vienna (which I have heard only on the recording) was quite as good, though I do think the performance of Strauss's *Metamorphosen* on the same disc is one of the recordings of the century. He had done that piece in Rotterdam less than a year before and I know he was incredibly angry with me for saying that it sounded like so many yards of sausage meat, which in that performance I'm sorry to say it did. But the Vienna recording was nothing like that, it was pure chamber music with a very great orchestra.

One of the things he said to me was that he thought his own work had now become more consistent . . .
Yes, certainly that's true, and when for instance I went down to hear a

rehearsal of the Berlioz with the Orchestra of the Age of Enlightenment I
was simply amazed, and it certainly brought me round to the view that this
is the only way to do this music these days; the conventional approach is so
boring now. With his technique he was apparently doing nothing to help
them at all. I took some students along and they couldn't believe how little
he was doing. But nowadays no one, not even musicians of that high calibre
in the OAE, would say, 'You're not clear there.' They would say,
'What's wrong with me that I can't get this?' It's a complete reversal of the
conventional situation with orchestras.

November 2000. The Maida Vale Studios, London. Another Rattle
family is here, in a former skating rink – not one of the most inspiring
London rehearsal venues, but one of the most familiar and reliable. The
BBC's Maida Vale Studio 1 has recently had a facelift, a shock of orange
paint and some new bright lights. It makes the place look almost cheerful, but you can't say it has done much for the acoustic, about which
conductors and players have always complained. Since the 1930s the
studio has been the home of the BBC Symphony Orchestra, housing their
rehearsals and their most adventurous invitation concerts, where Sofia
Gubaidulina and Harrison Birtwistle jostle for Radio 3 airtime. Rattle
came here as a student to hear Boulez rehearse. But this morning the
place is filled with a profusion of old harps, and a completely different
sound only rarely heard before – the lavish but crystal-clear sonorities of
Berlioz on original instruments. As Rattle put it later of the *Symphonie
fantastique*, 'I had no idea I had been conducting a transcription for all
these years!'

Rattle's relationship with the Orchestra of the Age of Enlightenment –
he is one of two principal guest conductors, and will continue to be when
he goes to Berlin – is a very close one and it has had a huge impact on
orchestral life (see chapter 9), helping to create a sea-change in performing styles and offering Rattle a laboratory in which to try some of his
boldest experiments. The collaboration has grown and flourished for
over a decade now, and it is clear that these are players with whom he
feels completely at home.

It's early days in the rehearsals, so there's plenty to learn from a standing start. At the coffee break, the players are still a bit worried: 'Simon
gets us to sight-read better than anyone else, but we're still usually pretty
embarrassed because it will take us a while to settle down and actually

play together. If he's come straight from the Vienna Phil or Berlin, it can be a bit of a shock for him.' What comes through is the sheer originality of Berlioz's writing and the zest with which Rattle recreates it. As another player puts it, 'Ten years ago we were struggling through Berlioz with Roger [Norrington]. Roger did some marvellous things, and it was great, pioneering stuff, but we are so much further on technically now. Simon's not afraid to be passionate about this music, and for a period-instrument orchestra that's so welcome.' Almost everything Rattle says in rehearsal is about using details of bowing, fingering and ensemble to get the sound to become more sophisticated and then to loosen up. 'That A can't be all white tone. By all means start like that but then for God's sake do something with it . . . Just make that the quietest pianissimo you have ever played. Any bowing you want! . . . More concentration here. This is no time to fill up the jacuzzi and just float around!'

Once again Rattle's sense of impetus in a rehearsal, something the public never sees, is crucial to the success of the process. The BBC Singers and Symphony Chorus are brought into the picture, sitting around the players so as to make their vocal contributions as tight as possible. As one player said later:

> We feed each other when we're playing, and he keeps up an amazing energy level. When he came to do this Berlioz period I think he was actually very tired, and I remember one day at Maida Vale, he was already rehearsing the choir when we got there, the double-basses and cellos during the lunch break, a whole afternoon with us all and he never flagged. But then suddenly as soon as the rehearsal was over he looked about ten years older, and so drained. It's as if he's only in his element when he's plugged into the music.

Rattle has already persuaded the Berlin Philharmonic to play Rameau, which is strange. But here is something almost stranger: persuading the Vienna Philharmonic to change the way they play Beethoven. After a superlative cycle of the piano concertos with Alfred Brendel, and several performances of the symphonies, Rattle has committed himself to recording a Beethoven symphony cycle with the Viennese orchestra over the next few years – and he has maintained that commitment in spite of noises from his new colleagues in Berlin that it could be transferred to them. Rattle's relationship with Vienna is very close and very intense, and indeed during the 1990s, when he was experiencing occasional tensions with Berlin, it seemed quite possible that Vienna would break the habit of a lifetime and offer him a title (see chapter 9). There have been many memorable collaborations, including the extraordinary Beethoven Ninth on the site of the Mauthausen concentration camp, which excited passionate controversy in Austria.

So here he is in the heart of Beethoven's Vienna, tackling the Fifth Symphony on its home territory, a worrying moment. This is an orchestra, remember, that used to claim quite genuinely that its tradition stretched back to Beethoven's Vienna and that therefore it embodied the truth about this music. A couple of generations of early-music players claiming an equally privileged status with the composer has certainly dented that argument, though the idea that either can claim to know the truth about the composer is now recognized to be misguided. Rattle's EMI producer Stephen Johns is watching closely:

STEPHEN JOHNS I arrived in the middle of the rehearsal process and found it very interesting. The major impact was, having heard Simon perform some Beethoven recently with the Orchestra of the Age of Enlightenment, that he was rushing away from the way that the Vienna orchestra normally played his music. You'd hear comments like, 'I sense you've always done a *ritardando* here, and I think it's not in the score, let's see how it works without it.' He was very clear that there was a different playing style required. But, at the same time, as an orchestra they provide so much that he loves – a glorious sound, a wonderful tradition. It seemed to be a question of adding new life to that.

I think they can be . . . 'lazy' is certainly not the right word but their attitude can sometimes be: 'We won't do anything different unless you really ask for it.' For example, he gets them to play extremely quietly, which is something you don't normally hear, and then the power in the louder passages can be overwhelming. The sheer range of sound he elicits, with new ideas of phrasing and bowing a familiar work, is astonishing.

It takes a little time to make it work. Within the orchestra, and I think this is true in Berlin as well, there are a number of people who are very go-ahead, young musicians who see the future and want to make that journey. It's a question of convincing all the players that they can produce their wonderful individual sound, but then getting them to try something different. In the scherzo from the Fifth Symphony, there is an open string note in the cello and bass opening. Simon knew quite clearly that they didn't like doing it as an open string, because it hasn't got any Vienna gloss on it! It's just an open D in an otherwise smooth phrase, and it sticks out like a sore thumb. But it makes an important musical point and this is why he makes it convincing, because they all appreciate the effect.

The first concert after a decent set of rehearsals was absolutely spine-tingling: it was edge-of-the-seat stuff, almost too frenetic in the urgency to get the music out. We sat there in the control room simply amazed by what was achieved; it was almost falling over itself with sheer excitement. The second performance was then the mid-afternoon of the next day with no further rehearsal. If I were a boxing judge I might have given this one to the orchestra on points. It felt as if they were less willing to be so extreme! And then by the third performance the next day, we reached the best stage of all. It had suddenly become an ideal partnership: the orchestra offered what they had to offer and Simon offered what he had to offer and it made total sense: the sheer virtuosity of their playing, Simon's aural vision of the sounds he wanted, the architecture of the work.

Simon Rattle's view is that the Vienna Philharmonic provides a unique interaction between past and present:

SIMON RATTLE We've been playing Beethoven together for five years, including all the piano concertos with Alfred [Brendel]. For them this Beethoven Fifth was the most surprising so far. And certainly the very first rehearsal was a little bit of a shock for me, and probably a great deal more of a shock for them, in realizing that what I was asking from them was so out of the ordinary for them. But then by talking a lot more I found what they really meant was that it just hadn't been their recent style. Earlier in the century there had been more freedom, not just more strictness. Once they'd blinked and shaken themselves to see what we'd got to offer, one of the older players said, 'It makes me think we have been playing it in the wrong way all these years.' Why should you phrase Beethoven 2 differently from Haydn's *Creation*, which was written just a few years before? You can't expect people to take the idea of tempo for granted. Changing tempo from what you're used to is very difficult. One of the older players just looked at me very wearily and said, 'Could we not just play this as we played in former times?' And then he gave me a look which said, 'Oh, all right then.' They will let themselves be persuaded. I'm a chameleon and it's easier for me. I have so much to learn from their approach, their energy and love and finesse and power.

The atmosphere in the Royal Festival Hall in December 2000 was indeed electrifying, and the only point at which Stephen Johns's reservations might have been true was in the orchestra's difficulties in adapting to the acoustic of the Festival Hall, now drier than ever as the electronic enhancement system which goes back to the mid-1950s is not working and has been switched off. (When Karajan came back to the Festival Hall after taking part in the opening concerts, shortly after the electronic system had been installed, he said the hall's acoustic had 'mellowed like an old violin'.) Sandwiched in between the Haydn 88, which John Carewe thought the perfect performance, and the Beethoven 5, was Berg's *Lulu* suite, without vocal soloist but for a huge orchestra – one shudders to think of the cost of bringing all those Viennese players around Europe just for one piece in the programme.

That recording of Beethoven's Fifth appeared very quickly, coupled with Brahms's Violin Concerto played by Kyung-Wha Chung. An entire Beethoven cycle with Vienna followed, recorded in 2002 and performed complete in Vienna's Musikverein during the Vienna Festival – coincidentally, Rattle reached Beethoven's Ninth with the Vienna Philharmonic there, just as Claudio Abbado was completing his journey with the Berlin Philharmonic in Mahler's Seventh. The two concerts occurred on successive days in May 2002, and Rattle was able to attend, unobtrusively, his predecessor's farewell. So Rattle got to record Beethoven's Fifth twice in two years, and we can be sure that eventually a Berlin version will follow. In addition, the Sixth was re-recorded after the Vienna concerts, because Rattle was not totally satisfied with the results. Such lavishness, like bringing Vienna players to London for a single work in a programme, seems extraordinary.

But Simon has never let those sort of practical considerations stand in his way, and while money has never mattered a whole lot to him personally, he has never – from the Vienna Philharmonic touring unused players to the Salzburg Festival rehearsing Rameau for weeks on end – minded encouraging the spending of other people's money in the cause of his art. Indeed, one of the central, unavoidable facts about Simon Rattle is that he has always got his own way. And as he claims Peter Sellars once said to him, 'You know, what we have in common, Simon, is that we don't really comprehend the word "no".' So far, he has had it, musically, all his own way. But in Berlin?

CHAPTER TWO

'This is the orchestra that claims it created Karajan'
Towards Berlin 1987–2001

'He makes the music dance': Rattle in action with the Berlin Philharmonic
(photo Reinhard Friedrich)

There is no more exciting city in Europe today than Berlin, as it seeks to recreate itself, and to distance the memory of the Cold War. It is determined to obliterate the two-cities mentality of the post-war period, literally to pave over the remains of the Wall, and to reconstruct the entire city as the German capital. The look of the place reminds you of one of Simon Rattle's favourite encores, the *Scene with Cranes*, though it wasn't this sort of crane that Sibelius had in mind. All sorts of buildings are going up across the city, many of them built too quickly. The biggest current building projects are new government buildings stretching right along the river past the Reichstag and vast new railway tracks which will unify the two halves of the city. Berlin has always argued about its buildings, and the city is prone to long, fierce architectural debates – the spectre of Albert Speer's megalomaniac scheme for reconstructing Berlin as Germania still looms large. Every major development seems to have roused passionate political antagonism, but once a decision is taken there seems no limit to what can be achieved in spite of the city's recurrent financial crises.

The Philharmonie, home of the Berlin Philharmonic Orchestra, is lucky – just. It was built at the extreme east of West Berlin, not far from the Wall. It used to be more isolated than it is now: in the old days there was little more outside it than a bus stop back to the old centre of West Berlin. Now it is near that part of the city where the major renewal is taking place. It is just across the road from the huge Potsdamer Platz redevelopment, where some of the ugliest new buildings in Berlin are being thrown up. Media companies including the Film and TV Academy, the Cinematèque and a new cinema are now in the Filmhaus near by. Past the Potsdamer Platz is the area of the Reich Chancellery and the eerie deserted plot under which Hitler's bunker lurked, near to the site where a Holocaust memorial has been fought over by the Berliners for years. Meanwhile a building of unrivalled eloquence and genius, the Jewish Museum of Daniel Libeskind, has risen next to a baroque museum in another part of the city. It is reachable only by an underground passage from the older building and was visited by crowds from around the world even though it was entirely empty; it is now open with a permanent exhibition.

So the Philharmonie has not been stranded in post-Wall Berlin, as has the Deutsche Oper in the Bismarckstrasse, outside the newly fashionable centre around the Brandenburg Gate. It is not far either to Norman Foster's renovated Reichstag in the old West, whose dome (in melancholy contrast to London's fiasco in 2000) is currently the biggest tourist attraction in the city, or to the ever-extending shops of the Friedrichstrasse in the old East. This was formerly a gloomy avenue leading down to Checkpoint Charlie, but here you can now buy your upmarket (and to many Berliners unaffordable) clothes in a surreal whirlwind of a conical building designed by Jean Nouvel, architect of the Lyons opera house and the superb new Lucerne concert hall.

The site of the Philharmonie dates back to proposals for a 'cultural-forum area' drawn up by architect Hans Scharoun in 1946 and 1957.

Various areas of the city were, in a Germanic sort of way, to be dedicated to different areas of activity, creating an urban landscape to contrast with the regularity of the nineteenth-century city. The building of the Philharmonie in 1963 was the cornerstone of that cultural policy; Mies van der Rohe added the Neue Nationalgalerie in 1968 nearby, solid and impressive. The cultural-forum plan kept being argued over; the nearby Gemäldegalerie was opened only in 1998, and has not been a great success. There is now a proposal to relocate its pictures to the restored Museumsinsel, and to link it instead to the Nationalgalerie. Certainly the surroundings of the Philharmonie need renewal, as does the inside of the building.

Scharoun's now famous hall was designed from the inside out, and became a symbol of 'organic' architecture. But the Philharmonie is still a relic of the 1960s because of its adherence to Scharoun's purist view that there should not be commerce in the foyers. The spaces feel cold and antiseptic: they are scarcely inviting and make you feel guilty buying a coffee, let alone a CD. There is no restaurant. The lighting makes everyone look yellow. There is little of the sense of bustle and welcoming activity found in the concert halls of London and New York. This is all part of what Rattle wants to change, but the relationship between the hall and the orchestra is one of the many complex unresolved matters in Berlin.

It is over a decade since Rattle first conducted the Berlin Philharmonic in November 1987. He had conducted in Berlin just once before, many years earlier, at a concert in 1976 with the RIAS Berlin orchestra which his agent Martin Campbell-White says was so badly received that he had to hide the newspaper criticisms from Rattle. The Philharmonic début should have happened long before, but there was a continual war of words and intentions before it could be brought about. The orchestra wanted Rattle on their terms; he wanted them on his. This is now a familiar story. He wanted to come to Berlin with the CBSO first, which he achieved in the Berlin Festival of 1984, but then insisted the orchestra was reinvited in 1987. He wanted to conduct the Berlin Philharmonic in something it had never done before: Mahler's Tenth Symphony in Deryck Cooke's completion, a piece in which he passionately believed. This, for the moment, he did not achieve. The Berlin orchestra did not share his confidence in the piece. Rather than reject it outright, they claimed there was limited rehearsal time and all parties settled on

Mahler's Sixth Symphony. It was an uneasy truce and one that suggested there might be more conflict ahead.

The CBSO's own visit to the Berlin Festival in 1987 with Rattle was extremely memorable, because Rattle insisted on bringing the music of Berthold Goldschmidt, who had been exiled from Berlin in the 1930s and had been disgracefully neglected as a composer since. He was living quietly in Belsize Park in London. The music programme of the Berlin Festival was at that time run by Elmar Weingarten, who was later to become intendant of the Berlin Philharmonic.

ELMAR WEINGARTEN It was a kind of blackmailing situation, one must admit that. The Berlin Festival had invited Simon to conduct the Berlin Philharmonic several times and he refused, or rather he said that he wanted to come with his own orchestra. And they said, 'Well, you can come with the Birmingham orchestra but you have to also agree to come to the Berlin Philharmonic.' So actually the CBSO came first, to the Berlin Festival, and the appearance was an enormous success. And the Festival was very altruistic about it, because he then made his début with the Berlin Philharmonic in November 1987, not in the Festival as we had hoped.

He did something very special in the CBSO concert. I was not at all aware of Berthold Goldschmidt, but Simon had told me about him, as had David Drew, who was very active in reviving his music. The Birmingham orchestra came to Berlin, and Goldschmidt was there sitting in the rehearsal. Now for years nothing had been played by him in Berlin and Simon made a little speech hinting at the importance of this situation which was really very, very touching. The *Ciaconna sinfonica* was played. And when the run-through was over, Berthold Goldschmidt got up and said this one marvellous, unforgettable sentence: 'You, Simon Rattle, and you, the orchestra, are picking up a thread which I left here sixty years ago.' He was really moved to tears. We were all moved to tears.

From then on Berthold's career in Germany started again, he became a star in Germany and all his pieces were played again. There were revivals of his operas and he got in contact with other cities where he had been. So Simon, by insisting on doing this piece at the Festival, did here a spectacularly marvellous thing for somebody who really deserved it.

When Rattle finally arrived at the Berlin Philharmonic in November 1987, the reviews were mixed. The English press was as usual very positive, the German press far more reserved and cautious but in the end won over. 'BERLIN TO RATTLE'S BEAT' was the headline of Hugh Canning's review in the *Guardian*:

It would be hard to imagine a performance of Mahler's most hysterical, angry music so far removed in temperament from that of the von Karajan recording. The composition of the orchestra may have changed to some extent in the last decade, but the unique Karajan sound is hardly to be dispelled in three rehearsals. Yet Rattle achieved just that . . . Rattle is himself dedicated in Birmingham to the kind of continuity that has made the Berlin Philharmonic phenomenon possible. They played magnificently for him at the Philharmonie, with a relentless intensity and grim rapaciousness rarely required of them by their principal conductor. At the close the packed auditorium cheered the young conductor with genuine warmth, and Rattle seemed genuinely surprised when the public called him back for a solo bow after the orchestra had left the stage.

The *Volksblatt Berlin* thought that

> for a conducting début, one could hardly think of a greater challenge. But one can say that Simon Rattle with the Philharmonic was on the whole quite up to it. The thirty-two-year-old conductor confirmed his position as a very promising talent. Still in some stretches he conducts the orchestra more than the music . . . the great test of endurance, the half-hour finale, was a triumph.

The *Berliner Morgenpost* said:

> It was about time for this début. The young maestro Rattle made things extremely difficult for himself [by choosing Mahler 6]. Rattle succeeded brilliantly again and again in combining every single event and drawing them together. A colossal symphony was brought under one huge musical arch, which embraced everything written in the score . . .

But as Simon Rattle recalls, that successful first concert was the prelude to serious problems:

> SIMON RATTLE What is important to remember is that this was still the Karajan time, and very much his orchestra, an older orchestra, and I was dealing with Mahler 6, which they had done a good deal with him. Now all of these things are positive statements! I was simply staggered by the level not only of their orchestral machine, but by the individual parts and the interdependence of all those parts. It was the type of response that I had always dreamt of and never experienced. Everyone was just looking up to see from my gesture what sort of attack they should use. It went: here's a point where we play it this way but there could be many different ways; what does he want? He makes this gesture. He wants this sound. And if people were in any doubt they would stop and ask.

The thing that was hysterical was the pizzicatos; they just would never do them when I wanted, but about five minutes after when the leader felt the moment had come. And it was quite difficult to describe the sound I wanted: I remember saying to them at one point when I wanted one of those particular sounds and I couldn't get it, 'Look, I am in a rather hard position here, because when I want this from any other orchestra I say, "Can you give me one of those Berlin Philharmonic sounds?" But what am I supposed to say to you?!' That broke the ice well.

That Mahler 6 really was an unqualified success for all of us together. It was only later that there were problems. People said to me, 'Now be really careful what pieces you choose to do next.' I couldn't believe that an orchestra that could play Mahler at that level couldn't necessarily play Bartók at that level, let alone Sibelius or French music. That was a real ignorance on my part of German culture and German habits.

What happened between my first and second visits was that Karajan died, and so there was a huge amount of turmoil, thinking about what the orchestra should be, looking for a successor. And EMI was very keen for me to record something with them at this point and Peter Alward, bless him, was very excited about the possibilities. So we decided on Bartók – *Music for Strings, Percussion and Celesta*, which was a Karajan repertory piece, and *The Wooden Prince*, which they had never done at all. At quite the last minute the concert programmes were changed to include the Bartók pieces so as to allow the recordings to take place afterwards.

I had no idea what this meant, and it was only about a week before the performances when they admitted, 'Well, you do realize that not all the players will be quite the same people who played the concert?' So my response to that was, 'Ah, do you think you could tell who those different players will be exactly?' The response to that was the most enormous explosion from the media committee: 'How dare you, you little * * * *, ask who's that going to be?' I had to say, 'I need to know whether this will be possible.' And it turned out that, of the string principals, eight out of ten were going to be different. What I didn't know then – not having even tried Bartók with them at this point – is that it would have been catastrophic, even worse than I then thought.

So I cancelled the recording and this was a major thing for them. There was this very strange attitude from the media committee that the orchestra really didn't need rehearsal for anything, and the idea of asking for a string sectional for *The Wooden Prince* was just incredibly insulting. In retrospect I realize that I was actually completely right! But we ended up doing Brahms 4 in the concerts, which was a completely formative experience for me, because there was so much for me to learn . . .

Was it any good?

I certainly wasn't any good, but it was very important and there were so many fascinating conversations with the players about Furtwängler and Karajan and how they did particular things. And what I realized at that point was that the only reason for my doing one of those pieces was for me to learn more about it from them. This was not really fair; this was not the way to go.

So you started introducing new pieces to them?

Claudio [Abbado] wanted me to come very regularly during the nineties and there were several things that were first performances for them, the Szymanowski *Stabat Mater*, the Janáček *Glagolitic Mass*. They didn't like everything I was offering, actually they had very set views of what was real music. I had never come across this attitude that Sibelius is simply second-rate!

What had been taken for granted was that when Karajan was with the orchestra he had a great deal of time to work with them. No one was allowed to leave the city, even if he was doing a Mozart symphony, in case he decided to do the Strauss *Alpine Symphony* instead. Which sometimes happened. But it also meant that no other conductor had much rehearsal, so what was possible was very limited. When he died there was very much a struggle for the soul of the orchestra and, as happens after the death of any autocratic father, there was an immense debate and free-for-all over what it all meant. There was no feeling for what a real functioning democracy might be. We all knew that Claudio was inheriting a very difficult position. He had always said that Karajan's followers would have a terrible time, but it didn't occur to him that he might be it.

A lot of younger players came in, and the orchestra changed a huge amount in Claudio's time. He is an extraordinary mixture of great stubbornness and great detachment, and he would suggest something, there would be a furore, and then he'd withdraw and the furore would die down. Then he'd carry on in exactly the same direction he'd always wanted to . . .

Everyone would say that man for man, player for player, the orchestra is now individually stronger than it has ever been. No orchestra comes close to that individual level, the level of ability is breathtaking, I mean almost vertigo-inducing.

Among the British artists Simon Rattle took back to Berlin on subsequent visits was the pianist Imogen Cooper, with whom he had worked over many years. She found herself in the middle of one incident where Rattle, having agreed to conduct a Haydn symphony, found that the orchestra had cancelled a rehearsal for that piece, apparently because of scheduling problems but basically because they believed they knew how it went. And that was not the only problem in that concert:

IMOGEN COOPER The situation was quite tense, because they cancelled rehearsals without asking him and then, when we came to do our first rehearsal of the Mozart concerto, K595, I didn't look around too much but I saw Simon going very white. And he asked this rather difficult man who was on the first desk of the second violins what was going on, because there were too few firsts and seconds. So this man answered, 'Well, we always do this piece with this many strings, so I told them they could go.' Simon said, 'Excuse me, who is conducting this orchestra?' He was, for once, absolutely furious and the atmosphere was electric, really electric. He was being upstaged, he was being tested, you could see that, and there wasn't anything that could be done there and then because the players had gone and we needed to do the rehearsal. But I'm pretty certain he made sure they were back the next day.

They were good concerts in the end but to say it was like falling off a log would give the wrong impression. The first rehearsal sounded pretty rough, I can tell you. The point is that you may have old traditions going way back when, but there are moments when you want to shake things around a bit and try something different, and Simon is always like that.

We go back a long way, twenty-five years now. We both feel we can pick up with the best trust and the best enjoyment whenever we meet. And that if there are seminal things in our lives, he would be the first person in an ideal world I would want to see, especially now he is so much more relaxed and happy with Candace.

However optimistic he may seem, in Berlin Rattle is stepping into a snake-pit of controversy that has claimed many artistic lives. The last years of Karajan's rule were marred by internal feuding and tensions, with Karajan playing off the Berlin and Vienna orchestras against each other in a way that still rankles. It would be a wonderful challenge for Rattle, who works so well with both great orchestras, to heal that rift and bring them together.

The root of the tension was that the orchestra members had great freedom in the choice of work they did, and their independence often appeared to rival the existence of the Philharmonic itself. A new intendant, Peter Girth, a protégé of Karajan, arrived in 1978, and made himself unpopular with the players. The notorious 1981 Christmas issue of *Stern* featured a piece on the orchestra that quoted Girth as saying, 'This orchestra is a terrible collective. Many of them don't know how lucky they are to have Karajan. There's poverty, unemployment and war in the world but this orchestra is completely blind to it all. They're frightful and remote from life. But they all know how to count.'

In 1984 – only three years before Rattle first entered the Berlin arena – the much-discussed affair of Sabine Meyer had come to a head. She is the clarinettist Karajan wanted to impose on the orchestra against their wishes. The details are now irrelevant, but they symbolized an impasse between Karajan and the orchestra as to who was in artistic control. Relations between Karajan and the orchestra reached an all-time low. It was at this moment that he cancelled the Berlin orchestra's appearance at the Salzburg Whitsun Festival and invited the Vienna Philharmonic instead. The Vienna players did not refuse. This was regarded by the Berlin Philharmonic as a rank betrayal by Karajan and they asked him to reconsider his position. (The incident also claimed the career as intendant of Peter Girth, who resigned early. The former intendant Wolfgang Stresemann was brought back to heal the rift with the orchestra, but he was never fully trusted by Karajan and was publicly insulted by him on his retirement.) In June 1984 the orchestra voted to terminate its recording contract with Karajan with the immortal words, 'The orchestra's self-respect must take precedence over any financial disadvantages.'

The orchestra was alienating not only its conductor but also the (then) all-important record companies. The orchestra had a contract to be paid DM200,000 for each recording, and even when they fielded only twenty-four players for Vivaldi's *Four Seasons* with Anne-Sophie Mutter they still demanded the same amount. At that time the activities of the media committee, led by Hans-Jörg Schellenberger and Bernd Gellermann, were notorious. Richard Osborne's compellingly favourable biography of Karajan relates the manoeuvres that led the orchestra not only to sell themselves to CBS, but even to try to persuade Deutsche Grammophon to record them without Karajan, at a time when Karajan accounted for 25 per cent of all DG's sales. Nothing came of this, and an uneasy truce with Karajan was re-established around a somewhat hypocritical performance of the Bach Mass in B minor festooned with messages of reconciliation between Karajan and the orchestra. (A depressingly unspiritual use of the piece, until you recall that Bach had at least as many conflicts with those for whom he wrote his church music.) There were some continuing collaborations at the 1988 Easter Festival, in Japan and Salzburg the same year, but Karajan gradually relinquished power and stood down as a member of the Salzburg directorium. His health worsened. He continued to press for a formal definition of his role with the Orchestra from the Berlin Senate; in July 1989, the new Minister for the Arts, Anke Martiny, went to Berlin and Karajan handed her a final letter of resignation from the Philharmonic. He was rehearsing *Un ballo in maschera* for the 1989 Salzburg Festival, with a cast featuring the British soprano Josephine Barstow, when he died on 16 July.

One typical British attitude to Karajan was aptly summed up by Rodney Milnes's extremely direct obituary: 'He was I think a bad man and in the final analysis a bad conductor as well. He wielded power out of all proportion to his talent, and the musical world will be a better place without him.' Another harsh judgement, by the Berlin-based journalist Klaus Lang, is that 'no one realized that, in the last analysis, Karajan's sole concern was with his own reputation: the orchestra merely provided the pedestal on which to raise the hero's statue.' On the other hand, the arrogance of the orchestra through this whole period was equally unashamed. As one person who observed this episode from the vantage point of a record company put it, implicitly warning Rattle to tread with care, 'This is the orchestra that claims it created Karajan.' Another observer characterized the orchestra's attitude as 'greed on a huge scale. They were bigger than any of these conductors. They exulted in their power.' Yet at exactly the same time the record market was beginning to fall apart, and it was clear that a successor to Karajan would have to take a very different approach to the orchestra's range of activities.

As Richard Osborne, who tends to give Karajan the benefit of some pretty extensive doubt, observed with some world-weariness, 'Talk in the press in the summer of 1989 about the Karajan succession was almost entirely political: about the need to "liberalize" and "democratize" orchestra–conductor relationships after the demise of the "last of the great conductor–megalomaniacs".' That might sound patronizing now, but the note that followed about Claudio Abbado showed real foresight: 'How else could they have elected a distinguished and likeable musician whose Achilles heel, it had long been said within the profession, was precisely his inability to rehearse in the kind of rigorous and systematic way the old kapellmeisters were trained to do?' Abbado's flaw was identified even before he had started.

If this is all merely musical politics, it is politics far removed from the down-to-earth arguments with the Arts Council or West Midland Arts that had preoccupied Rattle in his Birmingham period (see chapters 5 and 8). This is a fight for the musical future, played out in a world-sized arena under the glare of the press. The intendant of the orchestra who saw through much of the Abbado period before resigning in 2000 was Elmar Weingarten, a highly intelligent and cultured musical administrator who now runs the Ensemble Modern. An acute observer of the Berlin scene, the music editor of *Die Welt*, Werner Brug, says,

> I do not know and most people do not know what went on between Abbado and Weingarten. What you can say is that Elmar did everything for Claudio. He paid for his most eccentric schemes, hiring a choir from Sweden when there was one at RIAS, letting him do huge expensive projects, like Schubert's opera *Fierrabras*, things that were not at all important to the orchestra. But Claudio is not a man of the spoken word. You have to work out what he means from the silences! And somehow they fell out.

ELMAR WEINGARTEN There are always strong feelings here. When Goldschmidt, whom Simon had brought back to Berlin after so many years, was attending a Mahler concert with us, I saw the opportunity to introduce him to the former intendant of the Berlin Philharmonic, Wolfgang Stresemann, two great old men of the same age. They had never met before but as soon as I introduced them I realized that they were yelling at each other. Berthold was saying, 'You prevented Mahler 10 in the Cooke version being done here in Berlin and that is wrong. This is unacceptable.' And Stresemann was yelling back, 'I am convinced it is wrong to complete the symphony. Bruno Walter said it should never be done.' And Berthold said, 'That is complete rubbish.' Actually it turned into quite an unpleasant encounter and I separated them to go back into the concert. I think Berthold finally saw the chance to tell him what he really thought after all that time and he did. It was very direct.

When Simon in the end did Mahler 10 for the first time with the orchestra, which was not until 1996, he really had problems. Players were saying, 'It's just ghastly . . . It's not by Mahler . . . Why are we doing this?' So when he came to do it again much more recently, in 1999, I told him this whole story 'and he made a wonderful speech before they started rehearsing, explaining the whole thing, how much was already there, that the continuous line for the whole piece existed, and so on. It took ten years but the orchestra finally took to the piece and the recording they have made now is a real triumph. They played fantastically for the Mahler, and Simon and the record have won many awards.

Did EMI always want to record Simon with the orchestra?
Of course, and this was one of the first difficulties. After the success in 1987, in January 1990 he came back to do two concerts with Rakhmaninov

2, and EMI wanted to record some Bartók. So the Bartók pieces went into the concert, but the recordings were outside the concert period, and from the way the recording sessions were set up Simon got suspicious that actually he might not have the same players in the recordings who had taken part in the concerts. He called me on Christmas Eve in Berlin – I always remember it was that day – to ask me what was happening. I was quite frank about it and said, they probably don't have the same principals, but that is the way they organize themselves. And then he called up Mr Schellenberger and found out that it was as I suspected it would be: the principals would change but he shouldn't worry if they were different people. These new people were just as good. And so Simon cancelled the recording. It caused quite a lot of bad feeling with this media faction. But the concerts went very well, I remember, and the Rakhmaninov was really impressive.

It was then a long time before the Berlin Philharmonic actually did a recording with him for EMI and to be honest this was one of the things that did not turn out so well. The first recording was Liszt's *Faust Symphony* in 1994. Here again the orchestra just doesn't believe in Liszt as a great composer for the orchestra.

So what were the things that went well?
Almost everything else! The big pieces, Mahler 2, Janáček's *Glagolitic Mass*, Szymanowski's *Stabat Mater*, these were really his pieces, but also early on he did a concert in the small chamber-music hall in 1991 with Imogen Cooper playing Mozart and Haydn 90, really terrific. He worked well with the orchestra, and they respected him, because Simon is someone who takes every bar seriously, in real detail. Claudio [Abbado] can be terrific in the evening at the concert, creating a wonderful atmosphere stirring up emotions with a big symphonic sweep. Simon works for this in rehearsal and this is something that Claudio was never brilliant at. There were so many new discoveries: another piece that was quite decisive for the orchestra thinking about a new conductor was Haydn's *Creation* in 1997. That was one of the best things I ever heard.

Are you saying that already in 1997 the orchestra was thinking about a new conductor?
Well, this is hard to be certain about. But long before Claudio decided not to continue himself there were questions in the orchestra about whether his appointment would be extended. It would be wrong not to admit this problem. There were a number of people who were really quite distressed with the rehearsal practices and the practicalities of leadership. And when you start talking about these things then alternative names come up.

But it was in 1998 that Abbado said he was going to go in 2002 ...
The situation was that there had been a very unfavourable article in the
press at the end of 1997 by a journalist who was quite unfriendly towards
Abbado at that point. She talked to some of the orchestra on a tour to Paris
and was very critical and described the whole situation with Abbado as
very difficult. And Claudio took this as a disloyal act by some of the players
and then decided for himself that enough was enough. This article was not
the decisive reason but it was one element. The main reason was that he
wanted to get rid of the burden of being a chief conductor and concentrate
on music and projects about which he cares intensely.

*Was a long period of uncertainty between 1998 and 2002 going to be a
problem?*
Not really, because the orchestra is quite strong in these situations. The big-
shot conductors kept coming and there were immediately a number of
them presenting themselves as possible alternatives. It also gave the orchestra the chance to decide how the election was going to be organized, which
they did very well, much better than last time, without any complications,
and that worked out very well. So they now know who they will have
before it actually happens, and that gives them time to plan.

It certainly had been a different situation the previous time. Then, with
the classical-CD boom still just at its height, the record companies saw
dollar signs rising in front of their eyes at the thought of the Karajan
inheritance. No one had yet realized that the rising graphs of classical-
record sales would be a temporary phenomenon as people replaced their
LP collections in the user-friendly new medium of CD. I vividly remember sitting in the dressing room of one of the candidates as executives
bobbed in and out discussing the latest odds, and he told me about the
bedroom farce of different record companies appearing at different times
and more or less forcing him into declaring himself a candidate, when his
heart was clearly not it in. It was not an edifying sight. At exactly that
point Claudio Abbado had been developing an ambitious plan with his
friend and colleague Hans Landesmann (see p. 294) to take over the
New York Philharmonic and to reorder concert life in that city. The call
to Abbado after the vote in 1989 came, so one was led to believe, rather
out of the blue, because Abbado was thought of as a compromise candidate. Abbado was not someone with an allegiance to a single record
company, and some in the orchestra's media faction thought this would
make it easier to play one company off against another as they had
threatened to with Karajan.

The newly emerging Sony, incorporating CBS, was at that point trying optimistically to outrank DG, and had first backed Maazel for Berlin, but when it became clear that the Berlin players would not touch Maazel with the proverbial barge pole, Sony switched rapidly to try to attract Abbado in spite of his continuing relationship with DG. But the moment was already beginning to pass when that level of recording activity could be sustained and when recordings would be so important to the orchestra's future. Abbado's recording activities with the orchestra were not as successful as had been hoped, and the DG recordings reduced in number. However the 2001 Abbado–Berlin Beethoven symphony cycle, though it had been thought scarcely necessary in advance and gave rise to much head-shaking within the company, turned out to be an interesting and original set, and the later live concert cycles and video recordings that followed in Rome and Vienna in the spring of 2001 were highly successful.

Faced with a new election for a music director in 1999, the orchestra changed its process and deliberated calmly but still emotionally. The two leading contenders all along were Rattle and Daniel Barenboim, who was not only music director in Chicago but also the music director of the Berlin Staatsoper. He had settled in the city some years before, some people believed, precisely to be around for the moment when the Berlin Philharmonic became available. He used his political contacts in the city to lobby; Rattle did not. From the beginning the casting of Barenboim in the role of the defender of musical tradition made things difficult for him. 'Even those who wanted Daniel Barenboim didn't really believe it would be great,' said one observer. 'They just felt he would keep things going as they had been, which wasn't really a reason for appointing anyone.' The press wrote up the contest excitedly as a two-horse race. The more interesting story would have been who might have been the third horse if one was needed, but in the end it wasn't.

Rattle left the lobbying to the players who supported him. He did not want a contest, did not want to use the Berlin politicians. The only weapon he used was his music-making. Both Rattle and Barenboim were conducting the orchestra around the crucial time for the discussions. Barenboim did some fine concerts including Mozart arias with Cecilia Bartoli and a new piano concerto by Wolfgang Rihm. But Rattle's two programmes at that moment were inspired: not only Mahler's massive Seventh Symphony (the many problems of which he had thoroughly sorted out, having done this work with the CBSO more often than any other Mahler symphony), coupled with a dazzling piece of Boulez, but also a classical programme of Haydn and Mozart arias sung by Thomas Quasthoff alongside a good new piece by a member of the orchestra, his friend the violist Brett Dean. One observer said: 'During the rehearsal and after the performances he showed very much that he felt deep solidarity with the orchestra. He was as friendly as he could be in the way he asked members of the orchestra to stand up during the applause. If he wanted to indicate he wasn't interested in moving to Berlin he could have done it differently.'

It was after these two concerts that Rattle really admitted – to himself as much as anyone – that he wanted the job. He sensed that he could do it, that he did have things to bring to this proud and difficult orchestra. Talking to him about other things (typically, he'd rung me at the time to recommend someone else for a job), it was clear that he recognized that this was the big opportunity, and he sounded inspired by the potential of the orchestra. He had been equally convinced, equally determined and equally enthusiastic twenty years before, when he told the new manager of the CBSO, his friend Ed Smith, that he would like the job in Birmingham.

The election process had already been begun with much discussion between the orchestra members at their regular monthly meetings, so that when they came to take part in a first written ballot the outcome was not unexpected. The press was on tenterhooks: 'By tomorrow afternoon the musical world should know who is to succeed Claudio Abbado,' breathed the *Sunday Telegraph*. 'In an election process characterized by wild speculation and more leaks than the *Titanic*, the chances are that the news will be out well before the news hits the wires.' In fact the process had been scrupulously controlled, and the first anyone knew of the result was when the orchestra's chairman, Peter Riegelbauer, appeared from behind closed doors at 4 p.m. on the day of the election.

The most amazing reasons were put forward for supporting one candidate or the other:

> Barenboim's possible appointment was trumpeted by some as a form of musical reparation for the Holocaust – a hubristic and ludicrous notion that entirely overlooks the fact that Barenboim is ensconced at the Staatsoper and regularly conducts at Bayreuth, once music's walk-in wardrobe for anti-Semitic skeletons. Meanwhile Rattle has unwittingly assumed the uncomfortable mantle of representing New Europe like a baton-wielding Tony Blair . . .

One gathers that most of the conductors initially suggested by individual orchestra members inevitably received relatively few votes – they included Salonen, Nagano and Maazel again, while those for Barenboim and Rattle (with perhaps Mariss Jansons as a runner-up third choice) predominated. Maybe someone wrote in the name of Carlos Kleiber: hope springs eternal. So that when a final vote was taken after a subsequent three-hour discussion, the result was clear: Andrew Clark in the *Financial Times* reported that Rattle gained 43 per cent of the vote compared with Barenboim's 25 per cent, giving Rattle the margin needed for a consensus. But no one can know whether those figures are correct. The debate, behind closed doors, was passionate, but in the end the vote was a clear mandate for Rattle.

The next morning, even the British press – which seemed to have forgotten what the arts were all about except when there was another scandal at the Royal Opera House – went ecstatic on their front pages:

RATTLE'S CAREER HITS CRESCENDO WITH TOP BERLIN JOB
Sir Simon Rattle pulled off the musical coup of a lifetime yesterday, when the 112 players of the Berlin Philharmonic Orchestra voted to make him their conductor, the most influential classical music job in the world . . . The selection process makes the hunt for a new director-general of the BBC look like a parish council by-election . . . there were two secret written ballots yesterday . . . The meeting was controversial and emotional, orchestral members disclosed. 'It was a real affair of the heart,' Axel Gerhardt, a violinist with the orchestra for thirty-three years, disclosed. 'The young people in the orchestra won. It's a defeat for the traditionalists. It was a huge and a very emotional decision.'

Guardian, 24 June 1999

(The letters column was quick to carry a few comments, and a correction from one of Simon's oldest musical friends, the principal percussionist of the CBSO, Annie Oakley: 'I have to point out that you cannot hit a crescendo. Sir Simon's career has been a crescendo which has climaxed in his appointment.')

The *Sun* wrote in an editorial:

EURORATTLED
A British classical music conductor called Sir Simon Rattle was last night given the top job with the biggest orchestra in Europe. Does that matter? Yes. A Brit has now got the BIGGEST job with Germany's greatest orchestra. It proves that Simon is a winner and that Britain should be proud of its musicians – from him to the Spice Girls. Bravo, Simon.

Headline treatment: in Britain and Germany, the news breaks
of Rattle's move to the Berlin Philharmonic

Why did the *Sun* editorialize on classical music? A letter to Rattle from the editor, David Yelland, revealed that

> Just over sixteen years ago when I was a student I sat through an entire week of your Sibelius performances at Warwick University Arts Centre. You may remember it – you conducted all seven symphonies over three or four days I seem to recall. The memory has always stuck with me. I am a huge fan of Sibelius and the CBSO series was a classic. Well done to you. You have done your country proud.

Apart from one negative piece by Joachim Kaiser, questioning the depth of Rattle's commitment to the nineteenth-century repertory, the reaction of the Berlin press was extremely favourable. The English reaction predictably concentrated on the revolutionary nature of the appointment, but in a letter to the *Daily Telegraph*, Karajan's biographer Richard Osborne tried to redress that view:

> Rattle in Birmingham revealed a similar passion and long-term vision [to Karajan's] in what is, sadly, the dying art of orchestral training ... It is wonderful to have an English-born musician leading the Berlin Philharmonic into the next century, but it is not a break with the past; rather, it is a return to the old ways of doing things. The appointments of Nikisch, Furtwängler and Karajan were no less exciting and radical in their day than Rattle's is today.

Rattle had played his cards close to his chest, saying very little except for one reported on-the-record remark that the orchestra would need to decide whether it wanted to be an artistic institution or a media enterprise. He managed, as usual, to be unavailable for comment at the crucial moment, as he was receiving an honorary degree from Oxford University, though photographers managed to snap him in his highly untypical robes. He left the country on a safari trip to Africa with his two children the following day. His statement of 24 June 1999 was clearly designed to be flattering to the orchestra, but balanced the appeal to tradition and the appeal to change with considerable skill:

> I have always believed trust to be the most important ingredient in musical collaboration. The fact that the BPO has reached its decision through such a long, thoughtful democratic process gives me immense optimism for our future together. The opportunity to spend the next part of my life with this unparalleled group of virtuosi is a thrilling prospect.

The orchestra's tradition is of course staggering. The legacy of Furtwängler, Karajan and Abbado is a living, breathing thing. But equally important is the orchestra's embrace of change, the sense that many new things are possible without compromising the foundations on which they are built. It will be an honour and a privilege for me to take this journey with such a great orchestra.

Looking back on the election process, observers feel it worked well.

ELMAR WEINGARTEN The main thing they did wrong last time was to go round asking everyone if they would be willing to come, and so a lot of conductors thought they were strong candidates but actually they were just making up the list. So this time they did not do that, and after some suggestions there were basically two or three candidates left. And in the end only if Daniel Barenboim and Simon Rattle had divided the vote equally would there have been a chance for another person.

In my opinion it was a very brave decision. Daniel Barenboim proposed himself as the bearer of Germanic tradition going back to Furtwängler and maybe even also Karajan, certainly interested in preserving the sound of this orchestra, full, rich, dark. He is very convincing in the German repertory. Simon is striving for something totally different: a light, crisp, clear, transparent sound with a lot of middle voices heard, discovering new elements in the music. He is also very interested in new and neglected music. Both decisions could have been defended, both decisions could have been presented convincingly to the public. But in the end the orchestra was adventurous. The question is now what the orchestra will sound like in four or five years' time.

Simon was very nice indeed about Daniel. He was one of the first people he rang after the election. He has been very skilful at establishing good relations with him, which is very important for the future of music in Berlin. Whatever happens with the Staatsoper, the orchestra wants to keep up a good relationship with Daniel so that he comes as often as he used to. I hope he will stay in Berlin and receive international acclaim from touring with the Staatskapelle. It could be very fruitful.

The chairman of the orchestra and the person who convened the election and finally announced the decision is Peter Riegelbauer, who will from now on be very influential in the relationship with Rattle:

PETER RIEGELBAUER From the very first moment we heard him – some of the players went to concerts by the Birmingham orchestra, and certainly when he did that first Mahler 6 with us – we were excited by him. Even when we voted for Claudio Abbado in 1989, and Simon Rattle had conducted us only once, he was present in the discussions as someone we should be thinking about. Everyone knew and he knew that it was too early but it was certainly worthwhile to discuss it. And every time he came back there would be new experiences for us and new pieces.

Was it the new repertory that was most interesting?
Mahler 10 was a problem for some players the first time and it took some time to get used to this piece. By the second time, when we made the recording, it was great, but it is a matter of taste for the players, it is their right not to like it! But I must say it was also great to do pieces the orchestra knew very well. *The Rite of Spring* was very strong because it was so emotional. You can do it cool, you can do it beautifully, but Simon made it still expressive but incredibly exciting. And in rehearsal he would have complete control, always searching for perfection, hearing the details of the playing. He is such a good collaborator because he is very collegial – it's not as if he is a teacher arriving from somewhere far off; he is one of the musicians. Sometimes you lose respect if you are too collegial, but Simon always has our respect and he keeps a very good balance.

Has he already changed the orchestra's style?
He is I would say one of those masters who have been changing the orchestra. Of course Claudio changed it a lot after Karajan, not throwing away the good things but helping us to play in different ways. Harnoncourt has been very important for our style, and has made us more flexible and open: this is what Simon likes. The Haydn that he did just around the time of the vote was so lively, and that made a great impression on us.

How well did the process of replacing Claudio Abbado work?
It was early 1998 when Claudio said he would leave four years later and somehow we were very shocked because we thought: how can we continue through those four years with him when he has said he is leaving? But now we know that we needed this time. We didn't start the discussions by mentioning names but by discussing a lot with the whole orchestra what we wanted to be in the future, the principles behind the orchestra's work, and this took a long time. Then we started to work out a very, very refined and complicated system of voting. It's almost funny that it is so complicated, far more than for a politician, because it is such a delicate matter for us. So there were very complicated discussions and several periods of debate. And it was very important for us that the public and even the individual players should not know at the end how it went, who voted for who, how many votes a conductor got, but only the result. We want to keep good relations with all conductors!

What do you hope for now for the future of the orchestra?
A very simple hope is that we shall have some wonderful concerts, but that's not as easy as it sounds. Everyone says our orchestra is number one in the world, or at least one of the best, and the danger is that you give some bad concerts and people think all that is going down very quickly. Now the potential of the orchestra is fantastic, so many young players, so many good players, that the signals for the future are good. We will do wider repertoire with Simon, both old and new, and I think that too was a very important part of the vote. We need young people in the audience: our audience in Berlin is old, and we love the old people, but we also need people who will be old in fifty years' time! So education activity will be important to us.

The Philharmonie has always been a closed temple. This must change. We want it to be an exciting communication centre in the city, to be alive and busy and to be there for the community in the city to use.

You are changing the structure of the orchestra . . .
Yes, so that all the different aspects come together better into one focus, which is more compact: the media, the concerts, the tours. This has been a problem in the past, more I would say for the outside world than for us on the inside. But the world of recordings is so different now. How that is going to be in the future, I really cannot say. What we know is that all over the world in different countries people want to hear this orchestra, to have them for concerts, and the situation with live music-making is very good. Perhaps people will prefer that now to CDs, and all those discussions about how Muti does this bar or Abbado does that note, it's all very interesting but there's something a little artificial about it. We want to make music for an audience.

How did you feel about the proposal that you could be funded by the state rather than the city?
Frankly speaking, at one point we would have preferred to have the state fund us, we thought this could have been better. But the city wanted to keep us, and I think we did some good work with the politicians, and in the end it was settled that the city would keep funding us. The orchestra is very important to the city, and now that this has been decided it will be a very strong future for us. They have to keep this institution on the very top level.

Simon will bring a lot of new ideas to this situation. He is very good with the politicians. He is so democratic and a good colleague and I think it will work with this orchestra's sense of self-government which has always been so strong. We will work well together. I have been talking to him for an hour on the phone today; this is very unusual for a conductor. He is so intense, I am exhausted already!

So now it begins. There is a whole raft of issues to be faced: the structure of the orchestra, the pay of the players, the relationship with the hall, the city and the state. Already this has provoked one major crisis in 2001; more are sure to follow. The financial situation is not rosy for the players, because salaries had fallen behind other musical organizations and have only just been increased to make them competitive once again. Above all, Rattle has found a new collaborator as intendant of the orchestra, the German Franz Xaver Ohnesorg, who after an extremely successful period as director of the Cologne Triennial Festival had a very stormy and controversial period as director of New York's Carnegie Hall. The offer from Berlin was an extremely helpful escape route for him, and one suspects he would have preferred to have gone there in the first place: he had certainly discussed it six years earlier, when Elmar Weingarten was appointed. This relationship will be a central factor in Rattle's success: Ohnesorg's reputation for getting things done in the face of opposition suggests that he will be effective, but does not necessarily offer the open and collaborative stance that Rattle is looking for.

In February 2001 I asked Rattle about the Philharmonie, the orchestra's home in Berlin:

SIMON RATTLE If you go to Berlin when the orchestra is on tour in October and you look at what goes on in the Philharmonie, it's humiliating for one of the great cities of the world and it has to stop. Even Cardiff wouldn't put this stuff on. How we can change it and work with other promoters is a big unresolved issue. In the past even Bruno Walter used to have his own series conducting the Berlin Philharmonic put on by a different concert agency. I'd rather like to see that again for Claudio, for instance.

Carte blanche for Abbado?
Carte blanche without bankrupting us please, Claudio! At the moment this is one of the great orchestras of the world and there is no coherent philosophy behind what it does. Karajan was interested in his own periods with the orchestra but not much else. The idea there could be for the first time in Europe a great concert hall run by a great orchestra – not like at the Concertgebouw where it's a different administration – this could be a revolution.

The programming has to be widened in all directions. As it happens my first guest conductor in my first season is Bill Christie [of the French baroque ensemble Les arts florissants] and he will have so much to give the orchestra in one area. Then there has to be new music: Xaver and I just agreed that we should do four new pieces a year, which has never been done before. Here's a modern city; Rebecca Horn is down the road and she wants to collaborate with Luc Bondy; we have to find a composer . . .

The musical situation in Berlin is enormously complex because of the duplicate institutions created since the Second World War, when the two halves of the city increasingly became separate. In 1946 RIAS was founded, and in 1953–4 Sender Freies Berlin, which joined ARD in 1954. Both these radio organisations had their own orchestras. The situation in opera was even more involved: the weighty history of Berlin's culture was to a large extent cut off in the East, with the Staatsoper in the Unter den Linden. The Deutsche Oper became the focus of operatic activity in the West: following the building of the Wall in 1961, it was given a new home and a new building (typically and now depressingly post-war in its architecture) in the Bismarckstrasse. Meanwhile the Komische Oper, just beyond the Brandenburg Gate in the East, was run as the personal fiefdom of Walter Felsenstein, even though he lived in the West – leading him to remark that there were three states in Berlin, the BRD, the DDR and the Komische Oper.

Now, over a decade since the Wall came down, all these institutions want to survive. But there is not the money to go round; the three houses cost an enormous amount of money, and culture ministers tasked to look at this have come and gone rapidly. One proposal was that the Deutsche Oper, currently conducted by Christian Thielemann, should be merged with the Staastoper. But Barenboim said, 'In my view that would be a death sentence for both orchestras. Then the Staatskapelle will cease to exist as such, and I shall no longer have a reason for remaining in Berlin.' The battle of the opera houses threatens to harm cultural life in Berlin, and forms a background to the Philharmonic's own battles for recognition.

The stakes were raised by a foolish remark made by Klaus Landowsky, the leader of the Christian Democratic Union in the Berlin Senate, who was quoted by a journalist as contrasting 'the young Karajan, Christian Thielemann', and 'the Jew Barenboim'. This caused an outcry, and Barenboim kept the issue on the boil by using the platform of *Die Zeit* and the *New York Review of Books* in March

2001 to write a thoughtful but polemical piece about 'Germans, Jews, and Music':

> I believe that many Germans lost their sense of patriotism, their affection for their country, during the second half of the twentieth century and did so partly out of fear of nationalism. This is unfortunate ... My hope is that Berlin will not lose its special status because of reunification – on the contrary. Because of the forty-year-long division and the existence of the East and the West side by side, Berlin, in my view, has a unique potential for encompassing differences, a potential that should now be made use of. Instead about complaining about the division caused by history, one should treat it as a positive force.

The fact that this plea could be read as a bid to keep Berlin's special funding of the arts intact was not lost on the city.

WERNER BRUG Because Berlin has so many orchestras of its own as well as chamber-music groups there has never been much activity by the main touring orchestras here. They will play in Dresden or Hamburg or Leipzig but not in Berlin. The main agent here, Adler, who also happens to represent Daniel Barenboim, is getting older and he always thinks it has to go as it used to go but in fact now it doesn't go at all! Even with the big Berlin Festival in September, it doesn't make sense to have a four-week orchestral-concert festival unless there is a tourist audience. So the Festival will change and the relationship between the Berlin Philharmonic and the Philharmonie must change too. That's where Ohnesorg will be good.

What's your assessment of the Abbado years?
The roster of guest conductors was good. It's very interesting to have a Brahms cycle by personalities as different as Abbado and Harnoncourt. To have the old giants, such as Kurt Sanderling and Günter Wand, in as well as Salonen, Norrington and Jansons is really high class. In the last two or three seasons the recording situation has become more difficult and you see this in some very silly concerts. At one concert, the first half was taped by EMI – Sabine Meyer's second recording of the Mozart Clarinet Concerto – and then DG taped the second half – the Strauss *Four Last Songs* with Karita Mattila. It was interesting to hear Bryn Terfel, but his Wagner concert was just a recording session filled out with some new things; the audience felt like spectators.

Why did the Berlin Philharmonic escape for so long the controversy about how much is spent on the opera houses?
Because Berlin, the city, wants to go on supporting the Philharmonic. They give it 25 million marks [to which the orchestra adds about DM13m in

earned income]. They could have said, 'This is an international orchestra, so the state should subsidize it, and then we can spend this money on opera or whatever.' But the city don't want to do that because they are very proud of the orchestra. Culture is now a battlefield in Berlin; there is so much fighting among themselves. The culture ministers think only in the short term and look only at the period when they will be in power. Not one of them has had a vision. And because the city is a coalition it is difficult to gets things decided. The situation with the opera houses is really bad too. The state puts in 240 million marks, so it is a very serious situation.

There are certainly too many orchestras in Berlin, but it's the old story: who volunteers to go first? No one is volunteering for abolition. In the old West the Deutsches-Sinfonie Orchester Berlin is the successor of the old radio orchestra run by RIAS, which was the second-oldest radio orchestra in Europe, conducted by Ferenc Fricsay and Lorin Maazel. It changed its name to avoid the 'radio' tag under Vladimir Ashkenazy. Now conducted by Kent Nagano, it has the freedom to do adventurous programmes and also finds itself leading a new agglomeration of some 350 musicians, bringing together the radio choirs and orchestras from the former West Berlin and East Berlin.

The Berlin Sinfonie-Orchester was founded in the East in 1952 and is based in the Konzerthaus near Berlin's new centre of gravity around the Brandenburg Gate; its conductors have included Michael Schönwandt and Eliahu Inbal. Less certain is the position in this new group of the East Berlin broadcasting orchestra which Rafael Frühbeck de Burgos used to conduct. The intention was to make it a smaller specialist orchestra, but that is not popular with the musicians, nor with Marek Janowski, who has been asked to conduct it. He feels it should be kept at a strength of 120 but most observers feel that this is impractical. The RIAS dance orchestra was abolished after the Wall came down, and its big band in 2000, so the numbers of musicians employed for broadcasting has already been substantially reduced.

WERNER BRUG Berlin is not a rich city. It lost its bourgeoisie after the Second World War because the only people who stayed were the people who couldn't afford to go. Young people come here to study at the university but then they go away to cities in the West. It takes a time to develop a new bourgeoisie. There will surely be one now with all the change in Berlin, but it won't necessarily be one that feels responsible for music, for the orchestras and the opera. There are plenty of politicians here now, but

politicians who are not so educated or interested in the orchestra. There is a
lot to look after: twenty theatres as well as all the orchestras. How the
orchestra adapts to this changing situation is very important.

SIMON RATTLE It's desperately important that the Berlin Philharmonic
and I go to play in Eastern Europe. When did they last play in Dresden?
When did they last play in the real East Berlin? They're not going to come
to us. We have to go out and give something back.

And will that be seen as treading on people's toes?
Probably. While my German is terrible, I won't be able to understand what
they're saying so I can just go and tread away ... I sat and talked to
Hartmut Haenchen, who is running the festival in Dresden, the other day. I
said, 'It's very painful to be an Englishman in Dresden because whatever
you say about war this was a profoundly unnecessary act.' He laughed and
said, 'God, not harder than being a German coming to live in Amsterdam.'
These things are all around us and we have to live with them.

I don't think the musicians yet know how much they really have a part to
play, it's important they realize they have to give something back. They've
lived on a very privileged island for a long time and it is no longer an island.
They have to reach out and give back as well in order to deserve all these
manifold gifts.

The city is going to change. To be in a city that is changing so much is an
incredible privilege. The only thing that is certain if you read back over the
history of Berlin is that it has been in a state of transition for its entire
existence. It is always about to become something wonderful. It is rebuilding itself and there is a real will to change. Maybe I can help this idea that
the opera houses might talk to each other. The last time I was there two of
the opera houses were playing the same opera the same night. It was a
scandal that all three did *Macbeth* in the same month.

Now you have appointed a new intendant ...
The first thing I did when I got the job was to go to New York and talk to
Xaver Ohnesorg but at that point it was impossible for him. He'd only just
started at Carnegie. And we got seriously down the line with another wonderful man. But Xaver helped me so much just to decode what was going
on in Germany. For me, it's a problem to find a partnership having had Ed
Smith [the manager at the CBSO for Rattle's entire period there] through
the whole of one part of my life. But Xaver said to me, 'You know, I'm an
only child and I've always wanted a brother.' That will be great. He
understands, and he's even more radical than I am.

Is the orchestra really not paid well enough?
You have to realize that in the past everyone had to be bribed to stay in

Berlin. Everyone was basically paid 10 per cent extra for living in that island behind the Wall. So, of course, the year after the Wall came down the Philharmonic had a 10 per cent pay cut. There is now a plan to get that restored, and I feel it's really important to do that. But they are still way down the list if you compare them with the American orchestras. Some of them are leaving for prestigious teaching jobs, so we have to take real care now. Berlin is not a rich city and when they say there is no more money they mean it. So there's sponsorship, but getting into that will be very strange for Berlin, almost like man-in-the-moon time. It is a different culture and it's no use thinking a new culture can be forced quickly, but they are thinking about it. I believe in the end that if we do something really wonderful artistically then the funds will follow.

The process seems to be working already. Geoffrey Norris reported in the *Daily Telegraph* in September 1999 on the performance of Mahler 10 with which Rattle finally converted the orchestra to this piece. Under the heading 'BERLIN ENRAPTURED BY RATTLE' he wrote,

> This concert on Friday night will come to be seen as one of signal importance in the orchestra's history . . . His reception in the Philharmonic's auditorium demonstrated that he has secured the public's confidence as well. Rattle has few dates with the Berlin Philharmonic between now and 2002, but this performance alone was evidence that the orchestra has made the right choice.

In the early part of 2001 events moved forward smoothly. In April Ohnesorg signed his contract with the Berlin Philharmonic at a unique occasion attended by the present and future music directors, Claudio Abbado and Simon Rattle. Rattle had just given another hugely successful concert, of Janáček and Beethoven's Pastoral Symphony, while Abbado, though still thin and wan after his struggle with stomach cancer, was rejuvenated and relaxed. (It was a terrible irony that Abbado, whom few had thought could survive his cancer, was alive and well when just a few days before another conductor, Giuseppe Sinopoli, who had not been at all ill, had collapsed and died of a heart attack in Berlin during a performance of *Aida*.) As Ohnesorg signed, Christoph Stölzl praised the orchestra as 'the flagship of the arts in Berlin', while Peter Riegelbauer welcomed Ohnesorg's arrival as 'a key step in the re-forming of the orchestra'.

There was only one major flaw in the picture: Simon Rattle had not yet signed his own contract. He was holding out to make sure that the increased pay for the orchestra for which he had lobbied hard would be guaranteed, and given the political climate in Berlin that seemed to be far from certain. Not only the Green Party but other politicians were making objections to increased subventions to the orchestra, and heavy lobbying was necessary. The politicians had to approve the new foundation or Stiftung that would control all the orchestra's affairs, whose constitution had been formulated in a typically dry German legal document. It had been presented to the city government's cultural committee for its approval, alongside the demands for increased funding to restore the players' salaries. But if everyone thought the approval would be plain sailing they were in for a shock. Unfortunately it was at exactly that moment in May 2001 that the fragile political coalition in the city collapsed, and the parties began jockeying for position. Major financial crises and corruption charges in the city only added to the tension, and at a meeting in June the committee dropped a bombshell by failing to agree the proposals for the Philharmonic and instead deferring them. The spectre this created was of endless political strife, which would not be resolved before new mayoral elections in the autumn at the earliest.

An intense period of activity followed, carried out under the daily glare of the international press. Peter Riegelbauer denounced the city, saying that 'Rattle's appointment has been endangered in a barely excusable way', and while Rattle kept his counsel he seemed to me genuinely uncertain about the outcome. However, the pressure behind the scenes on the city to deliver was huge, especially since it had only just made a big play to keep the orchestra's funding rather than handing it over to the state government. Various political solutions were proposed: the most worrying for the orchestra was the suggestion that a representative of every political party should be entitled to a place on the Stiftung. Ohnesorg for a while believed he could manage that situation, but in the first test of the collegiate decision-making Rattle has insisted on, the player representatives and Rattle convinced him that it was a recipe for disaster and continual political interference. The idea was shelved, and instead there were to be only two politicians on the Stiftung, representing not parties but the culture and finance committees.

Meanwhile the orchestra continued to behave with considerable arrogance, complaining that they were being treated like 'a school where we have to beg pardon to buy every pencil', an unwise characterization of arts subsidy during a financial crisis. And it became clear that among the main objectors to the structure of the Stiftung were not only politicians but also the other orchestras in Berlin, who feared that the Philharmonic's ambition to control the artistic planning of the Philharmonie hall would reduce their ability to appear there. The opera houses, and especially Daniel Barenboim at the Staatsoper, were equally dissatisfied that their problems were not being addressed. The prospect of internal conflict between the musical bodies among whom Rattle had done much to foster good relations so far was a depressing one.

Although those who knew Rattle well always believed that the situation would be resolved and he would eventually sign his contract, there was only one moment when he could exert maximum influence in the discussions, and that was before he signed it. So the pressure grew relentlessly until the new interim mayor of the city, Klaus Wowerweit (a cultured man who was also the city's first major politician to be openly gay), anxious for a propaganda coup, ensured the proposals were passed by the Senate at the very end of its pre-summer session in July.

There was a huge sigh of relief that both the Stiftung and the financial proposals had been accepted, and the process of negotiating Rattle's personal contract could now begin. His agents were cautious; Karajan was arguing about his rights and responsibilities in Berlin until the very month he died. But their persistence paid off: by the time Rattle conducted and recorded Schoenberg's *Gurrelieder* in Berlin in September 2001, the contract was ready to be signed. The ceremony, delayed by the events of 11 September in America, took place in the Philharmonie on 19 September. It was a lively affair with some music by Brett Dean and Piazzolla, speeches by Klaus Wowereit and the then culture minister Adrienne Goehler (who has already been replaced). Simon spoke partly in German (the first time I'd heard him do so in public) and partly in English, with warmth and passion, concentrating on the depth of his relationship with the players of the orchestra.

At moments like these, Rattle is both a brilliant advocate and an astute politician. Will it work? Only time will tell: it certainly began promisingly in Liverpool, less than half a century ago.

CHAPTER THREE

'Monomaniacal about music'
Early Years 1955–74

First notes: Simon at the piano in Liverpool (photo Denis Rattle)

I

1955–70

In previous centuries, Simon Rattle would have been called a prodigy. But there is something too normal about his voracious enthusiasm for music to make that term sound right. His home background was warm and supportive, far from the pressurized atmosphere associated with artistic prodigies, such as the young Mozart, with their hothouse training and forced development.

Where do musical gifts come from? Nature or nurture, inheritance or education? It is a long-running debate. Simon knew that both of his parents were extremely musical, but it was only a couple of years ago that he found out that his father also came from a very musical family. His father Denis's origins had been shrouded in doubt – the family knew he had been adopted, but not from whom or why – until a newspaper researched the subject in 1999. The *Daily Mail* came up with the modest but fascinating revelation that Denis's middle name, Guttridge, was actually the name of his original family. His natural mother was Kathleen Guttridge, born at the end of the nineteenth century, who left home in Bournemouth, came to London and became an actress. At the age of nineteen and unmarried, she had a child in October 1916, who was handed over for adoption to a middle-class couple, William and Elizabeth Rattle. This child was Denis, who soon developed an interest in music. The interesting fact is that the Rattles were not musical, but the Guttridge family had been keenly interested in music, and all Kathleen's brothers played instruments; her elder sister Maggie gave concerts with her husband and sang throughout her life. Kathleen married and went to Australia, but the marriage broke down and she returned to Bournemouth with two children. There was never any contact with the adopted Denis, who moved to Broadstairs with his foster mother after her husband died. His musical talents developed from there and he went on to Oriel College, Oxford, to read English.

So there is actually no Rattle blood in Simon Rattle's veins – which might be a odd feeling were it not for the fact that this situation must also be true of many others, including one of the best-known names in the country, Tony Blair. (It was also the *Daily Mail* which revealed, when he was about to become leader of the Labour party, that Tony's father Leo had been adopted. In his case he had been born as the result of an affair and the two parents eventually married, but they were unable to reclaim their son from his foster parents, the Blairs.) As Tony Blair's biographer John Rentoul puts it, the story of his grandparents is 'a colourful one, although of limited interest to all but genetic determinists'. Yet in the case of someone as prodigiously gifted as Simon Rattle, genetic determinism is not at all irrelevant. Following the revelations (which he claims he was unaware of for several weeks because no one he knows reads the *Daily Mail*!) Simon was fascinated to track down a new member of his family, his widowed aunt Berenice (Berry) Laney, who is his father's natural half-sister, one of the children Kathleen brought back with her from Australia. Sadly, however, the revelations came just a few years after Denis's death. ·

Denis grew up passionately interested in music but never made it his career. He was for many years the managing director of an import–export company that dealt with the Far East in a wide range of major items such as industrial machinery and medical equipment, as well as such minor, unromantic items as plastic flowers and bras. But he always had a passion for jazz, and when he was reading English at Oxford he

joined a university dance band called The Bandits (whose members
included Frank Taplin, a future chairman of the Metropolitan Opera in
New York, and Desmond Dupré, the lutenist). He considered a career in
teaching, and then toyed with the idea of a career in jazz, but put both
aside when the Second World War broke out. He joined the navy, and it
was from that point that his future moved in the direction of business
rather than teaching. He met his wife, Pauline, in Dover, where he was
on minesweeping duties and she was running a music shop. ('I had to
wangle a second year in Dover,' he recalled, 'which wasn't really allowed
because it was supposed to be so dangerous. I spent every penny I had as
a sub-lieutenant on records, just so that I could talk to her.') It was their
mutual love of music that brought them together. They married in 1941
and went up to Liverpool where he was sent to recover from his arduous
duties, arriving on the night of the famous thousand-bomber raid that
destroyed so much of the city.

Through contacts he met in Liverpool he was asked to help set up a
company shipping goods to China immediately after the war, though the
Communist takeover soon put paid to that and the focus of activity
shifted to Hong Kong. For many years the work proved challenging and
exciting, but it became increasingly irksome as he found himself dealing
mainly with creditors and debtors, and his mind turned once more to the
idea of a teaching career. It was not to be until he was fifty, however, that
he made the break, left the company, went back to college and re-
emerged as an English teacher – at a considerable salary drop – at a
school where he also became involved in music, teaching the recorder,
guitar and piano.

Denis Rattle had always played jazz on the piano at home, and
Pauline Rattle also played from time to time. Their first child, Susan,
born in 1946, had a major influence on the family's development. She is
highly intelligent and physically slightly disabled, with muscular problems that caused her parents to worry for a long time whether she would
be able to be fully independent. She trained as a librarian, undertaking
the demanding three-year course at home and obtaining a librarianship
degree. She has for many years now been extremely happy working at
the Central Library in Liverpool. She too has a passion for music: she
plays percussion and from her early years she was bringing home
records and scores that were to have a profound influence on her
younger brother.

Simon was born nine years after Susan, on 19 January 1955. In an

interview many years ago he spoke very candidly about the early influence of his mother:

> Because my father's business took him away a great deal when I was a child
> my mother was the more dominating force. I remember particularly that
> she never smacked me. Discipline in our house – which has always been a
> very gentle place – was always administered verbally. The worst punish-
> ment you could have was a really sharp word and my mother was always
> good at that . . . She's always said I was a good baby and didn't cry much.
> When I was a bit older I was too fat, though not from the diet my mother
> served me but because I was a sort of food kleptomaniac, relentlessly pilfer-
> ing food from the fridge . . . Right from childhood she influenced my read-
> ing tastes considerably. I was encouraged to read George Orwell and H. G.
> Wells. My mother used to leave books around in the hope that I would try
> them . . . As a person my mother appears very quiet on the surface, but
> underneath that calm exterior there is a good deal of turbulence and inten-
> sity. I know she is proud of me but she keeps it to herself. It's rather more
> obvious in my father.

> DENIS RATTLE Sad how things turned out! I thought I would have a jazz
> drummer to accompany me in my old age . . .

It was certainly Simon's father who first led him towards music. Playing
his Gershwin songs and jazz numbers on the piano, he noticed that the
two-year-old Simon would tap along on whatever was handy with a
distinct and firm sense of rhythm. It was definitely jazz and not classical
music that made the first big impression on Simon, and he remembers
reacting strongly against some of the classical records Susan brought
home. By the time he was four he had a small drum kit, bought for him by
his father. Simon managed to break it up within a short space of time.
However, he had a real aptitude for percussion, and it was this that led to
his first public appearance.

> FRITZ SPIEGL My daughter Emma went to the same kindergarten as
> Simon, and we knew the family well. I remember that whenever Simon
> came round for a party he would always perform; it was difficult to get my
> children to play anything but he would immediately leap up to the piano,
> harpsichord, organ or whatever. In 1961 I'd been asked to put together an
> entertainment for the anniversary of the Bluecoat School. There was an old
> Victorian Bluecoat march of which I had the music, so I scored it up and we
> had Simon aged six as the drummer. He was real extrovert, but I can't
> honestly say that I spotted him then as someone who would go this far.

DENIS RATTLE Simon had never had a lesson at this point, but I taught him the piece Fritz arranged. I'd played some percussion in my school orchestra very roughly, so I took him through it. At the end of the performance Fritz lifted him up on to the table and Simon got his own round of applause. I think that made a big impression, the applause! That was what decided us to go to John Ward, who was playing percussion in the Liverpool Phil, and ask him to teach Simon seriously. Another thing that very much influenced Simon just around this time was that I started to take him to Merseyside Youth Orchestra rehearsals on a Sunday morning; he must have been six or seven. And when he saw the chap up at the back playing the timpani Simon knew that he was the king – he was obviously in control of everything – so I think his attitude was: 'Never mind the conductor, that's where I want to be.'

By this time it was clear that Simon had real musical talent. He was beginning to learn the piano too, with ten-minute lessons at his prep school, Newborough. He had developed a great interest in twentieth-century music – Schoenberg's *Five Orchestral Pieces* he distinctly recalls as a piece he found 'just wonderfully beautiful' at that time. Among the pieces Susan Rattle recalls bringing home from the library around this time are Bartók's *The Miraculous Mandarin* and Violin Concerto, Schoenberg's *Gurrelieder*, Tippett's *A Child of Our Time*, Mahler's First, Fourth and Sixth Symphonies, Shostakovich's First, Fifth and Tenth Symphonies, Walton's *Belshazzar's Feast*, and Rimsky-Korsakov's *Capriccio espagnol* and *Sheherazade*, a fascinating list which includes pieces that are still among Simon's favourites. Susan gradually taught him to read the scores of these pieces. Denis Rattle recalls this happening 'very casually and normally. When listening to Proms or records at home he would borrow scores. But it was not long, with Susan's help, before he could sit and read a score, just as other children would read a comic.'

SIMON RATTLE Having a sister who was handicapped put me in the very unusual position of having someone who was nine years older, and intellectually nine years older – which is a huge gap – but who was willing to play with me the whole time. I think I was very much affected by what she would bring back from the library; that's why I started with twentieth-century music rather than anything else. (I remember at the Royal Academy, when I was seventeen, realizing I was hearing Brahms's Third for the first time, which was a real shock.)

   The thing I most loved to read – which is pretty scary now I think of it – was the great green bound copy of the Berlioz *Treatise on Instrumentation*, and that must have been when I was seven or so. I think if I found a child doing that I'd think, 'God, how ludicrous.' I really don't remember how Susan taught me to read scores, but she did. I just needed to know everything: I was absolutely monomaniacal about music in a way I'm not any more, thank God. That changed around puberty, but I still see it in some of my colleagues, and it's frightening.

DENIS RATTLE Simon listened to all sorts of music on the radio in these years. He must have listened to virtually every Prom during the summer for years from the age of eight or nine, and our household was organized round getting supper in and the homework done in order for him to be upstairs with his radio by 7.30! He must have absorbed an incredible amount of music then, and he knew it really well and would often be following scores.

SIMON RATTLE I suppose the first time I had a baton in my hands it must have been to other people's records. We had one of those records called 'Music for Frustrated Conductors' and it had a fantastic cartoon on the front with a chap in tails and a little mirror, and it had the *Sabre Dance*, *Ritual Fire Dance*, bits of *Carmen*; it's so embarrassing to think about it, but I did conduct to it. It sounds so horrifying . . .

Some of the most remarkable events in those years before Simon was eleven must have been the Sunday afternoon concerts in the Rattle household. At the weekend Simon would go with his father and Susan to the local library where they would choose records and scores of some twentieth-century display pieces, usually those which involved a lot of percussion. During the week, Simon would copy out all the percussion parts and build the pieces into a programme. With a neighbour, Sally Loader, and Susan, and occasionally with his parents as well, he would give a concert on the following Sunday which consisted of playing the records with 'live' added percussion.

DENIS RATTLE He would have the plum part, of course, and we would chip in and he would tell us off if we did anything wrong. We did all sorts of pieces – Shostakovich 5, Mahler 4, Respighi's *Pines of Rome, Fountains of Rome* – you name it, we were in there. We even did *A Child of Our Time*, and bits of *Rosenkavalier* . . . The programme for each concert, written out by Simon, would be pasted on the drawing-room door.

SUSAN RATTLE Simon would always write on the parts not only the kind of percussion instruments but the size of instruments on which he would have wanted to have played it. This was a result of John Ward, who was

always very precise about which exact instrument was to be used: if there
was a single gong in a piece he would line up a whole row of gongs and
would choose which it was to be.

The surviving scores of those sessions show some pieces that have gone
on being crucial to Simon: in addition to those his father mentioned,
Gershwin's *Porgy and Bess* was there, with its insistent xylophone
obbligato, Elgar's *Enigma Variations* and Holst's *The Perfect Fool*, and
even the three fragments from Berg's *Wozzeck*. It is astonishing to
think how much music the young Simon Rattle must have absorbed so
early.

Simon's first experience of playing in a live group was with a small
orchestra of very young musicians under the direction of Raymond
Mulholland. He played violin and percussion and made his very first
attempts at conducting as well. ('He was a very very bad violinist,'
recalled Denis later. 'He didn't practise scales.') When he went to Liverpool College he was entitled to play in the Liverpool Schools Junior
Orchestra, where he played percussion, but since rehearsals were on
Saturdays, and the college worked on Saturday mornings, he was rarely
able to attend. Denis Rattle explained the situation to Bill Jenkins,
conductor of the Merseyside Youth Orchestra (which was run under
the aegis of the Royal Liverpool Philharmonic), who allowed Simon to
join the percussion section there even though he was below the usual
age for the orchestra. He was ten and the usual entry age was fourteen,
but he was so keen that Bill Jenkins allowed him to start playing with
them at once, and he formally joined the orchestra in March 1966, at
the age of eleven, using some new drumsticks which his father had
brought him back from Hong Kong. 'People still have vivid memories
of Simon as a chubby boy playing cymbals nearly as big as he was,'
recalled his father. One of the other percussionists in the orchestra was
Annie Oakley, who for many years has played percussion in the CBSO
(and was one of the first to write in praise of Simon when he took over
the Berlin Philharmonic). 'She used to say that she always looked at the
stairs to see if they had been soaped before she walked down because
she knew that Simon's greatest wish was to take over the timps!'
remembered his mother. And so he did, by the end of the following
year.

Simon described playing with the Merseyside Youth Orchestra as his
most important early musical experience:

SIMON RATTLE I think I was a very solitary kid, probably rather strange because I was so obsessed. And I had very few friends of my own age until I was eleven and was playing in the MYO. That somehow opened me out, and made me a bit more normal. Bill Jenkins was a wonderful Welsh character, and he gave me many of my ideas, and many of my opportunities, too.

I used to listen to concerts on the radio, and badger my father to take me to Philharmonic concerts. I think my parents' expectations of me were enormously strong, especially having had a handicapped child. They very much wanted me to succeed.

Simon Rattle was remembered well at the Liverpool Philharmonic. From the age of eight or nine he would be at concerts: a performance by Charles Groves of Mahler's Eighth Symphony at Liverpool Cathedral in 1964 had Simon (in short trousers) and his father in the front row. By the time he was nine he would be going round backstage to get conductors' autographs, and to discuss with them – with some persistence, recalled his father – features of their interpretations with which he agreed or disagreed.

SIMON RATTLE When I first started going it was really only pieces with percussion instruments in them that interested me; for years I didn't think it was music unless it had three or four percussion and four trombones. So it was mainly twentieth-century repertory, and especially anything contemporary. I remember being thrilled to bits by Henze's Second Symphony, but more because it had percussion than for any other reason. I liked violent, garish music – *The Miraculous Mandarin*, that kind of thing. But I was so lucky growing up in [Charles] Groves's time there because we really heard a lot of adventurous music. There was the tradition of John Pritchard's *Musica viva* series, which was so enterprising. Gerhard's *Concerto for Orchestra* I think was the last piece I remember there. It just wouldn't happen now because the climate has changed so much. And when people give me credit for what I did in Birmingham it's all because of what I was able to hear in Liverpool.

DENIS RATTLE A week before his tenth birthday he went to hear Arthur Fiedler at the Philharmonic. He was one of the people most interested in Simon and had a really long talk with him and Simon queried some of his tempi, not in a critical way but asking, 'Why did you do that?' Just a week later I was off to America on a foreign leadership programme, with real red-carpet treatment all the way. I found myself at a dinner in Boston and at my table were Anthony Eden (by then Lord Avon), Adlai Stevenson, Walter Cronkite, the mayor of Boston and his wife, and on my left a white-haired man, very distinguished, and I knew I recognized him. So I whispered to the mayor's wife, 'Who's that?' She replied with all the surprise in the world, as if everyone knew him, that it was Fiedler. So I turned to him and did the usual 'You won't remember me, but . . . ' thing, and suddenly he stood up and silenced the table, Anthony Eden and everyone, and said, 'I'd like to introduce you to the father of a remarkable boy I met in Liverpool called Simon Rattle, whom you will be hearing of again.' And the sad thing is that Fiedler died just six months before Simon made his début with the Boston Symphony Orchestra in 1983. That was typical of the kindness with which people listened to Simon at that time.

It was at one of those Liverpool Philharmonic concerts, Simon recalled, that he had the musical experience that really set him on the road to conducting:

SIMON RATTLE I remember the Mahler 8, yes, and was extremely impressed by all the noise, but I didn't really know what it was about (and I still don't understand the piece at all). But when I was eleven my father took me to hear George Hurst conduct Mahler 2. And that was it. That was a completely transfiguring experience. It was the road to Damascus and it knocked me for six. I couldn't get the impression of it out of my mind for days, and I think that in serious terms that is where the seed was sown.

Meanwhile Simon's piano-playing really took off. From the age of nine he studied seriously with Geoffrey Arnold, music master at Liverpool College, who subsequently went to Australia to become chorus master at the new Sydney Opera House.

SIMON RATTLE We always felt he was a very remarkable musician. I think he has to have a lot of the credit for pushing me through, making me learn other instruments – it must have been around then I started the violin – getting me into other orchestras, forcing me at the pace he knew I needed to go. It's only looking back that one realizes how important teachers are in that way. It's not necessarily what they teach you, it's just what they put in your way, what's set up by them. Then to be taught by a Godowsky pupil, Douglas Miller, that was really extraordinary. He knew Rakhmaninov really quite well, he'd met all sorts of musicians, and I remember when I took him the Grieg Concerto to play and he said, 'Yes, when I met Grieg . . . ' – that was really one of the climaxes for me! Godowsky I knew about through Miller, and I learned the *Java Suite*. Once in Glyndebourne during the summer someone said, 'Mr Godowsky would like to meet you.' It turned out it was a relative of his who would have been about forty, who had subsequently married into the Gershwin family.

The violin I eventually gave up, though I played a good deal for Bill Jenkins and I remember leading the school orchestra for a while. I'm very grateful I learned the fiddle, but I think the problem really was not hearing what I was actually playing. One of my violin teachers, the one who made me give up, said, 'You have to stop playing Rattle and hearing Heifetz!' – which was true but a tiny bit hard as I was only twelve or so!

When he was eleven he won a music studentship offered by Liverpool Education Authority to young musicians of great potential. The prize consisted of lessons with the most outstanding teacher available on Merseyside. Simon had the good fortune to go to Douglas Miller (who was eighty-four when he began to teach him) and within a couple of years he was playing his first Mozart concerto, K488. Denis Rattle recalls questioning Miller about Simon's interpretation of a piece by Rakhmaninov and being told, 'Rakhmaninov was quite young when he wrote it. I have no doubt Simon has a better idea of how it should sound than we have. He seems to have a direct line to the composers.' In 1967, when Simon was twelve, he was elected Student of the Year by the Liverpool Youth Music Committee, in competition with instrumentalists aged between ten and twenty-two. He played Moeran's *Windmills* and all three adjudicators gave him 100 per cent. As a result of that he played Gershwin's *Rhapsody in Blue* with the Liverpool Concert Orchestra, a piece and a composer that were to remain close to him in the future.

DENIS RATTLE He was invited by the Birkenhead Music Society to play that Mozart concerto, and they had the nerve to ask him as well to play a short recital in the first half of the concert! So of course he did, and I remember one of the pieces he did was the Scarlatti *Cat's Fugue*, and to my absolute horror, halfway through the fugue he went back to the beginning and I thought, 'God, this is going to go on for ever, he's never going to get out of it!' But I think the third time round he found his way home. The band in the Mozart was extraordinary: no bassoon, so they used a trombone, who was brilliant, played every note.

When Simon was eleven he went on the first of a series of annual European Summer Schools for Young Musicians, with the encouragement of Bill Jenkins of the Merseyside Youth Orchestra, and under the watchful eye of a couple of players, Bill Overton and Wesley Woodage, whom his father had known at school and who had both become trumpeters in the BBC Symphony Orchestra. The school that year was in England, but subsequent ones were in Salzburg, and then Mödling, outside Vienna near the Czech border. Rattle recalled, 'Whether it was wise for my parents to send a kid off to Europe I think they've been wondering ever since.' The critic Geoffrey Norris remembers Rattle playing κ488 'impeccably', with Anthony Lewis conducting, at Mödling in 1967. A year later they were there when the Russians invaded Czechoslovakia. Rattle remembers that as an extraordinary experience, 'having people coming in and saying, "How much German do you know, do you realize what's going on?"' But politics rarely impinged on the summer schools:

SIMON RATTLE We had a wonderful time. In Mödling we were conducted by Malcolm Arnold: it was my first experience with a real live composer conducting his own music and discussing it with me. He was incredibly helpful, and we had all sorts of adventures, and played jazz too. I had some very important musical experiences on those courses. I met Maurice Miles who taught conducting at the Royal Academy, and had some of my own first chances to conduct. I suppose I was fourteen and just before I went off to Vienna again that summer I thought, 'I'm going to take some music and get some people together.' And true to form, ever ambitious, the first piece I tried to do was Ravel's Mother Goose.

The first symphony concert Simon Rattle conducted in this country took place when he was just fifteen, in April 1970. This was the beginning of some extensive press attention in Liverpool for the young prodigy:

MAESTRO SIMON DRUMS UP AN ORCHESTRA JUST FOR CHARITY
A charity gave fifteen-year-old Simon Rattle the go-ahead when he asked if he could put on a musical evening for them. But they got a shock five weeks later when Simon came up with a seventy-piece symphony orchestra. 'We thought he had a small concert in mind,' said one astounded official of the Liverpool Spastic Fellowship. 'He has shown tremendous enterprise.'

SIMON RATTLE I had with a couple of my schoolfriends the harebrained scheme of doing a concert for charity with what was originally going to be a chamber orchestra. The thing mushroomed and ended up being a full-scale symphony orchestra! I remember the Vaughan Williams Tallis Fantasia which I couldn't conduct, and the Schubert Unfinished which I nearly could. I asked people from the Liverpool Phil to play, and I think they were so astonished at the cheek that they agreed. Anthony Ridley, who is now a conductor in his own right, led the orchestra and gave me a few tips on how to conduct at the same time – my first teacher – and John Ward played the timps and Robert Braga played the wonderful viola solo in the Tallis Fantasia.

Maestro

Simon drums up an orchestra jus[t

By GERRY HUNT

'A CHARITY group gave 15-year-old Simon Rattle the go-ahead when he asked if he could put on a musical evening for them.

But they got a shock five weeks later when Simon came up with a 70-piece symphony orchestra.

'We thought he had a small concert in mind,' said one astounded official of Liverpool Spastic Fellowship. 'He has shown tremendous enterprise.'

As well as providing the orchestra Simon announced that he would also conduct it.

His line-up includes five musicians from the Royal Liverpool Philharmonic Orchestra, members of top amateur North-West

orchestras, conductors, and two of his schoolteachers.

In all he has rounded up 26 violinists, 11 cellists, nine viola players, five bass players, and others on woodwind, percussion, and a harp.

And to complete the Simon has had programmes tickets printed by two school pals, Stephen B 17, and John Williams

The concert will next month at the

Schoolboy Simon Ra[ ] action—he hopes to make conducting a career.

Simon, 15, makes the big time for one wonderful night..

THE musical evening arranged by 15-year-old Simon Rattle staggered the officials of a spastics society.

They were expecting him to organise a small amateur concert to help the fund.

But Simon is going to turn up with a seventy-two-piece symphony orchestra, including leading musicians.

And the conductor will be—Simon, a sixth-form college boy, of Menlove avenue, Liverpool.

Spastics Fellowship said: "To say we are astounded is the understatement of the year.

"This boy has shown tremendous enterprise."

Simon is a timpanist in the National Youth Orchestra and the Merseyside Youth Orchestra.

Joining him will be twenty - six violin'sts, eleven cellos, n'ne viol

a harpist. They include five musicians from the Royal Liverpool Philharmonic.

"Simon said: "Once I started my idea with phone calls and letters it just snowballed . . .

"I want to make a career as a conductor and this is going to be a wonderful opportunity, conducting an orchestra

mind that I am so young."

Simon expects to raise over £100 from his symphony concert to be held next month at his school —Liverpool College, Sefton Park.

MIRROR
22 April 70

The fifteen-year-old conductor: press cuttings of his first charity concert

The concert was quite an event. Rattle rehearsed for five and a half hours, and at one point the four-year-old son of one of the players disrupted the proceedings. Rattle quipped, 'I see our leader has arrived,' and the incident helped to break the ice with the mixture of amateur and professional players. Among the packed audience in Liverpool College Hall that evening was Charles Groves, principal conductor of the Liverpool Philharmonic. As well as Schubert and Vaughan Williams there was also Malcolm Arnold's *English Dances* and Mozart's Clarinet Concerto. There was a great deal of 'young star' coverage, but Rattle also had the benefit of his first critical review, from Neil Tierney in the *Daily Telegraph*. It was extremely prescient:

> The poise and dignity of fifteen-year-old Simon Rattle compared favourably with the ballyhoo publicity which preceded his advent as a conductor with his own orchestra, the Liverpool Sinfonia, at Liverpool College last night. He has a demonstrative but very discerning beat, a pleasing personality and a genuine gift with the baton which survived even the absurdity of having two flashlight photographs taken at the very start of the performance. There is a future conductor of real insight here and his development is not helped by the atmosphere of the circus ring . . .

After that Simon did not look back. A month later he was directing a percussion group he had got together, called Percussionists Anonymous, in a concert that included a work by his teacher, John Ward. In June 1970 he was asked to play one of his piano party pieces, Gershwin's *Rhapsody in Blue*, at short notice in Philharmonic Hall with the Merseyside Concert Orchestra after the scheduled pianist, Eva Warren, fell ill. In November that year he and a colleague from the MYO, the oboist Denise Burrows, received an award, worth fifty guineas each, under Pernod's Creative Artists Awards Scheme. The Pernod Award was presented at a Philharmonic Hall concert by the youth orchestra in which both of them took part. She played a piano solo as well as the oboe with Simon accompanying. He played three solo piano pieces: one of Rakhmaninov's Op. 32 Preludes and Ravel's *Le Gibet* and *Scarbo* from *Gaspard de la nuit*. He was also allowed to conduct the orchestra in the suite from Britten's *Gloriana*. Afterwards he immediately went out and spent his fifty guineas on a new gong.

The Merseyside Youth Orchestra subsequently took part in an International Youth Orchestra Festival in 1972. The young assistant manager of the Liverpool Philharmonic, who had the responsibility of running the

MYO and who was later to become general manager and then chief executive of the CBSO, was Edward Smith.

ED SMITH The first thing I ever remember him conducting was the Britten *Gloriana* suite in a little church in Brig, Switzerland. Simon came as a percussionist and a conductor and he was allowed to conduct that one piece and also played timps in the Vaughan Williams *London Symphony*. But you couldn't hold him back, even then: on the same course in Lausanne Simon decided to get together an international big band to play Henry Mancini arrangements. That made the biggest impression of all, and he really began to acquire a reputation.

In October 1970 we gave him his first job as an extra percussionist with the Liverpool Phil. In fact I think my first formal contact with him over that was to write to his games master at school asking for him to be given the afternoon off sports so that he could attend the rehearsal of Gerhard's Third Symphony!

Simon's strictly professional career had perhaps begun a little earlier, for Fritz Spiegl, who had first asked him to play percussion publicly as a very young boy, again engaged him to play percussion in a massive account of the Handel *Fireworks Music*; Simon's father certainly remembered that the modest cheque Simon received on that occasion was regarded as a landmark. Meanwhile, at Liverpool College, Simon's academic career proceeded by fits and starts:

SIMON RATTLE I really didn't enjoy school – I think I was too much of a misfit – until the last years, thirteen to sixteen, when I began to enjoy things and I was concentrating on the things I loved doing. It still felt as if there were two separate lives, the musical and the working life.

There was a bit more of a synthesis towards the end, but at the beginning I was completely isolated. I am glad, though, that I didn't go to a specialist music school. I know so many people from them and I've seen the problems they cause. After all, we musicians have to spend our lives with real people in the outside world, not just with other musicians. And we're a strange race.

PAULINE RATTLE It wasn't a musical school, more a rugby-playing school, but of a very high academic standard. Simon did have the good fortune to have a housemaster who was very interested in him and interested in music, and an English master who was also interested in music, and so he came through. He was talented but the academic work never meant much to him. We did think at this time that he would go to Oxford, and the

Latin master at Liverpool College gave him extra tuition. Simon was eventually to go, but in his own way!

He applied to go to the Royal Academy, and was accepted, and then I think for the first time in our lives – because you know how hard it is to persuade Simon to do anything he doesn't want to do – we did insist that he get his A levels if he wanted to go to the Academy. He knew if he didn't get them, well, sorry son, but you'll have to stay at school another year. And that had a remarkable effect on Simon. For three months he didn't go to any parties or anything – of course we couldn't stop him going to the Phil, and as usual we all went as a family on those occasions – but apart from that he just worked and worked because he was absolutely determined to get them and go to the Academy. Although he was only sixteen he got four grade As at A level, in History, English, Music and General Studies.

(Susan Rattle added that during the period he was preparing for his exams he was also conducting the Merseyside Concert Orchestra on Monday evenings, preparing for a concert in which she was playing percussion.)

Another feature of these years was that Simon began to compose seriously. There was a modest piece for strings, *Elegy*, Op. 2, which was performed in Liverpool. There were sketches for much more ambitious pieces, such as the Mahlerian *Episodes*, which included extensive parts for carefully specified percussion and petered out after the first few energetic pages. And there were some songs, written mostly for friends. In 1987 he was quick to dismiss the whole thing as a passing phase and was hard on the pieces themselves:

SIMON RATTLE They were duff. The sort of thing that's quite impressive when you're twelve, I suppose, but far less so by the time you're fifteen or sixteen. The songs I wrote for a singer I was very fond of. But I didn't have any application, and I didn't have any original ideas – I just rehashed other people's stuff. I did do some orchestration exercises, which I'm glad I did. And composing taught me that it's just as laborious to write impossibly bad, derivative music as it is to write masterpieces!

The summer before Simon went to the Academy he played for the only time in the National Youth Orchestra. ('On the whole I preferred the international gatherings; there was more sex, which wasn't a great feature of NYO courses.') The major attraction that drew Simon that summer was the presence of Pierre Boulez. They rehearsed in Croydon during August, and then appeared at both the BBC Proms and the

Edinburgh Festival. At the Proms Simon was given the solo piano part in Bartók's *Music for Strings, Percussion and Celesta*, while in the Edinburgh concert, which was televised, he played the cymbals in Debussy's *La Mer*.

JAMES ELLIS He was incredibly self-assured. On that course Simon got together a group and did the opening movement of the Janáček *Sinfonietta* before a rehearsal. He was always running around and already had that incredible energy which has been his hallmark ever since. I think he's got more intellectual focus since, but the energy is still there. There were a lot of very clever and active people on that course. Some have gone into music, like Stephen Barlow and Andrew Marriner, but some have gone on to be doctors. It was quite a milieu and Simon wasn't alone in rushing around doing things. But it wasn't the culture of the NYO. Ivey Dickson's attempts to keep the genie in the bottle only made the genie even more active!

He was terribly keen to have a conducting lesson with Boulez on *Le marteau sans maître*, and eventually this was fixed up. Simon tells the story against himself that he bustled in bright-eyed and bushy-tailed and said he really wanted to know how Boulez felt it should go and so on. And Boulez said, 'So, bar one,' and pointed above the stave, showed him the symbols and did the gestures. 'Bar two,' and he went through the whole first movement like that. 'There, that's all you do!'

It was not until 1977, when Rattle returned to conduct the NYO, that he really learned from Boulez (see p. 159). In particular he had a scheme to mount with his Liverpool Sinfonia a performance of Boulez's *Le marteau sans maître*: 'Madness! What a thought! In the end I couldn't do it because the singer was ill, but it would have been wonderful to have a try.' In the NYO Simon made many friends among the players who were to remain friends after he went down to London, and some of them played for him in the various orchestras he got together. And while he never managed to do the Boulez, he did mount one more ambitious programme of twentieth-century music which included Peter Maxwell Davies's *Antichrist*, the Milhaud Percussion Concerto (with his teacher John Ward as soloist) and the Falla Harpsichord Concerto.

There was one final Liverpool ensemble that was to prove vital to him in those hectic years before he went up to London to the Academy – the Liverpool Mozart Orchestra.

SIMON RATTLE Very important to me was a Liverpool family by the name of Dutch. David Dutch formed the Liverpool Mozart Orchestra and I very regularly played a lot of baroque music with him and his wife at their house, which we nicknamed The Baroqueries. I played continuo, or sometimes violin when we had a string quartet, though they had to be very tolerant! There was a long-distance lorry driver who played baroque violin so beautifully, David was a marvellous oboe player, John Grove was the bassoonist and Elspeth, David's wife, played the flute. The experience of playing really fine chamber music was vastly important to me. And it was on a course organized by David Dutch with many of those people involved that I first met John Carewe.

That meeting proved to be a turning point, a first step on the road to conducting maturity (see pp. 76–7). But John Carewe's lessons were not learned quickly or easily. Meanwhile London, with all the excitement it had to offer, beckoned. Simon arrived at the Royal Academy of Music in September 1971. He was still only sixteen.

II
1971–74

SIMON RATTLE It seems like a gigantic arrogance now, but I didn't apply to anywhere else; and it didn't occur to me that I wouldn't get in. There were very good teachers there and lots of people I knew: Maurice Miles for conducting, Jimmy Blades for percussion, Gordon Greene for piano, Fred Grinke, Sidney Griller for strings, John Gardner for composing – these were all people I'd met. So it was the obvious place.

I decided quite soon that, whatever I was meant to be studying, I would pick the brains of every professor in the building. I went and saw them all. And what was astonishing was the range of levels of teaching, how shocking the worst teachers were and how remarkable the best teachers were. I must have learned as much from that as from anything.

In the first year you couldn't do conducting as a first subject, but quite soon I was getting twentieth-century things together, and I realized I obviously had to fix the players myself if anything was to get done. I soon got involved in the conductors' course, just playing the piano, and then someone dropped out, so I got in . . . It all happened fairly quickly.

Gordon Greene and I parted company. We always ended up talking about politics and he said, 'You don't practise.' And I said, 'I do; an hour a day.' And he said, 'Well, an hour a day isn't practice. Promise me you'll devote five hours a day to it or it's really not worth it.' So we parted amicably. There was always a problem with my piano-playing. People used to be very impressed that I could play so many notes, and it didn't matter if some of them were wrong ones. It never really occurred to me to practise to make it a lot better, and by the time of the Academy I was really playing no better than I had when I was twelve or thirteen. I was a very good faker.

So I transferred to John Streets, who then ran the opera school. He was a person who had the speed of musical responses that I needed. He is one of the most complete musicians I've ever come across. I did still play the piano: I remember four of us took the Messiaen *Quartet for the End of Time* to him, and I realized I had no range of colour at the piano. If anyone played like that for me today they'd never be asked back . . .

JOHN STREETS There was this little person racing round the Academy with stars in his eyes. Someone like that always sticks out a mile, and one soon heard about this chap Simon Rattle. I think the first time I actually met him was when he came in to accompany a singer – some bits of Stravinsky's *Rake's Progress* or something – and I thought, 'Heavens, this is good.' He always accompanied a bit like a conductor: you know, he set the tempo! But quite soon I asked him if he wanted to come on to the opera course and do some playing and he leapt at that. At that time Steuart Bedford was my right-hand man, and I think the first thing Simon was involved in was Donizetti's *Belisario* at Sadler's Wells, where he was assistant conductor, doing all the offstage bands and so on. That was March 1972, pretty early, in his second term. Then in November 1972 he did an opera workshop with all sorts of things: bits of *Così*, *Louise*, and Michael Head's *After the Wedding*, which we commissioned. But he did all that himself, with a rather nice cast: Felicity Lott was there, and so was David Rendall. And then a Stravinsky *Soldier's Tale* in December that year.

In 1973 he worked on Janáček's *The Cunning Little Vixen*, which Steuart Bedford was conducting, and this was much more important because he did a lot of the coaching and a lot of the preparation. He was very involved in it and I think that gave him a love of Janáček – and then of course that was an opera he did at Glyndebourne very early on. Later in the year, in December, it rather surprised me to find that he actually conducted one performance of Offenbach's *La jolie parfumeuse* which David Lloyd-Jones conducted. So that must actually have been his first official appearance in the pit.

The first thing that was really noticed by the critics was the double bill of Ravel's *L'enfant et les sortilèges* and Stravinsky's *Pulcinella* in November 1974, because that was after he'd won the competition, and after he'd left the Academy. He was intending to do a further year – I don't know what he would have got out of it – but the competition changed all that. Then we subsequently invited him back to do the Poulenc *Mamelles des Tirésias* and Vaughan Williams's *Riders to the Sea* with John Copley.

What would you and he talk about in your sessions?
He would bring in whatever he was working on at the time, and then we'd
go off into long discussions about French music, style in Debussy and
Ravel; it's very close to me and at that time Simon didn't know as much
about it. I remember those occasions far more than the times he brought
Beethoven sonatas. I did encourage him to bring Mozart in the hope of
broadening things out a bit. We used to talk tremendously about literature:
I had met Pound and talked to him, and Simon was fascinated by that. We
talked about Joyce and poetry, and I think that may have influenced him
towards the idea of taking a year off and going to Oxford. He was always
interested in theatre and film at this time, and realized how much you
needed to know about these cultural things in order to do the music well.

Was his operatic conducting technique always assured?
Right from the word go; there was never any problem at all. And what he
also had besides the technique was this marvellous thing of communication
right to the back desk of the second fiddles. They always looked at him, and
that didn't always happen with some of our staff conductors ... And he
was happy in the pit; there were never false leads; the singers wanted to sing
for him. He was always very patient with directors or lighting people and
would just put down his baton and wait for it all to happen.

*Has it surprised you that Simon has not gone into an opera house on a
permanent basis?*
That's an interesting one. As he's probably told you, he wasn't very happy
at Glyndebourne initially and that possibly soured things. Would he perhaps have found the repertory a bit restricting? And the business of doing
ten or twelve performances in a row? Now he is in complete control of an
orchestra in a way that you can't possibly be, completely, in an opera
house; there are so many other things to consider. He may come to it in the
future.

By the end of his first term at the Academy he was already associated
with the conductors' course and the opera course, doing a great deal of
accompanying, and gathering ensembles together for twentieth-century
music. In an end-of-term concert that December he even took over from
an indisposed colleague at twenty minutes' notice and conducted
Beethoven 8 with one of the Academy orchestras. But he was not getting
on as quickly as he could have wished through official channels, so he
began the most ambitious of his activities to date by forming the New
London Chamber Orchestra, a forty-strong band with an age range up
to twenty-two, which drew on several people he knew from the National

Youth Orchestra course the previous summer, including the first violin, the first cello, and Philippa Davies as principal flute.

Then just before he came back to London after the Christmas break he was offered his first semi-professional work. Leon Lovett, the conductor, asked him to be *répétiteur* and chorus master for a modern double bill which the New Opera Company was putting on at Sadler's Wells Theatre: Elisabeth Lutyens's *Time Off? – Not a Ghost of a Chance* and Anthony Gilbert's *The Scene Machine*.

One of the people who took part in that production recalled:

> Leon Lovett was having a lot of trouble dealing with the Lutyens, which was a very tricky score, and so in came this sixteen-year-old boy wonder and immediately made sense of it at the piano. He could play the piano like a complete orchestra, could tell the singers what to do, and gave everyone confidence. In the nicest possible way he took over.

Lovett subsequently passed on to him another fun job: conducting for the Alvin Ailey Dance Theater when they visited London. 'The first serious professional thing I did,' Rattle recalled. 'But it was never followed up. Those years were full of things that led nowhere.'

He was busy everywhere with rehearsals and going to other people's rehearsals. He rarely had the time or money to go to concerts, but would often go in to BBC rehearsals at Maida Vale or the Festival Hall – especially when Boulez, who was then chief conductor of the BBC Symphony, was conducting: 'When I think about what I was doing each day in those years . . . I'd be hospitalized if I tried it now. Burning the candle at both ends in every possible sense!'

In 1973 the conductor of the Merseyside Youth Orchestra, Bill Jenkins, who had so greatly encouraged Simon and given him so many chances to play piano, violin and percussion with the orchestra, retired. Simon was given the chance to succeed him, and he eagerly embraced the opportunity. It was the beginning of his long-term collaboration with Ed Smith, who ran the MYO. They worked together subsequently, first when Simon became associate conductor of the Liverpool Philharmonic, and then when Ed Smith became general manager of the CBSO.

> ED SMITH The first concert he did as conductor of the MYO was during his second year at the Academy: the programme had Philip Fowke doing the Rakhmaninov Second Concerto, Shostakovich 10 and Tchaikovsky's *Marche slave*. You don't catch him conducting much Tchaikovsky these days! I think that's the first and last time he conducted that piece. And it

was as vulgar as it always is! He would come up from London every Sunday for rehearsals, and would often be around at concerts. What he really wanted then was to go on one of the conductors' seminars which we'd arranged very successfully in the previous years: in 1970 we had Howard Williams, Tim Reynish and Colin Metters, and the last one was in 1972 – Mark Elder, James Judd, Antony Beaumont and Barry Wordsworth – a good line-up. Simon was always after me and I had to sort of hide behind pillars because I knew he would say, 'And when's there going to be another seminar?' But sadly the Gulbenkian who funded them weren't able to continue so 1972 was the last.

I had to be quite strict about some of his activities, because I was assistant manager of the Philharmonic so I had other responsibilities. I remember him using one of the RLPO players' xylophones without asking: there must still be a letter from me somewhere saying, 'Please note that you are not under any circumstance to touch instruments belonging to members of the Liverpool Philharmonic without permission.'

But the Merseyside Youth Orchestra with Simon was a great success, and we decided to try some ambitious pieces: the next concert was November 1973, and we did the Berlioz *Symphonie fantastique*, and the Shostakovich Second Cello Concerto with Roderick McGrath. Then there was *The Rite of Spring* in 1974, and that was historic because it got tangled up in the Bournemouth Competition . . .

The first MYO concert was well received in the Liverpool press. 'A resounding success,' one paper called it, while Neil Tierney continued his advocacy of the conductor in the *Daily Telegraph* by praising his 'definite beat and expressive left hand. Conducting from memory, he showed a splendid grasp of the music.' Another paper, which referred to the Rakhmaninov Second Concerto as 'Rachmaninov's Brief Encounter', reported that 'Superlatives were tossed around the audience afterwards, and people were clearly amazed at Simon's conducting the Shostakovich [Tenth Symphony] without a score.' It has remained one of his most powerful performances.

Meanwhile, in London, he was stirring things up at the Royal Academy. As well as gathering together small groups for contemporary music, he started on his biggest project: performing Mahler symphonies with an orchestra he fixed himself.

JOHN STREETS It wasn't much done at that time, students actually getting their own people together to put on a concert. Maybe there was the odd Beethoven orchestra, but not a Mahler 2 orchestra and chorus! It was frowned on slightly, and I don't think there was any real co-operation; you know what these places are like if you try something unusual, especially if it turns out to be rather better than the official activities! But I don't mean to say that he ever had any real trouble with the authorities.

SIMON RATTLE Some ways they tried to stop it; other ways it was just gently ignored. And sometimes they would actually help and lend me parts and occasionally print a programme. But basically they just let me use the hall, and sometimes I had to hire the parts myself.

If there was a single occasion that put Simon Rattle on the musical map in London it was the performance of Mahler's Second Symphony which he conducted at the Royal Academy on 6 December 1973 at 2.45 p.m. Quite apart from the success of the event itself, in the audience that afternoon was someone who was to have an incalculable effect on his future – the agent Martin Campbell-White from Harold Holt Ltd, one of the most prestigious agencies in London. (The agency has since amalgamated with Lies Askonas Ltd to form Askonas Holt.) Like any good agent, Campbell-White had heard about Rattle on the musical administrators' grapevine, while discussing another conductor he represented, Andrew Davis.

MARTIN CAMPBELL-WHITE Stephen Gray, the manager of the Liverpool Philharmonic, came in to see me at the time when Andrew Davis was principal guest conductor there. We were chatting away and he said, 'There's this fantastic boy we've got working with us conducting the Merseyside Youth Orchestra and he's going to do *The Rite of Spring*.' And I said, 'That's interesting,' and, as a passing comment while I thought about the next hard negotiating point for Andrew Davis, I said, 'How old is he?' And Stephen said he was seventeen. He told me a little more about him, and I was sitting there thinking, 'Seventeen? *The Rite of Spring* with a youth orchestra?' He told me he'd been in the National Youth Orchestra with Boulez and had played percussion with the Liverpool Phil since he was fifteen as an extra, and that he'd left school and gone straight to the Academy.

So I did a little research and found out that Simon was doing this performance of Mahler 2. I made contact with him and found out that he'd asked permission of the lords and masters there if he could do it officially and they said no, probably because he wasn't in the right year or something. But he was determined to do it and had got his orchestra and chorus together. I went along to the performance and he had quite obviously galvanized them beforehand in the rehearsals. The performance was somewhat raw but, my God, it was fantastic. It really was, and I don't even think the technique was limited. The impassioned approach that is a hallmark of Simon's style was already there, and the ability to get those people to play with him, which is something very special.

It was tremendous. So I said to him at once that I thought we would love to do something for him at Holt's but that clearly he was much too young, and I wondered what he wanted to do. He said he wanted to study more and learn more repertory and so on. But I did begin to mention his name to one or two people and said that I thought there was this incredibly talented youngster around. And word began to spread: Nick Tschaikov, who was then chairman of the Philharmonia, heard him and said he wanted to offer him a Festival Hall début. Brian Dickie from Glyndebourne came to an opera Simon conducted at the Academy and offered him work there. Michael Vyner came to the Ravel–Stravinsky double bill at the Academy and that opened up the London Sinfonietta, and so on.

Martin Campbell-White's prudent scheme for Simon Rattle was to develop a very small amount of work, carefully paced and planned, with high-quality organizations in London. But the best-laid schemes ... Simon had never been content to do things by halves and in 1974, towards the end of his third year at the Academy, he entered for the newly established John Player International Conductor's Award in Bournemouth. This was part of a scheme established by the Bournemouth Symphony Orchestra to provide opportunities for young conductors and soloists. Unlike most conducting competitions, which guarantee only a few engagements, this one carried a substantial opportunity: to work for two years with the Bournemouth Symphony Orchestra and its smaller Sinfonietta alongside their regular conductors Paavo Berglund and Kenneth Montgomery. The competition was to be held in May 1974 in the Guildhall, Portsmouth, and there seemed little likelihood that Simon would not apply.

He obtained references from John Carewe, from Charles Groves, who wrote a letter asking them to accept him in spite of his youth, and from Norman Del Mar, who was conducting the Academy Chamber Orchestra at the time. Martin Campbell-White was not aware that he had entered:

MARTIN CAMPBELL-WHITE I didn't know, and if I had known beforehand I would most certainly have discouraged him. I would have thought he had everything to lose and nothing to gain. By then he already had the Philharmonia début fixed and there were a number of other things in the pipeline – the right progression for someone who was still only nineteen and a half. Anyway, I went down to the competition and there were a number of conductors who were, as they say in America 'concertizing regularly', but Simon was head and shoulders above the rest. It was absolutely clear that he had the talent to bring it off, and he did!

Of the two hundred conductors who applied, ten were selected to go to Portsmouth. Simon was surprised that he had been chosen purely on his paper qualifications, because the upper age limit of thirty-five meant that many of the other entrants would have had far greater experience than he had. His parents had not stopped him entering because, they said, they knew he was not going to win it. Interviewed before the competition Simon said, 'You have to be 50 per cent lunatic to want to be a conductor. It's such hard work and there are so few opportunities, but it's a bug, and once you have been bitten there's really nothing you can do except allow it to lead you forward.' Looking back on it now he finds the whole thing even more amazing:

SIMON RATTLE If there was any proof needed that I didn't take it very seriously, I lived in a flat with a cellist called Cathy Giles and I was about to go off to the competition and she said, 'Simon, you haven't packed your tails.' I said, 'Well, I'm not going to need them. I won't get past the first round and, in any case, I can't because I've got the last rehearsal of *The Rite of Spring* with the MYO in Liverpool so I wouldn't be able to do it anyway.' And she said, 'You really should take them.'

The line-up in the competition was impressive, and included plenty of conductors who have made professional reputations since: Richard Hickox, Ronald Zollman, Geoffrey Simon (who came second), Colin Metters (who also reached the finals) and a fine Japanese conductor, Hikotaro Yazaki. In the first round of the competition they had to conduct a variety of pieces, including Shostakovich 5, and accompany a Chopin piano concerto. At the end of the second day four of the ten were chosen to go forward to the finals, and Simon was among them. This was 28 May. In the final round all the four conductors had to direct Strauss's *Don Juan*. Simon conducted one of the fastest and brashest performances in living memory. George Hurst, artistic adviser to the Bournemouth orchestras, came up to him afterwards and said, inimitably, 'Simon, that was thrilling. And the other thing about it was, it was terrible. Don't ever do anything like that to me again!' The orchestra applauded. Denis Rattle recalled:

It was a splashy old show, but tremendously exciting and he was the star turn of the evening, no doubt. I think some of the others who were more experienced might have won it, but perhaps in their minds was the fact that this chap had to work with them for two years, and some of them were not so bright at English. Anyway, Simon got it.

ED SMITH This was the weirdest situation, especially in view of the later Birmingham connection. We'd done *The Rite* with the MYO in Liverpool, but we were due to go down to Birmingham and do a concert in the Midland Youth Orchestra's series including *The Rite*. We knew it overlapped with the competition but Simon said that as there was no way he was getting further than the first round it didn't matter; there was no question he'd be back for the rehearsals. We had a deputy conductor in Liverpool and every half day Simon was ringing me saying, 'Don't worry, I'll be back tonight.' And of course he wasn't. So we rehearsed in Liverpool on the Friday night without Simon and travelled down to Birmingham on the Saturday and he travelled straight up from Bournemouth having won the competition. So the first concert he ever conducted in Birmingham Town Hall was *The Rite of Spring* with the MYO the day after he'd won the competition! And Peter Donohoe was one of the timpanists!

Rattle's engagement in Bournemouth began in September 1974, so there was no question of his returning to the Academy for a fourth year. Thus it happened that what was to have been his first major official undertaking at the Royal Academy, the double bill of Ravel's *L'enfant et les sortilèges* and Stravinsky's *Pulcinella* in November 1974, took place after he had left. Both pieces were to become firm favourites: *Pulcinella* became one of his first commercial recordings, and the Ravel opera he returned to on a number of occasions, notably at Glyndebourne in the summer of 1987 (see p. 199). For the first time he received widespread attention from the London critics. The production was given on the open stage of the Duke's Hall because the opera theatre was out of action for renovation: perhaps he was in luck – as usual – for as conductor he was much more visible in this set-up. Summing up a remarkable year's progress, Alan Blyth wrote in *The Times*:

> Stories of the formidable talents of Simon Rattle, the conductor, who is nineteen, have been spreading widely in musical circles over the past few months. They were confirmed in no uncertain terms on Wednesday at the Royal Academy of Music [when] he showed talents of command and understanding beyond his years. Obeying Sir Adrian Boult's prime rule of leading with his right hand and letting it give all the important directions,

he drew uncommonly sensitive playing from the Academy's orchestra and saw to it that they and the singers made the most of the scores . . .

Other press comment was equally favourable:

Much of the musical success must be due to Simon Rattle, a young con-ductor of distinct promise, whose performance is remarkable not only for delicacy (he must be careful, though, not to slacken the pulse in slow music) but for the precision with which the offstage voices were handled. There was some most creditable playing from the orchestra, and if occasionally the singers were overpowered (hardly surprising with a low stage and no pit) it was enjoyable for once to hear detail that an experienced conductor would firmly keep down! (Ronald Crichton, *Financial Times*)

I wish more audiences could have witnessed another young conductor, Simon Rattle. His assured and delightful handling of student forces in Ravel's *L'enfant et les sortilèges*, probably produced on a shoestring, was nevertheless one of the Academy's vintage efforts . . . (Felix Aprahamian, *The Sunday Times*)

Greatest praise must go to the gifted young conductor Simon Rattle, who had his student orchestra playing like seasoned professionals. His attack, sense of rhythm, and ability to control large forces in the orchestra and on stage indicate an outstanding natural talent for opera. One can safely prophesy a future for him in his chosen profession so long as he does not go dashing ahead too quickly. (Harold Rosenthal, *Opera*)

Everything looked set for a glittering future. But far from dashing ahead too quickly, Simon Rattle's musical career was just about to hit his first major obstacle.

'The most vital meeting of them all'
John Carewe

Of all the influences on Simon Rattle's career, that of the conductor John Carewe has been probably the greatest. From a master–pupil relationship they have become close friends, and one senses that of all the people with whom Rattle is able to discuss music and conducting, with John Carewe he can be the most frank and open. Carewe has watched Rattle through the most difficult personal periods of his life as well as relishing the new maturity that arrived in the 1990s.

> SIMON RATTLE The meeting with John Carewe was the most vital of them all. Working with Boulez, listening to Furtwängler, yes, those things were important, but the truth is that it was Carewe: 90 per cent of what I know came from him. It's extraordinary for us to have turned the corner now and just be friends and colleagues.

John Carewe is sharp, intense and perennially youthful; quick to enthusiasm, quick to praise, and equally quick to rule out of court anything he regards as unworthy or unmusical. He was a pupil of two Schoenberg pupils, Walter Goehr and Max Deutsch, and later studied in Paris with Olivier Messiaen and Pierre Boulez. He has been one of the most active conductors in Britain in the field of contemporary music, giving many premières, especially for the BBC during the 1960s and 1970s. He was principal conductor of the BBC Welsh Symphony Orchestra for five years, and now conducts extensively abroad. He has been a regular teacher and coach of conductors.

> JOHN CAREWE I first heard of Simon when I went to conduct a summer orchestral course in 1972 at a place called Burton Manor near Liverpool, run by the Liverpool Mozart Orchestra. It was great fun; we were doing pieces like the [Alexander] Goehr *Little Symphony* and Gerhard's *Alegrías*. People were talking about this young percussion-player called Simon Rattle who, although he was only seventeen, had already done some concerts and was attracting attention as a conductor.
>
> I discovered he was going to rehearse a Mozart symphony during one of my free afternoon periods, so I dropped in. I'd heard a lot about how

talented he was and sure enough it was clear that this boy had real talent as a conductor. But I was horrified because everything he was doing was absolutely dreadful. I had a long internal tussle with myself, wondering whether I should interfere, and then I thought I must. So I said to Simon, 'I'm going for a drive, come with me.' So we got in the car and I had him there as a captive audience! I told him exactly what I felt, which was basically that he was obviously intensely concerned with what he heard inside himself but had absolutely no idea of what the orchestra was actually playing. And equally, I said to him, he seemed to have little idea of what the music really required.

Now the interesting thing, which is so typical of Simon, was his response; this is really the touchstone of the whole business. He was instantly aware that I was trying to tell him the whole truth and he was so grateful to have someone who didn't just tell him how marvellous he was. And so our relationship clicked immediately, I think. We came back after the car journey and sat down on a settee in the big room at the manor and took out the Mozart symphony, no. 39, and went through it in the way that I understood it. I explained it to him and analysed the harmony and phrase structure and talked about how a good performance should reveal these things. From that moment he was hooked on my teaching, or rather the teaching I had inherited from my study with Goehr and Deutsch. The main principle behind this is the idea that the conductor must have clearly grasped all the harmonic and tonal implications of a piece and must use these to organize the phrasing, the tempi and the nuances. When he has these things clearly in his mind, then there are relatively fewer difficulties physically. Young conductors either respond to this or they don't, and Simon was absolutely intrigued.

Was the next time you came across him at the Royal Academy?
Yes. He was there as a student ostensibly doing percussion and piano, and I started to conduct an ensemble for twentieth-century music which Simon got involved with as a player. We didn't discuss conducting at the Academy but he asked to come to me privately, so he used to trek down to Haslemere and we would go through scores and he would play me things and he would eat us out of house and home!

The next thing was that in the summer of 1973 I asked him to come along as my assistant to the Glasgow Schools Symphony Orchestra and play the Stravinsky Concerto for piano and wind. Now I suspect this reinforced a lot he already knew about rehearsing. We had lots of sectional rehearsals, and we would really pull pieces apart and put them back together again. It's not unique – any good conductor does it – but perhaps this is where Simon saw how you can build up with quite poor players to a very high standard of performance. Simon is a great sectional rehearser now and he knows just how useful it can be.

Then in the December of 1973 he did Mahler 2 at the Academy, getting everyone together for it. I didn't go for some reason so he brought me a tape of it down to Haslemere and he was very, very proud of it. I remember sitting in the living room there listening to it and wondering what on earth I could say about it that would be useful and not hurtful. In the end I decided to put on the old Klemperer recording. And of course he was rather devastated. But from there we were able to move on and discuss the shortcomings of his performance positively.

Can you specify what you thought was bad about it?
It lacked character and understanding. It was a young man's Mahler, very exciting but very bland. That was a problem Simon had to fight through, to give the music its 'nose', as Max Deutsch used to describe it, its own unique quality. There was another example around that time: he put on a Bruckner 4 somewhere in North London in memory of a horn-player who had drowned, a typical gesture of his. I went to hear the rehearsal and in the break I said to him, 'Look, you're not doing anything, you're just letting it roll by without giving it any shape; I mean, it's all very well just standing there looking very beautiful and getting everyone to play very beautifully but in actual fact it comes out terribly bland.' Well, he was very quick, and he immediately focused on the phrasing, tightened the whole thing up and it was much better. But that was the basic problem with the Mahler. Very intense and superficially very exciting, but he had not dug deeply into the essential musical content.

Given the depth of lack of musical understanding you felt he had, what was it convinced you that he was a born conductor?
Well, I didn't use that exact phrase but I'm not going to contradict it. You could tell that he just had this tremendous ability and tremendous enthusiasm and a desire to communicate. He had all the natural attributes you could hope to find in a young conductor. He could always make it happen, and get players to give their best for him. In that Bruckner symphony I was mentioning, at the back of the fiddles I met one of the better players in a London orchestra and he said, 'This is marvellous; we really want to play for him.' That's the point.

But he realized and I think he still realizes to an extent that his intellectual understanding of music is not what he would like it to he. Unlike certain other conductors I could think of, though, he's very conscious of that and does everything he can to overcome it. I think that was why he responded to my teaching, because I wasn't telling him about stick technique and that sort of thing but about how to analyse scores. I do regret, incidentally, not having interfered with his actual technique until much later! We were analysing scores from the point of view of performance: not as a musicologist might, or Maxwell Davies might from the point of view of the composer, but just from the point of view of understanding how the notes on the page are supposed to work.

We studied the implications of tonality, what makes a movement stand up as an arch form. It was a question of understanding the harmony and its implications, the fact that tonality is the outcome of very particular chord formations and their use. We did study some music outside this basic diatonic tonal system, but we mainly concentrated on Beethoven 1, 2, 3, 5, 6 and 7, Brahms 2, several Mozart symphonies, and we must have done the *Tristan* Prelude.

What's interesting about that list is that it did not become at all typical of Simon's repertory until the late 1990s . . .
He has always been conscious of how deep one's intellectual understanding of those pieces has to be, which is why he steered away from most of them for a long time. But he did Brahms 2 at the Academy. In his last year he did it in his final exam and I'm sure everyone fondly hoped he would run away with the conducting prize. The other two judges would probably have been overawed by his ability and given it to him, but I had to stand up and say it was awful and I absolutely refused to give him the prize. At that stage the music just wandered for him – lovely sounds, but no appreciation of how it was actually built up.

Simon's first big break came when he won the John Player Competition in Bournemouth in 1974. Did you try to put him off?
He asked me for a reference for the competition and I said I would give him one but I hoped to God he didn't win because he wasn't ready for it. I told him to go in for it by all means because it would be good experience conducting a professional orchestra. And I suppose we all like to claim foresight but I did write in that reference that whether or not this boy wins, he is a born conductor. It's all history from then on!

When I heard he'd won I was very pleased for him but worried too. He did have a difficult time in Bournemouth but he survived. I suppose I underestimated how quickly he could learn. That's one thing about Simon: I've given him various pieces of very considered advice at various times in his life, and always he's ignored it and always he's been right. After things had really taken off for him, I told him what he should be doing was just twenty-five to thirty-five concerts a year with the greatest orchestras in the world. He chose the opposite, which was to go to Birmingham and do masses of concerts a year. And he was dead right. And he will stay in Berlin now, and make that work.

Did he continue to come to you for advice while he was at Bournemouth?
Oh yes, and afterwards too. We moved in 1975 from Haslemere to Guild-
ford, with my first wife, Rosemary, and my daughters, and he came there a
lot, was marvellous company for the girls, and still ate an enormous
amount. There was a period when we drifted apart. This too was interesting about him, because it was when he was having his first big successes
and getting lots of offers, and I think he was genuinely embarrassed about
it because at that stage my career wasn't so hot. I don't think he quite
realized that I was very, very proud for him and didn't mind in the slightest.
We saw each other but not so regularly.

I remember he brought me a tape of Beethoven 7 which he'd done with
the BBC Scottish and he said, 'John, I know you're not going to like this.'
And I didn't like it one little bit. It was from this point, perhaps, that I
began to learn from Simon, because I had never realized consciously that
one of the essential things about the analysis we had been doing together
was that once you had done it and it had guided your instincts then you had
to forget everything and let it come through your subconscious. You're not
teaching the orchestra or the audience what you've learned in analysing the
piece! Your analysis tells you how the music goes, and then you've got to
put it across. But by this time it was a fault in the right direction.

When did you start to get at his conducting technique?
That was much later. I was back living in London, he had started in Birmingham, and we had established the very different sort of relationship we
have now. He would want me to go to concerts, and tell him what I
thought. I must admit I must have been very rude on occasions. But he did
have a certain tension and stiffness in his right wrist which is a drawback
with a big orchestra. You must be flexible and I told him very severely
about that and over a period of two or three years he did put this right: he
now has a beautifully flexible technique.

I remember when he did *The Rite of Spring* with the CBSO at the Festival Hall in 1981 I was very disappointed. This is a piece which we'd talked
about ever since he'd done it with the NYO and recorded it – not one of his
best records at all – and we had a long talk in a BBC canteen about it.
(There's still one bar I'm convinced he beats wrongly!) After this CBSO
performance I said straight out, 'I never expected *The Rite of Spring* to
sound like Rakhmaninov and I don't think I can survive this culture shock.'
It was very lush and rich and stripped of all its brutality; he did it from
memory and glossed over lots of things. He was trying to make it sound
good. This is something he had to do with the CBSO: he had to work hard
at making them *sound* fine, and this was a case where it got right in the way
of the music. About six months later he did it again, this time with the

Philharmonia, and it was exactly as I felt it should be. I was over the moon, because it had all the sound but that was secondary to the musical character. Very exciting and musical, with a real punch.

How did it go at first with the Berlin Philharmonic?
I think he was terribly nervous when he was finally going to do Mahler 6 with them after all the discussions there had been. He had just done it with the Philharmonia in London, so I rang him up and I said, 'Do you want some advice?' And he said, 'Oh yes, anything, please!' So I said, 'Just play through the first movement and then the adagio (which as you know he does second) and then do the scherzo and have a break. The orchestra will decide among themselves how they feel, then come back and really rehearse.' Which is what he did, and then he did another clever thing, which was to save the last movement until the second rehearsal. They were won over because he didn't talk to them at all for quite a long time and let them play. The orchestra said that at the first performance he was doing almost too little, but by the second performance it was quite different and he had really gripped them. The fact that it got better was very important to them and they wanted more.

But then there were all the terrible problems the second time he went with him cancelling the Bartók recordings [see p. 26], and I can't get to the bottom of how he ever got invited back after that! He was demanding conditions that they said Solti and Haitink never worried about, so why did it have to be 'special circumstances' when Mr Rattle conducted them? Simon would presumably consider his to be the normal circumstances! Then there was a problem rather later when he went back to conduct a Haydn symphony and without telling him they cancelled a rehearsal of it. The chairman said it was very unfortunate but the clear implication was that they didn't need the rehearsal. It was arrogance: 'We know how to play Haydn.' He couldn't do anything about it, but he said afterwards that players came up to him and said, 'We did need that rehearsal,' which he took as something of a vindication.

And of course they realized he had something extra to give them. I was there when he first did Rameau with them – without vibrato! – and the orchestra really enjoyed themselves. I think they had agreed among themselves that anyone who didn't want to try this stuff should not play, so they had a very young orchestra, music totally new to them, they wanted to learn and they had a fantastic time.

What was happening to his performances in the late eighties?
There were fewer swings of style, although this was the time when he was starting to work with period instruments but still doing pieces with modern orchestras in a very different style; the two hadn't come together yet. Soon

after he came back from Berlin he did a Beethoven piano concerto with the CBSO at the Barbican with twenty first violins – ridiculous! He had this idea it would make the orchestra sound better and it was godawful. So I had to say, 'You cannot make this orchestra play like the Berlin Philharmonic just by adding more strings!' There was an *Eroica* with the CBSO that was just like the Schubert Great C major Symphony, all beautiful melody; but there is more to the piece than that! I was slightly unhappy with the first movement of the *Eroica* later on with the Orchestra of the Age of Enlightenment, where he found an absolutely perfect tempo for the melody in the coda, and I wondered why couldn't he have started like that; it was too fast to be clear.

He's become more open-minded about the soloists and singers he uses . . .
Oh, I don't know. I think when he finds someone that he is comfortable with and can work with he will stick to that person. He has not been your standard conductor who will do concertos with anyone who is passing through, not at all, and in the earlier years I think people found that very difficult to understand; it was baffling, because they didn't understand.

Do you think it went on developing in Birmingham?
Yes, right up to the day he said he was leaving. After that, naturally enough, it became more difficult. Rather as if a husband or wife says, 'I'm leaving you in two years,' then it does put a different light on things; you don't have quite the same relationship. It could have reached a plateau but nothing Simon has done has ever reached a plateau. He had the attitude that there were still things to learn. He could have stayed longer. But this is where we get into the personal story, because his whole divorce was horribly difficult, and I'm sure that was the moment when he thought that he had to get away from Birmingham.

Everyone had plans for him: Covent Garden – like hell! Then we thought the Vienna Philharmonic might change their rules to give him a post. Philadelphia was definitely after him, and Simon would have been very tempted in some respects. If Boston had got its act together he would probably be there now; we are very lucky that Ozawa was so jealous! But one thing Simon kept saying was, 'I think I have more to learn in Europe.' And that was true. Vienna and Berlin were teaching him more.

What repertory will he now be looking at?
I've always told him he had to do *Tristan* and *The Ring*. *Tristan* has now happened. It took three months out of his life and he loved that because he was totally immersed in it, absorbed in it and now he will know that piece and it can be done again and no doubt differently! *The Ring* – I don't know how it will happen but I'm certain it will. He might look at Verdi, *Otello*

and *Falstaff*, maybe even *Aida* – no, perhaps not! – and maybe he'll come round to Tchaikovsky symphonies, who knows. But he will find new territory.

Has Simon himself changed?
Changed? Fundamentally, no. At root Simon could never change, but he's become much more secure, much more mature, and the way he has dealt with the Berlin politicians and the situation with the Berlin orchestra has been very skilful and shown a new side of him.

You must be one of the few people who can criticize him without getting your head bitten off . . .
He's never quite bitten my head off, but he has very strong views and dismisses things quickly. I think that is because he has to make up his mind. When you perform and when you conduct, you have to believe it is the only way. Sometimes when he snaps back at me I think it may be because I hit a raw nerve! And people who say something to him and have it dismissed might be surprised to find in ten years that he is actually doing it different-ly! I think he takes on good advice like a sponge takes water. And he comes back to you with all the positive qualities that he has. He is such a positive person, unbelievably positive, which is why the personal setbacks have been very difficult for him.

Now Berlin is happening for him, will Simon ever come back to London?
My great *cri de cœur* is: why can't we build a concert hall in London worthy of him? He will never work permanently anywhere that does not have an orchestral hall of high enough quality for him, and yet we know that he lives in London. However long Berlin goes on there would still be time for London in his future. Whatever they say about the Festival Hall, and whatever they do to it, it will never be a Stradivarius among concert halls. But it is not in the interests of those running the Festival Hall and the musical establishment to take the obvious route, which is that the Festival Hall would make an ideal conference centre and that is what it should be. By all means keep it, 'Grade One' list it, but it is not the answer to our concert hall problems.

Unless we build a hall we will never get the benefit, as Birmingham did, of the catalytic effect he had on the whole cultural life there. I know what is going to happen, which is that ten years after he dies there will be a concert hall built here in memory of Simon Rattle. And a fat lot of use that will be.

The John Carewe relationship, which has always been so important to Rattle, took another turn when Carewe took up the cause of Rattle and London in a formal document circulated to leading musical figures.

Called 'The Rattle Project', and written after he had announced his departure from Birmingham but before the Berlin appointment was likely, it raised all the questions about Rattle's relationship to London:

> Sir Simon Rattle presently has no exclusive contract with any orchestra, and in fact has nowhere to go ... London and the UK need a new orchestra whose structure is not controlled by its players but by its resident conductor ... London needs a new concert hall with a new acoustic. We propose that an orchestra be formed and structured to meet Rattle's requirements and talents in a purpose-built concert hall ... Given that our proposal could very well take ten years to fructify, it is possible that Rattle would in the mean time accept a prestigious position abroad for personal and financial reasons. This would not, however, invalidate the project.

As Carewe observed,

> The emergence of an independently structured new orchestra with adequate funding will create a furore amongst the existing orchestras. Yet for more than forty years there has been outspoken criticism of London orchestral provision, created in part from the piques and vanities of pre-war days. By introducing to the capital a new concert hall and a new orchestra under Rattle's direction and flair, Darwinian forces will be unleashed to which the existing orchestras will be obliged to adapt.
>
> Other vested interests likely to oppose our proposal include the South Bank, the Barbican and the Royal Albert Hall. Nevertheless strong arguments can still be made for another venue, and the dispersal of some component parts of the existing London orchestras elsewhere (either in the metropolis or further afield) might allow a more sustainable and yet more imaginative level of musical programming.

All this was highly speculative. There was the important disclaimer in the document that 'Rattle himself should not be expected to campaign for this project in its early stages.' In the present climate it seems unrealistic to imagine a wholly new hall will be built. Lottery funds are running dry for this sort of project – the present failure of the South Bank Centre to achieve its development being only the most depressing example of this – and if private support might conceivably generate a building, it would certainly have difficulty generating running costs.

But who is to say whether during the next decade or two, with Rattle triumphing in Berlin, the climate might change to allow a visionary project to proceed? Perhaps it should be somewhere that could equally house orchestral music and baroque opera, educational work and contemporary music workshops, reflecting the unique spread of Rattle's enthusiasms and their links into the wider community. Such a music centre could be an avenue for the exploration of all our musical gifts, with a firmly educational perspective, as well as the home of the very greatest performances.

CHAPTER FOUR

'It had to be hard sometimes'
Professional Start 1974–80

'Facing the limits of one's ability':
Rattle in action in his early professional years

I
1974–77

Simon Rattle did not need to win the John Player Conductor's Award. He was already known in London, and with Martin Campbell-White of Harold Holt as his agent he would have begun to receive some high-quality work. There were already possibilities in the offing, as he recalled:

SIMON RATTLE Maurice Handford asked me to go as his assistant to the Calgary Philharmonic, and I seriously thought about that. John Streets saw the possibility of getting me into Glyndebourne. I might have gone abroad to study, but though I might have learned a lot from Celibidache or Franco Ferrara later, it might not have been so then. People went too early and got submerged, especially by Celibidache. I toyed with the idea of going to university then, but after the competition all that changed.

Had he not won the competition he might have stayed at the Royal Academy of Music for a fourth year. He would have continued to conduct the Merseyside Youth Orchestra, and would have been invited by Stephen Gray to conduct the Royal Liverpool Philharmonic Orchestra. His London début with the New Philharmonia Orchestra was in place for the start of 1976, and interest had been shown by groups such as the Nash Ensemble and the London Sinfonietta. There is no reason to doubt that the rest would have followed naturally, and perhaps the development would have been more organic than it was.

But Rattle had a problem. He was a young, brilliant conductor with a certain amount of technical expertise but without a repertory. Though he knew a great deal of music, the sort of thing he was best at conducting – Mahler, Stravinsky, Shostakovich – was only a part of the staple diet of most symphony orchestras. So the chance to spend two years with the Bournemouth Symphony Orchestra and the Bournemouth Sinfonietta was an important one: a chance to learn the repertory away from the London limelight, and to deal for the first time with a professional orchestra. It encouraged him to turn down work in London and concentrate on learning. But it was a struggle, and it is possible that he might have learned more easily in other circumstances, with more sympathetic orchestras. Instead he went through what he admits now was the worst period of his professional life:

SIMON RATTLE The Bournemouth orchestras were the first professional orchestras I had conducted. And that's really why I went in for the competition, for the experience of conducting professionals. But I remember standing there at the beginning of my first rehearsal with them in the autumn and wondering what on earth I was going to do. We did eighty or so concerts a year and I'm sure they, who were incredibly nice about the whole thing, would say that seventy of them were bad.

There was a problem in that they were staggeringly unimaginative in repertory and couldn't for financial reasons do anything that involved extra players. So I sent them a list of what I would like to do and I knew when at the end I slipped in Dvořák 7 and Schubert's *Unfinished* that they'd choose them for the first concert! It wasn't their fault: Bournemouth was a place where they'd had protest letters about the Walton First Symphony. But it had the effect that, for instance, when the Sinfonietta was faced with Stravinsky's *Rake's Progress* they thought it was modern music.

In Bournemouth I faced the whole difficulty of the young professional coming to terms with the limits on one's ability. I'd done a certain sort of conducting, but I didn't realize that when you conduct professionals you have to start again completely. And the problem was that I wasn't good enough to conduct them, I know, but I wasn't bad enough for them to ignore me completely! It was the worst of all possible worlds: if I'd been worse they probably could have played better.

But it was a worthwhile experience. It had to be hard sometimes, and you have to learn. In this case I just learned the conductor's problems very fast. Some of the times were very difficult, especially with the Bournemouth Sinfonietta. They had a set way of playing, and I don't think they liked someone who wanted to interfere with that. They were rather distant and they didn't want to give the immediate emotional response to the music that I wanted.

I'm certainly glad that I didn't stay in London and take whatever things people were silly enough to offer me. I was offered four concerts with the London Philharmonic that year when Fischer-Dieskau cancelled. It didn't cross my mind to accept. If I had I wouldn't be here talking today; I would be a bitter percussionist somewhere, because I couldn't have done it and they would have seen through me in an instant.

I can look at it fairly dispassionately now, but during the Bournemouth period I very seriously toyed with the idea of giving up altogether. What partly saved me at the time was working on some of the same repertory with the Northern Sinfonia and finding that actually it was quite easy with them. And the fact that straight away, in the autumn after the competition, I was working with the Nash Ensemble, and found that I could give them something to chew on and I wasn't completely out of my depth. It was so refreshing to work with people like the clarinettist Tony Pay, and I think perhaps I didn't realize that everyone in the musical world doesn't work that way.

TONY PAY Martin Campbell-White had mentioned Simon to me, and the Nash were looking for someone to conduct *Pierrot lunaire* for us on a tour to Spain. So I suggested Simon to Amelia Freedman, who runs the ensemble. And the word came back that he'd like to do it but that he wanted two or three rehearsals. We were all incredibly busy and the piece was in our repertory and I really didn't think it was necessary to do more than one rehearsal. But he insisted and so we did them. He really had something to say about the piece and he wanted to change the way we played it. He had a view about it, and so it really was worth rehearsing it. That was the first of many times, with the Nash and with the [London] Sinfonietta, where having Simon conduct made a difference.

Meanwhile Rattle was getting to grips with the Bournemouth Symphony Orchestra and Sinfonietta. His programmes with them were uncharacteristic in that they included almost none of his favourite works or even music by his favourite composers. Some of the restrictions on him were explained in an interview he gave at the time:

> I was amazed at how much thought it takes planning the programmes. I spent three or four hours with David Blenkinsop, the concert manager, one day just sorting out four programmes. Of course it helps me that the Sinfonietta repeats programmes in different places. It means that the idiocies I do on the second night I don't do on the third. At the moment I'm learning the standard repertory because I've never really had time to do that. It's interesting to discover the limitations of programming for the orchestras. For instance, we can't do Mahler because we can't afford it, and we can't do Maxwell Davies because they say it'll send the audience away.

There is a note of frustration here that is amply echoed in the programmes themselves, although in the education concerts he did for schools some of his favourites do turn up: Janáček, Bartók, Milhaud, Stravinsky. For his formal début with the BSO, in Aldershot (which even the local paper admitted was 'not perhaps the most inspiring place to make a début'), the programme consisted of Schubert's *Unfinished*, Strauss's *Four Last Songs* with Linda Esther Gray, and Dvořák 7. The Schubert went back to his very first Liverpool concert as a conductor, but has rarely reappeared in his repertory since.

With the Sinfonietta the fare was even less typical and more problematic. For the first tour around the West Country he took Boyce, Vivaldi, Stravinsky's *Dumbarton Oaks* and Mozart's *Jupiter* Symphony to Totnes, Bodmin, Falmouth, St Ives, Tavistock and Chard. For an important first appearance at the Brighton Festival he had an entirely classical programme: Haydn's Symphony no. 60, Mozart's *Sinfonia concertante* for violin and viola, and the *Jupiter* again. This was desperately difficult and unfamiliar fare for Rattle at this time, and he acknowledges that his classical performances were probably poor. The programmes continued to be unrelentingly inappropriate: in the following weeks he did Haydn 86 and 95, Beethoven 4 and Mozart's Horn Concerto no. 3.

He had his first experience of Glyndebourne the following year, in the summer of 1975, preparing Stravinsky's *The Rake's Progress* with the Sinfonietta for the tour. He had considerable difficulty, as John Carewe recalls him mentioning at the time, getting them to play with a sharp yet flexible sense of ensemble. This was something that was noted during the tour: reviewing the performance at the New Theatre, Oxford, Gillian Widdicombe wrote in the *Financial Times* that Rattle was 'brisk and sensible, but not yet coaxing a virtuoso performance from the Bournemouth Sinfonietta, for one reason or another'. Later projects with the Sinfonietta included a Contemporary Music Network tour for the Arts Council with a programme that must have come at least as a welcome change to Rattle in its complexity: Schoenberg's *Accompaniment to a Film Scene*, Goehr's *Little Symphony*, Dominic Muldowney's *Music at Chartres III* and Henze's First Symphony. But he recalls the experience as 'a total disaster. We had fifty-one hours of rehearsal and at the end, as someone who heard it said, it still sounded like one of the fifties recordings which convince you how dreadful modern music is!' Then in 1976 it was back to Bach *Brandenburgs* and Schubert 5, along with Gerard Schurmann's *Variants*, and then a mixture of Haydn 91 and Mozart 38 with Jean Françaix and Dvořák. Haydn 22 and Mozart 39 followed, alongside a Bach cantata – something he has never done again, though Bach's music is finally back on his horizon, and he gave performances of the *St John Passion* with the CBSO, Berlin and the OAE in 2002.

With the Bournemouth Symphony Orchestra things were better and improved rapidly. Among the programmes were Berlioz's *King Lear* overture (with which he was to open his New Philharmonia début concert), Bartók's *Concerto for Orchestra* and Rakhmaninov's Second Symphony, soon to become a mainstream Rattle piece. At the beginning of 1976, when he turned twenty-one, he celebrated with one of the more successful of his Bournemouth series of concerts: music from Janáček's *Cunning Little Vixen*, Wagner's *Tannhäuser* overture, and Rakhmaninov's Third Piano Concerto, soon to be a favourite. That programme toured Plymouth, Camborne, Exeter and Portsmouth before ending up at Bournemouth where it was enthusiastically received. His final stint with the Bournemouth Symphony Orchestra included Kabalevsky's *Colas Breugnon*, Rakhmaninov's Second Piano Concerto, Mussorgsky's *Night on the Bare Mountain* and Dvořák's Eighth Symphony (one of the works from this period it would be good to hear him do again). His last programme consisted of Schumann's Second Symphony, Strauss's Oboe Concerto with Heinz Holliger and Elgar's *Enigma Variations*, an early calling card of Rattle's in his guest engagements around the world.

He was undoubtedly a better conductor at the end of the Bournemouth period than he was at the beginning. At one concert his father, meeting George Hurst (who had expressed his views on the performance with which Rattle had won the competition in no uncertain terms), said to him, 'Didn't they play well?' Hurst's reply was to the point: 'They had no choice.' But it is possible to wonder just how much Rattle really learned there that would not have been acquired gradually over the years. It was a harder schooling than strictly necessary, and certainly he experienced for the first time what it is like to be an unpopular conductor.

Reactions from the players varied, it seems, from tolerance to annoyance. At one extreme is a Sinfonietta player who recalled that 'we found him very irritating indeed, rhythmically very inadequate; we didn't like working with him at all'. Another opinion is that his Haydn and Mozart were poor – 'slow movements too slow, silly bowings and phrasings; they often came out deadly boring'· – but that he was obviously aware of his own failures in this area:

> He had even then a definite presence and authority which many established conductors lack; the opinion of many of the orchestra was that he was very intelligent but lacked technique and musicianship. But he knew his limitations and openly admitted in a most endearing fashion that some of the things he tried didn't work. He was down to earth, outgoing, direct, witty. One had the impression he had thoroughly thought out his interpretations (though sometimes with slightly absurd conclusions). He improved extraordinarily fast and at the end of the Bournemouth period it was becoming much more comfortable to work with him. He was always charming, unassuming and diplomatic.

Rattle's own view of this period is that the problems were inevitable and could not have been avoided. It might have been even worse elsewhere, he argues, and no young conductor can avoid the problems of facing professionals for the first time. As for the repertory, he felt there was a balance of opportunities and difficulties:

> SIMON RATTLE Some pieces I was scared off for life, others I began to get to grips with. My love of Haydn started here, so I have a lot to be grateful for. It was the beginning of the road with Mozart's *Jupiter* and *Prague*. The Schubert *Unfinished*, on the other hand, I've rarely done since. I realized

that so many orchestras play it so incredibly badly that I have to be a really very good conductor before I can make them do it better.

It is hardly surprising that Rattle learned fast in this period, since outside Bournemouth he had made great advances. Following his success with the Nash Ensemble he was invited to conduct part of a concert they gave in the Queen Elizabeth Hall in February 1975: this was his professional South Bank début, and *The Times* praised his 'clean and careful' conducting of Ravel with Felicity Palmer. (Later in the year he made his first recording, an all-Ravel disc, with the same players.) In January he had appeared at the Institute of Contemporary Arts with a section of the Royal Philharmonic Orchestra in a programme of new music that contained a pair of obscure works for brass and percussion. He knew most of the players so the engagement was not a problem for him. *The Times* noted of one of the pieces that 'There was never any real textural interest and Simon Rattle, the conductor, did well to obtain what sounded like a quite committed performance.'

Then in April he was approached at very short notice to conduct an English Chamber Orchestra tour of Spain: Pinchas Zukerman, who was to conduct, had fallen ill. Once more he took fright, thinking he would be eaten alive by these experienced players:

> SIMON RATTLE Martin [Campbell-White] warned me that Quin Ballardie who ran the ECO was going to ring and I said that I just couldn't cope with it, I was too young, it wouldn't work, and all that. But Quin rang up and said, 'You don't know me but I run the ECO and I hear you're a bit nervous about conducting us in Spain. I've told all the people you're coming and your name is on all the posters so let's just assume you're coming, shall we?' Amazing! I was completely blustered into it. But I enjoyed it, and they were tolerant of what must have been some of the worst Mozart Fortieths ever.

An orchestra with which Rattle was to try out some of his most ambitious projects around this time was the amateur Salomon Orchestra. In June 1975 he did a concert with them that included the Adagio from Mahler's Tenth Symphony (before the publication of the full score of Deryck Cooke's completion of the whole work, which Rattle later took up enthusiastically). This drew a warm notice from Stephen Walsh in the *Observer*:

> The Salomon Orchestra has a good record in bringing forward young con-

ductors. I doubt, though, whether even they have gone much nearer the cradle than Mr Rattle . . . Even he wasn't quite equal to the basic difficulty of securing deft and athletic playing from amateur players in a Haydn symphony . . . [but in the Mahler] he showed remarkable ability to sustain long melodic sentences and build them into coherent paragraphs. The searing climax was by any standards exciting.

Rattle still found it valuable to be involved not only with amateur music-making but also school music-making. During the summer he went up to Aberdeen to conduct at a festival of youth orchestras there, and in September took his first course with the London Schools Symphony Orchestra. This was something that Andrew Davis had previously done, and through Martin Campbell-White Rattle was asked to conduct the autumn course and to make his Festival Hall début as a conductor at the end of it. It was a bold programme which included Ligeti's *Atmosphères*, never before heard in the hall, and Mahler's First Symphony. Ronald Crichton in the *Financial Times*, pointing out that Rattle was only seven years older than the youngest schoolchild in the LSSO, praised the Mahler: 'Nothing was funked . . . Mr Rattle's secure and sensitive guidance of this tricky score was of the greatest value.'

This amateur début was followed, and naturally overshadowed in importance, by his professional début in the Festival Hall in February 1976, conducting the New Philharmonia Orchestra (which was soon to drop the word 'New' from its title). This was a landmark, an event that had been carefully planned by Martin Campbell-White to gain the maximum attention. Simon's parents came down from Liverpool, and there was a party afterwards attended by such luminaries as Sir Robert Mayer. Rattle had expressed his misgivings to an interviewer beforehand: 'What can a twenty-one-year-old have to teach Gwydion Brooke?' he said, referring to the orchestra's famous first bassoonist. But he did in the event have something to teach Brooke, because the bassoonist made a wrong entry in Shostakovich's Tenth Symphony and Rattle was able to steer him through it.

GAVIN HENDERSON He was going to conduct the piece from memory, with the greatest orchestra in Britain, who looked askance at this unknown boy. The most formidable person in the orchestra was the legendary first bassoon, but on this night, for the first time ever, he lost his way. And Simon quietly and calmly brought him back into the performance. It was a wonderful moment, which he handled with great delicacy and dignity.

Nobody in the audience knew what had happened. He won the heart of the orchestra from that point on.

He was the youngest conductor ever to appear with the orchestra, and this inspired some faintly contradictory comments in the papers from the critics who were, however, united in their praise of the new conductor. In the *Guardian* Hugo Cole wrote,

> Conductors, like swimming champions, mature younger and younger, and skills which were once acquired only over many years and laborious processes of trial and error are today picked up by conservatory and university students in no time at all. Yet Simon Rattle, at twenty-one, is still something rather exceptional ... the symphony was well and seriously performed, suggesting that the New Philharmonia Orchestra were taking their conductor seriously, and giving him the performance he wanted and knew how to ask for.

On the other hand, Robert Henderson in the *Daily Telegraph* underlined some of the problems when he noted that 'whereas brilliant soloists in their early twenties are a normal feature of concert life, the very difficulty of gaining the necessary practical experience makes the appearance of a conductor of similar authority at the same age a rare and, indeed, unlikely occurrence'. But he found the début 'strikingly auspicious', and felt that 'rarely had any apologies to be made for his youth'. Max Harrison in *The Times* wrote, 'Mr Rattle is a convinced advocate; he presented an altogether clearly thought-out interpretation and obtained superb playing from the New Philharmonia.'

This was indeed, as one writer put it, a 'glittering start'. Rattle's enthusiasm for making things happen as a conductor, and all those years of gathering together amateur forces and cajoling people to play for him had paid off to the extent that it had given him the necessary experience to face an orchestra like the New Philharmonia without any qualms. Martin Campbell-White was delighted: 'The buzz started and I remember I introduced him to Daniel Barenboim and one or two other people; there was a great deal of interest in him from the right quarters from an early time.' Barenboim was to take a further intense interest in Rattle's career in 1999. Campbell-White recalls that Rattle was very much his own master in the choice of work that he undertook, and his choices were usually right.

Later that same month Rattle gave his first account of a work that was to become central for him: Gershwin's *Porgy and Bess*. This was the beginning of a ten-year love affair with this opera, 'one of the twentieth-century's most neglected operas', as Rattle called it. It was the first time he worked with Willard White, who was to be his Porgy ten years later at Glyndebourne as well as several times in between (see pp. 200–3). The performance was put on by the Chelsea Opera Group in the old Town Hall in London's Euston Road, and it apparently had plenty of fizz: Alan Blyth in *The Times* wrote that it did 'nearly as much justice as is possible in a concert performance of the opera'. (Only in a concert performance were non-black singers allowed by the rules of the Gershwin estate, a major factor in delaying the first staging of the work by an English company.) In a prescient review in *Opera* magazine, Rodney Milnes noted that 'The vigour and total lack of inhibition that characterized both the orchestral playing and choral singing must be put down to Simon Rattle's inspired conducting . . . let us hope that more successful concert performances will inspire a new stage production of Gershwin's masterpiece.' They would, but it was to be quite a wait.

There was more opera that summer, with the English Music Theatre, newly formed from the ashes of the English Opera Group. First at the Maltings at Snape, home of the Aldeburgh Festival, and then on tour around the country before arriving at Sadler's Wells, Rattle conducted Kurt Weill's *Threepenny Opera*. He then returned to the Dartington Summer School, galvanizing the choir – which included his parents – for a performance of Janáček's *Glagolitic Mass*, a work that was to be among the first he recorded, and giving an exhilarating read-through of Rakhmaninov's Third Piano Concerto at two pianos with Peter Donohoe as the soloist and himself as the orchestra.

In August there was his first BBC Prom – or part of one – conducting the London Sinfonietta at the Round House in Lutyens's *And Suddenly It's Evening* and Birtwistle's *Meridian*: he was the youngest conductor ever to appear in a BBC Prom. That success was to be followed up by regular Proms with the Sinfonietta, including his first Royal Albert Hall appearance the following year with a Mozart, Schoenberg and Stravinsky programme in which he returned to *Pulcinella*.

But the major events of that autumn were the result of Martin Campbell-White's desire that, slowly but surely, Rattle's name should become very well known abroad. The London Schools Symphony Orchestra did an extensive and exhausting American tour that took Rattle to Carnegie Hall in New York for the first time, to Chicago (where his conducting of

Elgar's *Enigma Variations* was compared favourably to that of another recent English visitor, Edward Heath) and to Los Angeles where, as Simon recalled, 'Ernest [Fleischmann, manager of the Los Angeles Philharmonic] met us off the plane and immediately started asking me to go and do things with the Philharmonic. I was scared stiff!' Meanwhile he worked with the Scottish Chamber Orchestra for the first time, establishing a good rapport which was to become important for the future when he would try out major new projects such as Beethoven's Third and Ninth Symphonies with this group. And Martin Campbell-White arranged his débuts with a couple of foreign orchestras, starting with the Trondheim and the Sjaellands Symphony Orchestras in Scandinavia, both of which he enjoyed. The vistas were opening up rapidly.

Another important experience in this period was to be asked back to conduct an ensemble he had played in, the National Youth Orchestra; not only to perform *The Rite of Spring*, but also to record it in what was his largest recording undertaking to date. John Carewe was less than flattering about the end result (see p. 80), and Rattle recorded the work again with the CBSO, as well as giving a highly praised performance in one of his early concerts with the Berlin Philharmonic in the early 1990s. But he remembered it as a chastening experience because the NYO recording immediately preceded a course directed by Pierre Boulez:

SIMON RATTLE That orchestra is a mirror: they can adapt so quickly. There were some problems with the recording because of the sheer timelag in hearing what was happening. I remember I couldn't see the piccolo trumpet-player at all because he was so small, but I worked out that he was the one whose feet didn't touch the ground so I waved in that direction! Just after the recordings Boulez came to direct the orchestra. They played him what I had trained them to do, and I watched his face. I was very proud because they could produce exactly what I had done, and I wondered what he'd make of it. He spent about an hour making it worse and worse, and then a couple of hours transforming it. Mainly he worked on the 'Danse sacrale', and I learned a hell of a lot seeing him mould that in his own image – going for a feeling of weighting, his insistence that you could hear what all those chords actually were. In his work with the orchestra he was basically just pointing out my deficiencies in a very clear way!

II
1977–80

The first radical change in the pattern of Rattle's work happened in 1977. After his two-year stint with the Bournemouth orchestras came to an end in the summer of 1976 he did a modest amount of guest conducting, but he still felt the need to work himself gradually into the repertory before making any substantial commitments or accepting any major offers. So the two posts that came his way in 1977 were both very welcome: the more substantial was as assistant conductor of the BBC Scottish Symphony Orchestra in Glasgow, and the more public was as associate conductor of the Royal Liverpool Philharmonic Orchestra in his home town.

It came as a surprise to Martin Dalby, Head of Music for the BBC in Scotland, that Simon Rattle would want to accept an assistant's post at a time when his career was taking off so rapidly. In fact it was ideal for Rattle, for it gave him the rehearsal conditions and the work out of the public limelight in the broadcasting studio that he needed. He wanted to broaden his repertory, but also to explore those areas of it with which he felt at home, something that had been impossible under the constraints of West Country touring.

For their part, the orchestra responded with enthusiasm and did everything in their power to make him feel welcome. Only their principal conductor, Karl Anton Rickenbacher, was baffled by the choice of a twenty-two-year-old conductor for the orchestra. Martin Dalby made every effort to accommodate Rattle's wishes, and the results were programmes that included many of his best pieces. Dalby soon realized that Rattle's title was the wrong one: 'He obviously assisted nobody, so somewhere along the line we redesignated it as associate conductor.' He took up the post on 1 July 1977, and his contract was renewed in 1979 for a further year to 30 June 1980. The commitment, a substantial one, was to do twenty-five programmes in the studio as well as public concerts.

Part of Dalby's efforts to make Rattle as content as possible in Glasgow involved finding ways to augment the orchestra in order to undertake the repertory Rattle wanted to do. His first concerts included Bruckner's Fourth Symphony, Brahms's Second and Rakhmaninov's Second. Major undertakings in 1978 included Mahler's *Das Lied von der Erde*, Bartók's *Music for Strings, Percussion and Celesta*, Messiaen's

Oiseaux exotiques and Mahler's Fifth Symphony (interestingly, a work
to which Rattle did not return in Birmingham until 1997, and which he
will record only in 2002, when it forms part of his opening concerts with
Berlin). Among the few classical works he attempted was Beethoven's
Seventh Symphony, in a performance in June 1978 which he was
unhappy with, and he later did Beethoven's Fourth and Brahms's
Fourth. But these were the exceptions: more typical were Strauss's *Don
Quixote* and Berlioz's *Symphonie fantastique*, for which nothing was
stinted in terms of players. Rattle must have felt much more at home
with this repertory than with that in Bournemouth.

There was also an element of contemporary music in these
programmes, but it was not extensive. Thea Musgrave's *Night Music*,
Lennox Berkeley's Flute Concerto, John Maxwell Geddes's *Lacuna*,
Peter Maxwell Davies's early *Five Klee Pictures* and Elisabeth Lutyens's
Echoi were among the recent works tackled. But more significant than
this for the future was the core repertory he developed in the early
twentieth-century classics: Debussy, Ravel, Stravinsky, Berg, Prokofiev,
Janáček, Shostakovich and Bartók. This was the music with which he felt
most at ease, and it was surely his skill in this area that made it possible
for him to tackle contemporary works with such comparative ease.

One of the contemporary works he undertook caused something of a
fuss. He wanted to use the orchestra to prepare himself for the first
performance of Peter Maxwell Davies's very complex First Symphony,
which he had been asked by the composer to première in London with
the New Philharmonia Orchestra. The Scottish Symphony Orchestra
performance was to be broadcast later, but the glory of the first performance would go to Rattle with the London orchestra. Although Maxwell
Davies expressed his appreciation of the Scottish orchestra's work, some
of the players apparently regarded it as 'a gross and insensitive insult'
that their orchestra was used in this way as back-room preparation for
the achievements of a London orchestra. The performance in London,
however, was exceptionally strong, and it is surprising that the work –
which Maxwell Davies himself criticized for its thickness of texture – has
not been returned to more often, for its emotional weight is certainly
greater than that of many of the symphonies that followed it in sequence.

Another minor controversy surrounded Rattle's determination to do
The Rite of Spring with the BBC Scottish. In January 1980 he spent a
week rehearsing and then performing the work, for which a large number of extras was needed. Dalby managed to obtain all except one (the

bass tuba-player) from Scotland, but word got round the BBC that the expenditure had been lavish. In an interview with *The Times* in 1982 about the reorganization of the BBC's orchestral resources, the BBC's Controller, Music, Robert Ponsonby, said that the orchestras had to rationalize their repertory to suit their size: 'When the BBC Scottish did *The Rite of Spring*, extras were brought in from the four corners of the Empire.' This infuriated Dalby, who protested vigorously that that was untrue, and that in any case such demarcation of repertory between the regional symphony orchestras was impossible to put into practice. Was the BBC Symphony Orchestra going to stop playing Mozart? And in fact that policy was gradually eroded: in an interview in the 1987 Proms prospectus, John Drummond, who had by then succeeded Ponsonby at the BBC, said, 'Of course the BBC Scottish wants to play *The Rite of Spring* and the BBC Symphony Orchestra wants to play Haydn symphonies and no one's going to stop them.'

That saga produced what Rattle regarded as one of his finest *Rites*:

> They'd never done it before and they'll probably never do it again. We rehearsed it for five days, and we built it up chord by chord until everything had this weight and depth and richness, and then we were able to put the punch on the top of it.

Besides that work there were several others that have turned out to be Rattle favourites: Sibelius's Second and Seventh Symphonies, Stravinsky's *Petrushka* and, perhaps most notably, Shostakovich's Tenth Symphony, which he took to the Proms with the orchestra in 1979. Already by that time there had been strong hints that the BBC was going to attack the orchestras as part of a package of economies the following year. Martin Dalby remembers turning to Pat Ramsay, the BBC's Controller, Scotland, after that performance, and saying, 'You're not going to let them touch it after *that*.' Ramsay did not reply, and ironically it was the Scottish Broadcasting Council of the BBC, rather than the BBC in London, that in the end recommended the sacrifice of the BBC Scottish Symphony Orchestra in 1980 – and that caused the Musicians' Union strike which led to the cancellation of some of that year's Proms.

Rattle was in Los Angeles in January 1980 when he heard the news of the proposed cuts. He was outraged, and told an interviewer:

> It only proves the people who run the BBC are philistine. It's not the music department; they're fine. It's the top management's fault. It's a first-rate

example of the damned bureaucratic mind. Extraordinary if you think of it
in humanitarian terms. Here's eighty people put out of a job, and in Glasgow; they don't stand a chance of finding other employment at short
notice. And what happens to the area's culture? The country's?

Rattle went back and wrote a letter to *The Times*, making the same
points in more measured terms.

One of his last acts before his contract in Scotland expired in mid-
1980 was to take part in a gala concert in May at the Theatre Royal,
Glasgow, in aid of the strike that had by then been called. It was a grand
gathering of conductors: Christopher Seaman, Sir Alexander Gibson and
James Loughran, with a splendidly miscellaneous programme of lolli-
pops. Then during the following week, Rattle concluded his Scottish
work with an entirely typical collection of pieces: David Matthews'
September Music, Elgar's First Symphony and Mahler's *Das klagende
Lied* and Fourth Symphony. Rattle has said, 'I found everything that I
consider to be at the centre of my repertory with the BBC Scottish, and I
remember vividly the sensation of welcome . . . they had amazing vitality
and great warmth.' It was a fruitful time, but once again Rattle was
lucky: the orchestra took a long time to rebuild itself following the
settlement of the Musicians' Union strike later in the year (which left it
still in existence but without some key players) and the post of associate
conductor has never been revived. The orchestra, however, has survived
further merger plans and threatened economies, and was invigorated
under the inspiring leadership of Osmo Vänska It has brought on such
major conducting talents as Martyn Brabbins, but it is a challenge for it
to have quite the same effect on the conducting scene as it did when
Rattle, Andrew Davis and others learned their trade in Scotland.

Rattle's other post, which he took up in April 1977, was as associate
conductor of the orchestra with which he had grown up, the Royal
Liverpool Philharmonic. The post was less onerous in terms of appearances – some twelve concerts a season – but far more public and rather
more problematic. It had been specially created for him as part of the
changeover from Sir Charles Groves, who retired as principal conductor, to Walter Weller, who succeeded him. Rattle had already
returned twice to the orchestra in 1975, the year after winning the John
Player Award, first with Sibelius's Fifth Symphony and Rakhmaninov
played by his friend Philip Fowke, and then with a Ravel centenary
concert including a complete concert performance of *L'enfant et les*

sortilèges which was perhaps less effective than the one he had given a year earlier at the Royal Academy. Nevertheless, he impressed Stephen Gray, the orchestra's manager, who had been one of the first people in the professional musical world to notice him, and whose mention of him to Martin Campbell-White really started the wheels rolling for Rattle as a professional conductor. He was well aware of Rattle's skills as a programme-builder, and wanted to give him his head:

STEPHEN GRAY Simon is a natural entrepreneur. He was always tremendously interested in the business of putting on concerts, from his teenage years, and he was very shrewd, and had a terrifically enquiring mind. I remember very clearly discussing the cast for the Ravel opera and being so impressed with the maturity with which he knew who could do what, and who he wanted to sing which part.

I think the orchestra regarded him as their son rather than their father, and there was a little bit of that in their attitude to him. In the three years he conducted us very regularly he did some fascinating programmes, and they were such events. (I remember every one of his concerts, which is more than I can say about a lot of the others.) He asked for a great deal of rehearsal, for example for the Strauss *Metamorphosen*, and I generally agreed. Mahler 10 we didn't have enough time for, and it wasn't one of his best performances. But Mahler 2 in Liverpool Cathedral was the greatest thing he did for us.

The performances were pretty rough, and little things went wrong, but they always hung together. I haven't had anyone to work with since who had that sort of flair for sparking me off with programme ideas. In fact I don't think I've ever met anyone quite so gifted in every way.

Rattle's associate conductorship was inaugurated with another performance of Gershwin's *Porgy and Bess*, as part of the Hope Street Festival. Once again Willard White was Porgy. 'A triumph for all concerned,' reported a local paper. And in his first season in 1978 there was Mahler's *Das Lied von der Erde*, Rakhmaninov's *Symphonic Dances*, Dvořák's Cello Concerto, and a typically thoughtful symmetrical programme:

Strauss	*Don Juan*
Ravel	*Shéhérazade*
Messiaen	*Et exspecto resurrectionem mortuorum*
Ravel	*Three Mallarmé Poems*
Strauss	*Metamorphosen*

In July 1978 he conducted Janáček's *Jenůfa* for the first time, in a concert performance with Pauline Tinsley. 'A triumph of closely involved, inspirational conducting,' wrote Neil Tierney in the *Daily Telegraph*. Rattle several times came near to conducting it in the opera house – in New York, at Covent Garden and at Glyndebourne – and it was finally seen in Paris at the Châtelet in a highly praised production. But it is typical of Rattle's determination to wait for the right conditions that even this opera he feels so close to his heart is one he has not conducted in Britain; for that we must still wait.

The 1978–79 season included Janáček's *Taras Bulba*, Walton's *Belshazzar's Feast*, Sibelius 1, Mahler 10, and a lively Bernstein–Gershwin evening. A novelty of that period was the extraordinary fantasy by H. K. Gruber, *Frankenstein!!*, which Rattle also conducted in a chamber version in London with the London Sinfonietta. This brought the national critics up to Liverpool to be amazed: in the *Financial Times* David Murray wrote that this 'pandemonium for baritone and orchestra' was

> singularly charming . . . Nearly half an hour long, it is a setting of wicked children's rhymes by the Austrian surrealist H. C. Artmann . . . Traditional monsters rub shoulders with Batman, Robin and Jimmy Bond, with lashings of simple horror . . . Bright-eyed scores like this suit Simon Rattle to a T, and the performance by the Royal Liverpool Philharmonic under him evinced infectious relish.

The 1979–80 concerts all included some Stravinsky: the *Firebird* suite alongside Rakhmaninov's Third Symphony, *The Rite of Spring*, *Petrushka* with Beethoven 7, the Mass with Mahler 6, the *Symphony of Psalms* with the Fauré *Requiem*, and the *Symphony in Three Movements* alongside Brahms's Violin Concerto.

Though there were many successes among these performances, and though the fascinating juxtapositions of works made up the first fully characteristic Rattle public concert programmes, the collaboration with the orchestra was not entirely a success. One player recalled:

> We found his rehearsal technique rather exhausting. His brain is so quick that he'd say 'Two bars before A,' very quickly and there would be a downbeat before anyone was ready. So he'd stop, repeat the instruction and again he'd be off before the violins had the instruments under their chins. He spoke in a clipped, jerky way which was quite taxing on the nervous system . . .

Many of us definitely did not enjoy rehearsing with Simon. But the shows, during which he couldn't talk so much, were good. He was excellent at getting good performances. I remember he spent a long time trying to get the orchestra to play one long phrase as one long phrase, not twenty short ones. Unfortunately many of us were rather unwilling to accept his authority.

This friction caused problems when Walter Weller was suddenly snapped up by the Royal Philharmonic Orchestra in London, since it then looked as if Rattle was the obvious person to succeed him as principal conductor.

PAULINE RATTLE [The management] was pressing him a lot, and pressing us too. We were very close to the Philharmonic at that time, and twenty or thirty people would come back home after Simon's concerts, so we knew them well. It was a great embarrassment to us: we were very happy when he was offered it but I quite saw his point that it wouldn't have been right.

SIMON RATTLE I'm sure Stephen Gray was very upset when I didn't do it: he had given me *carte blanche* with those programmes and had showed absolute faith. But I had to say that I wasn't going to be rehearsing Stephen Gray or conducting Stephen Gray. They all remembered me as a bumptious little kid running around backstage collecting autographs and listening to every rehearsal. In some ways there was a good rapport, but I never felt, as was somehow obvious with the other orchestras I was working with, that I really knew how to make that orchestra better. It was obviously not going to work.

The orchestra, for their part, decided in a majority vote that they did not wish him to be appointed. (This was something that he was unaware of until he read it in the first edition of this book. He said he was relieved, because several members of the orchestra had said strongly to him that they did want him and he had felt bad about being so convinced it would not work.) Probably for the best, both sides of the possible marriage realized in advance that it should not happen.

In any case, other orchestras were on the scene by then and Rattle's career was racing ahead. In 1978 he had made his first visit to the Rotterdam Philharmonic, where he had been offered a music directorship in succession to David Zinman. He declined but accepted a principal guest conductorship. That relationship produced some outstanding and enjoyable concerts, as well as, much later, his first Wagner operas, when he used the Rotterdam orchestra as one of the opera orchestras for the

Netherlands Opera. *Parsifal* was mounted in 1998, with an unforgettable repeat concert performance with the same orchestra at the 2000
BBC Proms. *Tristan und Isolde* followed in 2001 (see pp. 310–15).

   The following year he returned to Los Angeles for his long-awaited
début with the Philharmonic, and Ernest Fleischmann again wooed him
with the offer of a post. Chicago followed later that year, and Toronto
and San Francisco were planned for 1980. It might have been thought
certain that his future lay in that direction, in picking up a music directorship, as Andrew Davis had done, with a respected foreign orchestra
before returning to take up a major post in Britain. In fact the engagement that really mattered in this period had taken place in December
1978, when Rattle conducted the City of Birmingham Symphony
Orchestra for the first time in Birmingham.

CHAPTER FIVE

'I didn't realize how important it would be to be here'
Birmingham 1980–90

Rattle, conducting the CBSO Proms in the Town Hall, Birmingham,
1982, complete with added slogans (photo Alan Wood)

I

1980–86

Crater no. 357 on the Moon is officially entitled 'Birmingham Crater'. There are towns named after Birmingham in Saskatchewan, Canada; Jefferson, Alabama; Los Angeles, California; New Haven, Connecticut; Miami, Indiana; Jackson, Kansas, Oakland, Michigan, and many other American states. No one could argue that the city's reputation does not extend far afield. But it is a reputation that, in recent decades, has taken some hard knocks. In the industrial recession that hit Great Britain in the 1970s, Birmingham and the West Midlands slumped; with declining productivity, high unemployment and a lack of economic prosperity, it became the poorest area in the United Kingdom outside Northern Ireland.

Such a decline was perhaps inevitable for a city that had been built on the boom of the Industrial Revolution in the nineteenth century and that was wholly dependent on manufacturing and trading industries for its early prosperity. 'The City of a Thousand Trades,' they called it, and among the many testimonies to its success came one from the composer Antonín Dvořák, who visited Birmingham in 1890: 'I'm here in this immense industrial city where they make excellent knives, scissors, springs, files, and goodness knows what else and besides these, music too. And how well! It's terrifying how much these people here manage to achieve.'

There was indeed a remarkable history of achievement in Birmingham dating back to the late eighteenth century, when its prosperity first took off. Lying as it did at the heart of the country's canal network (it still likes to boast that it has more miles of canal than Venice) it became a centre of communications, and the place where scientists, men of ideas and entrepreneurs gathered: Joseph Priestley, who discovered oxygen; James Watt, who invented the steam engine; Josiah Wedgwood, the potter; William Murdoch, inventor of gas lighting; John Baskerville, the printer; Matthew Boulton, the industrialist – all these lived and worked in Birmingham. Soon, too, it was at the heart of a railway system, and there seemed no limit to what it could achieve. Large food and drink companies such as Cadbury's originated here – the Utopian village of Bournville was the centre of the Cadbury operation – and brewing, metalworking, engineering, car manufacturing and all kinds of light- and medium-scale industry became important parts of the city's economy.

So it was scarcely surprising that when industrial decline hit Britain it should hit Birmingham hard. But although economic circumstances are still extremely difficult for many, there has been a determined effort to adapt to changed circumstances and find a new role for the city. The foundation of the 350-acre National Exhibition Centre marked a turning point, and that complex now houses a large percentage of Britain's major exhibitions. For years now Birmingham has been promoting itself heavily as a venue for new business, offering 'a total workforce of around half a million with experience and skills in every type of industry . . . [and] some of the lowest industrial rents and rates in the country'. There is a major science park at Aston devoted to the emerging 'sunrise' industries in the fields of electronic, computer and precision engineering which it is hoped will replace the traditional industries now in decline. The Science Park has close links with Aston University, and can call on advice from its scientists and technical experts. The International Convention Centre containing Symphony Hall, which opened in 1991, turned out to be the biggest and much the most crucial part of that equation (see pp. 230–35).

But for all this determination and resilience, it still cannot be argued that Birmingham is a remarkably attractive city. In interviews Simon Rattle has had to fall back on the assertion that 'It's not a pretty city. On the other hand, it's not as ugly as Cleveland or Detroit.' A long-time observer of the Birmingham scene is Beresford King-Smith, the former deputy chief executive of the CBSO, their historian and archivist, who published a book, *Crescendo*, on the story of the CBSO:

BERESFORD KING-SMITH Birmingham is the spider in the middle of the motorway web and people come here because of their jobs. There was a strong civic pride in the nineteenth century – that's where all those big Victorian buildings come from – but then after the Second World War something went wrong, and the planning was I think a disaster. We're not the only city that's suffered from it but it was very bad here. Somehow the city got cut in two by the ring road and there's us up at this end and them at that end, and that is a bad thing in any city.

But those things are now gradually being healed. Some good buildings are going up; architecturally it is still not anything to write home about but the feel of the place is improving. A few open spaces are being created – that's something we lack in the middle of the city, a bit of grass, a few trees – which make a tremendous difference. But the really encouraging thing has been to see the political parties working together on all this. In the past a change of power from Labour to Conservative in Birmingham, or vice versa, was a very serious thing for us because Birmingham has always been a hung parliament. There's a feeling that we need to co-operate to survive, and that's very healthy.

It has been very healthy too for the City of Birmingham Symphony Orchestra. As Birmingham's reputation as an industrial centre declines, the city has been anxious to find other roles, other areas where it can show its expertise. And in the partnership of the CBSO and Simon Rattle it found, for eighteen remarkable years, an outstanding export. George Jonas, chairman of the CBSO for much of that period, likes to tell a story:

> GEORGE JONAS I arrived in San Francisco and got into a taxi. The taxi-driver started talking: 'Where are you from?' 'England.' 'What part of England?' 'Birmingham.' 'Oh, Birmingham. Would you know a guy called Simon Rattle?' He'd conducted there, you see. Birmingham was known in San Francisco by Simon Rattle. The orchestra is as good an investment for the name of Birmingham as anything here, and we can be the city's ambassador abroad.

The CBSO in the period before Simon Rattle arrived was not altogether a happy orchestra. In March 1978, very suddenly, both the general manager, Arthur Baker, and the principal conductor, Louis Frémaux, had walked out, leaving the orchestra without direction. The story of the dispute is murky, and it finally blew up over the question of who should play principal viola in a particular session. Frémaux declared briefly: 'The orchestra refused to accept my direction, so I left.' To this day he has not commented further on the matter. It was more than a matter of one viola-player, however. A player who was involved remembered:

> It was a revolution. The players took matters into their own hands because they didn't think that the orchestral manager had things under control. The diary was looking empty, and we were very discontented with the quality of the work we were getting. Essentially we expressed no confidence in the general manager, and he left. He was closely involved with Frémaux, acted as his agent as well as managing the orchestra, and Frémaux walked out in sympathy. Our relationship with Frémaux hadn't been bad until his last couple of years, and he had improved the orchestra a great deal, but it was never ideal.

We could understand his action but it left us in a very difficult position. However, there was also a major opportunity to rebuild things, with the players more involved in the whole process of management. The chairman ran things in the interim. There was player representation on the board that chose the new general manager, Ed Smith, who appeared out of the mist, as it were. Then we got a new constitution together, in which the players were more involved. [There were already two players on the council of management, but they were excluded from certain items of discussion.] The new set-up gave us a real part in the running of the orchestra. And players were on the subcommittee that advised on the choice of the new principal conductor as well. So if things go wrong now it's pretty much our fault.

The man who took charge of the CBSO during that difficult period, and who headed its council of management through a vital period of change, is the Birmingham lawyer and former councillor George Jonas.

GEORGE JONAS I came to Birmingham in 1952, strictly for one year. And I've stayed ever since. I remember going to the CBSO in Birmingham for the first time with [Rudolf] Schwarz doing the Beethoven *Choral* Symphony in December 1952. I also heard one of their first London concerts, just after the Festival Hall opened. That was in the George Weldon days and a pretty awful sound they made; it was a poor orchestra. Then I came on the management committee some twenty years ago when I was a member of Birmingham City Council. When the electors gave me up I stayed on the orchestra's council as an elected member. The orchestra was always thought of as something good, and there was a feeling that it had to be kept going, but without any of the sort of enthusiasm that followed once Louis Frémaux had been appointed and which, of course, is even greater now. It was my predecessor as chairman who supported Frémaux's appointment, and there was a lot of opposition to it. I remember I came out of a hospital bed to vote at a crucial meeting. After Frémaux came things improved. It began to record again; it became more of a national orchestra.

But it was always a bit of a fight to keep the thing going. There was no sponsorship. We had to make all sorts of economies, keeping down the number of extras and so on, but the sticking point with me – and I've fought for this often – was cutting down the number of players. I always resisted that violently as a way of saving money and I would have resigned if it had been done. It was proposed several times in the early years but was never actually carried out.

After Frémaux left relations between the players and the management were truly appalling. We had quite a struggle to bring them together but in the end we persuaded both sides that it wasn't a good idea to have a them-and-us feeling, so we got two orchestra representatives on to the board of directors, as it now is. And that has worked extremely well. But the situation was horrendous with both conductor and manager leaving at the same time. First of all we appointed Ed Smith. And then we took a conscious decision about a new conductor: either we could find someone to succeed Frémaux pretty quickly or we could ask the sort of man whose diary would already be full for the next two years. We took the view that we'd already reached a reasonable standard with Frémaux and we had Erich Schmid as guest conductor. Even though he wasn't with us all that often he did a remarkable job and kept things together. So we worked on the new constitution, and then we formed a small subcommittee to look for a new principal conductor.

Simon was not an obvious choice. We had a long list of conductors, which became a shorter list and was then reduced to two. Ed Smith knew Simon, it quickly emerged, and felt we had a genius in our midst. The greatest credit for the appointment must be the fact that Ed kept on pushing and pushing for it. We certainly felt we were taking a gamble. I had gone to hear two of Simon's concerts in Liverpool and I thought they were a total disaster: I later found out he had trouble getting that orchestra to play for him. But what changed my mind was that he came to Birmingham with Glyndebourne Touring Opera in 1978 and did Mozart's *Così*, with the Bournemouth Sinfonietta, which if I may say so is not the greatest orchestra in the world, and that was a revelation. That was the turning point for me, and I was then prepared to take the risk. But what a risk!

I remember when I first met Simon and had lunch with him he made the point: 'Don't expect me to conduct Beethoven symphonies and all the great works.' He has a great respect for that music, which is part of his marvellous modesty. But those things didn't worry us. What we weren't quite aware of was that Ed was right and we actually did have a genius.

The first concerts he did gave off an incredible, electrifying atmosphere. It was so exciting to see music-making of that sort, and very soon we snapped him up for a longer period. Any doubts we had were very quickly dispelled.

BERESFORD KING-SMITH Somebody gave me a document called 'Birmingham and its Civic Managers 1928'. The headings at the front start with 'Schools', 'Finance', and so on, and it ends, 'Sewers, Mental Defectives, Cemeteries, City of Birmingham Symphony Orchestra'. So we've moved up a notch since then.

The whole set-up is so different now from the days of Weldon and Schwarz and even Frémaux. Then you had your permanent conductor and if you had a good one you were on a growth trip up, and if you didn't it must have been murder. And we were doing things like the Prom season where we gave five concerts a week for three weeks, and in practice some of them were not very good. It's interesting that now we have such a success with the subscription series that the one thing we have trouble selling out are the Proms. Perhaps people assume they're sold out, or perhaps we've gone too far up the river the other way. And the orchestra is so used to rehearsing extensively that they have a real problem getting a concert on with just one three-hour rehearsal.

One thing, for instance, that has changed radically is the number of choral-society dates we do. One of the very serious things in British musical life is that choral societies now can't afford symphony orchestras. And it was in fact rather a nonsense because we did *Messiah*s all over the place, which meant that thirty or forty people were sitting at home being paid to do nothing. There are plenty of freelance and chamber orchestras who can do that sort of thing better.

We were also doing split dates, half the orchestra in one place, half in another, even in the seventies, and I don't think that did the orchestra much good. But one doesn't want to deprive the people in those small towns we visited then. It's a difficult situation. Now we have much more important series of concerts in the halls in Nottingham and Northampton and Warwick, which we do with the full orchestra. And that gives us another problem – the strings are having to play too much.

Orchestral music in Birmingham has a long tradition. But it was essentially as accompaniment to the great local tradition of choral singing that orchestras were first used there. Mendelssohn's *Elijah* and Elgar's *The Dream of Gerontius* are only the most famous of the many works that have been first performed in the Town Hall. There was a Birmingham Festival from 1768 onwards, when a little band of twenty-five accompanied choral music by Handel. It was with a view to making these triennial festivals 'finer and more perfect than any that have taken place in the kingdom' that the Town Hall was built in 1834. 'The New Room and Organ were opened last Friday; there were 3000 persons in the room, it will seat ab't 5000 & is a splendid room for sound – not the least echo – O how it will appear with 200 of a Band & 250 Chorus Singers,' wrote one player enthusiastically. (The present seating capacity of the Town Hall is now only 1,750.) From that date onwards the Birmingham Festival did indeed become the grandest of its kind in the land: an orchestra of 147 featured in the 1834 Festival when Handel's music was complemented by that of Neukomm and Spohr. Mendelssohn first came in 1837 to direct *St Paul* and to play Bach on the organ. The first performance of *Elijah* was in 1846, and by that time the orchestra's strength was around 130. Many rare choral works were performed over the succeeding festivals, directed first by Sir Michael Costa and then by Hans Richter. The première of *The Dream of Gerontius* in 1900 was a famous disaster, performed without sufficient rehearsal by an unconvinced choir and conductor, and a tenor soloist who, as Vaughan Williams nicely put it, sang 'in the correct oratorio manner, with one foot slightly withdrawn'. Nevertheless, the occasion sealed Elgar's strong links with Birmingham.

The first purely orchestral concerts in Birmingham seem to have been given by William Stockley's orchestra from 1873 onwards: in Stockley's Popular Concerts, as they were known, Elgar played among the first violins and some of his pieces were performed there, including the Suite in D in 1888. A Birmingham Symphony Orchestra of seventy players gave its first concert in 1906 under Sir Henry Wood, and Julian Clifford was its conductor until the First World War broke out. During the war that great orchestral entrepreneur Thomas Beecham stepped in with the New Birmingham Orchestra, but it failed to establish itself. It was not until 1920 that the City of Birmingham Orchestra was formed under the conductor Appelby Matthews, who had gathered together the players by adding strings to the police band of which he was the conductor!

From 1920 the City Council gave the orchestra £1,250 a year, making it the first orchestra in Britain to be truly supported by a local authority. Elgar was invited back to give the orchestra's first concert in November 1920: it consisted entirely of his own works. Among early visitors to conduct the orchestra were Granville Bantock, Gustav Holst, Ralph Vaughan Williams and Jean Sibelius (whose Fourth Symphony had first been performed in the Town Hall back in 1912). But Lyndon Jenkins, the Birmingham critic who, with Beresford King-Smith, knows most about the orchestra's history, writes, 'Financial difficulties soon loomed large and Appelby Matthews was quickly at loggerheads with the committee. By 1923 matters had reached a point where legal proceedings were necessary and though Matthews won his case, he and the orchestra parted company.'

It was clear that a new direction was needed, and the orchestra found it in the young Adrian Boult, who had been conducting the Choral Society in Birmingham following Henry Wood's abrupt departure. Boult recalled in his memoirs:

It was during this winter season in Birmingham that it became clear that all was not well there, and I very soon sensed that the direction of the orchestra might be offered to me. I didn't need to think it over: fifty concerts in the six winter months with nothing to do in the summer except prepare for the next season was a plan which suited me perfectly.

Among the letters Boult received to encourage him was one from Granville Bantock which had some resonances for Rattle:

> It has long been my dream to make this city our English Weimar, and the prospects for the realization of this idea were never brighter than they are today. Your advent will bring new life and culture into the place . . .

Boult's stay in Birmingham from 1924 to 1930 was distinguished by performances of important pieces such as Bartók's *Dance Suite* when it was only a year old, Mahler's Fourth Symphony and *Das Lied von der Erde*, which was then very little known in England. His main problem turned out to be that summer break: 'It was not at all good for the orchestra to split up and go off to the four winds during the summer, and I always dreaded the first few weeks of the season, when root principles had to be re-established and seaside habits unlearned.' Boult modestly said that if ever he wanted to hear a good orchestral concert he took the train to Manchester. Nevertheless, he did much to improve the orchestra and to give it permanence.* But when he was offered the directorship of music of the BBC in 1930, and subsequently the conductorship of its brilliant new symphony orchestra, he could not refuse.

Boult was succeeded by Leslie Heward, who seemed young at thirty-five, though he was a decade older than Simon Rattle would be in 1980. Economic stability for the orchestra in this period was helped by the BBC's decision to found a Midland Region orchestra in 1935 based on City of Birmingham Orchestra personnel. Not until 1944 was the orchestra placed on a full-time basis, however, and by then Heward had died tragically young, having just accepted the conductorship of the Hallé in Manchester. Lyndon Jenkins says that Heward 'was noted for his complete honesty and integrity: it was nothing for him to stop a performance in the middle and restart it, saying to his startled listeners, "I'm sorry, we can do better than that."' Felix Weingartner and Nikolai Malko came during his period, and the orchestra began to make records.

---

* There is fascinating information on Boult's Birmingham years in Michael Kennedy's biography, *Adrian Boult* (Hamish Hamilton, 1987).

Under Heward's successor, George Weldon, the orchestra became the City of Birmingham Symphony Orchestra, and gave its first London concert. But standards proved hard to maintain in this period, and the best that is said of Weldon is that he was 'a tremendously hard worker' who did 'frankly popular programmes'.

Rudolf Schwarz became conductor in 1952. He had rebuilt the Bournemouth Orchestra after the war, and was much respected by musicians (including, incidentally, Simon Rattle, who has the highest opinion of his musicianship), but he was less popular with the public, who stayed away from his concerts – all the more disappointing as the repertory he included was more interesting than Weldon's. But it was clear that a new force was needed in Birmingham to restore the slipping attendance figures, and when Schwarz was appointed to the BBC Symphony Orchestra in 1957 the management lighted on the Polish composer and conductor Andrzej Panufnik, who had arrived in the West and needed a stable base for his operations.

In his memoirs, *Composing Myself*,* Panufnik had some entertaining things to say about his experiences in Birmingham:

> The committee had suggested that my first task would be to improve playing standards in Birmingham. The string sections especially lacked precision and produced a poor sound quality. Spoilt perhaps by my experiences with great orchestras such as the Berlin Philharmonic, L'Orchestre National in Paris, the LSO, RPO and Philharmonia in London, I was determined to make use of the potential talent in Birmingham and concentrate on bringing the playing up to the international standards of which they were fully capable.

Unfortunately Panufnik fell foul of the leader, who would not co-operate: 'The atmosphere during rehearsals became unbearable and I was often frustrated in my struggle to improve the quality of our performances.' This culminated in a battle that resulted in the leader's removal at the end of Panufnik's first season, and though he had a much happier second season and felt he was achieving something, the burden of the post prevented him having enough time for composition and he decided not to accept a third season. Among the presents the players gave him on departure was a blank sheet of manuscript paper, with good wishes for his continuing success as a composer.

* Methuen, 1987.

Once again Birmingham had problems finding a successor, and Sir Adrian Boult at seventy returned for a year before Hugo Rignold came from the Liverpool Philharmonic. By this time the orchestra's strength was up to eighty-eight and Rignold made some strides in training them. His concerts were apparently not much enjoyed: 'It's a shame to have to say it, but in those years we went when there were guest conductors,' said one regular attender. Nevertheless, the orchestra certainly improved during Rignold's eight years. It was ripe for real development when in 1968 Louis Frémaux was chosen as the next principal conductor. Under him the orchestra improved vastly, went back to the recording studio and made some splendid recordings of French music. Simon Rattle is the first to agree that Frémaux was the decisive force in improving the orchestra, and that it was only the level to which he had brought it that made possible Rattle's job of improving it still further.

LYNDON JENKINS The orchestra played very well for Frémaux and he worked tremendously hard for them. He did sixty concerts a year and was at all the auditions. He auditioned all the chorus members too for the new CBSO Chorus. It wasn't just French music he was good at: romantic symphonies by Dvořák, Schumann and Tchaikovsky were excellent and he had an affinity for Shostakovich, Walton and Britten. It's perhaps not generally known that he was to have recorded the Britten *War Requiem* in 1978, but left before that happened. Among the recordings the Saint-Saëns Organ Symphony, of course, and the Berlioz *Requiem* were outstanding. He was one of the old-style permanent conductors and, as I wrote when he left, 'Whatever the circumstances of his going, he was the man who raised the CBSO to the highest point of prestige in its history to date.'

Simon Rattle's relationship with the City of Birmingham Symphony Orchestra began in May 1976 in the unlikely surroundings of Oxford Town Hall, with an unlikely programme consisting entirely of Beethoven, in the unlikely context of the English Bach Festival. The director of the festival, Lina Lalandi, had a young pianist she wanted to present, Cyprien Katsaris, and with the infallible nose for new talent that marked her festival for more than twenty years, she thought she would present Simon Rattle as conductor 'and together the conductor and soloist would be younger than I was!' The concert went well, and Rattle remembered it as a surprisingly positive experience in view of its being a programme he should never have agreed to conduct. Others recalled that at the time he was worried by the orchestra and found them a little stand-offish, but that the actual performance was a success.

He was asked back by them the following year to do two more dates away from their home base, in Cheltenham and Newcastle, but it was not until December 1978 that he conducted them in Birmingham in a concert that included Nielsen's Fourth Symphony, and by then the crisis of Frémaux's departure had overtaken the orchestra. It was, as Rattle recalled, 'my audition concert':

> SIMON RATTLE I remember the moment when Ed Smith was going to Birmingham from Liverpool. I knew they were without a conductor and I said to him, 'I really want to do that job.' I can't believe I did that. But I told him that if he wanted to work with me I would like to do it. For some reason I had a very good feeling about it and thought it would be possible. I'd done Shostakovich 10 with them and that had been a lovely experience. It all just felt right. I didn't think I would get the job, but I knew that with Ed there we would be on the same wavelength. We were very inexperienced, but we could get it to work. I'm sure I didn't think at the time it would become what it has. I didn't realize how important it would be to be here until I got here.

Rattle's appointment was due to be announced in Birmingham on 2 July 1979. But on 22 June the *Birmingham Post* published the story in advance under the front-page banner headline 'NEW CONDUCTOR HERALDS CBSO HARMONY': 'After months of debate, the committee of the orchestra has chosen Mr Rattle, twenty-four, for the prized post abruptly vacated by M. Louis Frémaux last year. The orchestra's full council of management is expected to ratify the appointment on Monday afternoon.' Barrie Grayson, the *Post* music critic, who had previously hailed Rattle as 'one of the most exciting conducting talents to emerge in recent years', commented, 'That this young conductor should take this position is a compliment to the CBSO's stature.'

Rattle was introduced to the press on 2 July as planned, and said, 'It is my intention to promote mixed programmes. We have eighty years of music which still needs exploring. I want to establish a sense of musical adventure. Even London concerts, returning time and again to the established classical warhorses, do not attract new audiences.' Predictably these remarks caused some alarm among those who imagined that Rattle was going to throw out the classics altogether, and there was anxious comment in the local press. Ed Smith found it necessary to write to the *Birmingham Post* with a cooling letter:

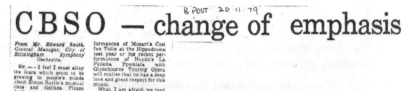

CBSO — change of emphasis

B POST 20·11·79

From Mr. Edward Smith, General Manager, City of Birmingham Symphony Orchestra.

Sir, — I feel I must allay the fears which seem to be growing in people's minds about Simon Rattle's musical likes and dislikes. Please don't imagine that Mozart, Beethoven, Brahms and Tchaikovsky disappear from programmes very ... audience ... To disappear stupid at ... Anyone ...

formances of Mozart's Cosi fan Tutte at the Hippodrome last year or his recent performances of Haydn's La Fedelta Premiata with Glyndebourne Touring Opera will realise that he has a deep love and great respect for this music.

What, I am afraid, we tend to forget is that the twentieth century is now 80 years old ...

From the work of Pierre Boulez (left) to the genius of Mozart (right) . . . the range that the new principal conductor hopes the CBSO will span

'I do consider it important that an orchestra should have a repertoire of pieces from all over the place'

New conductor heralds CBSO harmony

What makes Rattle tick

Baby Rattle comes to Birmingham: the press announces his arrival

I feel I must allay the fears which seem to be growing in people's minds about Simon Rattle's musical likes and dislikes. Please don't imagine that Mozart, Beethoven, Brahms and Tchaikovsky are going to disappear from CBSO programmes. If we allowed that to happen we would naturally very quickly see our audiences diminishing. To dismiss these composers as worthless would be both stupid and arrogant and I am sure Mr Rattle is neither . . . What I am afraid we tend to forget is that the twentieth century is now eighty years old and its composers include Mahler, Sibelius, Elgar, Ravel, Rakhmaninov and Stravinsky, all of which will feature in Mr Rattle's programmes for his first season . . .

For his part, Rattle defused the row in a subsequent interview in the *Sunday Mercury*: 'It's strange what people think they hear. Perhaps I should have said more clearly that at the age of ten I found it difficult to appreciate Mozart, just as a child finds it difficult to grasp Shakespeare. I did my O levels when I was fourteen but how are you supposed to understand plays like *King Lear* at that age? These things come later and so it was with music. Now I revere Mozart above all the others.'

Rattle's relationship with the orchestra was sealed in a notably successful series of performances of Mahler's Tenth Symphony in the Deryck Cooke version in early 1980, prior to his recording the work with the Bournemouth Symphony Orchestra. He began his tenure as principal conductor in September 1980 with everything to gain but, arguably, quite a bit to lose if it all went wrong.

Before taking up the new post there was an equally major landmark in Rattle's life: in September 1980 he flew into Scotland from the Hollywood Bowl to see *Wozzeck*, and the next morning 'charged down on the first flight to London'. He was married at Finsbury Town Hall to the Marie from that *Wozzeck*, Elise Ross, the singer, composer and expert in the music of the Italian avant-garde, whom he had met when she was singing in an opera by John Tavener at the Bath Festival some years earlier. She was often to appear with him on the concert and operatic stage before a painful divorce separated them in the mid-1990s and Rattle remarried. Rattle moved from the friendly chaos of a flat in Manor House, on the Marylebone Road, to a small Georgian terraced house in Islington, appropriately enough just off Liverpool Road. Here he settled into domestic life, though as a subsequent purchaser of a house in the road was told, 'You live near a celebrity . . . he's not too popular with numbers 42 onwards because he leaves his bins on the street!'

1 An early thirst for words . . .   2 . . . and music

3 Prize pianist: Simon at twelve, winner of the Merseyside Student of the Year

4 A table-tennis session during Rattle's first fraught season at Glyndebourne, 1975
(photo Greg German, *Sunday Telegraph*)

5 'An essential and crucial relationship':
Ed Smith and Simon Rattle at work at the CBSO, 1986
(photo Jason Chenai)

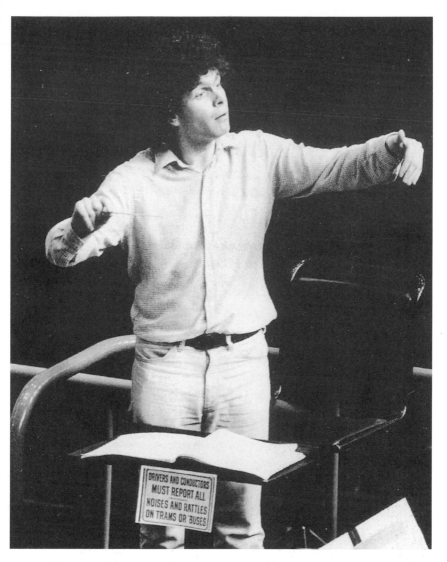

6 Rattling noises: Simon Rattle at the Los Angeles Philharmonic

DRIVERS AND CONDUCTORS
MUST REPORT ALL
NOISES AND RATTLES
ON TRAMS OR BUSES

7 Conducting isn't all a piece of cake . . .

8 'I'm not saying he hasn't got a lot to learn, but he's smart': John Willan, who produced Rattle's early recordings for EMI

9 Meeting Bess: after the triumphant performance of *Porgy and Bess* at Glyndebourne in 1986, Rattle and the cast meet the original Bess, Anne Brown (photo Guy Gravett)

10 A taste of things to come: Rattle at the Philharmonie, Berlin, 1984

11 'Simon is the most stunningly gifted young conductor I know': Alfred Brendel rehearsing with Rattle in Birmingham Town Hall, 1986

12 'He has inexhaustible appetite for rehearsal': Rattle enthuses the CBSO, 1990s
(photo Alan Wood)

13 The audience of tomorrow: Rattle meeting children after a CBSO family concert

14 John Carewe (photo Sally Cavender)

Rattle had also committed himself, before the CBSO post was final-ized, to taking a long-promised break from conducting during 1980–81 to study literature at Oxford University for a year. ('It's hard concentrat-ing on Joyce on the train to Scotland with beer cans flying around me,' as he put it.) The CBSO situation rather compromised that. He kept the terms free for study, making only exceptional appearances during them, but the holidays were packed with activity as a result, and he often travelled up to Birmingham to see how the orchestra was progressing in his absence. In all, though Rattle enjoyed the study, it wasn't quite the year away from it all that he was envisaging. He has always felt that he needed periods of study out of the limelight, but they have always been difficult to achieve.

In the years, eighteen in all, during which Rattle guided the CBSO, the principle in planning concerts with Ed Smith was always to create out-standing musical events, and to programme works that would advance the orchestra's learning process. Looking back on the seasons in Bir-mingham provides an indication of how far the plan succeeded. (The following lists do not include CBSO concerts with guest conductors, or Rattle's out-of-town and festival dates, when the programmes were normally based around those for Birmingham.)

1980–81

Janáček	*Sinfonietta*
Rakhmaninov	Piano Concerto no. 3 (Philip Fowke)
Sibelius	Symphony no. 5
Boulez	*Rituel in memoriam Bruno Maderna*
Mahler	Symphony no. 2 (Alison Hargan, Alfreda Hodgson)
Dvořák	Cello Concerto (Lynn Harrell)
Stravinsky	*Symphonies of Wind Instruments*
Elgar	*Enigma Variations*
Beethoven	Overture: *Leonore* no. 3
Mendelssohn	Violin Concerto (Mayumi Fujikawa)
Britten	*Variations on a Theme of Frank Bridge*
Ravel	Suite: *Daphnis et Chloë* no. 2
Haydn	Symphony no. 60

Mussorgsky	*Night on the Bare Mountain*
Janáček	*Glagolitic Mass* (Felicity Palmer, Ameral Gunson, John Mitchinson, Malcolm King)
Beethoven	Violin Concerto (Stoika Milanova)
Rakhmaninov	Symphony no. 2
Weill	*The Seven Deadly Sins* (Elise Ross)
Sibelius	Symphony no. 2
Delius	*Brigg Fair*
Beethoven	Piano Concerto no. 4 (Paul Crossley)
Stravinsky	*Petrushka*
Fauré	Suite: *Pélleas et Mélisande*
Mozart	Piano Concerto in C minor K491 (Stephen Bishop-Kovacevich)
Schumann	Symphony no. 2

SIMON RATTLE Ed and I knew absolutely nothing about training orchestras and what they needed. What we planned at first was affected by what we had learned in Liverpool, though you could scarcely find a more different orchestra from Liverpool than Birmingham. It was only when I got there that I realized how desperate they were to work. The whole business of re-establishing a style was vital because that had all slipped. They wanted to be told how to do things and work at things. I remember Felix [Kok, the leader] saying that if he asked them to play things in the same part of the bow they would laugh and ask why. This was all a long struggle, but the attitude is transformed now.

Ed allowed me to have a week of rehearsals before the first concert, and I think they reached every downbeat before I did! We got a lot out of our systems in that period, and there was immediately a feeling of achieving something. For the Boulez *Rituel* we had to do a lot of sectional rehearsal, and that helped such a lot. You met people face to face and assembled a piece from the beginning. You built up trust in that way.

What I wanted to do was to conduct the pieces I knew very well, and which could develop the orchestra and me together. *Rituel* was an exception because that was a recent piece and a dramatic gesture for the start of the season. All the other works were my showpieces: Sibelius 5 and Rakhmaninov with Philip Fowke – that had been my first Liverpool concert; Janáček and Elgar I'd done in Los Angeles; Mahler 2 I had done a lot already, and so on. These were things with which I could really work the orchestra and which would show us in the best possible light. The Sibelius was terribly important because I think Ed and I had already planned that we would do all the symphonies and would be living with this music. The *Frank Bridge Variations* – they made the strings work and work – and the Dvořák Cello Concerto too were such a help in just working out how to play.

One of the things we instigated in the first year was that we would have rehearsals with just the principal string-players, and work on bowings and marking the parts. That hadn't been thought of as something that was important. And in spite of all the problems it worked. I remember doing the Britten on no rehearsal at all a few weeks after we'd learned it in a church somewhere when the instrument van had broken down. And they pulled it off. Mahler 2 was the highlight. We took it down to London as well but the one I remember was when we did it first in Leeds. Players came up and said that was the best concert they'd done for years and years, and it certainly felt like it.

ED SMITH We will never know what would have happened if we hadn't changed a lot of things all in the very first year. We had our new conductor, but we also changed our publicity from the rather beautifully produced syllabus one had to buy to the free broadsheet everyone does now. And we much increased our subscription marketing: we used to have about three hundred subscribers to our Thursday series and it was received opinion that there were only three hundred people in Birmingham who would be prepared to commit themselves to a weekly concert. So the marketing manager, Julianna Szekely, and I were determined to turn that on its head and really go out aggressively to get the committed regular subscriber. We changed the pattern of the concerts from a weekly Thursday series to a fortnightly Tuesday and Thursday series, so for all the people who for decades had not been able to come on a Thursday there was a chance to attend. Those things all happened in 1980, and it's difficult to disentangle them, but together they worked. The rise in attendances was startling:

Series	1978–79 %	1979–80 %	1980–81 %	1981–82 %	1982–83 %	1983–84 %	1984–85 %	1985–86 %
Tuesday			81	88	78	95	97	96
Wednesday								97
Thursday	62	75	96	94	95	96	98	98
Saturday	60	83	90	80	85	95	93	98
CBSO Proms	70	77	91	78	85	85	86	77

Looking back on it now, it is clear that the success of Rattle's first few concerts with the orchestra was crucial to the whole relationship. Morale soared, and the concerts were events of a kind that fully justified the risks inherent in the appointment. They were not, perhaps, fully finished events, but they had a raw energy and commitment that created great excitement in Birmingham. The reviews were uniformly ecstatic: under the headline 'GAMBLE PAYS OFF', Lyndon Jenkins reported for *Classical Music* that the concerts

> have provoked an extraordinarily favourable reaction both in the city and elsewhere, and while this was in one way tinged with relief that an exciting gamble was paying off so quickly, there is no doubt that enthusiasm was extensively justified on musical grounds. In four wide-ranging programmes [Rattle's] rapport with orchestra and chorus seemed complete, and while not everything he did reached the same level, the performances of Sibelius's Fifth Symphony and in particular Mahler's Second displayed an astonishing maturity that held the promise of stimulating days ahead.

Jenkins was also impressed by Rattle's concerts in the second half of the season, though never uncritically so:

> His grasp of the scale and idiom of Rakhmaninov's Second Symphony was so satisfying it was easy to forgive him a cheap trick or two, and he illuminated many points of interest in Beethoven's Violin Concerto . . .

Kenneth Loveland wrote in the *South Wales Argus*:

> When someone makes the impact on a nation's music that Simon Rattle has in so short a time, there exists a danger that he will be dismissed as a whizz-kid. The depths his interpretations already plumb, the sincerity of his approach and his evidently ingrained musicality should be the answer. Neither whizz nor kid . . . Birmingham is in for exciting times.

Just a month later Rattle and the CBSO took Mahler's Second Symphony to London, pairing it this time with Szymanowski's *Stabat Mater*. In the *Financial Times*, David Murray felt that Rattle's interpretation of the Mahler was 'as yet too quick, too impatient to pounce, for the visionary scope of the work to be fully rendered. But it gripped the attention brilliantly.' And Christopher Grier in the London *Evening Standard*, observing how the 'playing, the singing, the conducting and the choice of programme were alike of the first order', added, 'I don't mean that the Berlin Philharmonic should immediately make way for the CBSO, but these Birmingham instrumentalists had not only been impeccably rehearsed but sounded excitingly alert and responsive.' This was just the sort of comment the orchestra needed at that time.

By the summer of 1981, when Rattle brought the CBSO to the BBC Proms for the first time, their relationship was already fixed in the minds of the critics as something potentially fruitful. In *The Times*, Paul Griffiths wrote:

> Simon Rattle has made no secret of his intention to bring the CBSO up into the first division. Already his programming puts many of the London orchestras to shame with its daring abundance of twentieth-century works, and last night, at the end of his first year with the orchestra, he brought them to the Proms to show what wholly magnificent standards they are achieving together.

The summer also saw the first year of Rattle's tenure as artistic director of the South Bank Summer Music season in London, the Greater London Council's answer to the BBC Proms, which brought small-scale music to the halls on the South Bank. Andrew Clements wrote in the *New Statesman* that

> At the moment Simon Rattle seems to be the answer to every jaded orchestral manager's prayers, revitalizing anything he turns his baton to. But his appointment as artistic director of the GLC's South Bank Summer Music was nevertheless unexpected; what had settled into a comfortable and middle-of-the-road fortnight of chamber music promises to have many of its conventions shattered

– as indeed it did, for Rattle introduced a larger proportion of contemporary and twentieth-century works and more orchestral concerts, featuring the CBSO, than in previous years. Among the highlights of this first season with the CBSO was a concert performance of Gershwin's *Porgy and Bess*, subsequently brought to Birmingham.

Everything had gone sensationally well with the CBSO in that first season, and before the new season opened in the autumn there was an announcement that Rattle had signed a new contract as principal conductor for at least another five years. 'We had a marvellous season last year and the spirit of Simon Rattle was responsible for it. We are absolutely delighted that he will be staying with us,' commented George Jonas. But probably even he did not realize for how long Rattle would actually stay.

The second season's programmes were still more wide-ranging:

1981–82

Haydn	Symphony no. 95
Enescu	*Romanian Rhapsody* no. 1
Elgar	Symphony no. 1
Gershwin	*Porgy and Bess* (Willard White, Laverne Williams, *et al.*)
Ravel	*Mother Goose*
Mozart	Piano Concerto in B♭ K450 (Imogen Cooper)
Brahms	Symphony no. 2
Mozart	Symphony no. 38
Messiaen	*Turangalîla Symphony* (Peter Donohoe, Jeanne Loriod)
Mussorgsky	Prelude: *Khovanshchina*
Shostakovich	Violin Concerto no. 1 (Ida Haendel)
Stravinsky	*The Rite of Spring*
Berlioz	Overture: *Roman Carnival*
Debussy	*Danse sacrée et danse profane* (Robert Johnston)
Beethoven	Piano Concerto no. 2 (Alfred Brendel)
Sibelius	Symphony no. 4
Britten	*War Requiem* (Ameral Gunson, Ian Caley, Thomas Hemsley)
Haydn	Symphony no. 22
Strauss	Oboe Concerto (Heinz Holliger)
Lutosławski	Concerto for oboe and harp (Heinz Holliger and Ursula Holliger)
Beethoven	Symphony no. 4
Britten	Sea Interludes and Passacaglia from *Peter Grimes*
Mahler	*Das Lied von der Erde* (Alfreda Hodgson, John Mitchinson)
Dvořák	Overture: *Carnaval*
Mozart	Piano Concerto in B♭ K595 (Tamás Vásáry)
Sibelius	Symphony no. 6
Strauss	Suite: *Der Rosenkavalier*

Wagner	Prelude and *Liebestod* from *Tristan und Isolde*
Berg	Three Fragments from *Wozzeck* (Elise Ross)
Mahler	Symphony no. 1
Britten	*Canadian Carnival*
Bartók	Violin Concerto (Iona Brown)
Rakhmaninov	Three Symphonic Dances

SIMON RATTLE Ed and I had so many ideas. Many of the things we wanted to do from the very beginning took ages to get round to. The Liszt *Faust Symphony* only happened much later, and in the end it was my first recording with the Berlin Philharmonic. One would think that during a season we could fit in everything, but it just wasn't true. And especially as we went on, we found the orchestra really needed more rehearsals and I needed to work more with them. They seemed happy enough rehearsing more, though I'm sure some of them were absolutely miserable. But the problem was also to find guest conductors who are actually willing to rehearse the orchestra and make good use of the time. And who are good enough to change the orchestra. I soon found out the difference between coming back to the orchestra after I'd been away for a time, and coming back to them when in a space of three weeks they'd had Jimmy Conlon, Paavo Berglund and Kurt Sanderling.

What Ed and I did was to aim for one or two major contemporary pieces each season; that was a long-term plan, and we had to grapple with what was important. It was very clear that we could choose only what we believed was the very greatest of this music. So that was *Turangalîla* in this season – the work we did on that piece . . . and the response! We tended to do these big pieces near the start of the season, because we had extra rehearsal time. Ed found it very difficult to accept at first how much rehearsal I needed, but for the orchestra to put standard repertory together was very difficult. We had a difficult time with *The Rite of Spring* this season, because we missed one rehearsal with a problem over the Town Hall and I thought they knew it well and I knew it well. But we didn't have time to get it right as I felt I had in Scotland.

One thing I had to guard against in all these designs to get the orchestra to play well – and this is something I discussed a lot with Mark Elder [then music director of the English National Opera] – is that you so want the orchestra to be well thought of that sometimes you adapt the way you conduct towards making that happen, making things easier for them. The trouble is that it might be temporarily easier for them, but you don't build up, you don't take the risks.

The Rakhmaninov Symphonic Dances at the end of the season were very important. If I had to specify a work that created the orchestra's sound as it became it would be that. All round this time was very fruitful, and really cemented us together. I think they had almost unrealistic expectations of what we could achieve. We were doing such hard pieces: I remember very clearly rehearsing Berlioz's *Béatrice et Bénédict* for that year's South Bank Summer Music and thinking that sooner or later there was going to come a crunch and we would have to talk about standards and it would be a problem. But that didn't arise until after the climax of this first period, which was the European tour in October 1982. That was marvellous and we hit new peaks in spite of being very tired.

An impression of Rattle's success with the orchestra this season can be found in some remarks by the players quoted by the press in 1981. 'Simon Rattle is 100 per cent honest. He is a complete professional,' said one player. 'He is simply a brilliant young man. He is completely committed and lets nothing stand in the way of the music.' 'His ability to hold complete scores in his head is absolutely phenomenal.' Lyndon Jenkins's summary of the early part of the season for *Classical Music* praised the Sibelius 4:

> Not only did he assess its size and scale very accurately but he also managed to reveal the toughness of the argument and the passion behind the spareness. This outshone the success that he had with Stravinsky's *Rite* and Messiaen's *Turangalîla*, both of which predictably found him in his element, and certainly eclipsed other symphonic scores by Elgar and Brahms which were nowhere near in the same exalted class.

Jenkins regularly criticized what he saw as weaker performances of the classical and some of the romantic repertory, and felt that the Britten *War Requiem* was under-prepared: it preceded the recording by a couple of months and was performed with a different team of soloists. Later, Jenkins felt, Rattle 'still seemed a little unsure as to how he wanted Beethoven's Fourth to go', but thought Sibelius's Sixth 'admirably authentic-sounding'.

For the Proms in London in 1982, Rattle revived *Turangalîla*, to which, the *Financial Times* reported, 'the Birmingham orchestra responded with great enthusiasm and no little virtuosity'. Then there was Berlioz's *Béatrice et Bénédict* for South Bank Summer Music, which the *Daily Telegraph* praised for its 'refreshingly alert, supple and graphically etched playing', and the *Financial Times* for its 'verve and buoyancy'. Then they worked hard towards the coming climax – the European tour – and the beginning of their third season.

1982–83

Mozart	Serenade for thirteen wind instruments
Sibelius	Symphony no. 1
Stravinsky	*Symphonies of Wind Instruments*
Stravinsky	*Apollon musagète*
Stravinsky	*Petrushka*
Knussen	Symphony no. 3
Mozart	*Sinfonia concertante* (Mayumi Fujikawa, Nobuko Imai)
Brahms	Symphony no. 2
Haydn	*The Creation* (Margaret Marshall, Philip Langridge, Stafford Dean)
Sibelius	Symphony no. 7
Walton	Cello Concerto (Yo-Yo Ma)
Donizetti	Concertino for cor anglais (Peter Walden)
Mozart	Symphony no. 41
Holloway	*Clarissa* Symphony (première) (Eileen Hannan, John Mitchinson)
Beethoven	Symphony no. 3
Debussy	*Prélude à l'après-midi d'un faune*
Sibelius	Symphony no. 3
Dvořák	Cello Concerto (Lynn Harrell)
Britten	*Sinfonia da Requiem*
Mahler–Cooke	Symphony no. 10
Weill	Suite: *The Threepenny Opera*
Strauss	*Four Last Songs* (Helena Döse)
Ravel	*Shéhérazade*
Debussy	*La Mer*
Beethoven	Piano Concerto no. 4 (Emanuel Ax)
Ravel	*Daphnis et Chloë* (complete)

Stravinsky	*Scherzo à la russe*
Prokofiev	Piano Concerto no. 3 (Janis Vakarelis)
Shostakovich	Symphony no. 10

The European tour in October took the orchestra to Holland for three concerts, then to Bratislava, then to Vienna for one concert, and then for three in Germany. All the programmes were demanding, and the repertory included Oliver Knussen's Third Symphony, Brahms's Second, Rakhmaninov's Symphonic Dances and several Stravinsky works. Rattle was already well known in Holland because of his connections with the Rotterdam Philharmonic, and the concerts were full. The hall in The Hague proved exceptionally difficult for the musicians (offering some lessons for the design of Birmingham's new hall), but in Amsterdam's Concertgebouw everything sounded much better. The final concert in Rotterdam was very well received, and the Dutch critics commented that they could see why Rattle had turned down the offer of the post of principal conductor in Rotterdam when 'the Birmingham ensemble is an excellent orchestra which gives the young conductor a permanent chance of demonstrating his ability on the British music scene'. Another wrote: 'It is difficult to see how Rattle can produce such exquisite clarity in every composition. Nothing is left to chance, everything is given great consideration and is expertly carried out by the English orchestra.'

There were problems getting to and from Bratislava because of border troubles, and the concert there started late, but it was rapturously received. In Vienna an all-Stravinsky programme was part of the Stravinsky Festival in the Konzerthaus (see pp. 294–5), and the warmth of the reception led to an unexpected encore: as someone noted, it was probably the first time that Delius had been heard in a Stravinsky festival. The concert in Frankfurt, consisting of Knussen, Rakhmaninov and Stravinsky, took place in the studios of Hesse Radio, and was attended by a large contingent of City Council representatives from Birmingham. The Frankfurt concert provoked a fine review in the *Frankfurter Allgemeine Zeitung*:

> The generally accepted notion that outside London is musically provincial is fostered consciously or otherwise by the media and on occasion by the record industry . . . A minor flutter was caused some time ago by the news that EMI had entrusted Mahler's Tenth to the Bournemouth Orchestra. The outcome was a pleasant surprise. Many people who experienced the

CBSO the other day may well have come to a similar conclusion. A well-tuned body of musicians, lacking in nothing except perhaps a reputation. The orchestra has throughout its sections musicians of the highest calibre and ability, who are capable of transforming these qualities into an unmistakable sound of their own. The same could certainly be said of the conductor, a highly talented orchestral trainer with the gift of formulating his very complicated interpretational intentions clearly, and transforming them convincingly into sound . . .

No one could doubt the boost in morale the tour had provided; as Lyndon Jenkins, who accompanied the orchestra for the *Birmingham Post*, noted:

> The overriding impression is that we have been listening to a different CBSO from the one we hear at home: this has nothing to do with playing standards, but everything to do with locations. Put straightforwardly, the orchestra sounds good at home; this weekend, in halls with good acoustics, it has sounded superb.

The return to Birmingham for the rest of the 1982–83 season was bound to come as an anticlimax but it proved more painful than had been expected; several matters came to a head.

SIMON RATTLE This was one of the great hard times. It was the point where after the euphoria of the tour we came back to earth with a bump. We made the first changes, seemingly simple things like reseating the first violins. Until then the relationship had been ludicrously sunny, but now things came out in the open. It was the day after the performance of *The Creation* that it all blew up. We insisted that things had to be done because of the standard of the orchestra, and suddenly everyone was churned up and asking why standards should really come into it. That's the big difference between the orchestra then and now: then there was still the feeling of: 'We're willing to do anything as long as you don't compromise the comfort of our work. We're still a provincial orchestra and we came here to avoid this sort of problem. How good do you want us to be? How good do we want to be?'

This was the start of our growing up, the fact that these questions came out. There was still really a taboo about talking about the actual abilities of any player, and admitting that there might be a problem. We had begun to reach the first ceiling by this point, and without raising these things we would not have got any further. It caused chaos and difficulties, but by the time I came back in March the following year it was already much improved. The end of that season was difficult again. We had the first sacking of a player, the first time the problem arose of a player having to leave the orchestra because of his lack of capability. I don't think it had happened quite like this before in a regional orchestra. The orchestra having to face that sort of difficulty and realize that playing standards had to be talked about was a big step. Perhaps some of them never really recovered, but then there was such a different feeling. I'm glad we waited a couple of years and made the changes when we did.

The première of Robin Holloway's *Clarissa* Symphony, drawn from an opera that had not been performed, attracted a good deal of interest from the London critics, and for the first time the developments in Birmingham demanded their attention. Among many comments, Andrew Clements in the *Financial Times* reported that 'Mr Rattle, his singers and orchestra, coped with the manifold difficulties of the score with great enthusiasm and assurance.' Peter Heyworth in the *Observer*, while reserved about the piece, praised the 'stirring account' of the work, while Bayan Northcott in the *Sunday Telegraph* noted that the performance 'was not without occasional roughnesses of detail, but glowing with the conviction of all involved'. Desmond Shawe-Taylor in *The Sunday Times* noted the 'impassioned playing of the orchestra under Simon Rattle's inspired guidance'. This sort of coverage of the CBSO's regular subscription-series concerts, rather than just of their occasional visits to London, was valuable and welcome as well as being encouraging.

1983–84

Brahms	Symphony no. 4
Stravinsky	*The Firebird*
Berlioz	Overture: *Le corsaire*
Debussy	*Prélude à l'après-midi d'un faune*
Henze	Symphony no. 4
Beethoven	Violin Concerto (Kyung-Wha Chung)
Britten	*An American Overture* (première)
Mozart	Violin Concerto in A K219 (Iona Brown)
Rakhmaninov	Symphony no. 2
Elgar	*The Dream of Gerontius* (Janet Baker, Dennis Bailey, Willard White)
Webern	*Passacaglia*

| Beethoven | Triple Concerto (Young Uck Kim, Yo-Yo Ma, Emanuel Ax) |
| Nielsen | Symphony no. 4 |

Ravel	*Valses nobles et sentimentales*
Mozart	Horn Concerto no. 3 (Hermann Baumann)
Strauss	Horn Concerto no. 1
Brahms–Schoenberg	Piano Quartet in G minor

Delius	*Walk to the Paradise Garden*
Elgar	Violin Concerto
Grainger	*A Lincolnshire Posy*
Ravel–Grainger	*La vallée des cloches*
Grainger	Suite: *In a Nutshell*

| Mahler | Symphony no. 6 |

Berg	Suite: *Lulu*
Rakhmaninov	Piano Concerto no. 2 (Shura Cherkassky)
Sibelius	Symphony no. 5

SIMON RATTLE We were really getting somewhere at this time. We had put together the Sibelius cycle and we did it in Warwick over a weekend, and in London during South Bank Summer Music. The last concert of that festival was a landmark: three Sibelius symphonies, and a superb response from the press, public, everyone. That was when John Willan decided to do the Sibelius cycle for EMI with the CBSO rather than the Philharmonia, which was the original plan. We had a big, big summer and it helped with the season. We realized that there were areas of the repertory where the band had special expertise and that those should be toured, and others where we just experiment at home. I wouldn't have dared to take the Brahms 4 to London because so many orchestras play it well. Now I *have* taken it to London because I think we've got a real contribution to make to that piece. If we had a healthier musical climate in London I wouldn't be searching so hard, but you have to make something that's different.

An example of that was the Brahms–Schoenberg Piano Quartet. I think I was very much looking for unusual works that would make an event, and also looking for recording opportunities for the orchestra. It was a matter of finding works that this orchestra would play well but others didn't. There were big landmarks this season – Mahler 6 in particular. You can measure them by what the orchestra is likely to achieve and how much it improves in the process.

The Warwick Sibelius weekend was a major undertaking that brought to fruition one of Ed Smith's and Simon Rattle's first major plans: to perform all the Sibelius symphonies as a cycle. In three concerts on successive days they were all played, though not in chronological order. In an interview at the time, Rattle spoke about the importance of the cycle to him:

> For a long time now I've had strong views on how Sibelius should be performed. I've felt that generally he's not taken as seriously as he deserves. I'd go along to performances and then look at the scores, and I'd find a great discrepancy. Details would be smudged, or else considered just to be background noise, instead of it being shown how everything grows out of the very tiniest cells. I learned a lot from Paavo Berglund in Bournemouth. He taught me, for instance, how a great many of Sibelius's melodies have to do with Finnish speech rhythms. And that's important in the woodwind chorale in the finale of the Second, where you have to take account of the fact that there's no anacrusis in Finnish. The music has had a romantic tradition foisted on to it, and orchestras have developed traditions you have to try to get rid of.

Lyndon Jenkins reported:

> What intrigues me about Rattle's Sibelius is that he is more successful with the greater challenge of the Fourth, Sixth and Seventh than with the others ... The revelation was the Seventh, which had evidently been rethought after disagreeably sleek and Latinized accounts. If he can do that with the Fourth and, yes – *pace* the rest of the world – the Fifth, and sort out some more convincing tempi in parts of the Sixth, this would be an immensely distinguished cycle.

What reservations were expressed about the Warwick cycle were quite swept away by the acclaim that greeted the London cycle, given this time in chronological order during South Bank Summer Music, and culminating in the Fifth, Sixth and Seventh Symphonies in one concert to end the festival. This single event surely marked the maturing of the partnership between Rattle and the CBSO, and turned his work in Birmingham from an interesting provincial experiment to an event of national significance:

> For a London listener the first thing to say is how much the success of the Sibelius series owed to the orchestra. On this showing ... the Birmingham orchestra under Rattle can match almost anything we hear from our regular orchestras. The refinement of the strings in particular – so vital in Sibelius whose poised paragraphs so often hang by the thread of the

pianissimo tremolo on high violins – was a consistent delight. (Edward Greenfield, *Guardian*)

Simon Rattle was equal to every interpretative challenge. Crucial questions of balance and pacing were expertly settled; the musical flow was ordered with passion and precision; and the tonal quality of wind and especially strings was full, fresh, and enthusiastic . . . In building up this cycle, Rattle has also built up his orchestra into a major rival for the London bands. (Paul Driver, *Daily Telegraph*)

One of the many odd things about Sibelius is that the better his music is performed, the more difficult it is to understand. Any number of conductors can show his Fifth Symphony as a triumph of heroism, his Sixth as Olympic games in fairyland, his Seventh as a long labouring colossally gratified. But these perhaps are the symphonies Sibelius wished to write: the ones he actually composed are a great deal more enigmatic, as indeed they appeared in the magnificent and important concert with which Simon Rattle brought his directorship of South Bank Summer Music to an end . . . Simply to play these last three symphonies together is a feat in itself, but the CBSO have proved before that they thrive on such a challenge when Mr Rattle is conducting, and the audience on this occasion responded with mounting concentration. (Paul Griffiths, *The Times*)

One young student listener to those Sibelius symphonies was later to be editor of the *Sun* (see p. 38), and wrote an editorial when Rattle became music director in Berlin. The acclaim spread internationally as well:

Rattle . . . must be the best thing that has happened in English conducting since Beecham. He inspires players and elates audiences, holding them intent on every line, every colour, every turn of the argument. (Andrew Porter, *The New Yorker*)

Then the orchestra went up to the Edinburgh Festival for the first time, taking programmes that included Mahler's Tenth, Britten's *Sinfonia da Requiem* and Sibelius's Fifth. These too received high praise in the press: morale could scarcely have been higher as the following season began.

1984–85

Schubert	Symphony no. 5
Takemitsu	Concerto for guitar and oboe d'amore (John Williams, Peter Walden)

Rodrigo	*Concierto de Aranjuez*
Debussy	*Ibéria*

Webern	Six Pieces, op. 6
Brahms	Violin Concerto (Henryk Szeryng)
Walton	Symphony no. 1

Mozart	Overture: *Idomeneo*
Haydn	*Sinfonia concertante* for violin, cello, oboe and bassoon
Sibelius	*The Oceanides*
Sibelius	Symphony no. 1

Mussorgsky	Prelude: *Khovanshchina*
Rakhmaninov	Piano Concerto no. 3 (Peter Donohoe)
Stravinsky	*The Soldier's Tale*

Skryabin	*Nocturne*
Shostakovich	Violin Concerto no. 1 (Victor Lieberman)
Haydn	Symphony no. 89
Ives	*The Unanswered Question*
Bernstein	*Prelude, Fugue and Riffs*

Mahler	Symphony no. 7

Copland	*Appalachian Spring*
Stravinsky	Concerto for piano and wind instruments
Beethoven	Symphony no. 3

Berlioz	Overture: *Le corsaire*
Martin	Three Dances for oboe, harp and strings
Mozart	Oboe Concerto (Heinz Holliger)
Ravel	*Daphnis et Chloë* (complete)

Mozart	*Requiem* (Elise Ross, Mary King, Alexander Oliver, Henry Herford)
Ravel	*L'enfant et les sortilèges*

Tippett	Concerto for double string orchestra
Walton	Viola Concerto (Nobuko Imai)
Strauss	*Don Quixote* (Robert Cohen)

SIMON RATTLE It was at this time that we began to think seriously about the future, about how things could improve radically for the orchestra so that the learning process could continue. It was clear that we would hit the ceiling again quite soon and this time it needed a plan. So that was the beginning of the famous development plan – really just a scheme for keeping growth going. We needed to pay people more. An orchestra isn't a charity, and our rank-and-file strings were earning less than Birmingham bus-drivers. That side of things is outrageous. And it was clear to me what a difference just having one or two really good people in important positions in the orchestra made: perhaps a system of co-principals could help to lift the thing on to a new plane. The players needed to work less hard, not to do absolutely every date.

An interesting piece in this season was the *Eroica*. I'd hacked it a few times as a student, and then it was the only piece I seriously learned during my time in Oxford. I did it with the Scottish Chamber Orchestra, as I did the Ninth in 1987, and I think it started all right, got worse when we first did it in Birmingham in 1982 and then gradually got better again. I rethought a lot of it. I was hearing a lot of Reggie Goodall's performances around then, and I think I got terribly influenced by the steadiness and the measuredness and the thing of giving every note time to speak. As a result I must have done some colossally boring and soporific performances of Beethoven and Brahms during that time! We did a *South Bank Show* partly on the *Eroica* and it was all very broad and I was showing that the metronome mark for the first movement couldn't possibly work. But I've changed my thinking a lot since then and it came out in this second Birmingham performance and in the one with which we opened the following season.

The thing now is that this orchestra will work endlessly at something that is going to be horrendously difficult; they will even work against easy virtuosity in a piece – for example in the first movement of Mahler 7, which is ludicrously difficult – and come out with something that sounds absolutely marvellous. On the other hand, one of the hardest things we did was the Strauss *Don Quixote* with Yo-Yo Ma, who has a technical ease we couldn't match; it was very difficult to cope. The only times you can't ask for the whole lot from them are the rare occasions when there's simply not the technique to carry it off.

Other highlights of that season included a pair of important foreign visits in the autumn of 1984. The CBSO was invited both to the Paris Autumn Festival and to the Berlin Festival, appearing for the first time in Berlin's famous Philharmonie. The Paris concert included a work by Iannis Xenakis as part of the continuing exposure of his work in Paris: Rattle's handling of the horrendously complex *Synaphai* (a work even he has not dared to import back to Birmingham) was praised as revealing his 'qualities as an analytical technician'. 'SIMON LE MAGICIEN' was one headline; 'UN JEUNE PREMIER BRITANNIQUE...' another. 'I really believe that the musicians of the CBSO are the kings of the *legato*. I have rarely heard such a sonorous texture so lovingly blended, in the manner of those sauces which mysteriously reach their· optimum consistency. That the strings should achieve this supreme flow fairly easily one can accept, but that one could obtain from the woodwind and brass the same lines, tenderly and subtly intertwined, was much more surprising,' wrote the critic of *L'Aurore*. *Le Monde*, noting that Rattle's reputation in France was built entirely on his records, was impressed by his technique: 'His supple and economic gestures seem to synthesize and encompass the entire music while rising above it . . . [He has] a delicacy of articulation, but also a sharp precision in his accents, which are the salt of his interpretations.'

No less remarkable was the orchestra's reception in Berlin, where Sibelius's Fifth and the Brahms–Schoenberg Piano Quartet were coupled not with Xenakis as in Paris but with Britten's *American Overture*, a local novelty. 'Triumphant success,' wrote the *Morgenpost*, while in a long review *Der Tagespiegel* praised both orchestra and conductor: 'The phenomenal Simon Rattle, his baton held like a sceptre in his hand, was called out again and again; with amiable modesty he directed the applause to the orchestra, which was then able to show off again in two encores.' The paper concluded that 'This concert, in which right up to the last note orchestra, conductor and audience were involved with the greatest concentration, must surely rank among the musical climaxes of the festival, and will surely be remembered for a long time.' Slowly but surely the CBSO was making a major reputation abroad, and the appearance in Berlin was noticed by the players of the Berlin Philharmonic, an omen of things to come.

1985–86

Beethoven	Symphony no. 3
Rakhmaninov	*The Bells* (Elise Ross, John Mitchinson, John Shirley-Quirk)
Beethoven	Overture: *Leonore* no. 1
Sibelius	Symphony no. 3
Beethoven	Overture: *Leonore* no. 2
Sibelius	Symphony no. 7
Beethoven	Overture: *Leonore* no. 3

Berlioz   Overture: *Béatrice et Bénédict*
Ravel   *Pavane pour une infante défunte*
Dutilleux   *Métaboles*
Bartók   *Duke Bluebeard's Castle* (Maria Ewing, Willard
                 White)

Mozart   Symphony no. 40 in G minor
Debussy   *Jeux*
Brahms   Piano Concerto no. 1 (Alfred Brendel)

Haydn   Symphony no. 70
Brahms   Violin Concerto (Kyung-Wha Chung)
Bartók   *Concerto for Orchestra*

Murail   *Time and Again* (prèmiere)
Messiaen   *Turangalîla Symphony* (Peter Donohoe, Tristan
                 Murail)

Webern   *Passacaglia*
Beethoven   Piano Concerto no. 4 (Alfred Brendel)
Debussy   *Images*

Mahler   Symphony no. 2 (Arleen Augér, Felicity Palmer)

Ravel   *Alborada del gracioso*
Holloway   *Seascape and Harvest* (première)
Brahms   Piano Concerto no. 2 (John Lill)

Mozart   Serenade for thirteen wind instruments
Mozart   Piano Concerto in C minor K491 (Radu Lupu)
Mozart   Symphony no. 38

For this season, because the Tuesday and Thursday series had regularly been sold out in previous years, the orchestra decided to add a Wednesday series. A small grant was received from the Arts Council to help with the marketing of the new series. Much to the orchestra's surprise, this too was almost immediately sold out.

SIMON RATTLE This was a tremendous season: so many mountains to climb. Those very big things, like Mahler 2, were vastly important things for us. Our re-establishment of *Turangalîla* was also very important, particularly because I really cannot imagine anywhere that piece could be better played. One small thing was working on Haydn 70, and finally establishing that a symphony orchestra could really play like a good authentic ensemble, and that has been absolutely seconded by the orchestra's recent experience [1987], working with Nicholas Kraemer, whom they adored. This could be a terribly important step forward, because it shows that it can be done and that the symphony orchestra doesn't just have to go into its post-Brahms shell. The other highlight was to be able to work with Brendel – we took that programme with the Brahms concerto to Paris – and to be able to do what he asked instead of *nearly* being able to do it, which was always our experience before! I would be very happy to conduct the Beethoven symphonies the way he plays the sonatas. That would be my ideal: to have that sort of flexibility, and that type of joy and life and daring.

At the time, Rattle talked about the special challenge of Messiaen:

SIMON RATTLE We've done *Turangalîla* a good deal together now: five times altogether, including the Welsh première! We sent Messiaen a copy of the big poster all in Welsh which is quite some curiosity. We very much hope he'll be able to come over when we do the piece later in the year for the Bath Festival. [He did, and players recall his visit as a highlight of the year: 'As if Mozart walked in when you played the *Jupiter*!']

One of the things I remember about all the performances has been the incredible response of the audience. Here in Birmingham there was something that sounded like an Indian war whoop at the end. The orchestra know it very well now, so it's more like rehearsing a very complicated big-band arrangement by Stan Kenton – actually it sounds like one too, I'm glad to say! – than putting together a 'difficult' piece of modern music. It really is like falling off a log for them now, which means we can concentrate on just getting it perfectly dead on, absolutely accurate, rather than having to start from square one.

It staggers me to think that when the Philharmonia played it in London they did it on two rehearsals. When we first did it we had seven rehearsals, spread over some time. The thing that surprises people about the piece is that the orchestra is not huge. It's nowhere near as large as the orchestra for *The Planets*, though it makes as least twice as much sound (and at least ten times as interesting a collection of sounds). There is obviously a huge percussion section but I think it's really the use of the brass section that makes such a difference. In fact we use a trumpeter who's playing in the show *Cats* to do the piccolo trumpet part and it's marvellous. He can play any note at any volume, any time, and so he'll be blasting out Lloyd Webber one night, and by ten o'clock in the morning he'll have driven up the motorway and be slamming out *Turangalîla* for us. One needs that; one needs a jazzer's nerve to go for it.

I first heard the piece in Liverpool in the 1960s, done by Charles Groves who did so much there for contemporary music, which we tend to forget. *Turangalîla* was done when I was ten or eleven, and I'd seen the score but never heard it, so I bullied and badgered my parents into letting me go and it was one of the most thrilling experiences I remember. I nearly jumped out of my seat in the way I see audiences doing today. What a great Mars Bar of a piece!

By the end of this season the CBSO were receiving notices in the press that were remarkable by any standards. When they visited the BBC Proms in September 1986 Robert Henderson in the *Daily Telegraph*, under the headline 'BIRMINGHAM BIG GUNS', wrote:

That the CBSO is at present in peak form, equal to every challenge offered by any other British orchestra, was again instantly confirmed at the start of their Prom . . . a performance [Debussy's *Images*] of an imaginative precision of detail, of a magic realism in the phrasing and texture, that meticulously reflected the composer's own description of the music, that here he was attempting something quite new.

And *The Times* agreed: 'They really are in the top league.' The stage was well set for the orchestra's leap into the national limelight.

II
1986–90

1986–87

Debussy–Constant	*Pelléas et Mélisande* Symphony (British première)
Beethoven	Symphony no. 9 (Alison Hargan, Louise Winter, David Johnston, Willard White)
Stravinsky	*Symphony in Three Movements*
Gershwin	Piano Concerto (Peter Donohoe)
Stravinsky	*Petrushka*
Ravel	*La valse*
Haydn	Symphony no. 60
Henze	*Barcarola*
Brahms	Violin Concerto (Ida Haendel)

Wagner	Overture: *Die Meistersinger*
Brahms	Piano Concerto no. 1 (John Lill)
Haydn	Symphony no. 60
Ravel	*La valse*
Brahms	Songs for female voices, two horns and harp
Bruch	Violin Concerto no. 1 (Oscar Shumsky)
Beethoven	Romance no. 2 for violin and orchestra
Sibelius	Symphony no. 4
Sibelius	Symphony no. 6
Mozart	Piano Concerto in C K503 (Stephen Bishop-Kovacevich)
Brahms	Symphony no. 4
Strauss	*Festival Prelude*
Delius	*On Hearing the First Cuckoo in Spring*
Knussen	*Choral*
Strauss	*The Three Kings* (Elise Ross)
Gershwin	*A Cuban Overture*
Varèse	*Offrandes* (Elise Ross)
Canteloube	*Songs of the Auvergne* (Elise Ross)
Prokofiev	*Scythian Suite*
Birtwistle	*Dinah and Nick's Love Song*
Mahler	Symphony no. 6
Berio	*Sinfonia* (Electric Phoenix)
Berlioz	*Symphonie fantastique*
Strauss	*Don Juan*
Elgar	Cello Concerto (Ulrich Heinen)
Beethoven	Symphony no. 6
Schoenberg	*Five Orchestral Pieces*, op. 16
Brahms	Piano Concerto no. 2 (André Watts)
Sibelius	Symphony no. 5
Haydn	*The Creation* (Margaret Marshall, Philip Langridge, David Thomas)
[Mozart	*Haffner* Serenade, directed by Iona Brown]
Mahler	Symphony no. 1

Bernstein   Overture: *Candide*
Sibelius   Violin Concerto (Yuzuko Horigome)
Brahms   Symphony no. 4

Tchaikovsky   Suite: *Nutcracker*
Shostakovich   Suite: *Age of Gold*
Stravinsky   *The Firebird*

SIMON RATTLE Beethoven's Ninth is one of the works I always said I wouldn't tackle until I was much, much older. But, as Giulini said to me once, there comes a time when these pieces come knocking on the door telling you to conduct them. It was Kurt Sanderling who really changed my mind, because he said that it would be a struggle whenever I did it, so I should start now and it would have much more of a chance to get better. So from that point of view, if I'm likely to have to get lots of bad performances out of the way before I get anywhere with it, we may as well do them now!

I was incredibly lucky with Beethoven 9 in having a series of Scottish Chamber Orchestra performances earlier in the year. I'd been right out of action for a while, so there was quite a lot of time to think about it, and then I went up there and worked with an orchestra that had never played the piece before. It makes a real difference. A couple of people in the band had played it, and they found it difficult to take all the rehearsal, I think, because they knew how it went. It was very different, of course, doing it with a chamber orchestra. They added some strings but still it was light at the bottom end. But I think we made people listen freshly, and there weren't players saying all the time, 'That's not what we did last time!' And I was able to sort out quite a lot of problems.

In *The Times*, Paul Griffiths, who had actually come to Birmingham to hear the first half's première of a symphony drawn from Debussy's *Pelléas et Mélisande* by Marius Constant, devotes his whole notice to the Beethoven. It is spot on:

What we heard was not an 'interpretation' of the work: it was far too simple for that – too open, even too obvious – if at the same time constantly and joyously surprising. Interpretation would imply a secondary experience, whereas this had the flat authority of something primary . . . I am at a loss to know how Simon Rattle achieved this immediacy, this sense of the music speaking for itself, searching and finding its own tempo (even through some extreme rallentandos), its own phrasing, even its own colouring from the strings.

No doubt the secret lies somewhat in the shared sensibility of conductor and orchestra, their working so closely in harness (and how well

Rattle's stay-put policy justifies itself). But the triumph is also a personal one, dependent on Rattle's ability to be desperately and personally involved and yet to be so on behalf of something much larger than himself . . . The music, the continuing comprehension of this music, was all that was important.

That notice summed up very precisely the remarkable results of Rattle's work with the orchestra. One other person I knew would be watching this Beethoven performance closely was Rattle's mentor, John Carewe:

JOHN CAREWE I think for Simon this was a make-or-break endeavour, and it had to be a make. And I think he knew that his role model in this had to be Furtwängler. Obviously he wasn't going to do it in the same way as Furtwängler – nobody could – but he realized (and I'm sure he sifted through various recordings of the piece) that of all the conductors of this work it was Furtwängler who provided the insight.

The architectural element is so important: it builds to a point and then goes back, and what was so amazing about Simon's performance was that he managed all that. I wonder if Simon remembers what Walter Goehr said about Beethoven 9, which was so illuminating, which is that it is not poetry, or drama, or a novel, but that it is philosophy. And it is a Germanic concept of philosophy, which is that you pursue an idea to its logical conclusion, and then another and another, until in the end you have assembled a total world view. And he made it like that.

Were there things in the performance you disagreed with?
I have to admit that I disagreed with him about the tempo of the scherzo at the first performance in Birmingham, and in discussing it with him it emerged that he was unhappy too. I was very puzzled as to *why* it was too fast and not quite articulated, and I came to the conclusion that the reason was quite simply that he was throwing away the shape of the phrase, which must go to either the third or fourth bar of every group, not just the first; you have to encourage the orchestra to notice those middle bars. And I suggested that to get that you should go a little slower. He agreed, and in the next performance I heard in Birmingham it was absolutely perfect.

One thing I felt in the rehearsals was that he was always striving for this long, sustained sound, and neglected all the accents and the sforzandi, *the light and shade.*
You've put your finger on something I don't think Simon has quite sorted out. Of course in this case Simon later added to this basic sound the elements that give greater clarity and character, as was clear from the

performance. But it is true that he wants a most beautiful sound and hasn't always got round to realizing that sometimes it's appropriate and sometimes it's quite wrong. One of his strengths is that he gets this gorgeous string sound because he insists on them playing through every note like a German orchestra would. But now he can afford to do something with that, to relax a bit. You can't make everything sound like an old Giulini or a Karajan, though there was a period, I must say, when I thought he would. But he's moving away from that characteristic now, and I have a hope that very soon he will acquire the courage of a Bruno Walter: to attack the notes occasionally with no regard to their sonority! And it was thrilling to hear him do Mahler 6 in January [1987] at the Festival Hall and to find that he could be utterly brutal with the sound, really using it in its right context.

With their performances of Beethoven's Ninth Symphony, it would be possible to argue, the relationship between Rattle and the CBSO came of age. The initial 'ludicrously sunny' period, as Rattle describes it, lasted from 1980 to the autumn of 1982. There was one difficult season with several changes, and then on a new level the partnership grew and matured from 1983 to 1986. Many of the events of 1986 were highlights, but whereas some of the big achievements – the Mahler 2 and *Turangalîla* recordings, for instance – looked backwards and summarized a period of work, the Beethoven 9 pointed forward to the future which was then wide open. A Beethoven symphony cycle beckoned, an ultimate challenge for both orchestra and conductor, but one for which they were nearly ready. For Simon Rattle, on a personal level, Beethoven's Ninth marked an engagement with one of those great works of the central repertory which he had always said he would be extremely cautious about – and it was also a great triumph. He too was moving from the group of works he had known and loved from his earliest days – the Mahler and Messiaen were among the earliest classical pieces he heard on record – and into the new world of pieces he had previously considered unapproachable.

After a tour, which again involved Sibelius symphonies, including a visit to the composer's home in Finland, the orchestra ended up at the Berlin Festival for the memorable concert that was the price Rattle exerted for making his Berlin Philharmonic début a couple of months later. It featured a work by Berthold Goldschmidt, the impact of which has been recalled by Elmar Weingarten (see p. 24).

1987–88

Brahms	Symphony no. 1
Brahms	Symphony no. 2
Takemitsu	*A Flock Descends into the Pentagonal Garden*
Bartók	Piano Concerto no. 2 (András Schiff)
Stravinsky	*The Firebird* (complete ballet)
Brahms	Symphony no. 3
Brahms	Symphony no. 4
Mozart	Symphony no. 40
Strauss	*Four Last Songs* (Maria Ewing)
Stravinsky	*Four Etudes* for orchestra
John Adams	*Harmonium* (UK première)
Mahler	Symphony no. 9
Robin Holloway	*Seascape and Harvest*
Wagner	*Die Walküre* closing scene (Phyllis Cannan, Willard White)
Schoenberg	*Five Orchestral Pieces*, op. 16
Mahler	*Rückert Lieder* (Dame Janet Baker)
Brahms	*Alto Rhapsody*
Nielsen	*Pan and Syrinx*
Shostakovich	Suite: *The Age of Gold*
Berg	Suite: *Lulu*
Dutilleux	Violin Concerto (UK première) (Isaac Stern)
Stravinsky	*The Rite of Spring*
Stravinsky	*Petrushka*
Beethoven	Piano Concerto no. 4 (Alfred Brendel)
Lutosławski	Symphony no. 3
Haydn	Symphony no. 70
Schumann	Piano Concerto (Peter Donohoe)
Wagner	*Die Walküre* closing scene (Phyllis Cannan, Willard White)
Sibelius	Symphony no. 5
Sibelius	Symphony no. 6

Sibelius	Symphony no. 7
Webern	Six Pieces, op. 6
Berg	Violin Concerto (György Pauk)
Stravinsky	*Apollon musagète*
Ravel	Suite: *Daphnis et Chloë* no. 2

The question that was in everyone's minds during this period was whether the partnership between the CBSO and Simon Rattle could rise on to a new plateau. Rattle had already expressed his confidence that it would, in agreeing to extend his contract, but only on the secret condition that a major development plan would be put to the Arts Council and other funders: if it was rejected he claimed he would move on in 1989. If it was accepted by early 1987 then he would renew until 1991 and perhaps beyond.

So the scheme for a development plan was conceived in some secrecy, because Ed Smith was fully aware of the problems it could cause with other orchestras: 'We had to take the position, though, that other orchestras were not our concern – not because we don't like them, or anything silly like that, but because our prime concern is the welfare of the CBSO, and nothing ventured, nothing gained.' By May 1986 the plan was ready for submission to the Arts Council, and on 21 May there had been a meeting of the Arts Council's music panel to which, very unusually, Ed Smith and Simon Rattle were invited. (Clients rarely have the opportunity of putting their own case verbally to the panels, and this certainly indicated a predisposition on the part of the Council towards the plan.)

The main proposals were to establish new posts in the orchestra for co-principals and associate section leaders, so that these leading players no longer had to do 100 per cent of the work in the orchestral contract; and to raise the rates of pay throughout the orchestra, ensuring that better players joined the orchestra. The latter was bound to be controversial with other orchestral managements who felt themselves starved of Arts Council funding. In the end, the problems of the plan came down to two points: the principle, and the money. On the principle, there was the matter of the imbalance such a plan would cause with the other regional orchestras and, as far as the money was concerned, there was the problem of where it was likely to come from, how much was needed, and when. The total cost of the scheme was £600,000 per annum, of which the Birmingham City Council and the Arts Council were each being approached for half.

But on 5 October 1986 the secrecy had been blown by an exclusive
story in the *Observer* by Peter Watson, headlined 'SUPER-ORCHESTRA
PLAN WILL RATTLE LONDON RIVALS', which revealed what the report
called a 'secret plan, kept even from the members of the orchestra', to
turn the City of Birmingham Symphony Orchestra into a world-class
orchestra. 'It will be created by a large injection of cash by the Arts
Council, among others, to enable Birmingham to retain its luminous
young conductor, Simon Rattle, and to hire the best players and soloists.'
One of the more remarkable features of the story was the strength of the
endorsement the plan received from Sir William Rees-Mogg, chairman
of the Arts Council:

> I am very enthusiastic about the idea. Simon Rattle is one of the greatest
> young conductors in the world. Birmingham audiences have been very
> enthusiastic – all performances are now virtually sold out. I also applaud
> the idea of trying to build a British orchestra so that it can rival the inter-
> national greats like Chicago. I suspect, too, that it can only be done with a
> regional orchestra where the players are on salary. With the London
> orchestras, where players are paid by the session, the quality goes up and
> down too much. It is noticeable that Chicago and Berlin are salaried
> orchestras.

The fact that no one quoted in the story denied that the intention was
to create a super-orchestra in Birmingham sent shock waves through the
British musical world. Everyone was aware how overstretched the Arts
Council's resources were, and how little money was available for orchestras generally. Small wonder that London's orchestral managers initially
reacted violently. John Willan of the London Philharmonic Orchestra
said, 'If this is the advice the Arts Council is getting from its music
advisory panel, then I find that very alarming. It's a slap in the face for
London's orchestras. I just don't understand why it's necessary to go out
of London, which is the musical capital of the world, and use resources
which are desperately needed here.' And Ian Maclay of the Royal Philharmonic Orchestra said, 'One can't help jumping to the conclusion that
the Arts Council finds it fashionable to support half-baked plans in the
regions when they make it the policy to reject new and interesting
formats submitted by the London orchestras.'

It was only over the next few days that the truth about Birmingham's
proposals began to trickle out. As it happened, the day after the revelations Simon Rattle himself was on public view in London, at the press

showing of the new television series, *From East to West*. I think he thought that because I worked for the *Observer* at this time, and was writing the first edition of this book, the story must have come from me. In fact, I was slightly embarrassed not to have known anything about it at all until the paper called me the night before the story went to press. On the other hand, the story is much more likely to have been leaked by the Arts Council itself, in order to flush out any likely opposition to the scheme. During the lunch break Rattle skilfully parried some intelligent questioning about the scheme from Terry Grimley, arts editor of the *Birmingham Post*, who subsequently wrote the clearest piece about the scheme, accurately reflecting Rattle's feelings that the Sunday newspaper story was unhelpful in its sensationalist aspects, but never dismissing the idea that the orchestra could, one day, become a world-beater. The only reservation was about the idea that such an orchestra could be bought, or that it could be transformed overnight. Grimley wrote:

> The picture being painted is that of the CBSO being picked out for groom-ing as Britain's premier orchestra, with its four London rivals desperate to torpedo the plans. But the reality is more complex and less dramatic, according to the man around whom the plan revolves, the CBSO's princi-pal conductor, Simon Rattle: 'The report was ludicrously over the top . . . You have only to consider that Munich spends £4.9 million on its one orchestra and Britain spends £4.7 million on all its symphony and chamber orchestras put together to see that there is not the sort of money around to make that dramatic a difference. We basically want a bit more to enable us to do more of what we are doing already, to enable the players to be paid better and to give us more rehearsal time. I will believe it all when it actu-ally happens.'

The internal politics of the situation, however, revolved around the pitting of regional orchestra against regional orchestra, a question Ed Smith had foreseen very clearly. Other orchestras in the country had been campaigning for an increase in their grant – the Hallé in Manches-ter had achieved a paltry £22,500 in the aftermath of the Arts Council initiative *The Glory of the Garden* – and the Association of British Orchestras and the Musicians' Union had been trying to publicize the appalling pay of regional orchestra members. But they realized that the Birmingham development plan, if it was approved by the Arts Council, would change the whole delicate balance of power within the country's orchestral structure. Meanwhile in the media the fall-out from the leak of the development plan continued. In his published comments Ed Smith sought to remove the idea that they were trying to create an 'élite' orchestra. 'That's just an interpretation that had been put upon it. All we are trying to do is to develop the work we are doing here already, and to keep Simon Rattle here after 1989. I don't think we should just sit back and wave goodbye to Simon.'

As it became clear that it was Arts Council *development* money that was being talked about, the orchestral managers became less unfriendly. John Willan changed his tack, and was quoted in the *Guardian* two months later as saying, 'Good luck to Birmingham. The Arts Council should reward success.' Clive Gillinson of the LSO saw past the immediate threat when he said, 'I'm delighted by any new money that comes into music, but not money that is taken from elsewhere.' And that was also the attitude of Christopher Bishop of the Philharmonia, after the dust had settled.

A week after their initial story the *Observer* returned to the attack with a full-scale leader-page profile of Simon Rattle (anonymous, as is the custom, but written by Gillian Widdicombe), which at last got all the details right and included an immortal quote from one of the London orchestral managers, who said that the plan was (figuratively) 'a load of old bassoons, because everybody knows that to make the Birmingham compare with the London orchestras you'd have to fire half the orchestra, not just add a few more players'. This quote was so near to what all the London managers probably felt privately about the plan that in a subsequent *Guardian* piece one of them denied 'using those exact words' when the quote had not come from him in the first place.

1988–89

Brahms–Schoenberg	Piano Quartet in G Minor
Janáček	*Glagolitic Mass* (Helen Field, Linda Hirst, John Mitchinson, Neil Howlett, Thomas Trotter)
Jonathan Lloyd	Symphony no. 1 (première)
Mozart	Piano Concerto in B♭ K595 (Imogen Cooper)
Haydn	Symphony no. 90 in C
Debussy	Incidental Music to *King Lear*
Rakhmaninov	Piano Concerto no. 2 (John Lill)
Franz Schmidt	Symphony no. 4

Britten	*Sinfonia da Requiem* (première of original version)
Schubert	Symphony no. 9
Debussy	Incidental Music to *King Lear*
Rakhmaninov	Piano Concerto no. 2 (John Lill)
Schubert	Symphony no. 9
Boulez	*Eclat*
Bartók	Violin Concerto no. 2 (Kyung-Wha Chung)
Debussy	*Images*

CBSO Benevolent Fund Concert

Debussy	*Rondes de printemps* (*Images*)
Brahms	Violin Concerto (Kyung-Wha Chung)
Beethoven	Symphony no. 7
Michael Torke	*Vanada*
Debussy	*Jeux*
Elgar	Violin Concerto (Oscar Shumsky)
Mozart	*Le nozze di Figaro* (Arleen Augér, Dale Duesing, Elise Ross, Stephen Roberts, Helen Field, Neil Jenkins, Susan Lees, Alastair Miles)
Busoni	*Berceuse élégiaque*
Alexander Goehr	*Eve Dreams in Paradise* (Feeney Trust commission, première; Ameral Gunson, Philip Langridge)
Shostakovich	Symphony no. 5
Heinz Holliger	Two Liszt Transcriptions
Dvořák	Cello Concerto (Lynn Harrell)
Brahms	Symphony no. 2
Elliott Carter	*Remembrance*
Elliott Carter	*A Celebration of some 100 × 150 notes*
Mahler	Symphony no. 7
Bernd-Alois Zimmermann	Ballet: *Roi Ubu*
Mahler orch. Berio	Early Songs (Willard White)

Berlioz   *Symphonie fantastique*

Peter Maxwell Davies   Suite: *The Boyfriend*
Gershwin   *Rhapsody in Blue* (Wayne Marshall)
Stravinsky   *Ebony Concerto* (Colin Parr)
Bernstein   *Prelude, Fugue and Riffs* interspersed with a
                                     selection of Paul Whiteman numbers

In 1987 Rattle had made his débuts with the Berlin Philharmonic as
well as with the Orchestra of the Age of Enlightenment. He was being
profiled in the *New Yorker*: 'If Christopher Robin had become an
orchestra conductor, he might have looked a lot like Simon Rattle, a
slight, soft-spoken Englishman with a mop of curly brown hair who is
one of the fastest-rising stars in the musical firmament . . . ' But Rattle
was as usual quick to pin his allegiance to Birmingham:

> Almost all of the great orchestras of the past have been built by individuals
> working away for many years, and it's this tradition that appeals to me. It
> lingers on long after the conductor has left. I mean, Fritz Reiner is still there
> in Chicago; Stokowski stayed on in Philadelphia, and Szell's ghost is still
> alive and kicking every time the Cleveland Orchestra plays Mozart . . . A
> conductor can have an extraordinary impact on music if he stays in one
> place long enough, and I want to do just that.

He took the CBSO on a triumphant first tour of the United States, a
fifteen-concert tour that went from Los Angeles and San Francisco to
Boston, Washington and New York. In the *San Francisco Chronicle*,
Robert Commanday summed up the mood, writing that 'We were convinced that the Birmingham Symphony was a distinguished orchestra, its
leader one of the major conductors of the day.' The New York critics
were more reserved, as they had been for Rattle's début with the Los
Angeles Philharmonic, but *Newsday* was favourable: 'If you haven't
heard them yet, beg, borrow or steal a ticket.'

After the tour, Rattle managed to have a sabbatical of nearly six
months in 1988. The family, Simon, Ellie and son Sacha, spent some
time on the West Coast, and then travelled to the Far East, where the
Rattles encountered the musical tradition of Bali at first hand. The family
studied gamelan music, became totally absorbed in the traditional
musical life and, as Rattle put it to me when back in London, 'After that,
nothing much back here seems to matter any more!'

In May 1989 Rattle did something he practically never does: he took
over a concert from another conductor. He had been conducting Berlioz

with the CBSO, and the LPO, which was increasingly the London orchestra with which he worked, found itself without a conductor when Lorin Maazel was unable to appear. Rattle saved the day with *The Damnation of Faust*, a substitution that could not have come at a better time as the work was one he had at the very top of his mind, and which he had just conducted at the Brighton Festival, drawing praise from Max Loppert in the *Financial Times*:

> The concerts, exhilarating experiences both, demonstrated that Simon Rattle is on his way to becoming the one of the world's important Berlioz conductors . . . the keyed-up musicians of the ensemble and the light (in the best sense) quality of the orchestra's tone colours offer an ideal starting point for the exploration of this composer; the conductor's native feel for the cutting edge of his sounds and rhythms, his determination not to smooth them over, made of both the symphony and the dramatic legend two thrilling Berlioz journeys.

Things were looking good in Birmingham. The development plan seemed to be working, and new players had been auditioned. The orchestra won many awards, notably for its Mahler 2 recording, which raced away with the 1988 Record of the Year award from the *Gramophone* magazine, presented to Rattle by Jeremy Isaacs. The year 1989 also saw a whole string of performances of Mahler 7 in Birmingham, Leeds, London and Paris (nine performances in one tour), which reached a climax in an astonishing televised performance at the BBC Proms in September, which the press praised as a 'marvellous interpretation with a transfigured CBSO . . . Rattle and players responded with an insight and virtuosity which were breathtaking'.

Rattle took his first dip into the waters of Glyndebourne with period instruments in July, for which he had prepared with two concert performances of *Figaro* with the CBSO in March, and recorded the soundtrack for Kenneth Branagh's film of *Henry V*, a score by Patrick Doyle that did extremely well as a CD recording. Over the summer the orchestra gave four highly praised concerts at the Edinburgh Festival before returning to Birmingham. But there were storm clouds on the horizon, at least financially. As the achievements of the orchestra reached ever greater heights, it was clear that its financial problems had failed to be solved by the development plan. The rise in grant for 1987–88 from £775,000 to £885,000 had been talked of as a first phase, but turned out to be a one and only phase. Was this the beginning of the end for Rattle in Birmingham, as the world beckoned?

1989–90

Ravel   Alborada del gracioso
Mozart   Piano Concerto in G K453 (Mitsuko
                     Uchida)
Messiaen   Oiseaux exotiques
Schumann   Symphony no. 2

Beethoven   Overture: Leonore no. 3
Mark-Anthony
    Turnage   Three Screaming Popes (première)
Brahms   Symphony no. 4

Bartók   Ballet: The Wooden Prince
Bartók   Ballet: The Miraculous Mandarin

Webern   Six Pieces, op 6
Ravel   Shéhérazade (Maria Ewing)
Mozart   Mass in C minor (Lillian Watson, Maria
                     Ewing, Maldwyn Davies, Henry
                     Herford)

Strauss   Oboe Concerto (Heinz Holliger)
Liszt   A Faust Symphony (Patrick Power)

Sofia Gubaidulina   Offertorium (UK première; Gidon Kremer)
Stravinsky   The Rite of Spring

Mahler   Symphony no. 6

Messiaen   Et exspecto resurrectionem mortuorum
Rakhmaninov   Symphony no. 2

Mahler   Lieder eines fahrenden Gesellen (Bernadette
                     Greevy)
Bruckner   Symphony no. 7

Ravel   Fanfare: L'eventail de Jeanne
Ravel   Ballet: Mother Goose
Ravel   Piano Concerto in G (Cécile Ousset)
Ravel   Piano Concerto for the Left Hand
Ravel   La valse

Bach	Concerto in D minor for two violins and strings BWV1043 (Victor Lieberman, Peter Thomas)
[Schoenberg	*Verklärte Nacht* (directed by Victor Lieberman)]
Webern	Five Pieces, op. 10
Beethoven	Symphony no. 7
Haydn	*The Creation* (Arleen Augér, Philip Langridge, David Thomas)
Schoenberg	Chamber Symphony no. 1 (BCMG)
Mendelssohn	Violin Concerto (Midori)
Dvořák	Symphony no. 7 in D minor

On 22 October 1989 Rattle's second son Eliot was born – as the orchestra recorded with some relief, on about the only free day in the schedule. The orchestra was in London for the festival of Hungarian music at the Barbican, offering Bartók ballets and Liszt's *Faust Symphony*. (These pieces were in Rattle's first recording plans with Berlin. The first never happened and the second was less than a total success – see p. 32.)

During 1990 Rattle was back in Berlin twice, for two series of concerts with the Berlin Philharmonic, then travelled to Los Angeles, and finally made his début at the Royal Opera House, Covent Garden, in Janáček's *The Cunning Little Vixen* (see pp. 307–8). But he still managed an extremely rich series of CBSO concerts, including the première of *Three Screaming Popes*, a new work by Mark-Anthony Turnage marking the beginning of his composer-in-association scheme in Birmingham (see pp. 260–62).

One important début of the season was the first concert Rattle himself conducted with the recently formed Birmingham Contemporary Music Group. Drawn from members of the CBSO, this ensemble had so far been conducted by Peter Donohoe, with Rattle as artistic adviser. But in 1990 Rattle found time to conduct them. The mastermind behind the group was Rattle's friend and colleague, the long-time CBSO cellist Simon Clugston.

SIMON CLUGSTON Somewhere in the back of my mind there had always been an ambition of having a contemporary ensemble based in Birmingham. The late eighties was very much a time in the orchestra when we were pushing ourselves to do more and do better. Sectional rehearsals became quite normal, and Simon had decided that it would be a good idea to bring people in to work in special ways with the orchestra. Nick Kraemer started to do early music; Iona Brown came in as guest director, and Victor Lieberman [from the Concertgebouw] came and did masterclasses with the string section. There was a special ethos around that period. I remember an ABO [Association of British Orchestras] conference at which Ed [Smith] and I were talking and there was a lot of discussion of how orchestras could become more humane and more interesting and less destructive to individuals.

So one night Ulrich Heinen [CBSO principal cellist] and I were sitting at the back of the bus coming back from Northampton having just done a performance of the *Eroica* and arguing about whether the first performance of the *Eroica* would have been the best. And he was saying we must do more new music, more first performances. So by the time we got home we had decided to see if we could make a contemporary music group from the orchestra work. West Midland Arts gave us a small grant, which was incredibly supportive, and it was just at the time when Ed was taking the development plan to the Arts Council, so he was able to say that as well as a better orchestra you would get all these other benefits as a new music group. And that really helped to kickstart the group.

What did you start with?
I remember we put it off. It was clear to me that if we were to do this it had to be excellent and we had to hit the ground running. The orchestra was in the ascendant and it was no good bringing into existence a group that was any less good and was only slowly going to find out how to do it. There was some additional funding difficulty. Anyway, in the end it was 21 June 1987 with Peter Donohoe conducting a programme Gerald Larner said wasn't contemporary at all: Berio's *Folk Songs*, Ravel and Stravinsky, with Elise Ross. Boy, have we moved on since then!

What was Simon's relationship to it?
He was enormously enthusiastic, and as far as he was concerned this was exactly the community-of-musicians idea that fitted with what he wanted to develop. And he was keen that more and more players had the opportunity to play chamber music. And finally I think he felt it could feed back into the orchestra: some of the strength of the orchestra in twentieth-century symphonic repertory has been due to the fact that something like half the orchestra has at some time played in BCMG. We always wanted it to be a very flexible format and could go down to one or two players or up to seventy for Bernstein's *Wonderful Town*.

Was it mainly organised in the orchestra's free time?
Part of the development plan was that players should get more time off. It
was a more flexible contract, especially for section leaders. So everyone had
more time off. They could choose their own time and that helped BCMG to
schedule itself. Simon wanted players to play with BCMG and bring that
experience back to the full orchestra. He wasn't actually going to conduct a
lot himself, but then he did *The Soldier's Tale* as part of the second decade
of the *Towards the Millennium* project and it developed from there. We did
some very high-profile things very early on: for instance, *Pierrot lunaire* as
part of the orchestra's concerts on the American tour with Ellie and Manny
Ax playing the piano!

Gerald Larner's welcome to the new group in 1987 had been guarded,
and his review of Rattle's first concert with them had an acerbic note:

GERALD LARNER (*Guardian*) Simon Rattle's first concert with the BCMG
[which included Colin Matthews' *Hidden Variables*, Judith Weir's *Con-
solations of Scholarship*, and Schoenberg's First Chamber Symphony] was
treated by the BBC like a royal investiture. The live broadcast on Radio 3
was fulsome in its introductions, flattering in its commentaries, and assidu-
ous in canvassing favourable opinions from distinguished witnesses and
eliciting pious hopes from the principals.

1990–91

Britten	Overture: *The Building of the House*
Rakhmaninov	Piano Concerto no. 3 (Artur Pizarro, Leeds Competition winner)
Walton	Symphony no. 1
Nicholas Maw	*Odyssey*

CBSO Seventieth Anniversary Concert

Haydn	Symphony no. 90
Beethoven	Symphony no. 9 (Alison Hargan, Alfreda Hodgson, Robert Tear, Willard White)
Bernd Alois Zimmermann	Symphony in One Movement
Bartók	Piano Concerto no. 2 (Peter Donohoe)
Brahms	Symphony no. 1
Haydn	Symphony no. 70
Mozart	Piano Concerto in E♭ K482 (Imogen Cooper)

| Goldschmidt | *Ciaconna sinfonica* (UK première) |
| Shostakovich | Symphony no. 1 |

| Mozart | Incidental Music for *King Thamos* (Amanda Roocroft, Elise Ross, John Mark Ainsley, Henry Herford) |
| Ravel | *Daphnis et Chloë* |

| Beethoven | Piano Concerto no. 3 (Peter Donohoe) |
| Beethoven | Symphony no. 7 |

| Varèse | *Déserts* |
| Messiaen | *Turangalîla Symphony* (Peter Donohoe, Cynthia Millar) |

Towards the Millennium 1900–1910

Sibelius	*Night Ride and Sunrise*
Schoenberg	*Erwartung* (Phyllis Bryn-Julson)
Stravinsky	*The Firebird*

Towards the Millennium 1900–1910

| Rakhmaninov | Piano Concerto no. 3 (Cécile Ousset) |
| Suk | *Asrael* Symphony |

Towards the Millennium 1900–1910

Webern	Six Pieces, op. 6
Berg	*Seven Early Songs*
Mahler	Symphony no. 7

Once again Rattle and the CBSO returned to the BBC Proms, this time bringing the London première of John Adams's thrilling choral classic, *Harmonium*, and once again they lit up the hall, as the press reported:

> After eleven days of moderate success and minor disappointments the Proms burst gloriously into life last night. More than life: this was an evening when everyone from Simon Rattle down to the humblest music critic seemed to be breathing pure oxygen. The CBSO played with magnificent unflagging spirit in steaming temperatures . . . the Albert Hall was packed . . .

The tenth anniversary of Rattle's becoming chief conductor in Birmingham was heralded with fanfares by the press, and another anniversary was celebrated during the season with the seventieth anniversary of the orchestra, marked with another Beethoven Ninth Symphony in the Town Hall. Nicholas Maw's *Odyssey* – which occupied an entire concert, as one of the longest single spans of orchestral music ever written – was a landmark, and the remarkable *Towards the Millennium* festival was launched (see pp. 238–42). Rattle renewed his contract yet again, and this time added to his role by becoming music director of the CBSO Society: 'Ten years with the CBSO have disappeared in a flash, surely because our relationship has been such a happy and productive one ... Rarely can a conductor have experienced such sympathetic colleagues ... '

But it was a moment to look forwards, not backwards, and the most exciting development in Birmingham was happening just down the road from the Town Hall, where the International Convention Centre – including Symphony Hall – was springing into life. It was to prove the decisive factor in transforming the CBSO in the 1990s.

'The music business is competely unnatural . . .'
Rattle on the Record

On Conductors

Herbert von Karajan

I met Karajan only once, when I went to Berlin after I made my début. What I didn't know at the time was that he had listened to that performance. He knew a lot about my work and I had no idea he had found time to listen to those things. I had met him and I spent a few days watching him rehearse and record Brahms, which I thought would be instructive. Actually he found it amusing that during my sabbatical in Oxford I chose to go to my last tutorial rather than meet him, and that made him chuckle and say he wanted to meet me. So we talked a lot and he was very generous with his time. I had no idea when we would meet again but suddenly there came this message that he was about to phone me.

I was in my little flat in Birmingham recovering from pneumonia at the time, so I was in bed when the phone call came. He wanted me to conduct *Figaro*. He said, 'Look, my body is giving way, I can't do this any more, I need you to do *Figaro* at Easter with the Berlin Philharmonic and in the summer with the Vienna Philharmonic, the usual arrangement, and a wonderful cast and whatever conditions you need.' I explained to him that *Towards the Millennium* was just starting, and the problems. That was fine. Then he said – and he must have known the answer – 'Are you conducting the Mozart operas anywhere else?' I could have just said, 'Yes, at Glyndebourne, over the next few years.' It would have done. Instead (typical!) I started baring my soul, enthusing about period instruments, worrying about what would happen if I tried the same thing with the Vienna Philharmonic. Well! There followed a long diatribe mostly but not entirely in English, and he was very, very angry. He seemed to think it was a personal insult, as if I was saying to him, 'Your style is history,' which I really wasn't. He said, 'Well, I don't know what style you think you are doing it in, but I just play it in Mozart's style. Thank you. Goodbye.' And put down the phone.

I sat in bed and thought: I've just had the phone put down on me by Karajan. What do I do? Should I write a letter, or what? Well, eventually I got a message from one of his entourage via my agent saying, 'He sends his regards. You're completely crazy to be doing this period-instruments nonsense, but he wishes you well.' I suppose I felt I'd encountered General Patten, or some gnarled old soldier. Is this a person you would trust anything with? Probably not – but what I'm now hearing from the Philharmonic is that in the best years there was a really close connection and a feeling of everybody working together. They were co-conspirators in the music-making. You hear that in the music-making at its best.

Rudolf Schwarz

Rudolf Schwarz used to come and conduct in Liverpool, so I had been watching him since my earliest days. And then in my year with the National Youth Orchestra, when I was sixteen, I had Pierre Boulez and Rudolf Schwarz. Can you imagine a more wonderful pairing? My love for Bruckner was born with Rudi's Bruckner 7. Very shortly afterwards – staggeringly so, at nineteen – I was in Bournemouth, and so he was another grandfather. Chris Seaman, who became a very good friend, knew Rudi well and brought us back together again. He was in so many ways a deeply conservative man, such a contrast to another of my old men, Berthold Goldschmidt, who couldn't have been more different. He was so radical, so modern, and Rudi was so different. But they were Jews of a certain generation and that was the similarity. Rudi had such humanity and humour. Everything needed to take time. The idea of music being grounded on the bass line and sustained – this idea of a long, singing line – is part of me to this day, which is why as a young man I listened to Bruno Walter and Furtwängler, and I was simply stunned by my experiences of Giulini.

Pierre Boulez

There is a whole generation of us who were completely educated by Boulez. The expectations he brought to us are so strong. The people he trained in the NYO are now in the London Symphony Orchestra and what you can see is that he trained people to hear in a different way. He has given people a completely different sense of the exactitude of rhythm and of a rhythm that not only has pulse, but that you can calculate. His programming also had a huge impact. It's impossible to think how anyone could conduct *The Miraculous Mandarin* and the Berg *Three Pieces* quite so often in their life and yet his influence has shot through all our music-making. As people we couldn't be more complete opposites. He is so at ease with so many people in so many different situations, and now looks like everyone's favourite Parisian uncle. Pierre at a barbecue in Pasadena talking to people who knew nothing about music: that was a wonderful sight! His complete lack of the maestro ethic is utterly irresistible.

Bernard Haitink

I had a wonderful experience as a young *répétiteur* at Glyndebourne doing *The Rake's Progress*, coaching endless Tom Rakewells. There were a few things in the score that I would practise and practise but I could never play them – except when Bernard was conducting and then I could play all the notes! He just made that happen. I've now seen this time and time again. Orchestras are suddenly able to do things they never thought possible. He just has it. It's one of those uncanny gifts, and he creates this huge sweep in his music-making. When I was preparing *Tristan* he said to me, 'You'll find there are some bits in the middle that are really not normal music.' Now I think I know what he meant!

Nikolaus Harnoncourt

Harnoncourt has made such a difference to the way orchestras play today with his originality and intelligence. He pushed open the doors that I am going through now. There's always some extraordinary new discovery that he wants to share and that's wonderful. We did have a day where I wanted to talk only about Rameau and Mozart and he wanted to talk only about *Wozzeck* and *Porgy and Bess*! We came to the conclusion he should stick to *Fledermaus* and I should stick to *Porgy and Bess*. We talked about the vernacular in music and what that means. He is a incredibly generous person and never feels threatened at all. I've taken on so many of this ideas – and also the verbal ideas that are so important. He's never anything but thrilled to find that there is someone from the other side of the world who is interested in what he has got to offer.

William Christie

Over the last couple of years Bill Christie has become a very close friend of ours. Candace hit it off so well with him, as they had so much in common: smart Americans, Harvard-educated, you name it. He was such a friend, guiding me through Rameau, that slowly but surely over the coming years I will pay him back for that. But so many of the people who began with early music are important to me. For my return to Bach after all these years, listening to Ton Koopman was enormously important.

On the Repertory

The repertory is in a terrible state. Most conductors, with the exception of someone like Esa-Pekka Salonen, aren't really committed to new music. In London the question is usually: 'Have we got time to get through it?' And the answer is usually: 'No.' So unusual things don't get done. But that doesn't excuse the conductors who are a bloody sight more powerful than I am, who travel the world without doing a scrap of music by living composers. That's the most dangerous thing for our musical culture.

On Musicians

What most musicians lack is a sense of the cultural background to what they're doing. It's not their fault: none of that is taught at the colleges. You can go through those places knowing nothing except how to make your reeds and how to play the notes. It's frightening. They didn't even teach foreign languages at the Royal Academy. And not much proper analysis: Schenker I don't remember being mentioned. But without some knowledge of art and literature and so on it's difficult to make sense of music. One of the things I've tried to do in television programmes is to provide the beginning of that sort of background, to treat music in an organic way as part of the culture it springs from. But it really needs a lot of hard work, and musicians are playing so much and so hard they don't have the time.

On Learning

You have to make many, many mistakes. Whether you have to make as many as I did, I don't know. I can remember my incomprehension at not being able to get what I wanted. I can remember the physical sensation of it not working. And what you have to learn is that 90 per cent of it is your problem. The problems for other kinds of young musicians are quite different. At least they can play their instruments. And gradually they come to musical maturity. For conductors it's the other way round: your musical maturity, such as it is, is all you have to protect yourself against your complete incompetence technically!

It is very hard for young conductors and you must have to have this opportunity to make mistakes. That's why British orchestras, who almost to a player are contemptuous of young British conductors, are crippling themselves for the future by not allowing themselves to work with them. Where are they going to learn? They are people with things to communicate. But faced with opposition and an obviously ironical attitude from the players, it's hard for them to communicate anything.

On Rhythm

Setting a pulse is so different from just beating in time. I think at first I had a very brittle-izing effect on orchestras, because I was very insistent about rhythm. But you need to feel the pulse, and the more you try to impose rhythm on an orchestra, on the whole, the less you get. One of the major problems I've had with some orchestras is that if you don't get back what you want from them, you feel completely crippled. You can't function. So you have to try other things, to do less. With Furtwängler – I've seen him on film – there is absolute economy of motion. And take a quite different conductor, Rudi Schwarz: he really set a pulse for anyone who cared to notice it. It's an incredibly personal thing, a sense of rhythm.

On the Future

In Japan the idea of the virtual girlfriend is very popular. Many relationships are suffering from the man having a girlfriend who exists only in virtual reality. And just as I don't believe the future lies in cyber-sex, I do believe that there are certain things – such as human discourse, friendship and music – that are meant to be live. The problem with the new technology is that musicians have used it for profit rather than for raising the art. Karajan was a great man, a great conductor, but he has got a lot to answer for. His media empire built up the expectation that electronic reproduction would provide the best of all possible worlds. But to be limited to recordings is like choosing snapshots of your children over the children themselves. The point is the real, live thing.

But what will remain is that concert-going will have an element of ceremony about it. It will remind people in a noisy age that there is a place where you need silence, and that places in the modern world where there are ten seconds of silence are shockingly unusual. That doesn't mean it has be to be a nineteenth-century ceremony. It's likely to be closer to Théâtre de la Complicité than to Sarah Bernhardt, with that sort of rough vitality. You need to hear the rough edges. To have a chauffered-limo drive through Beethoven's symphonies or string quartets means you've missed something. We can't know what the next revolution is. I cheerfully look forward to being considered grotesquely out of date.

[to John Whitley, *Daily Telegraph*, February 1999]

On Friendship

The music business is completely unnatural. There's no opportunity to build on relationships, which is what most people do in ordinary life, and you don't get any initial stages followed by a 'getting to know you' period. When I was twenty-four I took a sabbatical in Oxford which made me realize how different was the world I inhabited. Suddenly I had the time to make new friends at the normal rate of the rest of the world . . . My friendship with Imo is one that has always managed to survive the long absences that are part of the music business. She is one of a handful of real friends who go back a long way and always turn up at the most important times of my life . . .

['How We Met', with Imogen Cooper, *Independent on Sunday*, 1994]

CHAPTER SIX

'It will drive people back to live performance'
Media Old and New 1986–2000

Rattle rehearsing under the gaze of TV cameras

I
In the Recording Studio

SIMON RATTLE [1987] For me, the important thing about recordings is that they are the most effective way to make an orchestra play better. We make great strides when we do a difficult record. The increase in confidence and technical ability, just to assimilate all the things you have to do in the course of a session: that pushes the orchestra on so much. None of these recordings I'm making now is my last will and testament. I'm afraid I'm not so interested as I should be in the finished product, perhaps, because the work has been done. I must admit I fell asleep listening to my test pressing of *The Planets*, but that was a long time ago. Some of them I've never heard again after the pressings.

The awful thing about recordings is that you listen to them afterwards and you really can't tell what were the bits that went well in the studio and everyone was thrilled and you thought, 'This is a great performance,' and which bits were put on with everyone feeling totally whacked at the end of the day and playing with gritted teeth. You just can't tell, and maybe there's something wrong with that. But we try now to do more and more straight performances in the recording studio, with as few retakes as possible. That way we preserve the feeling of the live occasion. Mahler 2, for instance – well, I think you came to a session which did least to recreate that feeling; it was hard work. But the last movement with choir and everyone, we just did most of that in one long performance and it was really superb.

Do you think recordings in general are a good thing?
Oh yes. I grew up with them and I still learn a lot from listening to them. I couldn't possibly know the music I do if they weren't around. The problem is the effect they have on people's performances: everything tends to come out sounding more and more the same, and conductors seem unwilling to be really different. A conductor like Harnoncourt is an exception: he's certainly different! But on the whole there's less and less individuality, and recordings just veer towards some sort of norm. And the worst thing would be, for myself, if I ever thought that I'd 'done' a piece because it's recorded, so it's over and finished with. There's a finality about records that isn't very healthy. For me they're just a stage along the way. For the orchestra I think they're bad if it makes them think they have to play carefully without ever a wrong note. We do want the notes right, but if it stifles your sense of live music-making and adventure then recordings are not a good thing at all.

In the early days Rattle's recording work was with several orchestras, with a special emphasis on the Philharmonia with whom he then appeared regularly in London. He was originally going to record all the Sibelius symphonies with them. The very earliest discs were ones in which the orchestras were able to provide their services as part of their contract arrangements, so that the only costs to EMI were Rattle and marketing. That arrangement produced one of his first records, of Stravinsky with the Northern Sinfonia, as well as the record that first really alerted EMI to his potential: his original recording of Mahler's Tenth Symphony in the Deryck Cooke version with the Bournemouth Symphony Orchestra, recorded in June 1980, just before Rattle went to Birmingham. (That recording has now been supplanted by the magnificent live recording with the Berlin Philharmonic which won a Grammy and the Record of the Year award from *Gramophone* in 2000.)

With the release of that Mahler recording in 1981, EMI made a determined effort to promote Rattle, and it paid off. The record did well and encouraged them to make more. But that was just at the time when Rattle was becoming completely committed to the Birmingham orchestra. Some other collaborations had taken place, including an unlikely one with the London Symphony Orchestra in a recording of Prokofiev and Ravel piano concertos with Andrei Gavrilov. (Rattle had conducted the LSO only once more in the intervening years before the relationship was successfully revived at the end of the 1990s.) With the Philharmonia he recorded *The Planets*, Sibelius's Fifth, Shostakovich's Tenth and a splendid Janáček coupling of the *Sinfonietta* with *Taras Bulba* which the players much enjoyed making. He made Rakhmaninov's Second Symphony with the Los Angeles Philharmonic as their principal guest conductor, but that was the only recording there, and it was not especially well reviewed.

Rattle's recordings with the CBSO began with large-scale choral undertakings: Janáček's *Glagolitic Mass* and Britten's *War Requiem* (a work EMI had, coincidentally, already arranged to record with Rattle's predecessor in Birmingham, Louis Frémaux, before his abrupt departure in March 1978). These were followed by Weill's *Seven Deadly Sins* with Elise Ross; several piano concertos with Cécile Ousset; Vaughan Williams with Thomas Allen and Robert Tear; Nielsen's Fourth; Mahler's *Das klagende Lied*; and early Britten, including several first recordings of pieces such as the *Four French Songs* with Jill Gomez, *Young Apollo* with Peter Donohoe, *An American Overture* and *An Occasional Overture*. Many of these were prepared for by concert performances at the time of recording. (The Britten overtures, for instance, were heard in Birmingham, one of them conducted by John Carewe in the concerts he took over when Rattle's son Sacha was born, and the *Four French Songs* were slipped into a Cheltenham programme.)

Rattle's EMI producer for all the early recordings was John Willan, who later became managing director of the London Philharmonic Orchestra. Older than Rattle, he had been at the Royal Academy with him ('I was doing what was laughably called a postgraduate course') and is a good colleague and friend of his. He has observed Rattle from the beginning: 'Simon was always racing into the Academy canteen saying, "I've got the Duke's Hall for an hour, does anyone want to play Bruckner Seven?"'! It was seeing him conduct that put me off for good trying to do it myself.'

JOHN WILLAN [1987] I don't think Simon would mind me saying that we had a lot of problems with the first recording we did, which was *Pulcinella* with the Northern Sinfonia. He'd done a lot of conducting by then, but not in the studio, which is a very different thing. I was surprised, for example, by his inability to match the speed of one take with the next, or to remember exactly what he'd done half an hour ago. It was fine in a sense, because what he was wanting was to do it differently, but it made it awkward for us. Then there was a problem with one of the players, and eventually we had to give up and come back for another session later. But it all came out very well in the end, and I still listen to the record.

I did a *Planets* with Simon and the Philharmonia at Kingsway Hall, but I'm not sure that he ever liked it. That was typical record-company stuff: young star, got to do a popular piece. The orchestra played stunningly, of course, but I don't think it was technically very good from our point of view.

It's quite surprising that he wanted to make any records at this stage.
I don't think he did, really. And it was only because he was soon allowed to do the things he passionately wanted to do, like Mahler 10 and the Janáček *Glagolitic Mass*, that we got him into the studio at all. If EMI had gone on doing what they tend to do with young artists, and said, 'Now you listen to us, lad; make a Beethoven 7 and we can sell that,' then I think he wouldn't have stayed in the studio long.

It was a struggle to get that repertory through EMI. They weren't so worried about Mahler 10 because it hadn't been done properly before. It was a big thing for us, and they hyped it up and in fact it sold very well. But when we got on to things like the *Glagolitic Mass* [there were] a lot of problems. And that's just so upsetting and stupid because here's Simon, he's on television and so on, and you've got a real chance there *not* to do the standard repertory and have it compared yet again with the Karajan version.

Was EMI worried about his lack of international profile?
Yes, very. When I was there they were extremely concerned that he should – not my words at all – stop mucking about with a regional orchestra and get to the Berlin Philharmonic and all the other places who were desperate to have him. But Simon was always very firm about that, and he just said, 'What for?' There was no point for him. Records with Berlin or Amsterdam would have sold better, I suppose, but it's probably three times as expensive to go to Berlin as to go to Birmingham, so you'd have to sell three times as many records. Then you have to think in the long term of your relationship with the artist, which is what EMI eventually did. They realized that if Simon had such a very clear idea of what he wanted to do, they should

respect that if they wanted to be with him in ten or twenty years. The mistake with a young artist is to push him into the big-time circuit too soon.

Presumably Simon quickly became much more professional in the studio?
Oh yes, incredibly quickly, which is part of his strength. He picks up on things so rapidly. One impressive thing with the CBSO was that he knew very quickly what was possible for the orchestra. I remember I would say to him, 'It's not together there; are you worried about that?' And he would say, 'No, it's impossible, leave it.' Or if I said that the trumpet sounded a bit flat there, he'd just say, 'Have you tried to play it?' Simon is absolutely on the ball and he usually knows what's gone well. If you tell him over the phone that the trombones are too loud, he'll adjust it. But if he then comes in to listen to the take and finds that the trombones weren't too loud, he can be quite straightforward about it!

Some people have said that Simon's knowing what he wants does mean he can be very stubborn.
Oh, absolutely, he's incredibly stubborn. If he decides he wants a particular singer then that's the singer he'll have. So you make a straightforward choice: if you want to do that piece with Simon, you do it with that singer. And usually he's right. We did Mahler's *Das klagende Lied* in Birmingham Town Hall with Helena Döse, and Simon could tell I wasn't happy with the choice, but he would never explain. I just said, 'You're sure?' And he said, 'Yes.' And she was very good for that piece. He's pretty idiosyncratic about singers. I'm not saying he hasn't got a lot to learn, but he's smart.

When John Willan moved to the London Philharmonic, Rattle's records for EMI were made in collaboration with David Murray, who was previously a music producer for BBC Radio 3, and recently moved back to the BBC as Director of the BBC National Orchestra of Wales. He told me about the typical working methods of Rattle and the CBSO in the studio:

DAVID MURRAY [1987] He comes to a session with an incredibly precise idea of what he wants to do. He'll take suggestions, but more than once I've felt that it's us, the producer and the engineer, who are slowing things up and standing in the way of getting the thing done. For half an hour or so he'll warm up the orchestra and go through a few difficult bits while we balance and check things. Then we will do a test take of a section of the work to see if we agree on balance. Once he's made his comments and we've made our adjustments Simon will record a complete performance of the work, or at least a complete movement. Then he'll come in and listen to that, and people from the orchestra will come in too (which is very differ-ent from the usual thing with some orchestras, where mainly wind-players who are worried about their solos will come in and listen to a take). Then he'll go back, but he won't just do the bits that didn't work. He'll do another performance. And usually, as with *Petrushka*, that's the one that is the basis of the recording. Then we will do small patches for editing, but it is always better to do those small adjustments on the basis of a full performance rather than trying to stitch the whole thing together from this or that take. He hates that: he wants to get the feeling of a performance.

And does he change things a lot while the recording is happening?
They're mostly minor adjustments rather than anything radical, because the interpretations are already there and the orchestra now will have done a lot of performances of anything we record. But he is very realistic. He knows what happens at sessions, and when he comes in to listen to the final tapes you don't find him asking for some other mythical performance he and the orchestra never actually gave! And that also shows up in the way he runs the sessions. One of the most remarkable things about Simon is his ability to listen critically while he's conducting. Many conductors find this difficult, and because there isn't time to play back everything they rely on the producer. But at the end of a take Simon will tell me what went right or wrong from his point of view, and then will listen to my opinion of what we have to do. And he's absolutely open with the orchestra, so that they know what went well or badly, and he'll expect that after he's corrected it, it'll go right every time. They get better together all the time and the final 'com-plete' take is virtually always the master. It was like that with Sibelius 3. We'd done a performance and sorted out the difficult bits, but rather than leave it there Simon suggested we should put all the 'correction' takes back into context by doing another complete performance. And it was by far the best.

So is he realistic in what he asks for from the orchestra?
He's good at pacing them. Sometimes I think he overestimates what they'll be able to do: for *Turangalîla* he initially suggested just four sessions, but I insisted on five because we needed at least half a session for balancing, which is very complicated in that piece. But he knew which bits to do at the start of the session, or early in the morning, when everyone was relaxed and not too tense. And some movements we actually did on one take, with a couple of patches, because the orchestra was so much at home with it. In Mahler 2 each movement was done as a continuous whole, except for the finale which had to be split before the chorus section. But there too we were building on concerts they'd just done, and there were very few takes. And I

must say it was really thrilling, with all the atmosphere of a concert performance, unbelievably exciting. Even the tape editors got worked up about it!

The new element in Simon's relationship with EMI, at the time when the CBSO's recording activities were at their height, was the appointment of Peter Alward, and this was in the beginning not a very happy relationship. And at the same time there was an increasing concentration from the record companies generally on core repertory and a period of unwillingness to risk new things, which to Rattle was what recording was all about.

PETER ALWARD [2001] I became head of A&R in 1985, and I was actually rather young, rather green and certainly rather arrogant. I think I approached Simon in the wrong way. One assumes you would just say to an artist, 'We'd like you to record x,' and he will do it. That's not the way one works with Simon. At that time, although he was regarded as an incredibly talented conductor, there was a certain resistance from the Central European part of our company who looked rather askance at the CBSO and regarded it as something rather provincial. It was actually difficult in those days to make the records sell. So our relationship for a number of years wasn't the rosiest, and I largely blame myself.

By the start of the 1990s I think we understood one another. We had one dinner which was brilliantly arranged by Martin Campbell-White just to clear the air between us and the ground rules were that Simon would tell me exactly what he thought of me and I would tell Simon exactly what I thought of him, which is what happened. Since then everything has been wonderful and we collaborate very well indeed.

There was a moment when he said he would not renew his contract with EMI unless you recorded Nicholas Maw's Odyssey?
That's not quite true. It was blown up by the press into far more of a crisis than it actually was. He certainly put a lot of pressure on us to do it. We knew it wasn't going to sell and we were very cautious about committing. In the end it isn't a world bestseller, of course, but it's still in the catalogue. Simon is one of those rare people who will actually go on performing works he believes in, which helps an enormous amount, and he revived *Odyssey* as part of *Towards the Millennium*.

It was part of the bigger picture, which was that this was the tail end of the boom period for the CD when people felt that the central German repertory would be the most commercial thing for him to do and he quite rightly resisted that. He preferred to explore his own well-trodden paths, and he also resisted recording anything that he hadn't already done in a large number of concerts. Which is why the recordings that are made are so good, because the interpretations have matured over time.

When the CD boom stopped in the 1990s, and you had to persuade con-ductors to be realistic and make fewer records, how did Simon react?
He was the most sympathetic and co-operative and practical. First of all, he has never wanted to record too much. Second, I don't think money plays a huge amount in his thinking, and so the idea of losing some vast income had never been there and wasn't a factor. Nowadays conductors make their income from standing on the rostrum, and recordings come very far down the list. Simon is driven by the artistic vision and that is paramount. Of course he realizes now that the Berliners are going to want to see him bring-ing recording income to the orchestra. But I don't think that will be upper-most – as it was for instance with Karajan. In the boom years of the CD when we were all making too many recordings, people felt there was 'gold in them there hills', and we probably agreed rates and terms we are living to regret now. No one wants to pay people below the market rate, but the market rate has changed and we want to see a greater culture of risk-sharing. I certainly see my role in the next few years as trying to adjust to that situation.

So what will be the implications for you of recording with the Berlin orchestra?
Well, Simon is coming into the mainstream repertory but he is also coming to an orchestra that costs almost three times as much as the CBSO, and this represents for EMI a major increase in investment. Of course we are very happy to make this because we totally believe in him, but it is at a time when the market is not in its most stable state. Whether sales will increase to match the costs remains to be seen. [The 2000 recording of] Mahler 10 has done incredibly well and is in profit already, which is great, but I would be naïve to imagine that when we record *Gurrelieder* in 2001 the same thing will happen so quickly.

And what about the Berlin Philharmonic doing crossover projects like recording with the Scorpions [a German pop group who hired the Berlin Philharmonic to make a disc with them]?
I must and I will defend the Scorpions because although it caused an almighty stink in certain quarters it hasn't done the orchestra any harm. It's made money for them and for us and it helps us to do other things which otherwise maybe we wouldn't be able to afford to do. It enables me to afford *Gurrelieder*.

The confidential sales figures for Rattle's recordings reveal that a few extremely bankable products – Patrick Doyle's score for the Kenneth

Branagh film of *Henry V*, the Glyndebourne *Porgy and Bess* – bankroll much of the rest. But they also show what marketing and publicity effort can achieve, for the big push that EMI was able to make with Rattle in 1994 bore fruit in unusually high sales for the disc of Szymanowski's *Stabat Mater* and Third Symphony. This was a marvellous recording by any standards, but not necessarily an obvious popular success. Even the Mahler 2, which sold increasingly well after its awards, did not do as well as that Szymanowski disc in its first year. In line with the tail-off in CD sales once LP collections had been replaced, Rattle's back-catalogue sales fell during the later 1990s. By 1997 EMI was beginning to worry seriously that the amount of promotional time Rattle himself was willing to spend on his recordings failed to match the huge commitment EMI was now making to the CBSO.

Frustratingly, critical acclaim and commercial success never seemed to walk hand in hand, although good coverage, both in the papers and in the specialist realms of *Gramophone* magazine and later the broader *BBC Music Magazine*, certainly helped each of Rattle's recordings to sell several thousands a year rather than one or two thousand. Among some of the highly praised recordings with the CBSO over the following years were to be the Sibelius symphonies, though those recordings did not sell well until the cycle was collected in a mid-price box. The 'foot-tappingly irresistible' *Jazz Album* with Peter Donohoe did well but never became a popular hit. Elgar's *The Dream of Gerontius*, with John Mitchinson near the end of his career as Gerontius, was successful neither artistically nor in sales terms, and even other choral works Rattle did with great success in concert, including Haydn's *Creation*, fared less well on record. Stravinsky's *Petrushka*, praised for its 'countless fresh observations of orchestral detail', sold poorly.

In the later 1980s and even in the more difficult 1990s Rattle's recording output, however, swept along with almost evangelical fervour. There was innovative Haydn making the CBSO sound as fresh as if they were playing on period instruments: 'I hope that Rattle and his orchestra will continue to give us recordings of Haydn symphonies as long as performances on modern instruments remain legal . . . Joyous, humane readings, gamely, often brilliantly executed by the CBSO bear witness to an exceptionally fresh, penetrating musical vision,' wrote Richard Wigmore. There was a finely detailed Elgar *Falstaff*, 'the most meticulously prepared and subtly blended *Falstaff* ever committed to disc, keen intellect and almost fanatical fidelity to the letter of the score', according to

Michael Kennedy. There were the contemporary composers for whom Rattle argued so hard: Nicholas Maw's *Odyssey*, 'simply staggering in its conviction and authority, exceptionally distinguished'; a Mark-Anthony Turnage disc, 'a stunning collection showing that Turnage is a talent of major importance'; and more recently – released just at the time of the Berlin vote – Thomas Adès, whose *Asyla* has been one of the most frequently performed of the Rattle–CBSO commissions, now taken up by other conductors.

Some of Rattle's most successful recordings were his reinterpretations of the Second Viennese School: in the Berg, Schoenberg and Webern disc, wrote Michael Oliver in *Gramophone*, 'the slight feeling of overcompensating by overstating lyricism and drama, the fly in the ointment of Levine's sumptuous recording on DG, is almost wholly absent from Rattle's . . . Rattle's lyricism, tender and at times poignant though it is, is cooler than Karajan's or Levine's and runs no risk of the heaviness that spoils the latter's performances.'

It was in the bigger repertory that Rattle's recordings were not so wholeheartedly received: *Gramophone*'s comment that in Rattle's ultra-quiet opening of Ravel's *Daphnis et Chloë* (also a vivid memory from the opening of Birmingham's Symphony Hall) there was too great a feeling of calculation was a criticism that was to recur. Bruckner 7 sounded to Stephen Johnson as if it emphasized the big sweep at the expense of the human. This was an interesting tension in Rattle's work; David Gutman remarked of the Mahler 3 recording on 'some edgy individualistic effects that sound just a little self-conscious on repetition, speeding through the final bars . . . a self-conscious manipulation of texture and irresistible forward thrust. He is not quite so good at serenity.' In Mahler 1 David Gutman again felt 'a lack of spontaneity evident here, with Rattle as the arch-manipulator, holding back, reluctant to let rip'. Then Mahler 4 arrived in 1998, stimulating and unusual, especially in the opening bars, where the usual tempo relationships were reversed, perhaps due to some thoughts of Berthold Goldschmidt.

A Grainger miscellany followed, full of good things, including ravishing orchestrations of Debussy and Ravel, then Szymanowski's *King Roger*, and Bernstein's *Wonderful Town*. The new Mahler 10 from Berlin, recorded live after Rattle had been elected, was a milestone that created a real event in the recording world; it won Record of the Year from *Gramophone* and then a Grammy in the United States, so immediately broke through to a wider public. The next Berlin recording, of Schoenberg's *Gurrelieder*, also created a sensation when it was released early in 2002, with virtually unanimous reviews praising the performance, though there were some reservations about the crowded acoustic of the Philharmonie. (Because of the events of September 11, the intended soprano soloist was unable to travel from America; there was a rapid substitution for the concerts, but for the recordings, Karita Mattila's voice was added later to superb effect.) Now the plan is to record Mahler's Fifth at Rattle's initial concerts with the Berlin Philharmonic, and rush-release it in the autumn of 2002.

Rattle's attitude to live recording has shifted subtly over the years. In the wake of the experience of *Odyssey* he was very positive to Edward Seckerson in *BBC Music Magazine*: 'When there was actually a patch of forty minutes that didn't require retakes – can you imagine! – then I realized . . . several of the brass-players told me that they could never have achieved those results under studio conditions . . . You can feel an audience's involvement or lack of it immediately.'

However Mozart's *Così fan tutte*, recorded live with audience noise and laughter, was not nearly so well received, even though the concerts had been a roaring success. A few years later, in an interesting conversation for *Gramophone* with Rob Cowan and Imogen Cooper, Rattle added some thoughts on the increasing attraction of live recordings, about which he was now a little sceptical:

> One needs to play differently for microphones . . . the microphone is not the human ear. I often prefer live recordings because there's a certain going-for-broke quality about them, but it's like spying into someone's private diary. These things aren't necessarily meant to be repeated. Krystian Zimerman told me recently that he spent the last two or three years recording every concert he played in case it went really well! He'd listen to each one and tie himself up in knots.

A few years after that, Rattle's attitude has changed again, maybe because the whole idea of recordings as permanent or even repeatable is now fading a little. In 2001 he thought about the future media age for an organization such as the Berlin Philharmonic:

> I may be proved wrong, but I don't think there will be record companies in ten years' time any more than there will be Blockbuster video stores. Why would you go down to the store when everything is available on your wall

and you can dial up via the Internet the latest thing live? We'll have got beyond little people staring at computer screens, this will be big, and I think it will be live performance. What people will do is say, 'Hey, the Chicago Symphony playing Bruckner with Barenboim. I can't miss this.' And they will want to get it. In Germany there will be that thirst for knowledge around it as well, because they are slightly ashamed that they don't know everything. Here there's not quite the same feeling of shame but there is thirst for knowledge.

David Puttnam said to me that every artistic institution should be completely open by video link to every school in the country at least once a month, just so people can see what is going on. What is the artistic process? How does it happen?

We'll have to shout hard to be heard and to survive. But in the end I believe it will drive people back to live performance because that is where the real experience is.

II

Small Screen

It was Humphrey Burton, then running music for television at the BBC, who met Rattle after the John Player Award, and first realized that the young conductor might be ideal televisual material. He suggested various projects to him, though none in the end materialized. One of them was a gargantuan plan by producer Herbert Chappell for a series called *The Glory of Music* to be presented by Rattle. This was to consist of thirteen two-hour programmes of documentary and performance, taking in everything from Gregorian chant to punk rock, interviewing artists, watching them rehearse, and finally showing them perform. But in the end Rattle couldn't face the style of the presentation. The pilot ran: 'The glory of music is the simple fact that we can all share it . . . There are very few things that can match the excitement and the sheer thrill of listening to great music. And it's those qualities I want to communicate to you in this new television series.' But it was the producer Barrie Gavin who was to become Rattle's closest collaborator in making television programmes.

The local independent television station in Birmingham, Central TV (formerly ATV), was during the 1980s extremely supportive of the CBSO and Rattle, and under producer Jim Berrow they mounted some major projects. One of Rattle's earliest television films was a documentary for ATV, made very early in the Birmingham period, about the performance of *Porgy and Bess* that the CBSO mounted in 1981. This programme stirred up controversy locally because he was outspoken about certain aspects of the orchestra's work, about how poorly they were paid, and he questioned whether Birmingham really deserved them. Subsequently he has tended to confine his comments to the works in hand. Outstanding among the Central TV films was a documentary on Elgar that juxtaposed biographers talking about the more elusive aspects of Elgar's personality with some magnificent performances of his music, including Alexander Baillie playing the Cello Concerto.

The Barrie Gavin–Simon Rattle partnership then attempted something more ambitious musically: a four-part series for BBC2 of performance and discussion about the music of 1911. The programmes were based around two favourite Rattle pieces, Mahler's Tenth Symphony and Sibelius's Fourth, each of which had a programme to itself. The last programme was a straight performance of Mahler's Tenth, but the first was the most ambitious: a panorama of the music of 1911, bringing together all sorts of pieces written in that year, and juxtaposing them with paintings of the period. It was an extremely ingenious programme which captured a good deal of interest, though some felt that the approach was too kaleidoscopic and not sufficiently explanatory.

But the kaleidoscopic approach pleased Barrie Gavin, who set about structuring the next series he conceived with Rattle in the same way. *From East to West*, 'dreamt up in a Chinese restaurant', was an exploration of the impact of the East and its music on Western culture. It grew out of a conversation about Debussy but was quickly extended to include Mahler's Eastern-influenced *Das Lied von der Erde*. That work became the focus of a major documentary with the Mahler scholar Donald Mitchell and a complete performance recorded at the 1985 BBC Proms with Jessye Norman and Jon Vickers.

The most original programme in the series was the first, an uninterrupted sequence of music and images pointing up all sorts of connections between the music of the East and that of Western composers as diverse as Ravel, Debussy, Steve Reich, Holst, Messiaen, David Matthews, Koechlin and Henry Cowell, returning at the close to Ravel's evocation of *Asie* with which it started. A memorable sequence had split screens on which Rattle simultaneously conducted the five orchestral groups featured in one movement of Nielsen's music for *Aladdin*.

The second programme was very different: an exploration of the sound world of Toru Takemitsu, whose music Rattle had performed for the Aldeburgh Festival when Takemitsu was composer-in-residence there. It featured a single work, *A Flock Descends into the Pentagonal Garden*, which Rattle and the CBSO would bring to the BBC Proms in 1987. This was beautifully organized by Gavin into 'thirteen steps around Toru Takemitsu', in which different aspects of his work were matched with the corresponding sections of the piece.

BARRIE GAVIN It's a Mickey Rooney–Judy Garland act, though I won't tell you which is which! 'Let's do the show right here' – that sort of thing. Simon is incredibly practical and he thinks fast. He's good at deciding – 'OK, let's do it' – and then getting his players to respond. And he's able to communicate the enthusiasm. He's so stimulating to plan things with, like the first *From East to West* programme, where we chipped in with all our favourite pieces and then created the patchwork; that's a very enjoyable aspect of working with him. For television, I also need to have absolute confidence that a conductor will produce the goods on time. With everything there is riding on it, there's no point having a conductor who says he needs an hour to rehearse and three and a half hours later you're still waiting. Of course, Simon is absolutely efficient and he knows exactly what's needed.

How did it all start?
There was a meeting in 1981 summoned by Humphrey Burton in Oxford where Simon had gone to give himself a year's education. We went to an extremely expensive and not very good French restaurant and Humphrey said, 'We want you to be the André Previn of the 1980s.' And Simon, with a cherubic smile, said, 'I think I'd rather be the Simon Rattle of the 1980s.' Even then it was clear that he was a phenomenal communicator and a most attractive personality who had to be on the screen. There was a certain amount of pressure about being audience-friendly and the suggestion was we should do *The Planets*. 'Not a good idea,' Simon said. 'I made a record of it which isn't very good and I don't really like the piece and I don't want to tackle it again. I think I could do other things more interestingly.' So that was that.

What worked with him as an idea?
The first major successful idea we came up with was the idea of 1911, which was perhaps a godfather to *Towards the Millennium*. We were looking for a time when you could talk about all the artistic cross-currents that happened at the same time and 1911 was incredibly rich in them; that

became the genesis of the idea. The things were evolved with remarkable speed. It was clear Simon would want to do something big about Mahler 10, and also about Sibelius 4. So there was the project: a film about the cross-currents, with two more films on single works and a performance of Mahler 10.

How interested was he in television?
He wasn't very interested in television as such, and why should he be? He always said the important things were concerts, records, TV – in that order. He was keen to do it and he did it in a more striking way than I think any other conductor–presenter I'd come across, and that includes the very famous names like Bernstein because he did it without any egocentricity. In fact the problem was in the other direction – he was sometimes too diffident about having an opinion: 'I'm too young to tell people about these things.' But of course, having said he had nothing at all to say, he'd breeze in and give you forty-five minutes that were absolutely compelling.

He did have some odd ideas, which I suppose were to do with not wanting television to trivialize. For example, that there should never be speaking over the music. That's fine in principle but there are moments in the making of documentaries where you have to have certain kinds of elision. Music will drop away and come back. You can't do a film so that the music stops and then someone speaks and then the music starts again. That would be a very bumpy and stuttery sort of programme rhythm. So these things he came to terms with, I think, as we went along.

He never seemed quite happy talking to the camera . . .
No, he didn't. He looked a little uneasy and he realized it. People in television thought the programmes weren't really his own unless he talked to the camera – an absurd notion! Personally, I think that if what people say is interesting, whether they're facing the camera or not, it's of no consequence. But the bosses were obsessed with authoritative statements, so that was why *From East to West* had tacked-on introductions by Simon and he talked very *sotto voce*. They were dreadful. And of course that was a problem that was endlessly discussed with *Leaving Home* and eventually he talked to camera and to the producer Sue Knussen through a system of mirrors! It certainly worked better than what I had achieved previously.

How involved would he get?
He gave an interview once saying that we had a symbiotic relationship. I had to rush to a dictionary in case I had to sue him for that, but it turned out that it was a scientific term that described it pretty well. The choice of repertory and so on was absolutely vital and that was his decision. But

from then on all the stuff that directors love he found pretty boring, and it was my job to make the processes of actually recording the music as swift, efficient and painless as possible.

I have worked with a few conductors now and I don't think I have met anyone who has on the one hand an almost animal-like ability to get to the core of something – the sort of really inexplicable way in which he knows what Mahler should sound like or Janáček should sound like – and on the other hand a phenomenal ear that really hears what's going on. Everyone talks about Boulez's ears or Knussen's ears, and they are right, but Simon's are just as acute, and he has an absolute discipline about preparation. He will not take on a piece until he's ready to do it.

You were also involved in Simon's major Channel 4 programme on twentieth-century music, Leaving Home.

Leaving Home was for me very turbulent. There was such pressure, countless Channel 4 people talking about the mood and the style and the kind of nineties optimism we wanted and what colour shirt he should wear. There was a problem in that one director could not do it all and in fact we should maybe have had more than the three we had. A seven-part series is a phenomenal amount of work, not simply in front of the orchestra, but beforehand and afterwards for many months. Not that there was a moment when it was fraught with him or the orchestra. It was just the tension inherent in the set-up. It won a major prize. I was, shall we say, pleasantly surprised.

I've worked with him thirty-six times, including Proms and concerts and everything, and we have a wonderful working relationship.

When Rattle was asked by Melvyn Bragg to put together a history of twentieth-century music for Channel 4, he was initially daunted, and felt it would be impossible in less than twenty hours of television: 'Music is both a blessing and curse, in that it cannot be taken in at a glance.' So they both compromised, Bragg confining the story to orchestral music, and Rattle excluding many favourite composers and pieces whose cause he had championed over the previous years: 'With just seven programmes, it was important to concentrate on music that somehow drove the century forward, to make a narrative, a journey of the series, to encourage as many people as possible to join the expedition. If I aspired to be anyone in that, it was David Attenborough! TV is a tricky medium for music, but there is so much you can do in associating it with other visual images. You can help people hear if you can help answer the inevitable question, "Why does it sound like that?"'

As Rattle put it, '*Leaving Home* is the metaphor for a time in which all the certainties, be they social, political or artistic, have migrated. Music left behind the sameness of tonality and rhythm.' The original idea had been, as usual in these circumstances, extremely ambitious, with location filming in Vienna, Berlin and the great European centres. There was a projected programme called *The Borrowers*, with Bartók using folk music and Tippett using spirituals. Interviewees were to range from Gruber to Boulez and Takemitsu, Henze to Turnage. The final scheme was reduced from eight to seven programmes, and had to be produced with considerable discipline, because there were only two periods during which the orchestra would record the material for all the programmes. The problem of television assuming it could fill all Rattle's free time with work on the series also surfaced.

The crucial linchpin here turned out to be Sue Knussen, an experienced TV producer who became the link to Rattle in both the writing and the delivery of the material. She had previously worked on Bernstein's televised Norton Lectures, so there wasn't much she didn't know about television and temperament.

The final scheme for the project was defined by seven titles and seven groups of music:

Dancing on a Volcano
'The idea of moving away from tonality was not the destruction of some time-honoured law but a way of moving forward towards a new type of strength.'
Mahler 7, Strauss *Elektra*, Berg Violin Concerto, Schoenberg *Erwartung*

Rhythm
'Rhythm has long seemed something organic and regular, not to be meddled with. But in the twentieth century everything was to be questioned and all certainties were up for grabs.'
Stravinsky *The Rite of Spring*, Boulez *Rituel in memoriam Bruno Maderna*, Messiaen *Turangalîla Symphony*

Colour
'The idea that colour could be a form in itself must have seemed at the least slightly sinful, and at worst desperately revolutionary.'
Stravinsky *The Firebird*, Debussy *Jeux*, Messiaen *Et exspecto resurrectionem mortuorum*, Takemitsu *Dream/Window*

Three Journeys through Dark Landscapes
'Music can tell truths that written in words would have cost the authors their lives.'
Messiaen *Quartet for the End of Time*, Bartók *Duke Bluebeard's Castle*, Shostakovich 14, Lutosławski 3

The American Way
'American music is essentially a dialogue between cultures thrown together very fast. If European classical music is a slow marinated casserole, then American music is a fast, brilliant stir-fry.'
Gershwin *Porgy and Bess* and *Rhapsody in Blue*, Ives *Decoration Day*, Bernstein *West Side Story*

After the Wake
'In 1945 the war had spun the world on its axis and nothing could be the same again. But to survive at all, artists had first to bear witness to what had happened and to mourn what was lost for ever.'
Strauss *Four Last Songs*, Schoenberg *A Survivor from Warsaw*, Stockhausen *Gruppen*

Music Now
'At the end of the century's long journey, in happy absence of schools and dogmas, the myriad different styles and colours have emerged like rainbows after a storm.'
Hans Werner Henze Symphony no. 8, Mark-Anthony Turnage *Drowned Out*, Knussen *Flourish with Fireworks*

SUE KNUSSEN There were a lot of challenges, but the Simon part of *Leaving Home* was the totally positive part. The project was cooked up by Melvyn Bragg, who then got Michael Grade to commission it for Channel 4. Grade took the bold decision to allocate the prime-time slot and Melvyn kept saying that he wanted a history of twentieth-century music. But the first time Simon and I got together we agreed that there was no way we could do an entire history of twentieth-century music with a symphony orchestra. After all, so many of the significant landmarks are not orchestral. We thought it was dangerous to try to be comprehensive in seven hours with a symphony orchestra.

So I said to Simon that what will make it really interesting is if it's very personal and it's very much generated by you. But I think he felt the heavy responsibility of doing a series like this and a bit worried that it might be too personal. He was saying, 'We have to do this piece and we should do that composer,' and I had to keep saying to him that he should do any given piece only if it had a significance for him, in which case we'd find a way to fit it in the format.

The seven programmes were broadly chronological but it was thematically arranged and though we ended up in the present we started with the *Tristan* chord and went forward from there. The directors would make their own suggestions but it seemed important that Simon chose and ordered the repertory. We covered excerpts from about thirty-seven pieces in two periods and the logistics of actually recording that amount of music in what you can imagine was a very limited amount of time were horrendous. Simon was extraordinary in the way that he would switch across wildly different styles and repertories and get the band to change with him. That wasn't observed by many people but it was truly impressive.

Was he confident with writing it or did you do that?
What happened was that his confidence developed as we went through the thing. It started out with us talking and making broad outlines. He would then talk to me and we actually filmed it with me sitting underneath the camera so he could talk to me and it looked as if he was talking to the camera. But as we went along he gradually realized that through this series he was making an important statement that he wanted to be in control of – not in a control-freak way, but just to own it. And to make sure he was saying what he wanted to say. So he started writing more and he would memorize it just page by page. At the end we went back and re-recorded the first programme in this way.

He was so aware of his responsibility, it was very hard to get him to lighten up his tone. What he says is so metaphorically alive, and that needs to be done with a light touch. I would just make faces at him, anything to get him to lighten up. I was trying to get it a little more conversational, but he just felt the weight of it and that came out in the pacing. He's so good when he is very casual but in this case he really didn't want to be casual about it. It would be a century or two before a series of this size would be done again!

Leaving Home was always going to be a difficult concept to sell to the viewing public, so Channel 4 went down a well-trodden route and courted controversy on the choices of composers included in the series. 'RATTLE THROWS OUT BRITISH FAVOURITES', shouted *The Sunday Times* news pages helpfully, in one of those artificially fermented arguments beloved of arts journalists. 'Some of Britain's best-loved composers, including Edward Elgar and Sir William Walton, have been excluded from a history of twentieth-century music because they were not progressive enough. The decision by Sir Simon Rattle, the celebrated conductor, has shocked some musicians, who accuse him of self-indulgence and snobbery.' Actually the only criticisms that could be found were from bookseller Tim Waterstone, *parti pris* as chairman of the Elgar Foundation, who said he was 'horrified' there was no Elgar in the series – 'perhaps he is too popular for Sir Simon' – and one-time Beecham assistant and Lottery rent-a-quote Denis Vaughan who defended Walton as creating 'a style of choral music that has gone around the world. What is Rattle thinking?' One unnamed record producer suggested that 'when a charismatic character like Rattle sets out his opinions through television, it creates the orthodoxy for the next few years. It could create a benchmark of who is in and who is out, which will influence concerts promoters and radio programmers alike.'

It was hardly as if Rattle had not performed the music of Elgar, Tippett and Walton in his lifetime. He was telling a story, and the story was one that ranged far and wide without needing to include them. Did he sacrifice a broad appeal to the viewing public to the strong coherence of his theme? In the end, *Leaving Home* made less impact than it might have done had he started from more of the music his audience already knew.

After *Leaving Home* there have been two *South Bank Show*s on composers Simon Holt and Judith Weir, following the preparation of the new works they wrote for the final year of *Towards the Millennium*, providing excellent TV exposure for new British music and the CBSO. But the final television extravaganza of the twentieth century in which Rattle participated was the BBC2/Radio 3 Millennium Concert in December 1999, which came at the climax of the Radio 3 series *Sounding the Millennium*. This concert, devised jointly by BBC TV and Radio 3, was mounted in the historic space of Ely Cathedral under its famous octagon. It culminated in Beethoven's Ninth Symphony, but also brought together Haydn's *Te Deum*, Oliver Knussen's *Two Organa* (featuring the BCMG), and the première of a new work by Mark-Anthony Turnage, *About Time*, which united the forces of the BCMG with those of the Orchestra of the Age of Enlightenment for the first time ever in a BBC commission. Turnage began his piece when he was in Japan: 'I felt strangely unsettled and disturbed by a mini-earthquake that occurred during my visit. The inspiration, or rather the actual music, came to me in a dream. Nothing like that has happened to me before or since . . . '

As Fiona Maddocks reported in the *Observer*, the concert was an apt celebration of centuries of music-making ... The music in this grandly conceived event, complete with two ensembles and two choirs, did its own job of persuasion. Both contemporary works were of beguiling beauty, framed by Haydn's vigorous *Te Deum* and the Ninth Symphony. With *About Time*, Mark-Anthony Turnage has produced a twelve-minute work of aural radiance and airy vitality, grasping not only the millennial theme but the challenge of the building too.

CHAPTER SEVEN

'On the whole I'm in favour of monogamy'
Around the World in the 1980s

Rattle in the Royal Albert Hall, preparing for an early appearance at the Proms

I
London's Many Orchestras

October 1986. The London Sinfonietta's Britten–Tippett Festival has been, until now, a little patchy – some low-voltage concerts, and some low attendances. But the final concert in the Queen Elizabeth Hall is packed to the doors and provides some quite exceptional music-making. The tension in the hall is electric, and the atmosphere in the green room afterwards is ecstatic. The pianist Paul Crossley sums it up when he says to Rattle, 'Congratulations! We were hearing world premières. They really sounded like first performances!' In the typically long and generous second half of the concert were Tippett's *Ritual Dances* from *The Midsummer Marriage*, Britten's early *Four French Songs* sung by Jill Gomez, and then the famous *Young Person's Guide to the Orchestra*, which can scarcely ever have sounded so fresh. There is a vast throng of people waiting to see Rattle – including, it's reassuring to note, several members of the Sinfonietta who haven't just packed their bags and fled at the final chord but have waited to thank the conductor for an exhilarating evening.

'Phew!' exclaims Rattle. 'I was very depressed this morning thinking, "Oh, there's far too much to get through today." Tippett's so annoying: you rehearse and rehearse the difficult bits and in the concert they still sound awful, and the simple bits take no trouble and they sound just wonderful. There's still one bit in between two of the *Ritual Dances* where I really haven't a clue what's going on.' But it's the Britten *Guide* that has got people worked up: 'One of the most exciting concerts I've ever been to,' says the composer David Matthews. Certainly the fugue in the Britten raced away as never before, and as usual it's John Carewe who has observed the occasion most precisely. Over a crowd of well-wishers, he shouts to Simon, 'I heard you speed up in the fugato and you should have seen the look on the faces of the string-players when they realized how fast it was going!' Rattle ripostes, '*They* went that fast so I thought, "Sod it, it's your fault, I'm not going to slow it down!"'

It is this sort of electrifying, unpredictable partnership that made Rattle and the Sinfonietta such an exciting combination in the 1980s. He felt able to tackle almost anything with them, and the only reservation he came near to expressing about their playing was: 'They don't yet play Mozart as well as they play Stravinsky.' Rattle became a close friend and collaborator of the Sinfonietta's artistic director, Michael Vyner, until Vyner's untimely death in 1989, and together they cooked up some of the most stimulating brews in London's music-making in the 1980s. There was a sequence of BBC Proms; there were Rattle's contributions to regular Sinfonietta series and the Sinfonietta's contribution to Rattle's three South Bank Summer Music series. It was, for too short a time, a great creative partnership.

Perhaps the most characteristic Rattle–Sinfonietta collaboration was the Bean Feast of April 1985: 'knocking around favourite things without any attempt to make a theme', as Rattle put it at the time. 'We have pieces I wanted to hear the Sinfonietta play or works that have proved popular in the past. Most of the programming in London is so conservative that it's deeply depressing.' In *The Times*, Stephen Pettitt was rather dubious:

> First they lure crowds by creating a festival atmosphere, with the help of good publicity and puppetry and folk music in the foyer. Then they play easily palatable music by composers like Britten, Ravel, Weill and Gershwin, making sure that the programme tells everyone that this really is twentieth-century music in the hope that people will thus be encouraged to return to try things more adventurous another time.

Put that way it seemed a rather good idea! The main events included a wild staging of Weill's *Mahagonny Songspiel* by David Alden, and a more restrained one of Falla's *Master Peter's Puppet Show*. The final concert brought together jazz-inspired pieces: Milhaud's *La création du monde*, Stravinsky's *Ebony Concerto*, Gershwin's *Rhapsody in Blue* in its original arrangement for the Paul Whiteman Band, and song arrangements by Whiteman himself.

Almost two years later, in the first week of 1987, this programme formed the basis of the long-delayed first recording for EMI by Rattle and the Sinfonietta. Rattle conducted part of the London Sinfonietta's huge day-long birthday concert in 1988. ('After six and a half hours,' reported the *Daily Telegraph*, 'the jazz fun began at 9.40 p.m., almost an hour later than intended, but who cared when this was a celebration of such an all-consuming achievement . . . Simon Rattle's ebullient readings demonstrated the Sinfonietta's welcome eclecticism.') Together, Rattle and Vyner thought up the concept of *Towards the Millennium* (see chapter 8), and there was a collaboration with the group throughout the decade-long project, but Rattle's own relationship with the Sinfonietta became less close after Michael Vyner's tragic death, as the importance of the new Birmingham Contemporary Music Group grew in his life.

MICHAEL VYNER [1987] In 1974 I was rung up by Martin Campbell-White, who was on our board, to say that he'd come across this very talented boy, and Tony Pay also mentioned him to me about the same time as someone who was amazingly bright. I went along to hear him do the Ravel and Stravinsky double bill at the Royal Academy and all the drawbacks were those of a young person – lack of experience, lack of technique – but it was clear he knew exactly what he wanted, and he didn't want what everyone else wanted. Simon's *Pulcinella* was quite unusual: most people start with a sharp, pointed, neo-classical sound, but Simon's was smooth and elegant and *legato* – very original. He had a long way to go but it was obvious he would get there. He had a wonderful manner, a lovely smile, and if I'd had my violin under my arm I would have wanted to play for him.

Initially did you suggest programmes to him?
In the early days there were things I wanted to interest him in, but it soon became clear that he had a very definite mind of his own. What actually happened was that I would say to him, 'Could we have the Schoenberg Chamber Symphony in this programme?' And there would be a long pause – you know how difficult it is sometimes to work out what he's thinking – and either he would dismiss it out of hand and you'd start again or there would be another pause and then he'd produce some complete programme scheme which worked perfectly. He was very astute and planned very carefully: he would do pieces in Scotland or Liverpool and then bring them to us in the Queen Elizabeth Hall knowing them extremely well. It gave him great pleasure to plan to do things that were unusual or ought to be heard more often – like taking up Henze 7 – and his tastes are very strong. He has tastes as catholic as any conductor I know, but his dislikes are very strong too. If he believes in a work then he will insist. It was Simon who said to Claudio Abbado when we did a concert in the 'Mahler, Vienna . . . ' series that he wanted to do Alexander Goehr's *Little Symphony*. Most people might be slightly scared of forcing something on Abbado and would give up the idea because they wanted to keep in with him, but Simon just doesn't have to worry about that sort of thing, and in the end it was accepted.

So how did you plan programmes?
Simon isn't the sort of chap who will take fifteen lunches off you while ideas gradually work their way through. One cup of tea and perhaps a serious dinner and he'll have produced a week of programmes. Some of the things we've done together have been very much his idea: the Busotti *Rara Requiem*, which Ellie, who knows the repertory from at least 1400 to the present, was keen on, they talked me into doing. But he is such a wonderful suggester of programmes and builder of programmes that we could work together happily doing that for ever.

Have you seen his skills change and improve?
Oh yes. In the beginning the performances were always good. Whatever the

drawbacks from his lack of experience, they were still wonderful. But now he has become so much better a trainer of musicians, and Birmingham is the result. He knows what he wants, very clearly, but I think he's more willing to take what comes from a player and use that too. It takes two to tango: if Simon likes something he hears from a player he'll keep it and use it. He likes music a lot and he likes people a lot, and that is what gives his music-making such amazing communicativeness. When he steps on that stage and smiles he's got the audience there where he wants them, and he can use that in a completely musical way. He's a popularizer in the best sense of the word: he really wants to get through his enthusiasm about twentieth-century music.

Do you wonder what he'll do in the future?
The things I wonder about him are: Why does he never lose his temper? Why is he always so thorough? Why does he never let anything go? Why does he always buy his own cup of coffee at rehearsals and probably one for the players as well? Why does he go on working so hard? Those are the sort of questions about him. He'll go on helping composers and interesting audiences in Henze and Haydn. I do think he's got to do less, otherwise he'll work himself to death. But the thing is that I don't think the future for him will necessarily be drastically different: it'll just be a slow process of expansion.

Rattle's relationships with the London symphony orchestras have always been ambivalent: he had a Philharmonia period, a London Philharmonic period, and now appears to be closest to the London Symphony Orchestra. But he has never been committed to any of them, nor has he felt entirely comfortable with the conditions they expect or the lack of permanence they offer.

The Philharmonia, in the days when it was still the New Philharmonia, was the first London symphony orchestra to engage Simon Rattle and present him in the Festival Hall. That was thanks to the enthusiasm of the then chairman, Basil Tschaikov, and after the success of Rattle's début concert with them in 1976 there were immediately plans for more concerts, and particularly for recordings for EMI. Holst's *Planets* followed in 1977, but this was neither a piece nor a performance on which Rattle was very keen. There were reservations from the critics about some performances at this time: of Ravel's *Daphnis et Chloë* in the same Festival Hall concert Paul Griffiths wrote in *The Times*, 'The score is a long way from the Straussian opulence which Mr Rattle pressed on it.' One early Philharmonia project, undertaken when Gavin Henderson arrived as general manager in 1975, was the forging of a link with one of London's commercial radio stations, Capital Radio, which had an obligation in those far-off days to provide some live orchestral music and was keen to use the Philharmonia with Rattle for this purpose.

The event that drew most attention to Rattle's continuing work with the orchestra was, however, the long-awaited première of Peter Maxwell Davies's First Symphony in February 1978. (It had been commissioned some five years earlier.) Rattle was surprised to be asked to undertake the piece and described it as 'just about playable' but 'quite horrifically, quite cosmically difficult . . . It's not all pleasant music – part of the last movement is unbelievably violent . . . It's one of those works that scream from the page that it will still be played fifty years from now.' He gave a remarkably assured première (partly thanks to preparing the work with the BBC Scottish Symphony Orchestra) which received good notices everywhere: 'Simon Rattle did a masterly job conducting the Philharmonia Orchestra, taxed to the limit in each movement' (Edward Greenfield, *Guardian*); 'Simon Rattle conducted with evident skill and enthusiasm, and, far from exhausted by the experience, he and the orchestra returned refreshed to give us another hour-long symphony, Mahler's *Song of the Earth*, in a performance of considerable authority and touching delicacy' (David Cairns, *The Sunday Times*). It was impossible to tour the performance, and Henderson estimated that the subsidy per seat required to prepare the single Festival Hall performance was £150! However, it was subsequently recorded, and there was a BBC Prom performance as well as a foreign hearing at the Flanders Festival. Rattle took the orchestra to the Edinburgh Festival in 1979, conducting alongside Muti and accompanying Sir Clifford Curzon; all the season's concerts went well, and they culminated in a riveting Janáček *Glagolitic Mass* the following June.

While Gavin Henderson was manager of the Philharmonia he considered asking Rattle to become an associate conductor of the orchestra, as Andrew Davis had been. But the plan ran into problems with the principal conductor, Riccardo Muti, who was not in favour of extra appointments when Lorin Maazel, whom he regarded coolly, was principal guest conductor; the plan was quietly shelved. Gavin Henderson moved on and subsequently became artistic director of the Brighton Festival, where he regularly collaborated with Rattle and put on two of the CBSO's finest concerts in 1986. Rattle was eventually offered an arrangement with the Philharmonia when in 1979 the new general manager, Christopher Bishop – already a fan of Rattle's through his previous work for EMI – took over and negotiated an arrangement. The following year they signed an agreement, with no title attached, under which Rattle would work with the Philharmonia exclusively of the other London symphony orchestras for the following five years. It fitted in well with Birmingham and was welcome to Rattle, but any hope that it would produce extra EMI recordings for the orchestra soon dried up as Rattle did more and more of his recording work with the CBSO alone. In the end it led nowhere.

At this time, too, the Philharmonia decided to respond to the Arts Council's frequent accusation that the London orchestras did too little for contemporary music. It established a *Music of Today* series which featured open rehearsals and discussions; Rattle was an obvious choice as conductor. Along with Oliver Knussen (who at that time enjoyed the largely honorary title of the Philharmonia's composer-in-residence) and the critic and composer Bayan Northcott, Rattle formed part of the think-tank that chose the projects, and he conducted a couple of the concerts in the next two seasons. David Matthews' Second Symphony was rehearsed and performed in one such concert. Rattle was also in charge of the Philharmonia's contribution to the Arts Council's own series, *Music of Eight Decades*, giving the première of Maxwell Davies's *Black Pentecost*, a less successful offshoot of the First Symphony. Conflicts over the casting of this led to a cooling off between Rattle and the composer, and there have been few if any Maxwell Davies performances from Rattle since.

All these one-off concerts were enjoyable up to a point, but Rattle felt frustrated by the lack of continuity and connection between the various parts of his Philharmonia work. The chance to create something more coherent – and to set a whole new fashion for London concert planning which was to be of immense significance – came almost by accident in 1984.

SIMON RATTLE The Philharmonia had a tour of Spain planned, and it fell through. So one day when I was rehearsing, Chris Bishop came up to me and said, 'We've got this time and some dates free. Why don't we do a series of concerts at the Festival Hall, and add in a couple at the Queen Elizabeth Hall, with a theme? You think about it.' So in my bath that afternoon I dreamed up this collection of Mahler and Strauss and the Second Viennese School with all my favourite pieces in it, and I thought they would soon shoot it down. It was a marvellous opportunity, which you don't often get in London, to put together concerts that really make sense. Surprisingly they liked it, and some of the players like the trumpeter John Wallace said, 'We just must do this.'

CHRISTOPHER BISHOP It is typical of Simon that when I said, 'Can you let me have a few ideas for a possible series?' (and usually with a conductor you're lucky if the ideas turn up ever) virtually by return of post, on a filthy piece of paper which I've kept – this one was really historic – there came a scheme that was absolutely perfect and we did it virtually without a change. (In the end Simon couldn't face doing the Clinton Carpenter completion of Mahler 10, so we did *Das Lied* instead, but that was the only alteration.) He really is a superb concert planner.

We had one horrific experience in that series, which shows how difficult the situation is in London with repertory and contemporary music. We had a Mahler 2 with Simon which was sold out, and before the interval we'd put the Webern *Passacaglia* and the Schoenberg *Five Orchestral Pieces*. And at the start of the concert the place looked half full and I wondered what on earth was going on because I knew it was a sell-out. After the interval they all turned up for the Mahler. So these people couldn't even be bothered to come and hear some pretty early Webern and Schoenberg when they had already paid for their tickets. That is a ghastly story and it reflects very badly on the London situation.

The Mahler–Strauss series in April 1985 received excellent reviews and good attendances, and alerted London's orchestral managers to the virtues of a concentrated, thematic set of concerts over a short period of time. The Philharmonia immediately began to plan a new series, and that turned into one of the highlights of London's music-making in 1986: *Après L'Après-midi*, a survey of French music since Debussy. This changed slightly more than the Mahler–Strauss series between conception and realization. Rattle's original plan, sent this time in a telegram to Martin Campbell-White just a month after the success of the first season, included Messiaen's *Poèmes pour Mi*, for which Rattle indicated his preference for soloist with the line 'Jessye Norman or bust'. She was also the desired soloist for two other concerts, but she could not take part (though she did sing Mahler with him at the 1985 BBC Proms). This series was an exceptionally expensive undertaking: as Rattle put it at the time, 'They'll lose a colossal amount with this enormous rehearsal time. But without a real tradition of exploring and experimenting, great masterpieces go down the same hole of over-familiarity.' Of the Philharmonia's risk in undertaking the series, he said, 'If I was their accountant I'd have stopped them doing it.' A reasonable sentiment, especially in view of the fact that French music has always been of uncertain popularity with the London audience, and Rattle's series mixed the familiar with the unfamiliar in even measure:

Debussy	*Prélude à l'après-midi d'un faune*
Ravel	*Shéhérazade* (Maria Ewing)
Boulez	*Rituel in memoriam Bruno Maderna*
Ravel	*Trois poèmes de Mallarmé*
Debussy	*Ibéria*
Ravel	Fanfare: *L'éventail de Jeanne*
Satie	*Parade*
Duparc	Songs (with orchestra; Ann Murray)
Debussy	*Le martyre de Saint-Sébastien* (symphonic fragments)
Koechlin	*Les Bandar-log*
Ravel	*La valse*
Ravel	*Alborada del gracioso*
Poulenc	Concerto for two pianos (Katia and Marielle Labèque)
Debussy	*Jeux*
Ravel	*L'enfant et les sortilèges* (Elise Ross, Dinah Harris, Mary King, Ameral Gunson, Peter Hall, Henry Herford, Raimond Herincx)
Debussy	*La boîte à joujoux*
Messiaen	*Oiseaux exotiques* (Peter Donohoe)
Boulez	*Éclat*
Ravel	*Ma mère l'oye*
Poulenc	*La voix humaine* (Elisabeth Söderström)
Messiaen	*Et exspecto resurrectionem mortuorum*
Ravel	*Daphnis et Chloë* (complete)

CHRISTOPHER BISHOP I was petrified, because we planned it and were intending to go ahead but we had no extra money, no sponsorship and nothing extra from the Arts Council. Suddenly we got £40,000 from Chanel [the French perfumiers] just like that, and we got something extra from the Arts Council – difficult to say exactly how much, because it was put into the whole grant, perhaps £30,000 – so that we had the largest grant for that period of all the London orchestras. In the event the series did extremely well, had a great deal of attention, Simon conducted quite superbly, and there was an average 75 per cent attendance, which for those programmes was remarkable. Simon is very aware of the financial problems of the London orchestras, and he is very clever at arranging rehearsals so that not a minute is wasted, so it was all done as economically as possible.

The reviews of *Après L'Après-midi* were outstanding, reflecting something of the almost total enthusiasm with which the London critics now regarded Rattle: 'Conducting his first two concerts . . . Simon Rattle proved that he knows how to secure playing of French music with a perfect accent' (*Guardian*); 'Rattle has a special gift for making the simplest orchestral statement or instrumental combination resonate in a subtle and telling manner – and a special gift too for gauging exactly the right pacing for related gestures' (*Financial Times*); 'Simon Rattle's series has been marvellously enriching, with the standards of the Philharmonia Orchestra's performances over the fortnight remaining amazingly high, and perhaps most warming of all, near-capacity audiences greeting music by the likes of Boulez and Messiaen with something like rapture. And it came to a suitably glorious close last night' (Stephen Pettitt, *The Times*). Ravel's *Daphnis et Chloë* was 'a fitting conclusion to one of London's major musical events of the decade, and further evidence of Rattle's genius for planning programmes and then performing them with utter conviction' (Robert Henderson, *Daily Telegraph*). As someone wistfully put it, 'Can Simon Rattle do no wrong?'

Much to some people's relief, he could. His relationship with the Philharmonia had not been uniformly sunny between the Mahler–Strauss series and the *Après-midi* series. An awkward tour of Japan in 1985 was one problem. Rattle agrees that it was unhappy, and he puts the cause down to a relatively small matter: programming the Brahms *Haydn Variations* which he had not relearned properly and felt incapable of doing well: 'I couldn't even admit to myself that I funked it. It shows you have to be prepared.' However, another cause of tension might have been Rattle's open criticism of some Philharmonia appointments (though not that of his friend Esa-Pekka Salonen as principal guest conductor). Certain conductors, including former principal conductor Riccardo Muti, were drifting away from the Philharmonia at this period towards the London Philharmonic, where former EMI producer John Willan was newly installed as manager. Towards the end of 1986, Rattle unwittingly became a major factor in the talk of a takeover that erupted between these two orchestras.

At the end of 1985 John Willan attracted Rattle to the London Philharmonic with ready agreement to his requests for extra rehearsal. The two programmes he did, one of Stravinsky and one including Rakhmaninov's Second Symphony, fulfilled the highest promise. Many observers thought this was the beginning of an important new relationship:

> JOHN CAREWE He was suddenly conducting an orchestra that was really great, and which had probably seven-tenths of all his ideals already built into it. In the Rakhmaninov Second Symphony I have never seen a London orchestra so totally committed, to the last player. They really did for one night forget that they had to earn their living at ten o'clock the next morning, and I would not like to have been the conductor they had the next day! I think it was one of the greatest concerts I have heard him conduct.

At the end of that year John Willan made the suggestion to *The Sunday Times* – displayed with sensationalist headlines on its front page – that collaboration between the two orchestras, mooted for many years, should be in the form of an LPO 'takeover'. This soured relationships considerably, and there were more than a few who thought that Willan's pre-emptive strike might have something to do with his wanting to create the conditions that might lure Rattle to come and throw in his lot with an LPO-dominated London in the foreseeable future. In fact, Rattle was in sympathy with the ultimate aim of bringing order to London's musical life, but he felt the matter was much more difficult than the planned merger implied.

Richard Morrison wrote in *The Times*:

> If he decides not to renew his Birmingham contract, which is the subject of a financial hassle at the moment, he is likely to be everyone's first choice as music director of any South Bank resident orchestra. Hitherto he has done most of his London conducting with the Philharmonia. But if the LPO is building on its Glyndebourne association with him, working towards a tacit exclusivity in London, that could be the end of the war.

Rattle was annoyed by these speculations, as he was by a suggestion I made in an *Observer* piece at the same time that even if he renewed in Birmingham until 1991, he might be prepared to come to London after that if the orchestral situation there changed radically. To Terry Grimley of the *Birmingham Post* he said,

> What I find rather offensive about the speculation is the assumption that I would want to go. It's part of the arrogance of the London music scene that they assume I would jump at it. This [Birmingham] is where my life is, this is where my work is . . . The problem is that the London orchestras have some absolutely great players, and that's about it. They don't have the halls to rehearse in, and they don't have time to rehearse, it's just not good enough. I work with the musicians themselves with enormous pleasure, but in terms of trying to build something up as we do in Birmingham, forget it.

However, there followed a period in which Rattle did work quite often with the London Philharmonic, and achieved some spectacularly good results:

> On Saturday Simon Rattle conducted another wildly successful concert. It is becoming a little tedious to report these events – even musicians with no natural inclination to *Schadenfreude* must wish occasionally that Rattle would make a real hash of something. The London Philharmonic played superbly for him, and he designs his concerts with as much flair as he conducts them. (David Murray, *Financial Times*)

> Great risks and great rewards . . . the London orchestra of the moment was working with the English conductor of the decade. (Robert Maycock, *Independent*)

> An extraordinary event . . . it may not be fair to insist that among today's leading conductors only Simon Rattle could persuade the London Philharmonic into such a concert [of Boulez, Dutilleux, and Mahler] . . . but only Rattle, surely, could have made such a balanced success of both its parts. (Max Loppert, *Financial Times*)

Looking back from the perspective of some years later, John Willan reflects:

> JOHN WILLAN [2001] I talked to Simon a lot to try and persuade him that things could change in London. I did think that with the LPO's links with Glyndebourne that would provide an incentive to do things in London, like the *Porgy and Bess* concert performances which were so great. But ironically that was just when he began to distance himself from the LPO at Glyndebourne, preferring to do Mozart with the Age of Enlightenment. So that idea got nowhere. I think too the LPO was offering something he really needed at that time, a great sound where he could try out the classical

repertory such as the Brahms symphonies. We had a period, lasting several years, of doing some fine things with him. But in the end, with all the problems continually recurring, the funding difficulties, the same things coming round again and again, the London situation was impossible. He thought the whole thing was pathetic, and I had to agree.

II

Ups and Downs in Sussex

Rattle first went to Glyndebourne at the age of only twenty, the year after he won the John Player Award, to work on *Eugene Onegin* with Haitink and conduct *The Rake's Progress* for the tour.

SIMON RATTLE I very nearly didn't make it in Glyndebourne. I was almost sacked for not turning up to all the rehearsals, and insisting that I was going back to conduct the Liverpool Philharmonic. And I remember Martin [Campbell-White] ringing up. I was given the choice of leaving, or going back and having six weeks of my very little pay docked. The only thing that made me go back was that it seemed dumb not to have the opportunity to work with Bernard Haitink. But almost everyone has some horror story like that about Glyndebourne!

By the time he has finished there, following *Fidelio* in 2001 (see p. 309), Rattle will have some more horror stories, including the saga of a cancellation of Rameau's *Hippolyte et Aricie* he was due to conduct there in 2005. Although he will return in 2003 for *Idomeneo* with Peter Sellars, it seems unlikely that Glyndebourne will ever see him again after that.

It was Brian Dickie who first brought Rattle to Glyndebourne:

BRIAN DICKIE I'd gone to see the Offenbach opera he conducted one performance of at the Royal Academy in 1973, and was very impressed. Then there was the Ravel *Enfant* rather later, at the end of 1974, which was superb, but I think it had been fixed by then that he would come in the summer of 1975 to work on *Onegin* and *Rake's Progress* with Bernard [Haitink] and then do the tour of *Rake*. I may say it took a fair bit of persuading my colleagues and I had to be a little bit imprecise about his age ... And I was really pushing the boat out a bit in saying we should have this young chap not only as a *répétiteur* but also to do the tour. And I wasn't even sure I'd done the right thing when it happened.

I gather there were problems in the first couple of years . . .
Initially Simon made a tremendous impression: lots of energy, and for the younger members or the newer members of the company this was great. But the more established people, and some of the more insecure ones, found this young upstart extremely threatening and tiresome, and he soon made a few enemies. The thing about Simon was that his instincts were extraordinary, though, and he soon got a great deal of respect. His learning curve just zoomed upwards.

Then there was a rather tiresome period when he always seemed to be double-booked. This was after he'd won the Bournemouth competition, and he was conducting there and always trying to get back to Glyndebourne by British Rail – he's never driven, which is rather irritating. Oh, and then he would go off to Liverpool for the odd concert, that sort of thing. So I think we did become a bit annoyed by all that, and Bernard certainly found his unreliability annoying.

But he was just so good, and so talented, and so efficient when he did rehearse, that I think this sort of thing was gradually forgotten. He did some splendid things with the touring company: I particularly remember the *Così* in 1978. There came a time quite early on when we wanted him to become musical director of the touring company in succession to Kenneth Montgomery. But I don't think he felt that committed to it, and he had so much else going on. So we just established the pattern that he would come back regularly to the Festival, as often as he wanted, and we would do some special things, like the Mozart–Da Ponte cycle from 1989 onwards including the Mozart anniversary year in 1991.

When Bernard Haitink went to Covent Garden, did you want Simon as musical director of the Festival?
Certainly, yes. But by then he was fully involved in Birmingham, and I think it had become clear too that while Simon has the most marvellously invigorating effect on Glyndebourne when he comes and does something like *Porgy*, he preferred that the relationship should be regular rather than permanent. I know he has reservations about many aspects of our operation – playing to small audiences, the ticket prices, and so on. There is a set of values that prevail at Glyndebourne that are not necessarily Simon's. We've had this out with him and we know there's no real way we can greatly extend the scope of things or bring down the ticket prices. The way we get out to a larger public is first through the tours, and then through television, video and so on. So I don't think Simon could have been fully enough in agreement with the basis of things at Glyndebourne to want to be musical director of the organization.

Would his control over casting have been a problem too?
Any musical director *could* cast everything if he was around enough. If he
was free for all the auditions I go to, and so on. But usually they're not. As
we found with *Porgy*, in the end certain decisions have to be made, and we
have to take the responsibility. OK, sometimes we get it wrong, but I think
our casting is pretty good. No, I don't feel casting would have been a basic
problem with Simon, though I do think he has a lot to learn about singers,
and that does tend to be the area where we have what I can euphemistically
call our discussions.

Whatever the tensions at Glyndebourne, the results of Rattle's work
there were universally praised from the very beginning; in 1977,
Janáček's *Cunning Little Vixen* drew Max Loppert in the *Financial
Times* to say:

> Simon Rattle, young in years, is an excellent choice of conductor. From the
> lithe, clean, infectiously vibrant manner in which the London Philharmonic
> attacked Janáček's nuggety little cells and repeated rhythmic patterns, it
> was immediately and rewardingly apparent that he has an instinctive
> command of that eternally youthful rhythm. Some of the playing had
> rough edges, but the spirit behind it, energetic and also lyrical, was just
> right.

The Janáček was coupled with Poulenc's *La voix humaine*, which Rattle
was to revive in his Philharmonia French series in 1986. And subsequent
collaborations have ranged from Haydn's *Le fedeltà premiata* to
Strauss's *Der Rosenkavalier* and *Ariadne auf Naxos*. In the summer of
1987, he returned to one of his favourite operas, Ravel's *L'enfant et les
sortilèges*, pairing it with *L'heure espagnole* in a new production
designed by Maurice Sendak. That was an example where casting did
not quite go as Rattle had wanted, and he made a big issue of one singer
who turned out to be inadequate and disappeared before the first night.

Perhaps the most striking of all his Glyndebourne performances,
Mozart's *Idomeneo* in 1985, revealed that Rattle had an approach to
Mozart that was quite distinct from the Glyndebourne house style.
There were some real difficulties during the rehearsal period (recalled by
Philip Langridge on p. 217). Rattle remembers it as 'even worse than
Philip describes. Martin Isepp, who was chief coach, called a meeting of
the music staff to discuss how they could stop Simon doing these things
to Mozart.' Rattle got his way, and the intensity of the performance
communicated itself:

Simon Rattle ... intensifies the emotional thrust of Mozart's score, not with unwanted romantic mannerisms but with an extra rhythmic incisiveness established at the very start of the overture. Where Bernard Haitink two years ago took a broad, spacious view, Rattle has you registering with new excitement the close continuity of the piece. (Edward Greenfield, *Guardian*)

With Rattle in the pit the meticulous orchestration and sense of constant dramatic recharging unique to this score are revealed ... with Simon Rattle conducting the opera for the first time, it achieves the stature for which it has waited so long. (Hilary Finch, *The Times*)

Rattle made no secret of his intense admiration for Nikolaus Harnoncourt's recording of this opera. Fascinatingly, it was Bernard Haitink who had first encouraged him to listen to it when he was persuading Rattle to take on this revival and Rattle did not feel the opera would work for him at Glyndebourne. But Haitink's insistence had a far bigger impact than he could have imagined. The fact that it was Harnoncourt's revolutionary recording that made sense for Rattle, rather than any of the other available versions, drew him closer and closer to working with old instruments. This led eventually to the sensational concert performance of *Idomeneo* in 1987, as a result of which he persuaded Glyndebourne that they should use the Orchestra of the Age of Enlightenment for a cycle of the Mozart–Da Ponte operas beginning in 1989 (see pp. 287–90). Bernard Haitink responsible for a revolution; who would have thought it possible?

July 1986. The first night of George Gershwin's *Porgy and Bess* at the Glyndebourne Festival, conducted by Simon Rattle and directed by Trevor Nunn of the Royal Shakespeare Company, brings the audience to its feet in the most sustained, emotional reception of an opera I can remember there. Of all the extraordinary and gripping evenings for which Simon Rattle has been responsible, this is surely the most extraordinary and the most gripping. The thing was just magic. And yet it could have gone wrong at so many points, and initially the whole project seemed deeply suspect. As one press report put it, 'The arrival of Catfish Row at Glyndebourne must be the most spectacular geographical move since Birnam Wood came to Dunsinane.' The *New York Times* reported:

The denizens of George Gershwin's Catfish Row took possession on Saturday night of the English stately home renowned for its productions of classical operas, and what might have been seen as a gesture of musical condescension became instead the triumph of the operatic season. *Porgy and Bess* and the Glyndebourne Festival are almost the same age, having been born in 1935 and 1934 respectively, but until recently no one could have imagined their convergence . . . [but] as jointly conceived by Simon Rattle, the young British conductor, and Trevor Nunn of the Royal Shakespeare Company, who shaped *Nicholas Nickleby* and *Cats*, it was meant to demonstrate that *Porgy and Bess* did not have to be patronized either musically or dramatically.

BRIAN DICKIE It would be fair to say that we took the idea of *Porgy* from the English National Opera. In the summer of 1983 Frank Corsaro and David Pountney were having a picnic at Glyndebourne, and Pountney said that they wanted to do *Porgy* at the Coliseum with Simon. Corsaro came and told me, because I think he would have liked to do it for us himself. But just at that time we were looking for something for Simon and Trevor Nunn to do after they worked on *Idomeneo*, and I thought it would be a thrilling thing for us, though full of problems. (I think if I'd realized how many problems I wouldn't have gone on with it.) And it seemed to me unlikely that the Coliseum could possibly meet the Gershwin Estate's stringent conditions about performing the piece.

At that time we were also thinking of a Janáček *Jenůfa* with Simon and Trevor, so we discussed it and Trevor said that if we offered him either of those pieces with Simon he'd sign the contract tomorrow. So it was quickly fixed with Peter Hall, who was then away doing the Bayreuth *Ring*, that we should pursue *Porgy*. In November I flew out to Los Angeles and met the lawyers and everyone to do with the Gershwin Estate. Meanwhile I think George Harewood was still writing letters to them, and I think the fact that I went out there gave us an advantage. And we were prepared to do it with a completely black cast, whereas I think the Coliseum wanted to have a compromise with the chorus. So they agreed, and we'd crossed the first bridge.

Contrary to popular supposition, by the way, there was absolutely no mention of the all-black cast in the contract we signed with the Estate. I think they were just satisfied that we would do it in accordance with their wishes, but there would have been no legal comeback if we hadn't. There was no discussion about production style, or faithfulness to the text and so on, no instructions about that. Perhaps if they'd heard we were going to do it with someone called David Alden they might have enquired further. It just stipulated we had to give it a first-class production, which is rather nice. I don't know who would have arbitrated if they had thought it wasn't first class!

Was the casting a headache?
Yes, because it was a completely new cast. Think of getting a complete
chorus from scratch. We'd had a couple of black chorus members previously and about half a dozen came in for *Simon Boccanegra*. Apart from
Willard White, whom Simon had worked with and immediately said was
the Porgy, the rest was pretty well open, with not much to go on. Terrifying! So we planned a couple of days of auditions in New York with Trevor
around the time Simon was there with the LA Philharmonic, in December
1984, to get the principals. We found some – Harolyn Blackwell sang there
and we got her in at once – but there were plenty of holes. Bess was a real
problem, for instance, and in the end I was the only person who heard her;
and also the Crown – they were chosen only about a year in advance. And
the last half-dozen or so of the chorus I found myself last March in New
York in some 9 a.m. auditions.

When did you suspect it was going to be such a success?
Oh, from day one of the rehearsals. We had five weeks of ups and downs
but the place really buzzed as never before, and we knew we had it made. It
was extraordinary, the sheer energy that went into this production. And it
wasn't easy, because we're not a commercial operation like *Cats* or *Star-
light Express*, the sort of operation Trevor Nunn is used to. There were
very serious technical problems with the set, which is heavy and elaborate,
and things became pretty tense in the last week or so when rehearsals had
to be cancelled just to give time to make the set safe. But there's such a
different atmosphere in the place when you know a production is going to
work – and this one did. The cast were marvellous – total integration – and
they livened up Glyndebourne no end. There were a few problems down in
the village, I gather. Incredible, really.

For Simon Rattle it was the culmination of a ten-year relationship with
the opera that went back to a Chelsea Opera Group concert performance, again with Willard White, in 1976. He'd also done it in Liverpool
and Birmingham, and had brought it with Birmingham forces to London
for his 1981 South Bank Summer Music season. It was a work he knew
thoroughly and loved passionately.

SIMON RATTLE There are tunes in the opera I've known since I was a kid.
We must have had piano arrangements of it lying around at home, and my
father would play Gershwin songs day in and day out. It was very much his
kind of music. One of my earliest things as a pianist was to do *Rhapsody in
Blue* and my father would bash through it with me telling me how square I
was, so there is some of that in my bones.

Were the rehearsals lively?

Amazing in every way. Both Trevor and I at various times hit the tension of being white people telling black people what to do – particularly difficult in a piece they know so well. Very near the end was very tense and a very difficult time for me, and the problems with the stage and the set and cancelling rehearsals didn't help. But the problems certainly resolved themselves!

The moment I will never forget was the first meeting of the orchestra and the chorus. I insisted we had just one rehearsal in the rehearsal room rather than on stage so that the chorus and the orchestra could see each other, without the players being hidden in the pit. I had brought in some singers to work with the orchestra, but it was just seeing the effect of the whole chorus when they began to sing, the noise that came out of them. The players were sitting back, mouths wide open. It was one of those extra-ordinary atmospheres. I've never felt anything quite like it, and it makes me quite weepy to think about it now. When the orchestra did something marvellous the chorus would cheer and so eventually if the chorus did something marvellous the orchestra would cheer. After that there was so much contact behind every scene. I've never seen that orchestra enjoy itself so much. Down in the pit during performances it was incredible – people rolling around, tap-dancing – a real feeling of something going on and a masterpiece being rediscovered.

The point about the singers is that they were all great. I may never again conduct an opera where every member of the cast is a great singer in their own right. You don't get that in Verdi. And what is astonishing is that many of these people don't have much work, purely because they are black, and not for any other reason. There are people there I'll be wanting to work with in my next Janáček opera or whatever. That level of feeling and gener-osity is very rare, and the emotions were very close to the surface the whole time.

Leonora Gershwin said it was the first time the piece had ever been done properly: the first time there had been an orchestra that could really play it; the first time there had ever been a proper production, and of course the cast. It was still very strange to play that music to that audience, but in every way it was a milestone.

Two years later *Porgy and Bess* became a recording, a best-selling CD and video, and transformed everyone's understanding of how this great piece belonged in the mainstream of the twentieth-century operatic world.

III
Orchestras Abroad

November 1986. Simon Rattle is making his début with the Concert-gebouw Orchestra, the first major new orchestra he has conducted since his début with the Boston Symphony Orchestra three years ago. I have flown over for the opening concert of the second programme he is conducting, which consists of Mahler's Tenth Symphony in the per-forming version by Deryck Cooke. Since discovering the published score of this work in an Oxford music shop shortly after it appeared in 1976, Rattle has made it one of the most powerful and convincing performances in his repertory, and has conducted it many times as well as recording it. The hall of the Concertgebouw is packed and the audience is expecting something special: the orchestra, perhaps the most famous in the world for its Mahler performances, has never played the complete Tenth before.

But from the very beginning of the concert it is clear that something is wrong. Rattle gives a very slight upbeat for the violas' unaccompanied first line, and they don't enter together. The playing is tentative – profes-sional but scarcely committed. Rattle is having to work very hard. His gestures become broader and broader in his effort to draw the sound out of them. There are more fluffs and imperfections than one would expect from such an orchestra, and though some of the greatest moments make their impact, the overall effect is muted. Afterwards, Rattle looks exhausted.

Backstage, while we wait for Rattle to emerge, I ask Martin Campbell-White, his agent, how the first programme, which included Stravinsky's *Petrushka* and Ravel's *Shéhérazade* with Maria Ewing, had gone. 'Later, later,' he whispers, and introduces me to the orchestra's manager who is standing close by. He confirms that the orchestra has never played the Cooke completion of Mahler 10 before. There is to be a conference in Utrecht over the next few days at which all the attempts to complete this torso are to be discussed and some of them played. Rattle and the orchestra will give another performance of the work in Utrecht. But I don't learn whether the orchestra has enjoyed the experi-ence or not.

Rattle, tired but ever cheerful, comes to say hello to his friends. His first reaction is that 'It was all such hard work . . . ' He leaves the rest unspoken. We wander around Amsterdam looking for a place to have a drink and something to eat. It is noticeable that the crowd of Dutch friends who have come along are all players from the Rotterdam Philharmonic, with whom Rattle has had many happy experiences, rather than from the Concertgebouw. After many attempts to find somewhere with space enough for the whole crowd of us, we end up back near the Concertgebouw in a café where some of the orchestra are having a drink. One of the viola-players comes over to Rattle and apologizes for the beginning of the symphony. 'Well, at least you started!' says Rattle, putting a cheerful face on it. The player goes back to his friends. 'Was he the one who played together?' someone quips.

In conversation with the Rotterdam players I gather that while the first programme presented fewer problems, it didn't go especially well either, and that Rattle feels he simply hasn't made contact with the orchestra at all. 'He's had a bad time really,' admits Martin Campbell-White, which, given his customary discretion, is rather a major admission. It seems that the orchestra were not keen to play Mahler 10, which they didn't know, and thought that in any case it would be rather easy, which it isn't. It is fiendishly difficult, and that shows in performance. Rattle has worked very hard during rehearsals but the orchestra, which likes learning gradually and gently, has not responded to his businesslike approach. All in all, it's been a mismatch.

Back in London a couple of weeks later, Rattle reflects on the experience.

SIMON RATTLE I think they got the impression that I was very cold, which is very interesting, because that's exactly the impression that I got of them, so we must have been very mystified by each other. They couldn't understand why I was so no-nonsense all the time. I tried to explain that in England that would be a compliment. But the very fact that I take it for granted that the orchestra wants to use rehearsals to work and make it better was a problem. I really think they work in another way: rehearsals are used for playing a great deal, gradually homing in on things that they think are important. They are allowed to make their own shapes. They think in phrases, which is one of the things I liked about them. But their sense of rhythm I have yet to come to terms with.

They must consider themselves to be the greatest Mahler orchestra in the world; they play the other symphonies very often and sometimes very well. They probably thought that this would be just as easy, but of course it's no more easy than doing the Ninth Symphony for the first time – probably more difficult. One of the orchestra said to me that if I'd come expecting

English or American discipline it just doesn't happen there. He said, 'We're
used to making a lot of noise, playing on to the ends of phrases, and so on.'
They're not very disciplined, but Holland is a very liberal society so maybe
discipline like that is hard to imagine there.

   I was physically so tired. I have not had to move around like that for
years.

*Was part of the problem that you were handed too much by them, in the
sense of a playing style that was all there?*
Well, you heard it, did you think it was all there?

Certainly not in the Mahler . . .
Well, can you imagine what it was like in Stravinsky and Haydn? Maybe
there were playing styles I couldn't get to grips with . . .

Or as you said of some other orchestras, a style you couldn't unpick . . .
Absolutely. That was the trouble. I had to ask for it to be unpicked and
that's what they weren't used to.

Does it make you want to go back and try again or give the whole thing up?
My first reaction was to say, 'Fair enough, no hard feelings, but let's leave
it.' I said this to the manager at the end of the time and then there was an
enormous flurry of activity and I was rung at 11.30 p.m. by the chairman of
the orchestral committee asking to come over and see me the next morning.
I don't think anyone has ever said to them before that, without any preju-
dice, they would rather not come back again. I think that was a bit of a
shock to them, and their pride, and I think they wanted to try again. But life
is not endless, and there are many things I don't have time to do. Do I want
to battle with all that again? It's not even as if they are underprivileged.
They have plenty of conductors whom I admire much more than I admire
myself!

   I think I'm still mulling it over. It does strike me that perhaps as I get a bit
older I make it more difficult for orchestras to play for me instead of more
easy. I thought that as time goes on you learn more about how to cope. But
now I feel I have to demand more and I find the compromises more difficult
to achieve.

A close colleague of Rattle's has another perspective on the Amsterdam experience: 'The arrogance of that orchestra! They can't be
bothered to play and then at the end they turn sweet and say they'd like
to give him another chance. How patronizing! Why should *he* give *them*
another chance!'

Rattle's relationships with orchestras abroad were not universally sunny during the 1980s. It is interesting that the problems seemed to increase rather than diminish after he went to Birmingham. He perhaps became too used to an orchestra that wanted to play for him and to create an occasion for him. One example of those problems was with the Cleveland Orchestra. He had a successful first appearance with them in 1982, doing Mahler's Tenth once again, but when he returned at the end of 1984 the orchestra felt his style had changed considerably. His beat was no longer as clear, and he expected them to understand what he was doing without explaining it to them. One player told me:

> Precision is a byword in the Cleveland Orchestra and the players felt insulted. He did the Stravinsky *Symphonies of Wind Instruments* with the wind in one long line across the stage. One end couldn't hear the other end and they were very angry and very upset about the whole thing. I don't think they liked being experimented on, especially when he didn't tell them what he was trying to achieve. It was something to do with the fact that he wanted the orchestra to sense the feel and the pulse of the music. But perhaps he didn't know what the Cleveland Orchestra was taught by Lorin Maazel, who always said, 'You follow my beat and don't bother about listening to each other.' We were mystified, because the first time he came he was absolutely clear and it went well. But this time he was perhaps expecting something unrealistic. He gave the orchestra its head and it didn't know what to do with it.

Similar problems recurred when he went back there in 1987.

Rattle's experience with foreign orchestras is not as wide as might be expected of a conductor of his reputation. His first engagements abroad were arranged by Martin Campbell-White in the wake of the John Player Award win. There were visits to some small Scandinavian orchestras in Trondheim and Sjaellands, which Rattle enjoyed. Then there was the beginning of the very successful relationship with the Rotterdam Philharmonic, who would have been happy to have had him as musical director after David Zinman left. He settled instead for a principal guest conductor post, and has always enjoyed returning to Rotterdam, especially when the relationship moved into opera with *Pelléas*, *Parsifal* and more recently *Tristan*. The major orchestras came into view a little later, headed in the American area by the Los Angeles Philharmonic in January 1979 and followed by the Chicago Symphony that summer. On an American visit the following year he made his débuts with the San Francisco Symphony and the Toronto Symphony.

The following year there was the Israel Philharmonic, then the Cleveland and Montreal Symphony orchestras and in 1983 the Boston Symphony, to which he often returned. That, until the Concertgebouw Orchestra in 1986, was the sum total of the major international orchestras he had conducted.

A distinctly unhappy encounter among the orchestras Rattle has guest-conducted was with the Israel Philharmonic in December 1981:

SIMON RATTLE It was a horrendous experience. Circumstances conspired, and in every possible way it didn't work. There was snow in England and everything closed down, so I arrived there two days late. I was going to do Mahler 10 in the first programme, but as there were only two rehearsals left we had to change round the programme, so the first time I met this orchestra was conducting Brahms 2. I might have been able to get away with that a week later – I'd done the piece very successfully with the Philharmonia and was very happy with it – but it never would occur to me to go for the first time to an orchestra and do Brahms 2, even now. There was no time at all. I had brought the Prokofiev *Romeo and Juliet* which I was going to give myself the first ten days there to learn, and we had to do that straight away.

I really didn't know it, and I think they thought I was just a joke. They are up there, as another conductor said to me, with the hardest orchestras in the world to conduct. There's lots of noise the whole time. It was not a happy experience, and I was very lonely and miserable.

If guest conducting has brought Rattle a fair number of unfortunate experiences, it has also brought him some happy ones – with orchestras with which he has been able to build more than a temporary relationship. Best of all, the Los Angeles Philharmonic, the first American orchestra he visited, responded to him so warmly that when Carlo Maria Giulini left, the orchestra and their manager Ernest Fleischmann wanted Rattle as music director there. It must have been a difficult post to refuse, given the exceptional conditions and the financial security it would have offered.

Ernest Fleischmann was formerly manager of the London Symphony Orchestra and continued to run the Los Angeles Philharmonic for many years in spite of other offers. Rattle says, 'To understand Ernest you have to realize that he was once a conductor. Like incredibly few people in that sort of position, he looks at things from an artistic point of view. I think he believes that if he manages the orchestra well the first violins will play better. I really love the man.'

ERNEST FLEISCHMANN [1987] I first encountered Simon when he came to Los Angeles with the London Schools Symphony Orchestra in 1976, so he was still only twenty-one. The band wasn't so hot – we're used to really crack youth orchestras in the States – but it was clear from the way they responded to him in a very brief rehearsal that he was exceptional. So the next day I had lunch with the woman who ran the orchestra and with Simon and I said that whenever he felt ready I wanted him to make his American début with the LA Philharmonic. I knew he wouldn't do anything straight away and it was clear that he was a sensitive and intelligent musician, very different from the average career-oriented young conductor I come across here. Rather like Esa-Pekka Salonen these days, he had a completely honest emphasis on music and not just the career, which I greatly admired.

It must have been early in 1978 that Simon agreed to come and we planned the début for January 1979, with Sibelius 5 and the Elgar *Enigma Variations*, which he'd done on that tour. There was some murmuring from the older musicians that first time, but his total command and security won them over, and it was clear we would want to have him back often. He did the Hollywood Bowl that summer, but I think the occasion that really cemented the relationship was Simon's coming at very short notice to do Shostakovich 14 when Giulini cancelled in April 1981. That was one of those incidents. It was supposed to have been Giulini – a big thing to show that he didn't always do just classical repertory – with Jessye Norman and Simon Estes. First Jessye let it be known that although she was studying the piece it wouldn't be ready. Two weeks before, Giulini became ill and cancelled. I called Simon who was then on his sabbatical in Oxford and pleaded with him to come. He told me he was preparing the piece with Felicity Palmer, so I asked him to speed up the learning process. The first rehearsal was on a Tuesday afternoon. On the Monday morning I heard that Simon Estes had been in a TV gala the previous evening from the Met, and had lost his voice in the middle of it in front of millions of Americans on live television! So I called Simon again and we found a British bass who could sing it but he'd just left his wife and his score was back at his house so he had to drive through a hailstorm to retrieve it and fly straight out here on a tourist visa ... But Simon rehearsed it marvellously and created a superb performance, which was most moving.

Though I gather there were some problems with the audience?
Yes, that was one of the most shameful things that's happened since I've been in LA. People just kept getting up and leaving between the songs, and so Simon just stopped and turned round and said quietly, 'All those of you who are going to leave during this piece please leave now,' and then went on. Actually it heightened the tension.

What other highlights do you remember?
I can only tell you that I can hardly remember anything that hasn't gone well. Sibelius 4 was unbelievable; Shostakovich 10, Mahler 10, these were marvellous. There was the case of the Beethoven *Eroica* which when he first did it here was by no means formed. The first movement was very very slow and it didn't have that intensity and power that marks out all Simon's greatest performances. Mahler 10 we took to New York and that was Simon's début there. I take grave issue with the critics who disliked it because I just don't think New York critics are able to distinguish an orchestra playing with the special commitment they brought to it. I thought it was one of the greatest things he ever did and was in tears at the end.

It must have been a blow for you when Simon decided not to come as music director . . .
It was a blow, both musically and personally. It was such an obvious progression and I'm sure it would have worked well, but it was hardly surprising knowing Simon that he decided against it. Part of the problem was living in LA when they had a new baby, and part of the thing was the demands of a music director's post in America – all the PR and so on. But Giulini did little of that and between Simon and me we could have worked that out. More important perhaps was Simon's not feeling comfortable at that time with the classical repertory, which has to be central for us. In Birmingham that's different.

SIMON RATTLE There were many reasons why I didn't accept but the greatest is that I had my own orchestra and my work with them was nowhere near finished. I've seen what happened in Los Angeles when Giulini left and what a crippling blow it was. Giulini was doing wonderful things with them, but when he left the orchestra it wasn't yet able to play as well for everyone as it played for him. One of the things about that orchestra is that it could be one of the very greatest contemporary-music orchestras. That goes back to Zubin Mehta, who did remarkable repertory there. I heard some tapes of what they did with Pierre Boulez and that was quite extraordinary. They have a pretty good range now, I reckon.

Shostakovich 14 was a wonderful experience because two of the orchestra are Russian and one had actually played in the première. Those weeks set the seal on my friendship with the orchestra. The audience? Maybe not. They're always friendly but they just don't want to be bothered. André Previn was telling me that he had mass walk-outs during the Britten *Spring Symphony*, of all pieces, in New York and Philadelphia. And it's not just twentieth-century music: Bernard Haitink says you expect them to applaud after the third movement of the Tchaikovsky *Pathétique*, but in New York they put on their coats and left! Was it because they didn't know there was a last movement or because they knew they didn't like it?

Rattle's début in New York with the Los Angeles Philharmonic was an especially important occasion because he had turned down all previous invitations to appear there. Both the New York Philharmonic and the Metropolitan Opera had invited him, and the Met wanted him to do Janáček's *Jenůfa*, an important work for Rattle but 'there was no rehearsal time for the orchestra, and the performances were spread out over a ridiculous period. If I'm going to do something like that I want to do it as well as possible.' The New York Philharmonic was well known as a minefield for conductors, and Rattle determined to steer clear of it. So the two programmes he gave at the time of his thirtieth birthday in January 1985, one at Carnegie Hall and one at Avery Fisher Hall, were thus doubly important. On the whole, as Ernest Fleischmann indicated, the press was less than rapturous. Again, the choice of Mahler's Tenth might have been a problem, and it was prefaced by a recent work by Takemitsu, commissioned by the Los Angeles orchestra.

'Years from now many of us will be able to say with pride that we were there when Simon Rattle made his local conducting début,' enthused Robert Kimball in the *New York Post*, but others were less overt in their praise. In the *New York Times*, Donal Henahan wrote that Rattle's conducting of the Mahler

> showed that he can handle an orchestra with confidence in an immensely difficult, problematical piece and moreover can go beyond a competent reproduction of the notes into the realm of real interpretation . . . He is handsome, which gives him an edge with the audience, and he is a solid technician, which appeals to orchestral musicians. His baton divides the beat with oddly clipped and jerky movements at times, which inhibits the flow of some long-lined phrases and might take some getting used to by the players. But he conducted without referring to a score and threw important cues when they were needed without unnecessary showmanship.

A review by Peter G. Davis in *New York* magazine irritated Rattle's agents and supporters because his criticism of the orchestra was very fierce, but of Rattle he had this to say:

> Opinions differ on just how it happened, but Simon Rattle is generally regarded as the hottest young conductor to arrive on the international scene in years, a magnetic podium presence, an innovative programmer, and a maverick personality. He is a thirty-year-old British musician who

blithely rejects every glamorous offer that comes his way, makes all the 'wrong' career decisions by stubbornly remaining in the provinces, and continues to watch his reputation soar. Rattle finally made his New York début in a characteristically low-key manner . . . Expectations ran high but both events turned out to be disappointing . . . What these thoughtfully unspectacular New York concerts indicated to me is that Rattle prefers to work methodically at being the best musician he knows how to be rather than diverting his energies into over-exposure and aggressive career politicking. That sort of disarming modesty, and an earnest wish to make himself scarce, have only added to the conductor's mystique.

Rattle has always been shrewd about the reactions to his music-making, and though he has continued to return to New York, he has met persistent sniping there which resurfaced when the CBSO went back in 1992 (see pp. 242–3). Even his Mahler Fifth with the Philadelphia Orchestra, which came to Carnegie Hall in March 2002, was quite coolly received. It may well be that one element in his eventual decision not to take any of the American music-director jobs that were offered him would have been the uphill struggle he might have to establish himself critically in New York, on which so much depends in America. By the time the 1990s began, Rattle was able to leave behind the Concertgebouw, Cleveland and other orchestras with impunity. He went to no new European orchestras after the mid-1980s with the exception of the Vienna Philharmonic. Though he kept loyal to Los Angeles, the emphasis in America changed to Boston and Philadelphia, and Rattle's new world beckoned in Europe, based around the two great orchestras of the Continent, in Berlin and Vienna (see chapter 9). But that is another story.

'It's difficult for geniuses . . .'
Friends, Colleagues, Critics, Composers

Michael Ignatieff

I think Simon is acutely aware that he is genetically endowed with quite extraordinary charisma, and has a unique capacity for empathy. But he doesn't use his charisma as other people do. Certain conductors might say: here's my charisma. You get strapped to the electricity pole and thousands of volts will go through you for the duration of a concert, and before you realize it's over they've taken the plane off to the next concert. Simon uses his charisma; he knows it's an instrument a great conductor must use, but he uses it to build a social relationship with those people he is performing with. And that brings such results because what he does is based on community and the continuity of a shared musical life. Seeing him work with the Rotterdam orchestra on *Tristan*, that was how he achieved the extraordinary results he achieved, making that opera, which really is iconic for him, sound so different.

I've only met four or five people in my life who I have felt have this kind of weird genetic endowment. It's difficult for geniuses, because genius doesn't go all the way through a person; they may be quite ordinary at other things. But the thing about Simon is that he is absolutely normal; he is not a freak, not an *idiot savant*. He is the very ordinary father of two boys, scorched and scarred by a very painful divorce, building a new marriage and deeply in love – you know, the things we all experience. And another rare thing in geniuses: he is a very good listener, and when I was going through some of the same things that he went through he understood what I was feeling better than I did. Suzanna and I have now become very close friends with Candace and him and there is a totally normal friendship and respect.

He is not the sort of genius who is detached from life and struggling to communicate with other human beings. Communicating comes absolutely naturally to him. In fact sometimes he over-commits. He thinks he can be all things to all people and no one can be that. Then he just hits the wall. I think he was dumbfounded by the emotions he encountered in the course of the divorce, the feeling that there could be so much hate around someone you loved. There was real anguish there, and as a genuinely devoted father I'm sure that keeping hold of the children through that period and not losing them was desperately important to him. He grew through that, though I am sure he would say it didn't have to be as hard as that.

With musicians – and I am not a musician – it's another conversation. He is utterly, ruthlessly clear about music, and you would have to say that there is a cold-hearted clarity in the centre of Simon about his music-making because he knows so exactly what it is that he wants. I've sat in a rehearsal with the Boston Symphony and seen how hard he makes people work, every note, every little bit with the second violins. You could feel the whole temperature warm up gradually, as if he started with thin gruel but ended up with a rich, tasty soup. (The cooking metaphor is not unimportant, by the way, because he loves to cook and is incredibly good about timing, blending ingredients, bringing everything together at the right moment.)

He is very physical about his music. He has this small, compact, muscular form; it's almost like meeting a great athlete when you see him and hug him after a concert with the sweat pouring off him. Three thousand people in that audience want to touch the hem of his garment; twenty-five make it through the guards to the dressing room. He gives every one some piercing attention; he knows how to cope with all that now. But away from that situation, he is just totally relaxed and a very close friend.

Andrew Jowett

I think Simon and my daughter are clear evidence for reincarnation! They both just seem to know their way around so well they must have been here before. It's enough to make you want to be a Buddhist . . . Simon knows his place in the world; it's an almost predetermined thing with him. You can have a wonderful conversation with him in a quarter of the time you take with most people because he knows exactly where you're going and can almost predict the questions and ask ones back of his own.

Anon

This is something which is hard to talk about, because it sounds like pop psychology. Growing up in a family like his, with an elder sister who had a disability, gave him a different perspective on how to be and how to think and how to behave. And I think it also affected him in terms of his personal life because he always felt that he was the lucky one, he was the one who had all the breaks, and he felt a bit guilty about that. And he went on being the lucky one. That played itself out when his personal life got really difficult later on. He put off making a decision about it because he couldn't bring himself to face the fact that he deserved better. He always thought anything that went wrong was his fault, but it wasn't, and in the end he recognized that.

Annette Isserlis

He can communicate so well in the context of rehearsing music, and you can feel a real personal connection with him in performance, but it can be quite difficult talking with him outside that, even for people who've known him for long time. He gets incredibly engaged talking about things like theatre and books; he goes to a lot of art exhibitions, and has the most amazing memory for things and sometimes you can have a really deep conversation. There was a period when he was going through a difficult time and seemed very vulnerable, and I think it must have been a help for him to know that the Orchestra of the Age of Enlightenment had a lot of people who cared about him as a person, not just as a conductor.

Sue Knussen

You know the way that Leonard Bernstein had of making you feel as if you were the only person in the universe when he spoke to you? And then he would turn around and speak to the next person, and I think one of the reasons Bernstein got into trouble with so many people emotionally and personally was because they inferred from that attention some kind of emotional commitment that couldn't possibly be there. And yet he did need people in his life; if you went to a concert and didn't say hello to him this was terrible. Anyone who had a part in his life, he needed them to keep going. Now Simon is much more self-contained than that. But I don't think he's self-sufficient. There's just a sort of invisible shield around him. When we were working on the television programmes he was coping with his personal problems and I had been through mine, so we had a lot to talk about. It wasn't as if he spilled his guts to me or anything like that, but we just knew each other better because of all those things. I would never in a million years expect to hear from him, but I always feel a sense of real friendship whenever we meet.

Singers

Thomas Allen

I did Janáček's *Cunning Little Vixen* at Glyndebourne with Simon back in 1977. (One Janáček conductor said to me, 'Well, it was marvellous, but it wasn't Janáček.') Simon liked to do the final scene in concert, which worked so well. He had a fantastic instinctive understanding of the music, which was unusual for such a young person. That was the strange thing about Simon's maturity: he just had this innate understanding of an old man's music. The *War Requiem* recording was another highlight for me – I'd got to grips with that work very early as a student in 1964. All that last section we did in one long take, and for someone like me, whose family was very caught up in that period of history, it was something very satisfying.

After we (finally!) did *The Cunning Little Vixen* at Covent Garden in 1990 there was a period of talking about doing *Billy Budd* and I hoped he would do it, because there's been so much criticism of that piece, the inadequacy of some of the writing, and Simon would have been exactly the person to persuade us otherwise. We've waged a long campaign to get that piece established and Simon would have been the perfect ally.

For a conductor he hasn't got very good physical coordination, which is surprising. I know because I tried to play snooker with him once and he was hopeless. When we were doing *Vixen* at Covent Garden there was a regime where we would do exercises to start the rehearsals each day, pretending to be sheep or goats or whatever and he just couldn't get with this at all. A lot of what we do as performers, especially singers, requires coordination and a certain athleticism and it is very useful in a singer to have some kind of sporting ability. Conductors don't seem to need that so much.

Conductors are the pampered people: singers do feel that. Singers get it in the neck for being prima donnas but actually, really, it's the conductors who know the world revolves around them, and they have the nicest hotels and the best limos and the biggest fees. Now Simon is not remotely a prima donna but he will be very insistent and he does not suffer fools gladly; it is the music that comes first. And that is quite rare. He won't let anything stand in its way. I do feel there is an incredible aggression there, somewhere inside him. You can hear it in the explosiveness of his performances; you can hear it in those grunts when he's trying to get what he wants. I would almost say it is an anger in him. I know he has suffered. I'd had an upset in my married life and I'm sure Simon wouldn't mind my saying that he asked me once, just sort of out of the blue, how old were my children when it happened. Much later I realized what he had been thinking about. In situations like that you either lose it and it drags you down, or it causes you to focus and get through it. It made me knuckle down and fill my work diary and learn a whole opera for Covent Garden in three days.

Philip Langridge

I used to go to Birmingham before Simon's time and it was pretty grim. A lot of oratorio. It was a case of: 'Well, I suppose I'm free and I suppose it's money.' He completely turned that round. Then he did Janáček's *Osud* for more or less the first time here, in South Bank Summer Music, and I was singing quite a small part, but the lead tenor decided he couldn't do it. So Simon asked me to take it over and I learned it at very short notice and I must say that was the start of my believing that I could do larger-scale things.

What I really remember is the first *Idomeneo* we did at Glyndebourne. We went up and down on the train discussing it a lot, and Simon actually asked for proper rehearsal for the recitatives, just with the harpsichord and cello, and I think this was rather unheard of at Glyndebourne. And he wanted a feeling of passion; he really wanted me not to worry about the notes but to show what I was feeling. You're angry: you shout. You're suicidal: you weep. He wanted to find the real meaning of the piece. We went on stage quite early, and there I was trying all this shouting and screaming, and one of the vocal coaches rushed up to me, ignoring Simon, and said, 'You can't possibly do that in Mozart; that's terrible.' And a little voice from the pit said, 'Well, we're grateful for any advice of course but, excuse me, actually we are trying to do something slightly new here, and that's what I want.' I don't think that coach ever came back.

He is always like that, willing to take risks to find out how a piece should really go and not just blindly following how it has always gone. We're all a bit sick of the people who always beat this bit in three; it's always the same and nothing changes. It was like that with *Jenůfa* in Paris. I wondered, 'Well, honestly, can he make any difference to this piece?' And it was just staggering. He's a specialist in everything now, and he learns all the time as well. He's an obsessive musician, yes, and I think he's had quite a lot of sadness in his life, with the kids and so on. I remembering him borrowing my mobile phone to ring them because that was the only moment he was allowed to speak to them. But you have to say that he is searching for the truth. Everyone wants to find that, and he finds it so often in a piece of music that you just sit in wonder. You can't compete with the truth.

Willard White

Simon pointed out to me recently that I must be about the only singer that he's worked with every single year since I did the first *Porgy and Bess* for the Camden Festival. Many times I've worked with him on something new, and he says before we go out to the rehearsal, 'Gosh, I hardly know this piece.' You get there and he may not think he knows it but actually he knows it better than anyone there, just perfectly. As all great people do, he puts forward his ideas, and usually it's a happy marriage where you just completely follow what he says. That's what he's like. At Glyndebourne with *Porgy* I remember a big discussion about tempo in the group. He was very adamant about what he wanted and gradually everyone came round to his way of thinking, with just a bit of compromise from him. It was a very emotional time with Trevor [Nunn] and Simon not knowing how it would be received, just guiding us, painting the picture through to the end. With that sort of music you can't but have a true emotional release. He has changed over the years: any one of us who can go through the passage of life and not change is dead! He changed and developed so fast. I didn't find that he was an uneasy person before but he is certainly so much more at ease with everything that he comes across. He lets me do things – I remember a rather controversial gesture I made during the recitative of Beethoven 9 in Salzburg when it was being televised. I did it in the rehearsal and he said, 'Yes, go for it, keep it in!' Now we'll do Beethoven 9 in Berlin as well as *Parsifal*. So there's no end! Even when I die there's no end . . .

Critics

Edward Seckerson

I did an interview with him at the very beginning of my journalistic career for a now-defunct magazine and then, a weird coincidence, within a week I got a call from the Salomon Orchestra asking if I could play cymbals in a performance of Mahler's Sixth Symphony that Simon was conducting. At the first rehearsal he was very surprised to see me and said, 'Well, this had better be bloody classy,' and we've had a standing joke about it ever since. What was so astonishing even then was his understanding of the precise sound world and character of that piece: the way he was coaxing the orchestra into extremes of beauty and ugliness.

He can be quite obsessive about detail, especially if it comes from a respected source. And unless you are Alfred Brendel it generally doesn't do to disagree – however contentious the issue. I was once given the 'head prefect' treatment for questioning a detail in the fourth movement of Mahler's Third Symphony. I think it was Berthold Goldschmidt who told Simon that the repeated semitone rise from the oboe in this movement – like a sound from nature – should be played *portamento*. Now I have never heard anyone, however far back you go, do that – not any of the Mahler specialists, Bernstein, Tennstedt, Barbirolli, Horenstein, Schuricht or Adler – but he had it from Berthold so he was damn well going to do it. He insisted Mahler's preferred word for *portamento* was clearly indicated on the score. Never mind that in every other score *portamento* is clearly marked as such. But you just can't argue with him about things like that.

The order of the inner movements in Mahler's Sixth Symphony was another example: he was so insistent that the slow movement and not the scherzo followed the first movement and that anyone that did the scherzo second was just plain wrong. Mahler, he said, had reversed the movements after the first performance – which was true – and never again performed them the other way round – which was not. We now have that on very good authority. And yet when I tried to argue out with him the advantages of the original order as I saw them, I was smartly put in my place.

Simon's great gift is his ability to wipe the slate clean and start from a blank page, to make every time the first time, to make you the audience acutely aware of why everything is where it is. There are no preconceptions and generally no received wisdoms or ignorances. That is the most exciting thing about a Rattle performance – the way he reveals both the letter and spirit of the score and communicates that to his audience. You actually hear what you see with Simon. If he's alerting you to a balance or a textural effect he will do so in such a way that visually pulls focus on it with his body language. Sometimes before things settle, before he truly gets under the skin of a piece, early performances can be a little calculated. For example, in his recording of Mahler's Second Symphony the first movement is way too studied, too slow. At the very opening he articulates exactly what's written in the cellos and basses – including the little *accelerando* – but it sounds like an exercise. He usually knows when it's not working. He actually persuaded EMI to re-record his account of Mahler's Seventh Symphony for just such reasons. That was an expensive endeavour which really paid off because the live recording has the heat of something truly spontaneous happening.

His recordings of the three big Stravinsky ballets are among his most successful, but again there's a fantastic but somewhat overstated moment at the end of *The Firebird* – a good example of point-making not quite integrated into the finished reading. In the final cadence, he leaves you in no doubt as to where the climactic chord comes – hitting it with tremendous intensity – but rather too much so. Details like that need to marinate a little. Spontaneity is the key difference between a first- and second-rate Rattle performance.

Generally, as a journalist, one gets to know one's place. I've known Simon a long time and he once introduced me backstage as one of a dying breed – the nice critic. Even so . . . When I went to the recording sessions for Bernstein's *Wonderful Town*, there was a break and I was chatting to him and looking at the band parts and saying how scandalous it was that the orchestrations were not credited. His immediate response was: 'But he did them.' Meaning Bernstein himself. Now this is very much my field, and while it's true that in time-honoured Broadway tradition Bernstein will have given fairly detailed instructions as to how the orchestration should go, it is also true that he didn't actually do the job himself, not even on *West Side Story*. No Broadway composer of that period ever did. But I don't think Simon liked being caught out on this. I didn't get much attention after that, though when the record finally came out, it was all of course correctly credited!

When all is said and done, the fact remains that I would travel great distances and pay good money to hear Simon conduct because it is always a real event. There are very few of his kind about.

Hugh Canning

His conducting is always instinctively theatrical, whether or not he's conducting opera. When you think how he does the Mahler symphonies, it's as if they are operas without voices. And Wagner's *Tristan* in Amsterdam was a symphony with voices.

Some of my best early memories of him were in Oxford on the Glyndebourne tour, conducting *Cunning Little Vixen*, *Così* and *The Rake's Progress* better than they were done in the Festival. And you got a sense of the voraciousness of this young man's musical sympathies. The playing of the Rotterdam orchestra for him in *Tristan* was some of the most beautiful playing I've heard for years and I thought their *Parsifal* was the highlight of what I heard at the 2000 Proms; it was the thing that stays in the memory. So here he is scaling the heights of Wagner at the first attempt.

One thing that has remained constant is that he has been a wonderful Haydn conductor, and that links to the fact that he has opened his ears to the period-instrument movement. Rameau's *Les boréades* I didn't enjoy so much, because I thought the style of the singing didn't match the colours of the playing. I think a weak link for him can be his knowledge of singers, and he has sometimes made some quite serious casting mistakes. He's got that rare thing of being as good at opera as at being a symphonic conductor – like Abbado is, Giulini was and I suppose Karajan (not that you'd want to hear his Mozart after the early 1950s). He does conceive those big works like the Mahler Tenth, the Nicholas Maw *Odyssey*, on a vast scale. The *Towards the Millennium* series was a project of real vision, which marks him out as someone who just doesn't think short-term. You hear that in his music-making too. He thinks ahead and I'm sure it's going to get better and better.

The Berlin appointment shows that the orchestra finally came to its senses. Towards the end of the selection process I was convinced that Rattle would get the job, but knowing the music world and that players think primarily of their pockets, there was a chance that they would have been seduced by the idea of a return to the Karajan era with what Barenboim was offering. Barenboim wasn't even going to give up Chicago if he had got the job. It wasn't a realistic option.

The record company boom is over, they now think carefully about what to record next, and don't do it for the sake of conductors and their vanity. There is not the money out there. At the press conference in Berlin after Simon's Mahler 10, there was an obviously planted question asking what he was going to do about improving the income of the Berlin players and he just smiled in a quiet way. The Berlin orchestra isn't affected in the way that the opera houses are. I have very little sympathy for the opera houses, which together get more than we spend on opera in this country. They've been living in this welfare-state mentality; everyone is on a pension, lifetime contracts, everything hugely overmanned. Berlin opera has huge problems, so the Berlin Philharmonic now has the chance to be the artistic leader of the united city.

Artists

Bernard Haitink

It is a remarkable development, beginning from a very, very high point of achievement! I came across him first at Glyndebourne, I think, but I have since heard him with many different groups, with the Age of Enlightenment in London, and the Vienna Philharmonic, in the Mahler Festival in Amsterdam. He has such a quicksilver attitude; he is quick to grab the essence of a style, and he has an enormous thirst for a wide repertory. He is volatile in a good sense: alive in a way that speaks to a modern audience. He finds the style that suits each individual composer and doesn't impose a pompous style of his own. He has such an open mind, and a really incredible charisma.

Alfred Brendel

Conductors these days are steeped in Mahler rather than in the classics. There is not enough chance to work as regularly on the classical repertory as conductors used to do. The regular fare of orchestras is no longer Beethoven symphonies, and although the critics may complain about continual Beethoven, it seems to me to be so important for an orchestra and for a conductor to have that firm basis of what a symphony is about and what a symphony orchestra should sound like. Much as I can understand the reluctance of conductors today to deal with Beethoven, and their desire to give it a rest, I do feel they miss out on something important. Simon is very typical in that the Mahler symphonies seem to come more easily to him at the moment than the Beethoven symphonies. (For me, Simon has put Mahler 10 on the map; he has proved once and for all that this is a very remarkable score.) They may be nearer to us and to what we feel than Beethoven. But he knows he must now go back and find the roots of this tradition. One of the reasons for the unease of conductors and orchestras with Mozart and Beethoven is the question of performance practice, of 'authentic' performances using old instruments. Interesting and stimulating as this is, it can never be the only way to play the classics. My problem as a soloist is that I can find at present a dozen conductors who can do the Schoenberg Piano Concerto well, some of them very well. As for the Beethoven concertos, I am sometimes at a loss!

It is wonderful to work out classical concertos with Simon and the CBSO because it means breaking fresh ground. Simon is the most stunningly gifted young conductor I know, and my only reservation is that he spends too much time on repertory that I regard as second-rate; surely the first-class repertory is big enough to spend one's life with. I think the time has come to identify with what is really worthwhile.

I heard a tape of the first performance of Beethoven's Ninth he gave, in Scotland, and I would like to meet another young conductor who could bring it off in such a fashion; it was truly impressive. We also talked about one of his earlier performances of the *Eroica*, and I said to Simon that I felt it was too spacious. So, it seems, did he. Stronger concentration, greater tightness, more sense of the overall shape was needed – and, I'm sure, was achieved in the next performances. Simon loves the detail and pays great attention to it, to the point where he gets over-sensitive about it (in welcome contrast to certain other conductors!). He has a marvellous 'ear' for sound and nuance. [1987]

In recent years Simon has made himself at home in the classics. His performance of Beethoven's Ninth at the Proms in 1998 impressed me as the most extraordinary I have heard since Furtwängler and Bruno Walter's days. Who else would be able to present Haydn symphonies with such zest, imagination and humour? And then there is Simon the partner: a soloist's dream. Whether in Mozart, Beethoven or Schumann, he is wide awake and loving.

I see for him also a role in the cultural life of this country. If anybody can persuade the people on this island that culture is much more than entertainment, and the politicians of this country that the arts, music, musical education is grossly underfunded, then it is him. [2001]

Philip Fowke

If you ask me which of all the conductors I've worked with I enjoy best, then Simon is right there at the top. When you're out on the platform with him you have a feeling of complete security. It's like playing with a safety net, and when little things happen, as they invariably do, you know you'll be OK. If you want to take a little time over something, he's with you. He makes you be with him as well, of course; it's a complete collaboration. Musically he likes all the things I like – time to breathe, flexibility. He's a very passionate conductor; there's no holding back. And he's a superb accompanist: I remember Rakh. 3 in Birmingham, and the televised Prom when we did the John Ireland Concerto: the beginning of the slow movement sounded glorious.

We both studied the piano at the Royal Academy with Gordon Greene, and Simon was brilliant at slashing his way through an orchestral score at the piano, but couldn't play a C major scale to save his life (or so I heard). I used to go up to Liverpool for lessons, so it seemed natural we should do something together there. I remember Simon's complete professionalism even from the first Rakh. 2 I did with the Merseyside Youth Orchestra. He knew exactly what he was doing. There was a lot of movement, and a certain cockiness in his manner – I have always wondered how that went down with orchestras where the players were much older than him – but I'm sure people put up with it because he was just so glaringly gifted.

I never feel I've got to know Simon as well as I could wish. We've had some very nice times, and a couple of years ago I bumped into him quite by accident in the Piazza San Marco in Venice, and had a marvellous time with him and Ellie and Sacha. But there's something about him that overawes me, and I can't quite work out what he's thinking. You can be terribly friendly, but you feel you are only really communicating when you're actually playing. Yes, that's it: you feel you know him best through the music. [1987]

Composers

Oliver Knussen

Simon was asked by Michael Vyner [then director of the London Sin-fonietta] to do the premiere of my *Coursing* in one of his Sinfonietta concerts. So I took the first twenty or so pages of the piece, which was all that was ready a month before, round to him when he lived down on the Marylebone Road. It was rather early, and he answered the door in a dressing-gown and absolutely nothing else, which was, I thought, refreshingly un-conductor-like. That piece eventually got terribly stuck, and I was for giving it up, but it was Simon who insisted, 'Put a tempor-ary ending on and let's do it.' It's a horribly difficult piece, but he under-stood it at once; he had no apparent difficulty at all. As a composer that's the thing I like most about him: you don't actually have to spell out what the piece is about or what to bring out; he knows.

He did my Third Symphony in Birmingham – he was the first con-ductor in this country to take it up. I did some preliminary rehearsals with the orchestra (because he characteristically felt that they should have more time on it than he had). When he began his own rehearsals a few weeks later he said, 'Well, of course I had to start from scratch!' I know he can't stand composers who bounce up in the middle of rehearsals and ask for things, so I volunteered – and he accepted – a rather funny arrangement. I sat in the control room with the sound turned off and read a book while he rehearsed next door. We left it that he would come in if he needed to ask anything, which of course he didn't. I just went in at the end and it was fine.

He has a terrific sense of style; he knows the twentieth-century litera-ture very well, and he will know the antecedents of any piece he is deal-ing with – and is quite merciless in pointing them out! He instinctively knows what you are aiming for. There are a few people who can perceive things that quickly, but there's virtually no one who can also communi-cate them in rehearsal, as Simon does, without ever putting a player's back up. Of course there will be minor moans, like there are about any conductor, but I've never seen him irritate players with his sharpness, and that *is* a gift.

Once every six or nine months in the eighties we used to have a sort of listening orgy. He would bring me things – he brought the Debussy *House of Usher* fragments, which we then worked on together for South

Bank Summer Music, or tapes he's been sent by unknowns – and I will play him things. That was how he got on to Takemitsu, for instance. One day he rang up and said he was feeling terribly out of touch with the younger generation of composers (the ones now in their twenties) and could he come round for a 'crash course'. Now the point to make here is that when you fling a bunch of stuff at most people they might say, 'Very interesting, very promising,' but Simon knows at once what he likes and what he doesn't, and can say why, too. When something does strike his fancy there is a quite wonderful spontaneous warmth in his response, and he usually goes into action on that composer immediately. I should add, however, that any attempt to thrust something on him is likely to have a contrary effect. He is open to suggestion, but closed to hyperbole.

Writing an opera and rehearsing it at the same time is not an experience I recommend to anyone. In 1985 I was at Glyndebourne working on my *Higglety Pigglety Pop* and was in a terrible state, obsessed with the knowledge that this piece could not be finished in time and that it might not hold up. Simon came into a rehearsal, a particularly bad one for me. I saw him quietly sitting there, and I was rather nervous. I don't think he'd seen me conduct before. So I came out of the pit at the end and everyone was worried by what they'd seen, about whether the thing was going to happen. The actual music was the last thing on anybody's mind. Simon just came up and said, 'Well, I think that music is beautiful, some of the best you've done, and I can't wait to get my hands on it!' I don't know whether he really felt it, or sensed that I was very low, or whatever, but it was so unexpected for someone at that moment to comment on my music instead of all the problems that I just burst into tears. It probably embarrassed him terribly, but I'll never forget that sensitivity or that moment. [1987]

Simon has, without fanfare, consistently programmed my music over the years – curiously, the more I've conducted myself, the less 'real' conductors have had much time for it. A few years ago it occurred to me that in that particular season he had played four of my pieces. Now I had only heard one performance of one piece, and had found out about the others only from my publisher's lists. That's something for a composer to be grateful for in this day and age. [2001]

Tributes from four composers when Rattle came to the end of his time in Birmingham, in 1998

John Adams

When Simon invited me to conduct concerts with the CBSO in 1993 he did more than extend the usual formal invitation. He offered me a room in his flat, sent his driver to pick me up at the airport, and even stood in line with me at a local supermarket while I waited with jet lag to buy a few necessities to survive the week in Birmingham. I thought to myself, 'Would Karajan have done this?'

Hans Werner Henze

Thinking of Simon and the CBSO, memories spring to mind which contain some of the best, most enjoyable artistic experiences in my whole life – unforgettable performances, all of which had one thing in common: clarity. In Birmingham the music is irradiated X-ray fashion, so it shines, yet at the same time unfolds human proportions, human warmth, speech and truth. The music sings and dances in bright daylight. Even in works where the expressions of pain and sorrow are the prevailing musical subject matters, the sound of the score remains transparent, clear, openhearted and Apollonian.

Judith Weir

One of the pleasures of working in Birmingham has been the chance to sneak into early rehearsals and hear the music in little bits, the way the public never hears it. All of Simon's music-making is supercharged with energy, and even the most technical points in rehearsal can become fascinating and dynamic in his hands. His concern for the way music fits together, and whether it works is, I'm sure, why his performances of newly composed music are unparalleled among the conductors of today.

Nicholas Maw

The experience of working with Simon Rattle and the CBSO on *Odyssey* was a high point of my musical life. At the time of writing that enormous work I never imagined it would make its way so quickly into the world – in fact rather the opposite. That it has done so is in large measure due to Simon's championing it. I have often thought about the qualities that produced those memorable performances: musical gifts of a high order, of course, but also spiritual and intellectual curiosity, appetite, dedication, concentration, and the ability of all great conductors to make musicians give the best of themselves – to make them want to play. We are all fortunate to be living through the Rattle era.

CHAPTER EIGHT

'This is the place where ideas are allowed'
Birmingham 1991–98

Rattle's final concert as Music Director of the CBSO, 1998
(photo Alan Wood)

I
Symphony Hall

It must have been some time in the late 1980s that I zapped up in a lift with Simon Rattle and stood at the blustery top of Birmingham's Alpha Tower, the old Central TV building that looms over Centenary Square, looking down on the most spectacular hole in the ground, which was about to become Birmingham's new Convention Centre and would house a new hall for the City of Birmingham Symphony Orchestra.

SIMON RATTLE It's extraordinary to see the size of it. Looking down on it from a great height, it's a bit like a Christmas present for me, to realize the possibility that there really will be somewhere for us all to work. Somewhere for the orchestra to play. The Chief Executive of the city got the President of the European Commission to lay the first stone so his name was on it just in case they didn't give us enough money, so it would somehow be his responsibility. This is not the main city centre but the canal area, and there are many plans for opening the canals out more so that there's ever more water and piazzas. The hope is that the focus of the city centre will shift somewhat from the mess over there, and I think there's a chance it could be quite pretty.

How long is it since a new concert hall was promised to Birmingham?
The first thing I have a record of is in the 1920s when it was promised to Adrian Boult. He wrote me a very sweet note when I took over saying words to the effect: 'As you are now the second Scouse person who has got the job of principal conductor, can you see if you can have any more luck than I did with getting a new hall to replace the Town Hall?' And there was a little PS: 'I'm reliably informed that Mendelssohn also had problems with the acoustics there.'

What is wrong with the Town Hall according to Mendelssohn or Boult – or you?!
The Town Hall is a magnificent building, with a great deal of atmosphere, built for a certain time and a certain kind of music, which really is no more. Unfortunately no one can hear anyone else on stage; almost nobody on stage can hear what the orchestra's doing; it's immensely uncomfortable. There are all types of problems – everything from seating to heating and lighting. It really was never designed as a concert hall; it's a place for great occasions. But what the orchestra has deserved for many years is its own hall where it can actually be heard to advantage and go on growing and building.

15 Rattle in concert (photos Alan Wood)

16 Luther Henderson, long-time collaborator with Duke Ellington, with Rattle at their sessions for the Ellington jazz album (photo Alan Wood)

17 Rattle with Kennedy, recording the Elgar Violin Concerto (photo Alan Wood)

18 Rattle on the site of the new CBSO Centre, Birmingham (photo Alan Wood)

19 Composing mortals: Mark-Anthony Turnage (centre) with Rattle and Edward, Duke of Wessex, Patron of the CBSO (photo Alan Wood)

20 Rattle with his first wife, Elise Ross, his mother Pauline and father Denis (photo Alan Wood)

21 Rattle with Hans Werner Henze, Aldeburgh, 1986 (photo Nigel Luckhurst)

22 The triumph of time: Rattle with Harrison Birtwistle, Aldeburgh, 1991
(photo Nigel Luckhurst)

23 Bill Bryden's production of Janáček's *The Cunning Little Vixen*, Rattle's début at the Royal Opera House, 1980 (photos Clive Barda/Performing Arts Library)

24 At work in Berlin (photos Reinhard Friedrich)

25 The risks of the future: Rattle in Berlin (photos Reinhard Friedrich)

How will it work?
Down there is the part of the site where there are going to be eleven halls, of which ours is Hall 2. We called it 'Hall 2' very anonymously for a long time in the hope of getting the idea past people without their realizing quite how much culture they were going to pay for. There's a phrase at the start of the score for Elgar's Second Symphony where he says 'a massive hope for the future'. And corny though it may sound, I think, as it happens, that was the first piece he conducted with the orchestra, and now, sixty years later, it is coming true. It is part of Birmingham's commitment to us which always has to be a two-way thing. We will give back what we are given.

The building of Symphony Hall was, in retrospect, a tremendous gamble and a tremendous risk, which only just worked. It came to fruition on the crest of a cultural wave in Birmingham, at a time when the CBSO was gaining international recognition and acclaim, and when the mood and the moment were right. As Simon Rattle now says, 'It was only right for five minutes, but thank God they happened to be the right five minutes!'

ED SMITH It was very lucky that it happened at the right time. If the hall had opened, say, in the early 1980s when the orchestra was at the stage it was at then, and the hall had made it a policy to invite in the world's great orchestras, the CBSO would frankly have had great difficulty in maintaining its status with the public. That was a problem elsewhere – for example, in Manchester in the early days of the Bridgewater Hall – where the resident orchestra suffered somewhat because touring orchestras came in and there were invidious comparisons. But by the time Symphony Hall opened in 1991, the CBSO was able to be heard alongside all-comers with its head held high. And it had a great effect on concert-going.

The arrival of Symphony Hall and the provision of more concerts by visiting orchestras doubled concert attendance in Birmingham. The 1,750-seat Town Hall was used exclusively by the CBSO, apart from the occasional visit. So, from the 1991–92 season, the increased number of concerts that the CBSO did, plus the increased number of symphony concerts promoted by the hall itself, over the first two or three seasons doubled the number of symphony-concert attendances. For three or four seasons houses were 98 or 99 per cent. Then – let's not beat about the bush – there was a decline, and I think that's understandable.

The support of the city council, and of its newly appointed arts officer, Anthony Sargent, was vital both for the flourishing of Symphony Hall and for the other ambitious schemes such as the *Towards the Millennium* festival that flowered in Birmingham during the 1990s.

ANTHONY SARGENT Simon didn't just give Birmingham a concert hall; other conductors have done that in other cities. Because of his totally uncompromising association with the design process, he gave Birmingham an absolutely exceptional concert hall by the highest world standards, and the achievement was that he stayed right inside the design process, stayed very close to the acousticians and the architect, almost as if he had been the patron or the client, when in fact he was neither, and secured this completely outstanding result, which ten years on is still is the best performing base for music in the UK.

SIMON RATTLE We fought an enormous battle to get the acoustician [Russell Johnson, of Artec] appointed over the architect because, almost without exception, the big acoustical disasters have been where the architect was above the acoustician and they have said things couldn't be done. Everything is to do with Russell Johnson – the acoustics, the shape of the concert hall, what materials are used. It's such a success.

BERESFORD KING-SMITH The promise to Boult was made in 1924, but a civic-hall project had been on the stocks since 1919. We can probably be grateful now that a loss of nerve (or maybe a change of political control) caused it to be dropped. Some years ago I was shown the preliminary plans for the Civic Hall, whose exterior was designed in the monolithic style favoured in the 1920s and 1930s and whose interior, designed to seat five thousand people, would have served as a multi-purpose hall – implying, of course, a hall that serves no useful purpose known to man.

The building, now Baskerville House, was in due course erected to house various civic offices, and since then there have been several moves to initiate a new concert hall for Birmingham, but on each occasion initial enthusiasm was always dampened by the cost, which seemed to double every time you blinked. Only a supreme act of determination on the part of a few stubborn visionaries in the early 1980s finally broke the old mould!

It was Symphony Hall – as 'Hall 2' was soon renamed at Ed Smith's insistence – that had, in the end, the biggest impact on the CBSO's music-making in the 1990s, rather than the much-vaunted Arts Council development plan. It took Birmingham into a new league internationally. The new manager of the hall was Andrew Jowett, who already knew Simon and Ed Smith from his previous role at the Warwick Arts Centre where the CBSO had given many concerts and made some of their best recordings.

ANDREW JOWETT The CBSO was on a roll at the end of Simon's first ten years: the development plans were in place, the orchestral strength was there for the new hall and there was a real artistic vision of what it could contribute. There's always one moment when you know there's something special and I think it was 15 January 1991, the first rehearsal with just the strings and Simon played the beginning of the last movement of Mahler 9, and as that incredible string melody emerged we knew we had a real success on our hands. Then someone commented, 'Well, you can get rid of three of those double basses right away because it's so good at the bottom end.' On 15 April we opened officially and did two concerts on the same night – four thousand people to feed! The nerves were unbelievable. That week we also presented Cleo Laine and John Dankworth, a two-day youth festival with three thousand kids coming through to see the place, and finally on 12 June the Queen came to a rehearsal of Mahler 2 and then the Princess Royal came in the evening to open the hall. [Prince Edward became Royal Patron of the CBSO the following year.]

I think the biggest potential disaster area we were aware of was audiences. We might have split the audience. We were starting to promote another series of concerts with quite major orchestras and the CBSO was having to sell more seats for its own concerts in a bigger hall. So it could have been a disaster but it wasn't. We built a new audience. We looked at a business plan that had something between thirty-five and forty-five concerts a year, depending on their size and scale, and asked the city to underwrite that – which they did. They wanted to see the CBSO perform in an international context and that was what they were ready for and that was what they did, with the orchestra benefiting from being in the hall. The city was prepared to subsidize the operation and so by not charging the CBSO a commercial rent, they felt this was a win–win for the CBSO.

It's a privilege to work in a city that doesn't play silly buggers with its support for the arts. Irrespective of which politicians hold the purse strings, they have the same aspirations. The city views culture as being fundamental to the life of its citizens and adds to its image as a great European city in that tradition. It's not backed off at all from that aim, whatever the pressures from different quarters.

The project was an enormously complex one, which had its roots as far back as 1982 when a working group was set up by the city council to see if it was feasible to build a convention centre. A new Hyatt Hotel was built in the city just by the site, a major advantage for visitors to conventions. (This produced one amusing but little-noticed result: a bridge was built from the Convention Centre to the Hyatt above the road, but when it was designed it wasn't realized that the hotel had been built a few yards further back than originally planned. The extra bit of bridge that had to be added on is still clearly visible today.) The architects who formed the Convention Centre partnership were Percy Thomas Partnership and Renton Howard Wood Levin (who had designed many theatres as well as the Royal Concert Hall in Nottingham, where the CBSO frequently toured, and had collaborated there with Artec). The confirmation of the European Union's funding of £37.5m was received on 30 October 1986 – which marked the formal beginning of the project. (By the end the EU had contributed £49.7m.) The architects worked closely with Artec on all aspects of the acoustics and planning of Symphony Hall, while Ove Arup did the extensive engineering works which, among other things, balanced the whole hall on rubber pads as the mainline trains ran in a tunnel not far underground. At one time there was a plan to site the concert hall away from the railway line, which would have involved moving the Crown Pub – literally picking it up and taking it across the road – but that was resisted as it was a listed building, and the concert hall was moved to within thirty-five metres of the railway line. Two thousand rubber bearings were inserted to dampen any vibrations, and the piles had six metres of empty space around them. All pressure to make the hall a dual-purpose or multi-purpose hall was resisted, and Rattle's involvement ensured a purpose-built concert hall of the highest quality.

The city earmarked 1 per cent of the construction budget for works of art, both in the International Convention Centre and in the new Centenary Square, a splendid space opening outwards from the ICC and fronting the Birmingham Rep, leading a pedestrian path over the dreaded ring road, through a giant atrium (by the Birmingham Conservatoire where the CBSO offices were housed), and into the pedestrianized space by the Library and the CBSO's old residence in the Town Hall. The most famous result of these art commissions was Raymond Mason's dominating and somewhat Stalinist *Forward*, showing the industrial march of the people of Birmingham. Centenary Square has now become the regular venue for huge open-air events in Birmingham, from the BBC's Music Live to Proms in the Park.

The new hall opened, boldly, with a double concert so that two complete audiences could experience it on the same day: first Stravinsky's *The Firebird* and then Ravel's *Daphnis et Chloë*. In the *Observer* I wrote of the hall's 'overwhelmingly live, vivid, crackling ambience ... The sound combines to an electrifying degree qualities of reverberation and sharpness.' I noted that the artistic programming could throw up problems: 'The big unspoken challenge for Birmingham is that given new rivalry from the Concertgebouw, Los Angeles, Leipzig – and maybe even, who knows, the Berlin Philharmonic with Rattle himself – what will the effect be on the CBSO's marketing and profile? That will be the most interesting question as Birmingham races, with this huge new resource, towards its millennium.'

The shock of the hall was its bright reds and oranges, a dazzling display that composer Micháel Berkeley, presenting the official opening night's television broadcast of Mahler 2, described as looking like an art-deco liner. Some have always found it too busy as a visual space for music, but there was no denying the superb quality of the acoustic. The performance of the *Resurrection* Symphony for the royal opening in the presence of Princess Anne made for a tremendous occasion – although from my perch on one of the side balconies I could see musical dignitaries asleep in the front row as the symphony reached its massive climax.

Apart from the concerts transferred from the Town Hall towards the end of the season, the residence at Symphony Hall began in earnest in the 1991–92 season, in which the main novelty was the second year of the key project of the 1990s, *Towards the Millennium*:

1991–92

Beethoven	Overture: *The Consecration of the House*
Schoenberg	*Variations*, op. 31
Schubert	Symphony no. 9
Weill	Excerpts from *Happy End*
Weill	*Mahagonny Songspiel* (Elise Ross, Ameral Gunson, Damon Evans, John Graham-Hall, Benjamin Luxon, Nicholas Folwell)
Janáček	*Sinfonietta*
Tippett	*A Child of Our Time* (Roberta Alexander, Florence Quivar, Robert Tear, Benjamin Luxon)
Beethoven	Piano Concerto no. 1 (Alfred Brendel)
Schoenberg	*Variations*, op. 31
Beethoven	Piano Concerto no. 4

Beethoven	Piano Concerto no. 2 (Alfred Brendel)
Beethoven	Piano Concerto no. 3
Mozart	Symphony no. 40 in G minor
Mark-Anthony Turnage	*Momentum*
Beethoven	Piano Concerto no. 5 (Alfred Brendel)
Henze	Symphony no. 7
Verdi	*Requiem* (Andrea Gruber, Luciana D'Intino, Dennis O'Neill, John Tomlinson)
Berlioz	*Harold in Italy* (Yuri Bashmet)
Mahler	Symphony no. 1
Walton	Cello Concerto (Lynn Harrell)
Mahler	Symphony no. 1
Turnage	*Three Screaming Popes*
Mozart	Piano Concerto in C K503 (Lars Vogt)
Prokofiev	Symphony no. 5
Robin Holloway	*The Spacious Firmament* (première)
Mozart	Mass in C minor (Arleen Augér, Anne Sofie von Otter, John Mark Ainsley, David Thomas)

Towards the Millennium 1911–1920

Berg	*Three Pieces*, op. 6
Mahler	Symphony no. 10

Towards the Millennium 1911–1920

Nielsen	Symphony no. 3 (*Espansiva*)
Szymanowski	*Songs of a Fairytale Princess* (Eileen Hulse)
Ravel	*Daphnis et Chloë*

Towards the Millennium 1911–1920

Debussy	*Jeux*
Elgar	*Falstaff*
Stravinsky	*The Rite of Spring*

Simon Rattle was by now an essential part of the cultural furniture in Birmingham, but there was much more to be done to enable the CBSO's success to be integrated with that of the city, as Anthony Sargent, who arrived at the city council from London's South Bank, recalled:

ANTHONY SARGENT He was around. He had a house there unlike a lot of music directors; you met him in Sainsbury's; he took the kids to school, and he was part of the community. He went to other performances – you'd see him at the ballet, at the Rep, at black dance performances at the Arts Centre. He often said that one of the things he particularly valued in Birmingham was its culturally diverse traditions, and some of the young rock and pop people would say they felt he was their champion, which isn't something they would necessarily say of Barenboim or Abbado. It was just something about the openness of Simon's views that spoke very directly to the broad generality of artists working in Birmingham.

At the start there wasn't a sense that he was part of the arts world in Birmingham. People running other arts organizations didn't feel they could approach him. That was what really changed through the 1990s. It was partly because the CBSO itself had previously stood apart from the rest of the landscape as the only arts organization at that time that had the international profile in touring and broadcasting and recording. But all those doors opened during the 1990s, and that was through a series of collaborative projects, *Towards the Millennium*, but also the 'Sounds Like Birmingham' festival in 1992, the first BBC Music Live in 1995, and then ArtsFest in 1998: all these things were milestones that created a very natural and instinctive desire to collaborate across the city.

SIMON RATTLE So many things were happening to the arts scene that it became very exciting. And to the city as well. Did you ever wonder why there were so many young people wandering the streets at the weekend? Apparently the hotels offered their rooms to up to twelve people at a time so the place was crammed and the bars were all full.

The oft-repeated line is that in Birmingham Simon Rattle made audiences listen to everything, that they trusted him, and that whatever he gave they took. At the start it worked, while the curiosity value was high: over the first twenty-six promotions in 1991, the CBSO recorded 97 per cent attendances. But, as so often, that is one part of the truth:

ANDREW JOWETT It didn't work all the time. Simon's integrity was never in question, though perhaps I have slightly a more jaundiced view of the role of the record companies and the extent to which that activity dictated what went on in the concerts. But it was as if he said, 'You will want to listen to this.' And the audience said, 'OK, well, you've said that to us before and once or twice we've been disappointed, but three or four times we've really enjoyed it, so we'll take the chance.' People didn't follow, blindly. There was a choice, but in the end he delivered audiences for programmes that would have been unthinkable in any other venue in any other city.

The press responded quickly to Birmingham's new role. Andrew Clements wrote in the *Financial Times*:

> With the opening of Symphony Hall last spring and the continued prosperity of the CBSO, Birmingham had already placed itself at the very centre of our concert life. The new year promises to show how the musical profile is to be rounded out, so that the goodies are not confined to the juiciest programmes from Simon Rattle and the CBSO but can offer a truly varied diet of events.

II
Towards the Millennium

The big idea that Simon Rattle had already launched in Birmingham and which became a catalyst for change in the city was *Towards the Millennium*, designed originally as a collaboration between the CBSO, the South Bank Centre in London, and the BBC. Anthony Sargent was at the South Bank Centre at the time it was conceived:

ANTHONY SARGENT It was an idea that was around. I was at the South Bank and meetings were taking place but the idea didn't quite seem to have taken root, and actually in some ways it never did in London. When I went to Birmingham there was also a problem, because I talked to all the arts people, the art galleries, the theatres, and I sat down with Simon and Ed [Smith] and said that for whatever reason the CBSO hadn't really got to the point of engaging the wider community in the idea. So I said, 'Well, we just have to have a meeting with the main arts organizations, and Simon has to come and explain the idea from scratch.' Which he did, and there was suddenly a room full of tangible electricity. There was a palpable sense of excitement about a journey that could be embarked on over the ten years.

It was interesting that a few years later Simon and I were reflecting on why it had taken off in Birmingham and not in London. And he thought for a minute and said one of those things I've never forgotten, which is that in Birmingham the first question they ask is: 'Is the idea any good?' But in

London they ask, 'Whose idea was it first?' That conditions all their further reactions.

I think the original idea as conceived by Simon and Michael Vyner was of a classically composed festival, but of course once you got beyond the 1950s it was impossible to do anything that didn't take account of all the other cultural streams. Especially in Birmingham you've got black and Asian immigration into the Midlands which affects the city's cultural history fundamentally. Simon really had a feeling for this, and the project expanded as it went. In the 1970s festival the Midland Arts Centre re-created the Pink Floyd work *The Wall* in an old bombed-out department store with a cast of a hundred and twenty incredibly energetic youngsters and Simon was absolutely captivated by the idea. The fact that the festival rolled on with popular and world cultures increasingly absorbed into it just would not have happened with another kind of classically trained musician at the heart of it.

One collaboration on *Towards the Millennium* that in the event did not work – perhaps because of the issue that Rattle raised of ownership – was with the BBC. John Drummond, who had been director of the Edinburgh Festival and then of the BBC Proms, had dealt with Rattle over several successful seasons of CBSO visits to the two festivals, and was by then Controller of Radio 3:

JOHN DRUMMOND That was a sad story. I had spent a long time trying to get Simon to work with the BBC Symphony Orchestra, but he just didn't like them. He had been to a rehearsal once with Lutosławski and two or three of the players had been rude to Lutosławski and Simon never forgave them.

He came to talk to me about the idea of *Towards the Millennium*, and he sat in my office in an enormous great yellow oilskin raincoat. I saw it as the only possible way of getting him to the BBC Symphony Orchestra. The idea was threefold: it was meant to be the BBCSO, the CBSO and the London Sinfonietta. Three conductors – Andrew Davis, Rattle and Olly Knussen – each conducting all three groups. There were going to be nine concerts a year, three with each group: three with the BBCSO, three with the CBSO, three with the Sinfonietta. Well, two things went wrong very quickly. One was that the CBSO totally refused to accept the BBCSO in Birmingham as part of their series, so the financial implications of getting involved with Birmingham were extremely large: we would have to promote ourselves and that was a considerable risk. The second thing is harder to talk about but I think it should be said. Simon's attitude was that he would do the pieces he wanted, and Olly could then be allowed to do what he wanted, and Andrew would be left with the rest. There was a feeling that the BBC would be cast in a supporting role and we were not going to get adequate reflection of Andrew's ideas – or indeed mine.

I think in the end it was better that it ended up as Simon's personal view of things, and it certainly made it possible to plan the project. One afternoon we were in Andrew's house in Weymouth Mews for two and a half hours and we didn't get a single programme done. I pulled out – with great reluctance – and everyone sneered and got terribly annoyed with my attitude. I said, 'I'm not sure if the project will work.' Well, I was proved wrong. The project worked pretty well, and attracted a lot of interest for programmes that without that sort of context wouldn't have sold at all. I was rather wrong-footed and people would ask why we weren't involved and I couldn't tell the whole story. But it was the moment when I saw Simon's authoritarian side and I didn't like it.

Towards the Millennium was launched in December 1990, with the first concerts in 1991, and I spoke to Simon Rattle about it then, which was when the line that Michael Vyner and he had conceived it 'in a traffic jam in Birmingham' was born.

SIMON RATTLE I'm not exactly a systematic person in my life, but I liked the idea of planning it logically, decade by decade, and I was very conscious of the idea of lateral history. The two of us could have been accused of delusions of grandeur, but I thought, well, somehow I am going to be involved with those two musical institutions [the CBSO and the London Sinfonietta] over the period. It's such a mad idea that we can't afford not to do it. There won't be another chance.

But what we have found is that it's very difficult in London to get people together, and I was quite surprised by some of the reactions – 'Oh, London doesn't need this' – which is rather sad. What's been very impressive is the co-operation and enthusiasm in Birmingham. With the arrival of Anthony Sargent at the city council to help us, it's burgeoned beyond my wildest dreams, and the result will be more Birmingham-based than I had thought. The number of organizations taking part is quite fantastic, and just to have the city bring us together round one table to discuss it was thrilling.

There were two possible roads to go down, the didactic or the playful, and inevitably I chose the playful route. I think it's important that the gigantic diversity of each decade is reflected – *Peter Pan* the same year as *The Cherry Orchard*, expressionist music and the beginnings of jazz.

ED SMITH *Towards the Millennium* was a huge journey, a wonderful thing to have lived through. I think inevitably it was more successful in Birmingham than it was in London. The whole idea of having everything

that lives and breathes being part of the event really wasn't possible when
you took it a hundred miles away to London where so much else was going
on. Simon was obviously the catalyst of bringing together the cultural
organisations in the city – with Tony Sargent's great help, but it was
Simon's conception. It is a very close artistic cultural community in
Birmingham and easier to bring them together than it would have been in
London.

In *The Times* Richard Morrison thought that to call the approach
'playful' was too modest:

> He is the finest conductor of his generation, presenting a monumental sur-
> vey of the century in which he lives. Future historians will gleefully regard
> the choices in *Towards the Millennium* as a time capsule: 'Look! This is
> what those crazy late twentieth-century audiences were listening to.' For the
> only certain thing about the next century is that it will regard much of our
> taste in art as lamentable, quaint, or incomprehensible. Next centuries
> always do.

Taking a different tack on the programming for *Towards The
Millennium*, Bayan Northcott wrote in the *Independent*:

> According to hearsay, Simon Rattle and the late Michael Vyner thought
> up the idea of *Towards the Millennium* in a traffic jam. Symbolic, that?
> For here we are, less than nine years short of a century which is supposed
> to have seen an unprecedented acceleration of artistic change, and cer-
> tainly has witnessed a revolution in the technological diffusion and com-
> mercial exploitation of music, yet in some ways we still seem stuck with
> the same artistic conflicts, the same crisis of communication, as eighty or
> ninety years ago. The Storm Cloud of the nineteenth century was
> Ruskin's metaphor for the polluting, dehumanizing pall of industrializa-
> tion. Could one, culturally, speak of the Traffic Jam of the twentieth
> century?

Northcott was not entirely convinced by the planning of the first
decade's programmes:

> Yet where in the series is the music of the composer of the 1900s as his
> contemporaries saw it; that most daring, notoriously state-of-the-art mod-
> ernist Strauss himself? . . . Such imbalances suggest that, if the remaining
> nine festivals are to add up to something more unified that a succession of
> Simon Rattle's modern lollipops – with the inevitable Messiaen *Turangalîla*
> representing the 1940s, etc. – the contrasting ways of planning such a
> historical series need to be thought through more rigorously.

After giving his own view of the styles of the twentieth century, Northcott concluded wittily:

> Right now the stylistic traffic seems gridlocked again. Again at junction AD2000 a traffic cop looking suspiciously like Pierre Boulez keeps waving it on, but many vehicles prefer to U-turn down Post-modern Parade or to sheer off up Minimalist Mall (cul-de-sac) to chase one another round the bollards in ever-decreasing circles. The CBSO charabanc rattles away healthily enough as it waits, but one wonders whether the Sinfonietta minibus has enough petrol to make it. Ah well, the saying goes, it is better to travel hopefully . . .

The year 1992 was also Birmingham's Year of Music, designated by the Arts Council in its own millennial scheme that would run (with varying degrees of success) around the country up to the final Year of the Artist, which failed to make much impression in 2000. The confidence that Birmingham's music-making was in good shape and could withstand a year of special exposure seemed entirely justified, and the accolade was celebrated with 'Sounds Like Birmingham', an excuse for a rash of visiting orchestras, including a whole series of Russian bands. Andrew Clements wrote in January 1992 that 'certainly the omens look promising . . . The performance [by the St Petersburg Orchestra] was rapturously received, and the concerts attracted evidently large, enthusiastic audiences.' The Association of British Orchestras held its conference in the city at this time, and Simon Rattle was presented with its annual award for services to the orchestral community. Birmingham was becoming the musical, not just the geographical, centre of the country.

The big ambitious project of the spring was the CBSO tour of America, taking some of the favourite works of the *Millennium* series in programmes designed to reflect specifically the three years 1911, 1912 and 1913, to Boston and Carnegie Hall in New York. But financial pressures were beginning to bite, and the tour had to be reduced to two weeks from three. The critical response in New York was once again mixed, and it was clear that the Rattle magic did not necessarily work on the hard-bitten critics there.

Typical of the problems the CBSO faced in America was the patronizing reaction of Bernard Holland in the *New York Times*:

> The CBSO, which has been the beneficiary of British music's extraordinary public-relations apparatus, comes very close to being a victim of it. When

the clouds of praise clear away and only the Birmingham musicians are left, what we hear is an assemblage of very modest skills used so intelligently that it fulfils many of the functions of a first-rate orchestra. The sum, as one music professional said to me at intermission, is better than the parts . . . Marketing the Birmingham and the thirty-seven-year-old Mr Rattle as a starry international duo is, I think, a mistake that will in the long run backfire. All the cleverness and dedication in the world eventually runs into the limits of technique.

And Edward Rothstein echoed this in the same paper: 'I wanted to admire the playing more than I actually did . . . I found myself less than fully engaged . . . ' There was at least one dissenting voice, the British critic Andrew Porter, who found that '*Falstaff* was emotionally a knock-out to a point where I struggled to stifle sobs distracting to neighbours'. But he reported for *Financial Times* readers that the New York consensus 'seems to be that the CBSO is an excellent but over-hyped regional orchestra'. This was not the situation the CBSO felt it was in at all, and caution prevailed over future appearances there.

Much better reactions followed a tour of the European festivals later in the year, when Janáček's *Glagolitic Mass* was a huge success at the Salzburg Festival alongside Turnage and Mahler's Tenth (even though this was a work the festival had not wanted – see Hans Landesmann, p. 295). Throughout the 1990s, audiences in Europe began to appreciate fully the unique qualities of the CBSO, and regular tours of parts of the *Millennium* concerts reinforced that view across the decade.

George Jonas stood down as chairman at the end of that season, to be replaced by local businessman and musician Arthur Knapp, and subsequently by the former Director-General of the BBC, Sir Michael Checkland.

1992–93

Boulez	*Notations I–IV*
Mahler	Symphony no. 3 (Jard Van Nes)
Rameau	Dances from *Les boréades*
Mozart	Symphony no. 39
Bartók	*Concerto for Orchestra*
Mozart	Symphony no. 39
Szymanowski	Violin Concerto no. 1 (Thomas Zehetmair)

GHT

Bartók	*Concerto for Orchestra*
Berlioz	Overture: *King Lear*
Gerhard	*Don Quixote*
Brahms	Symphony no. 3
Bartók	Piano Concerto no. 2 (Peter Donohoe)
Wagner	*Die Walküre*: Act I (Manfred Schenk, Rita Hunter, John Mitchinson)
Nielsen	Symphony no. 1
Mahler	*Lieder eines fahrenden Gesellen* (Solveig Kringelborn, Olaf Bär)
Nielsen	Symphony no. 3 (*Espansiva*)
Nielsen	Symphony no. 2 (*The Four Temperaments*)
Mahler	*Kindertotenlieder* (Olaf Bär)
Nielsen	Symphony no. 4 (*The Inextinguishable*)
Nielsen	Symphony no. 6 (*Sinfonia Semplice*)
Mahler	*Rückert Lieder* (Olaf Bär)
Nielsen	Symphony no. 5
Beethoven	Symphony no. 8
Beethoven	Rondino in E♭ for winds, op. 146
Beethoven	Symphony no. 6 (*Pastoral*)

Towards the Millennium: the 1920s

Szymanowski	*Litany to the Virgin Mary* (Elzbieta Szmytka)
Bartók	Ballet: *The Miraculous Mandarin*
Sibelius	Symphony no. 7
Szymanowski	*Stabat Mater* (Elzbieta Szmytka, John Connell, Florence Quivar)

Towards the Millennium: the 1920s

Shostakovich	Symphony no. 1
Berg	Three Fragments from *Wozzeck* (Elise Ross)
Varèse	*Amériques*
Gershwin	*An American in Paris*

Towards the Millennium: the 1920s

Bridge	*Enter Spring*
Britten	*Four French Songs* (Lynda Russell)

Ravel　　　　　　*L'enfant et les sortilèges* (David Thomas, Elise Ross,
　　　　　　　　　Lilian Watson, Christine Cairns, Mary King, David
　　　　　　　　　Wilson-Johnson)

Towards the Millennium: the 1920s

Schoenberg　　　*Variations*, op. 31
Stravinsky　　　*Symphony of Psalms*
Janáček　　　　　*Glagolitic Mass* (Faye Robinson, Ameral Gunson,
　　　　　　　　　John Mitchinson, Stephen Richardson)

Mozart　　　　　Piano Quintet in E♭ K452
Mozart　　　　　Piano Concerto in C K467 (Robert Levin)
Mozart　　　　　Symphony no. 38 (*Prague*)

Haydn　　　　　Symphony no. 86 in D
Rakhmaninov　　*Rhapsody on a Theme by Paganini* (Joanna
　　　　　　　　　MacGregor)

Mussorgsky–
　　Ravel　　　　*Pictures at an Exhibition*

There were many challenges in this season – Rameau and Boulez in
adjacent programmes, a live recording of the Bartók *Concerto for
Orchestra*, and other works programmed in order to prepare for EMI
recordings – but the highlight was undoubtedly the Nielsen symphony
cycle. Assembled for the Barbican's outstanding *Tender is the North*
festival, which explored the music of Scandinavia, the cycle was then
toured by the CBSO around England. It coincided with the European
Arts Festival that was meant to celebrate Britain's presidency of the
European Union, but which became a controversial subject from which
the politicians backed away, leaving the festival somewhat exposed.
John Drummond reflected both on that festival, which he directed, and
the annual sequence of CBSO appearances at the BBC Proms:

JOHN DRUMMOND When they programmed the six Nielsen symphonies
with Mahler song cycles in 1992 it was a big risk. I put some money from
the European Arts Festival into it and was much criticized for doing so
because it would have happened anyway. But I'd seen the figures and I
know that taking Nielsen symphonies to Basingstoke and Cheltenham and
so on is not very good business. Can you imagine any one of the big
London orchestras putting on a Mahler–Nielsen series outside London?
But it was a brilliant piece of planning and I think you could only take that
risk with the confidence Simon had got out of Birmingham. It also meant

that when he came to London with the orchestra the programmes were not only thoroughly rehearsed but had been performed several times and of course that too gave them an edge over the London orchestras.

At Edinburgh and then at the Proms in the early stages, it was fun planning things with Simon. He'd have a central work and it was a question of what we surrounded it with. In the last twenty years or so it got harder, because eventually it became a sort of production line in which he decided everything a long way in advance. He had this remarkable relationship with Ed Smith where they went into a cupboard and planned the future of the world. The focus was tremendous, but it made him rather inflexible. It was an essential and crucial relationship and it's a very hard one to describe. It wasn't a subservient one, because Ed is very outspoken and very opinionated.

The really outstanding Rattle Proms for me were those with new music: Henze's Seventh in 1986 and then his Eighth in 1995; John Adams's *Harmonium* in 1990; Gubaidulina's *Offertorium* in 1991. And, of the big pieces, the *Glagolitic Mass* in 1992 and Shostakovich 4 in 1994 really stood out.

Conductors can be more difficult than most people: Claudio [Abbado] and Simon are two of the most stubborn men I've ever met when we talk about programming. Claudio is different because he seems to forget he's agreed something and the next time he sees me he's says, 'I'm glad we're doing this' – which is exactly what you spent the last day getting rid of. With Simon there's no discussion; he says we're doing that, full stop.

He's one of the most interesting talents I have ever come across. I watch what he does, I listen to what he does, with increasing admiration because I do think he's working on a wider scale intellectually now. I don't find any kind of falling off at all, as so often happens, from being a wunderkind to being a boring middle-aged conductor.

The *Towards the Millennium* adventures continued into the 1920s with more Rattle favourites by Janáček and Szymanowski (which fitted with EMI's recording plans), and Rattle did one of his now rarer concerts with the London Sinfonietta, including Stravinsky's *Les noces* and – most unusually for him – Vaughan Williams's *Flos Campi*. May and June were given over to Debussy's *Pelléas et Mélisande* at the Netherlands Opera, in a set inspired by Frank Lloyd Wright houses, staged by Peter Sellars in one of his perhaps less successful updatings. Rattle's then wife Elise Ross was Mélisande, but this was an increasingly difficult time for their marriage and it was soon afterwards that they parted. Nevertheless they both took to Amsterdam and loved the set-up at the opera under the direction of Pierre Audi (previously an Islington colleague who had created the reputation of the Almeida Theatre in North London, very near the Rattles' home). At this time it was much more in Rattle's mind that there might be a connection with Amsterdam – with either or both of the opera and the Rotterdam Philharmonic Orchestra – than all the many other glamorous connections that were being proposed for him by the newspapers, though Boston was still very popular with him: as well as conducting the orchestra he did a conducting class at Tanglewood that summer, working with talented young musicians.

III

Speaking Up for Kids

Increasingly during these years, Rattle became a vocal advocate for music education and a thorn in the side of the educational establishment. It started early in the 1990s when the music curriculum, like those for all other subjects, was being revised. The advice of the specialist committee set up to rework it, which included such luminaries as Sir John Manduell of the Royal Northern College of Music, was ignored by the National Curriculum Council. They were driven by a Gradgrind-like attitude to facts and learning, whereas the musicians wanted to stress all the advances that had been made in recent years in involving children in composition and in making music for themselves. An absurd and unworkable plan for the music syllabus was unveiled by the then education minister, Kenneth Clarke, clearly playing to right-wing sentiment with its emphasis on the Western classical tradition at a time when non-Western music was increasingly used in schools and appreciated by listeners. Simon Rattle was first into the fray, with strange results.

SIMON RATTLE I'd always been very involved in education. It goes back to being a teenager and teaching in the blind school in Liverpool. It was Dick McNicol [Richard McNicol, one of the longest-standing pioneers of music education with orchestras, who works with the LSO] who first alerted me to what was going on and he said, 'Will you do something on the *Today* programme?' So I said, 'When?' And he said, 'What do you think the *Today* programme means? Today! Here are the facts, put your money where your mouth is.' So I did. And what I remembered then was Peter Hall saying to me that there would be a moment when I would have to stand up and defend music. He had done it continually and found it exhausting, but he had looked at me at lunch one day and said, 'Your turn will come soon enough.'

I got a very mysterious phone call that same day from a civil servant who did not identify himself but he said, 'I want you to know for your own reputation and protection, go on doing what you are doing but do not meet Kenneth Clarke. Do not debate with him, do not go on television with him, because he will trip you up on some insignificant details and dispose of you.' I have no idea who it was, and it was the nearest to cloak-and-dagger I've ever been, but it was good advice. I don't think Ken Clarke believed I could have sat down and read that desperately dull document but I had. It was quite an easy call because everyone in music whose advice they had asked had advised a different course and his was being put forward with such a degree of ignorance. There was some point where the only two forms of music you were supposed to know about were the symphony and the oratorio. Really! It was important that someone was the spearhead for that opposition.

The second time round [towards the end of the 1990s] it was much harder work and even more important, because it was pointing out the real danger that was going on in the reduction of provision for music. I cannot tell you the number of extraordinary, despairing letters I received as services crumbled all over the country. To be attacked by Chris Woodhead [then the government's chief adviser on education] – well, that was a rite of passage no one should miss. And when we had our argument in *The Times*, the letters editor got in touch and said that they had had so many letters on my side that it was just ridiculous and they couldn't print them.

It may be unfair to say it, but I still think that there are people who really believe that music is a luxury we can afford to lose. And that it is only for a certain section of the population who can afford it. That is such nonsense. My friend Eddie Thomas turned up when he was a kid for a double bass audition for the London Schools Symphony Orchestra with a bass guitar, not realizing it was a different instrument! But they encouraged him to try the double bass; within three years he was in the LPO and now he's back at Liverpool trying to turn around the fortunes of my old orchestra. That's what it means to give a chance to people who don't know that they have got it in them.

One of the great disappointments about working on Ken Robinson's wonderful report [*Culture and Creativity*, published in 1999, in which Rattle was involved, along with Lenny Henry, Dawn French, and distinguished academics including Sir Claus Moser] was that it was just knocked into touch by the government and not acted on. We worked bloody hard for two years on the report, and no one worked harder than

Ken. But in fact what it was saying about the British education system was too radical for its time. If we try to stick to a system that was designed for a society that has not existed for twenty years, let alone the society that might be existing soon, then we are going to be in deep trouble. And employers everywhere are telling us that they need people with lateral thinking, who make connections, not straight-line people any more. And those are arts, music people.

Now I'm on the National Federation for Youth Music, which is really trying to do things, and pick up the pieces. One of the ideas they came up with is that of the Pied Piper, using the wonderfully inspiring but usually unknown people around the country and making more of their work. But as for classical music . . . The idea of doing anything specially for our repertory – like George Benjamin's brilliant idea that we could form a National Youth London Sinfonietta – well, that didn't cut much ice with them. It's a start. They're making a difference.

The sad thing in this situation is that you can't be a friend of government. I have to say thank you when things have happened but to remind them how much there is to be done. There are many people who are equally and more qualified than I am to speak out, but if I can be used as a weapon occasionally that is really important.

Simon Rattle has used every occasion to drive home the importance of music for young people. In 1993 he also received the prestigious Montblanc de la Culture award in Paris, and as part of his speech he dug into the pocket of his suit and read out a letter he'd received from some kids who'd come to a CBSO concert. As the press reported, 'Duane happened to mention that his friend Mark had fallen asleep during the concert, and he noticed that Rattle opened and closed his mouth like a duck when conducting, but the basic message was not lost on a high-profile Euro-audience.' To Beresford King-Smith (who retired in July 1993 from the CBSO) Rattle explained that

> we came relatively late to serious educational work – indeed it came about very largely at the insistence of the players themselves – but it's every bit as important as anything else we do and it has developed the members of the orchestra. Maggie Cotton was doing tremendous work with deaf kids, for instance, long before we started on the Adopt-a-Player scheme. If we're not in the business of changing people's lives, then I don't know what business we are in.

Back at the orchestra, playing standards too continued to rise. And praise was unbounded for the orchestra's BBC Proms that year, with the

Bartók *Concerto for Orchestra* and Nielsen's Fifth Symphony. 'The success of Simon Rattle's Prom with the CBSO on Tuesday night offered exactly the kind of reading that inclines one to elevate the symphony to the pantheon of masterpieces . . . the most majestic welter of sound heard in this hall all season,' wrote Edward Seckerson; while Michael Kennedy in the *Sunday Telegraph* referred to 'Simon Rattle, whose Proms programmes last week with the CBSO reached stratospheric heights of performance and interpretation'. Whatever the problems in America, in London it seemed the CBSO could do no wrong.

IV
Money Troubles

1993–94

Debussy	*Prélude à l'après-midi d'un faune*
Bartók	*Concerto for Orchestra*
Nielsen	Symphony no. 5
Schoenberg	Chamber Symphony no. 1
Mozart	Piano Concerto in C minor K491 (Maurizio Pollini)
Stravinsky	*Pulcinella* (Ann Murray, Philip Langridge, David Wilson-Johnson)
Knussen	*The Way to Castle Yonder*
Rakhmaninov	Piano Concerto no. 3 (Alexander Toradze)
Berlioz	*Symphonie fantastique*
Mozart	Piano Concerto in C K467 (Ricardo Castro)
Bruckner	Symphony no. 9
Sibelius	*Tapiola*
Turnage	*Drowned Out* (première)
Beethoven	Symphony no. 3 (*Eroica*)
Stravinsky	*Song of the Nightingale*
Schoenberg	*Erwartung* (Phyllis Bryn-Julson)
Brahms	*Song of Destiny*
Szymanowski	Symphony no. 3 (Jon Garrison)

Mozart	*Don Giovanni* (Thomas Allen, Willard White, Amanda Halgrimson, Lynne Dawson, Christine Schafer, John Connell, Christoph Homberger, Geoffrey Dolton)
Mahler	Symphony no. 9

Towards the Millennium: the 1930s

Hindemith	Symphony: *Mathis der Maler*
Bartók	Piano Concerto no. 2 (András Schiff)
Harris	Symphony no. 3
Copland	*Billy the Kid*

Towards the Millennium: the 1930s

Varèse	*Ionisation*
Berg	Violin Concerto (Gidon Kremer)
Shostakovich	Symphony no. 4

Towards the Millennium: the 1930s

Britten	*Sinfonia da Requiem*
Messiaen	*Poèmes pour Mi* (Faye Robinson)
Berg	Suite: *Lulu*
Gershwin	*In Memoriam Lily Pons*
Gershwin	*Walking the Dog*
Gershwin	*A Cuban Overture*

Towards the Millennium: the 1930s

Stravinsky	*Perséphone* (Nigel Robson, Stephen Richardson)
Walton	*Belshazzar's Feast*
Tippett	Symphony no. 4
Bruckner	Symphony no. 7
Britten	Serenade for tenor, horn and strings (Philip Langridge, Claire Briggs)
Liszt	*A Faust Symphony*
Rameau	Dances from *Les boréades*
Debussy	*La mer*
Haydn	Symphony no. 86
Bartók	Suite: *The Miraculous Mandarin*

The 1993–94 season was again full of magnificent things artistically, including some of the most memorable *Towards the Millennium* concerts. A review in the *Oldie* by Richard Osborne summed up the success both of that series and of Symphony Hall:

> Birmingham's new Symphony Hall is one of the seven wonders of the modern world: elegant, comfortable, and capable of delivering sound of astonishing clarity, vividness and depth. Never can the Byzantine colours of *Belshazzar's Feast* have glowed and dazzled more than they did here. You would need a month in Ravenna to experience the visual equivalent of what was conjured up for us by these prodigious musicians and this prodigious hall.

And in London too the acclaim for the series continued: in Shostakovich 4, wrote Rick Jones in the *Evening Standard*, 'The orchestra's rhythm was electrifying, their *fortissimos* overwhelming, their response as complete as satisfied customers to a hypnotist. This was an ecstatic performance which no one wanted to end.'

But all this was overshadowed in Birmingham by the question of money. A financial crisis blew up in the first months of 1994, the inevitable result of the Arts Council failing to deliver on the much-vaunted development plan some years before. The orchestra had been increasingly relying on sponsorship to cover the gap left by the Arts Council's lack of support, but the gap widened during this season and a deficit of over £250,000, a large sum for those days, appeared. The CBSO was unwilling to cut back on its now universally praised activities, so it was a question of lobbying boldly. As ever Rattle was pushed to the forefront to comment: 'I am not prepared to lead this wonderful orchestra into decline. The problem in this country is that arts organizations that do well are penalized. Birmingham has been tremendously supportive, but I think the Arts Council believes that the arts will be all right whatever happens. That's wrong. The Arts Council has to put its money where its mouth is.' The press was used with skill, and on the day when there was a key Arts Council meeting, 2 February 1994, an alarmist piece ran in the *Daily Telegraph*, warning that 'the money has run out and the political will is fast disappearing', highlighting the danger to Rattle and Birmingham if something was not done. The Arts Council did the usual thing: it set up a working party, recognizing that all the orchestras were in trouble, and asked for a report within a month.

By 9 March there was a strong article in the *Independent* suggesting that the current leader of Birmingham City Council had beaten the more right-wing Labour candidate 'on the platform of stopping the search for prestige'. This was a worrying omen for the future of the orchestra if it were true. Were the glory days of Birmingham rising to international fame on the back of its arts activity beginning to be over? The claims of education, the health service and much else were beginning to become severe in Birmingham, as Rattle himself realized, and the signs were that however much the council wanted to continue developing the arts, there were now other priorities and it was going to become ever more difficult as the years went on. In the end the temporary crisis was alleviated with an extra £125,000 from the city, but this did nothing to solve the underlying problem. Rattle commented:

> We do have plans for long-term projects, but if one has funding only from one minute to the next that can change everything. It is very depressing to think we could face the same scenario this year as well. I have no idea where we will get the extra money from. We are having to go hand to mouth, day to day. I never imagined that we would be in the state we are in. The Arts Council shouldn't be an arm of government; they should be battling at the sharp end. They should be there at the barricades with us.

As one newspaper headlined an interview with Simon at this time, this was the 'RATTLE OF A NOT SO SIMPLE MAN'. The increasing complexity of the political and financial situation became a daily worry, and meanwhile he was having to make the hardest of decisions about his personal life and the end of his marriage. However committed Rattle was at this point, it would be difficult not to see here, and in the personal situation that would soon remove his children from Birmingham altogether, the beginning of the end of his time with the CBSO.

ED SMITH We got the first tranche of money from the Arts Council; we got the first tranche of money from the city council, and many other things fell into place, especially the confirmation of the new hall, which was actually an important part of the whole development. We were able to increase the orchestra to a string section of 18.16.14.12.9. We were able to create an environment whereby things like the BCMG could fly, which it has done. The thing happened.

But isn't it true that the impetus didn't really sustain itself?
After the first year, there were changes at the Arts Council as so often in these situations, and I can say quite honestly that they did not deliver, they

did not honour their commitment. William Rees-Mogg had left as chairman; Luke Rittner had left as secretary-general; there were different people in different departments. Thank God for the Birmingham city council. They didn't entirely pick up the difference but they provided us with sufficient, I think, to achieve those developmental things we had conceived. And also we got a very big (in our terms) sponsorship from Merrill Lynch, which actually stood in place for what the Arts Council had reneged on.

But by 1994 there was something of a financial crisis . . .
This was the joint effect of the Arts Council not living up to its commitments, relying on sponsorship, which perhaps we shouldn't have done but we had no alternative, and other factors as well. We became in what – at least in UK terms at that stage – was pretty serious difficulty, with a quarter of a million pounds accumulated deficit. And it did coincide with the matter of Simon renewing his contract. We never played that card overtly in Birmingham but everyone knew it was the issue; it didn't need to be said. I think the line I used was: 'We have somebody here in Birmingham who has been here over a decade and has presided over the phenomenal growth of this organization. It doesn't take a lot of imagination to realize that he's not going to stay to preside over its decline.'

Wasn't the city changing politically as well?
Not as much as you might think. Symphony Hall was actually conceived by the Tories and the first discussions Simon and I had were with the Tories. They lost control in the mid-1980s, but by that time the seeds had been sown and the process begun. After that it was Labour-controlled throughout. The chief executives and political leaders of the city were always very well informed, not just paying lip service but fighting for the orchestra in a very tangible way. The orchestra was never a political football. It was always supported by both political sides very substantially.

Do you think the development took Simon where he wanted the orchestra to be?
It is interesting. I am sure that he would say that the orchestra must never reach a ceiling; we must never feel we've achieved everything. But I think he could leave with a very good feeling that he and the organization had actually achieved what we'd set out to do in the 1980s: we had got one of the greatest halls in the world; we had created this core of musicians and provided them with the ability to do contemporary music and other kinds of performance. We had created an environment where they could be something other than a member of a hundred-piece orchestra. We had created these wonderful choruses with Simon Halsey, and finally we had the CBSO Centre. I think Simon would acknowledge that by the time he left the

CBSO was as well equipped in terms of infrastructure as any orchestra in the world. It might not have the resources, the financial resources, to fly, but I think he could be very proud of the situation – hall, centre, the working environment for the players.

Your working relationship was obviously very close: did you ever disagree? You've got to remember it went back to when we were both growing up, and he played percussion at the age of sixteen in the Merseyside Youth Orchestra which I managed. I think the first concert he conducted that I organized was in a church in Switzerland! It was my job to do the enabling, to have the faith in the music director that he would deliver. And a lot was never said; we just understood each other. He could always tell if I hadn't enjoyed something or it hadn't gone well, but it was usually unspoken. And he could tell if I was annoyed, even though I didn't need to say so.

I do remember one absolutely ridiculous programme he conducted, costing the bloody earth. Loads of short pieces, and the Strauss *Festival Prelude* with ten trumpets – I mean, you could justify ten extra trumpets for some things, but not for six minutes of dreadful Strauss. Later he said to me, 'You were really cross about that, weren't you!' And I was, but it was so like him to wait until I'd got over it before he mentioned it.

ANTHONY SARGENT The support of Birmingham city council for the CBSO was a level of support unmatched by any local authority for any art form and that speaks for itself. There was real anger about the Arts Council situation, but it was very difficult to deal with because all the people involved had moved on. Simon recognized the financial pressures on the city – he was a realist, he had young children, he knew about problems with schools, the health service. But there was a great warmth from the councillors towards him and the CBSO and I must say he reciprocated that and treated them with enormous generosity. He would always get the best deal he could from them, for the orchestra, but there was a feeling that there was a limit beyond which he couldn't go.

There was a period at the end of Simon's time when maybe there was a feeling that the CBSO hadn't embraced some of the opportunities of Symphony Hall, that they were complacent about their marketing, and not very imaginative about their fund-raising – which they couldn't afford to be, because the other arts organizations were marketing increasingly strongly and audiences for other Symphony Hall concerts were creeping up at the same time as the CBSO's were creeping down. There was a feeling that the CBSO was suffering declining audiences for completely unnecessary reasons, that there wasn't a shrinking market for orchestral music in Birmingham, but the CBSO wasn't engaging with that market in an effective, purposeful way.

So it wasn't just that people went to easier concerts than Towards the Millennium *because they were on offer?*
No, that's not right at all. Some of the incredibly tough programmes in *Towards the Millennium* did well, because they were exciting events, and at the same time the visiting orchestras were not just offering popular programmes. I think it was more to do with the fact that people need marketing encouragement to come to anything, popular or recondite, and they were getting more energetic marketing from other quarters in the city than they were from the CBSO.

The pressures of life for a busy conductor are unimaginable. We see the performances, but there is the programme planning, the scheduling of rehearsals so that no time is wasted and everything gets done, the learning, the listening, the marking of scores and dealing with the parts, the rehearsals, the discussions with management and players, and then there are the perils of fame . . . One of the unimaginable things about a life like Simon Rattle's is the sheer number of things he gets asked to do, many but not all of them stupid. Of course artists' agents help to deal with all that. At Harold Holt Ltd, which later amalgamated with Lies Askonas to form Askonas Holt, Simon has one of the best teams in the business.

Just to pick a month almost at random during 1994, the year that he was knighted, and at a time when his life was under severe pressure because of the battles surrounding his impending divorce, he was: written to by John Selwyn Gummer to ask if he would be on the National Lottery Board; asked to contribute to a newspaper feature on his favourite car (this it was easy to deal with: 'as Simon Rattle does not drive or own a car it would be impossible to answer these questions truthfully'); asked if he would model shirts for a Jermyn Street shirtmaker (of course it would not take more than a few minutes of his time to be photographed); take part in a television programme in which *Birds of a Feather* stars Pauline Quirke and Linda Robson would be trained as singers and learn to sing 'Rule Britannia'; and address the Oxford Union about music education. All this while he was trying to rehearse a new production of *Don Giovanni* at Glyndebourne (see chapter 9).

This was just the tip of the iceberg. How many of these requests actually ever reached Rattle or were batted away before he saw them is difficult to say. Certainly the endless pressure to attend pre-concert receptions, post-concert dinners, often in worthy causes, to conduct totally unsuitable orchestras and ensembles (or even some highly suitable ones, dates that have come within a whisker of happening), and the relentless demand for press interviews, radio interviews, contributions to souvenir programmes ('Could he not write a few words remembering our wonderful Bruckner 7 . . . ') must be unbearable. It is always a feature of these requests that people cannot understand why they ever have to be declined, and while Rattle has always been good at saying no, except where the good of an orchestra or a project is at stake, the time demands must have added intolerably to the pressures at a difficult period.

It is obligatory to turn up at awards ceremonies: it is the least you can do for the record company that has invested so heavily in you. Simon always did that with deceptive ease, and whenever he accepted something – such as the Artist of the Year prize from *Gramophone* in October 1993 – he always had something striking to say, in contrast to the often self-serving speeches heard from others. In this case it was a stark warning of 'the death of culture' if the government failed to recognize that 'Passionate musicians only come from passionate five-year-olds. What has so patiently and inspiringly been built up in this country is slowly being demolished.' When, to please his record company, he conducted at the Classical Brit Awards in 2001, alongside Kennedy and others, his remark was 'and here for once is something *un*amplified'.

The mid-1990s were probably the most difficult period of his life so far, over which he would very reasonably prefer to draw a veil. None of the personal problems reached the public prints until the end of his first marriage was announced, though in retrospect you can see some touching indications of where things stood. In an interview with Richard Fairman at the end of 1994 about the knighthood he received that year, he said, 'It's just a shame that a knighthood can't be backward-looking. My mother would make an ace Lady Rattle.' Even allowing for the continual closeness within the Rattle family, there is a certain feeling of marital loneliness in that remark.

He deflected his feelings by accepting the knighthood on behalf of the orchestra, realizing the impracticality of bestowing a knighthood on a hundred musicians: 'My misgivings were personal. I considered very quickly what it meant for the orchestra, what it meant for my parents. The thing that convinced me was thinking of the use that Ian McKellen has made of his knighthood, turning it into extra ammunition for an extraordinary crusade.' Once again, he dismissed talk of Boston: 'I love going to Boston. I love the orchestra. But in case anyone hasn't noticed, there isn't a vacancy there. And I can't imagine a time in my life when I am not linked to the CBSO, one way or another.' No one actually had any knowledge at all of when or if Seiji Ozawa would make way for a new conductor (see chapter 9). It was to be several years before, not coincidentally one suspects, on the very morning of the 1999 vote in Berlin, Ozawa finally announced he was leaving Boston to take up a post at the Vienna State Opera.

V

Working with Composers

1994–95

Schoenberg	*Gurrelieder* (Rita Hunter, John Mitchinson, Christine Cairns, Ian Caley, Brian Bannatyne-Scott)
Berlioz	*Romeo and Juliet* (orchestral excerpts)
Brahms	Symphony no. 2
Rossini	Overture: *The Silken Ladder*
Elgar	Violin Concerto (Gidon Kremer)
Shostakovich	Symphony no. 15
Haydn	Symphony no. 102 in B♭
Prokofiev	Piano Concerto no. 3 (Martha Argerich)
Shostakovich	Symphony no. 15
Haydn	Symphony no. 102 in B♭
Schumann	Cello Concerto (Ulrich Heinen)
Brahms	Symphony no. 2
Tippett	*Fantasia Concertante on a Theme of Corelli*
Szymanowski	Violin Concerto no. 2 (Thomas Zehetmair)
Sibelius	Symphony no. 5
Haydn	Symphony no. 22
Gubaidulina	*Zeitgestalten* (Feeney Trust commission; première)
Beethoven	Violin Concerto (Anne-Sophie Mutter)

Towards the Millennium: the 1940s

Stravinsky	Ballet: *Orpheus*
Messiaen	*Trois petites liturgies*
Bartók	*Concerto for Orchestra*

Towards the Millennium: the 1940s

Pavel Haas	*Study for Strings*
Schoenberg	*A Survivor from Warsaw*
Tippett	*A Child of Our Time* (Faye Robinson, Cynthia Clarey, Philip Langridge, Benjamin Luxon)

Towards the Millennium: the 1940s

Copland	*Appalachian Spring*
Strauss	Closing scene from *Capriccio* (Felicity Lott)
Vaughan Williams	Symphony no. 5

Towards the Millennium: the 1940s

Britten	*Four Sea Interludes* (*Peter Grimes*)
Szymanowski	Violin Concerto no. 1 (Thomas Zehetmair)
Shostakovich	Symphony no. 8

Mozart	Symphony no. 33 in B♭
Strauss	*Ruhe meine Seele!* (Gundula Janowitz)
Strauss	*Waldseligkeit*
Strauss	*Morgen!*
Strauss	*Wiegenlied*
Strauss	*Befreit*
Schubert	Symphony no. 3
Wagner	*Good Friday Music* (*Parsifal*)

| Mozart | Piano Concerto in B♭ K456 (Imogen Cooper) |
| Mahler | Symphony no. 6 |

The season opened with a huge bang with Schoenberg's *Gurrelieder*, a work it would have been impossible to fit into the Town Hall. Rattle was developing an interpretation that would blossom in the succeeding years in Philadelphia, and eventually would be recorded in Berlin in 2001. The CBSO then toured Japan with Gidon Kremer and Martha Argerich playing concertos, luxury casting that was proof, if proof were needed, that the CBSO was now at the top of the world-class ranking of orchestras. Rattle marked his fortieth birthday in January 1995 by sweeping aside yet more press comment about his future movements: the London press continued to whinge that 'London is a nettle he simply has to grasp,' which was increasingly an out-of-date thought. He celebrated by renewing his contract until 1998.

There was the option to renew beyond then, but close observers thought it unlikely. The call of the European orchestras was now strong and, given the enormous success of his début with the Vienna Philharmonic as well as his continuing relationship with Berlin, the future for him was wide open. In February 1995 Simon and Ellie had formally announced their separation: another milestone creating an open future. Unusually, for someone who had never worried or much cared about money in the course of his career, Rattle began to confide to friends that he needed to accept some well-paid engagements abroad in order to safeguard the financial future of his children.

Towards the Millennium continued into the 1940s, with some massive concerts, to which Rattle added one of his funniest programmes: a coupling of Boulez's early cantata *Le soleil des eaux* and Poulenc's one-act opera *Les mamelles de Tirésias*, the last concert with the London Sinfonietta he conducted himself, though the ensemble continued to feature strongly in the project. These concerts were now becoming increasingly famous all over Europe, and the CBSO was in continual demand: Linz, Vienna, Munich and Innsbruck were on the *Millennium* route this year.

One of the most important projects influencing the development of the CBSO in the 1990s was the composer-in-association scheme funded first by the Radcliffe Trust and later by the Esmée Fairbairn Musical Trust. First Mark-Anthony Turnage and then Judith Weir were able to benefit in very different ways from close integration with the working life of the orchestra. In 2001 Rattle reflected on how his view of new music had changed since the first edition of this book:

> SIMON RATTLE It has been so exciting over the last decade to get to know some of the great composers of our time. We would never have talked about Kurtág fifteen years ago, would we? The only stuff we knew we thought was a parody of Max Davies's *Miss Donnithorne's Maggot* – the mad lady with the cimbalom. Now we see him for one of the real originals: beautiful, serious, funny music. Ligeti: the wonderful concertos; Heiner Goebbel, who we will commission in Berlin; Turnage's *Blood on the Floor*, John Adams, Hans [Werner Henze] and so many others.

We wanted to have a composer actually working with us, so we gave Mark Turnage a laboratory to create his very best music, let him go to rehearsals and meet players, so it wasn't just a matter of writing works in isolation. It produced some great pieces and others he'll tell you about, but we were able to make some big decisions, like cutting a whole section of *Drowned Out* on the day of the dress rehearsal.

Judith, on the other hand, said, 'I don't want to write for a large symphony orchestra. I want to explore other things.' And so she did. She wrote *Storm* for the youth chorus – an immediate classic. It's amazing how such a *mezzo-forte* person can have such charisma and enable people to do things they do not think themselves capable of.

MARK-ANTHONY TURNAGE The first piece of mine Simon did was *Three Screaming Popes* in 1989, and that was just when the scheme was starting so it would have been terrible if it had not gone well. What happened was that Olly [Knussen] put Simon on to me and played him a few tapes. For some reason he couldn't listen to the end because he had a taxi waiting or something, but he liked *Night Dances* on the basis of the first two movements, so it was OK!

He is the greatest rehearser of new works. He knows instinctively when there's a problem with a piece and sometimes you reject the ideas, but he's so technically hands-on that he really knows what's happening and you respect that. In *Drowned Out* we came to the same conclusion on the day of the dress rehearsal that the whole middle section was too long and so we made quite a crude cut, which I had to fix later. That was really a big thing for him to say and for me to accept, but he was right. I take criticism from people I really trust like Olly and Simon, because they always criticize me from the point of view of being really positive about the pieces.

I don't know him socially; I know him professionally and that is an element in the relationship. Because he's such a famous figure now I don't know how he deals with that. One thing I really admire is that he would never allow his children to be used, avoids them being photographed and so on, and I've almost copied that. I'm sure in that position it's quite necessary for his sanity. But I think he's become quite relaxed, and the question of how you behave in front of an orchestra has never been a problem for him.

The basic thing is that he really respects composers. He really believes that a score is important and in that sense there is no ego in him. The composer counts. When I was writing *About Time* for the BCMG and the OAE, he rang me up and told me to make it more difficult, to have the courage to make the difficulty of the tuning a real part of the piece. It was great that he felt strongly enough about it to take that trouble.

As part of my scheme I was on the artistic advisory committee of the orchestra, and it was fascinating to see him in action there because he had such a great way of putting his ideas across – quite firm but very tactful, so he gets his way in the end just because there is such quality in his ideas. People don't know the amount he has to do: the number of scores that get sent to him is unbelievable, with letters that are very personal, composers baring their souls to him – then they'd be quite indignant not to get a response. The unsuccessful piece I wrote was *Leaving* for the chorus. I loved working with the chorus but I found the piece very hard. I think it was a psychological block I had with the English choral tradition. Now Simon is going to do *Blood on the Floor* in his first season in Berlin and that's incredible. He determined to say, 'I believe in this.' He would take my pieces on tour; he would insist that they were in TV relays. When *Drowned Out* came to the Proms, for instance. I know for a fact they weren't keen on it, but he insisted. It's the same with EMI: Simon stands up for the new. I never push and I just wait for him. I just get on with the composing. That's all I do. I can't conduct! I look after my kids and write music.

JUDITH WEIR I did feel an ambivalence about working with orchestras, but by the end of this experience I had come through that. I had had some experiences that weren't great and so it's fair to say I did feel some doubts. So I approached the scheme in a slightly unusual way which was to do a lot of work with small groups from the orchestra, out in the country or in the suburbs, for instance with a village band in Alveley, Shropshire, where the collaboration with the orchestra is still going strong. By the end they would be organizing themselves to come up to concerts in Birmingham – not because it was part of the scheme but because they had got to know members of the orchestra and they wanted to come.

I was able to conduct a lot of these small-scale projects myself, which enabled me to be more involved, and I gradually got more and more bold in the things I would do. I worked with BCMG which was just becoming more independent. I also heard some wonderful concerts in Birmingham: the Beethoven symphonies, the Haydn *Seasons*. Simon would say, 'Well, we'd better get them off the shelf from time to time just to hear what they sound like.'

The later years of *Towards the Millennium* were brilliant, and I don't think people in London realized how completely they worked as part of the arts scene in Birmingham. For the 1950s I remember Terry Grimley in the *Birmingham Post* writing a piece about how knocking down Birmingham and building the ring roads was like the effect of total serialism in music – quite an analogy! There were concerts for the 1960s and 1970s that were a bit empty – not that Simon minded at all, though I was sorry more people didn't come to Nick Maw's *Odyssey*, which has grown so much as a piece.

A lot of the time Simon wasn't directly involved in my work, and it coincided with a period when he wasn't around so much in Birmingham, though a week of his time felt like ten of anyone else's. Then at the end there was my biggest piece, *We Are Shadows*, which he commissioned for the final *Towards the Millennium* and which he worked at so hard. He has a really great love of rehearsals and getting it sorted out. He is so committed and serious about solving any problems that I can get rather annoyed now if I don't get that level of attention from a conductor! A lot of conductors in the States do contemporary music but they would really rather be doing Strauss, and it shows.

1995–96

Beethoven	Symphony no. 1
Beethoven	Symphony no. 3 (*Eroica*)
Beethoven	Symphony no. 2
Beethoven	Overture: *Fidelio*
Beethoven	Overtures: *Leonore* nos. 1, 2 and 3
Wagner	Overture: *Die Meistersinger*
Debussy	*Danse sacrée et danse profane* for harp and orchestra
Beethoven	Piano Concerto no. 1 (Lars Vogt)
Mussorgsky– Howarth	*Pictures at an Exhibition*
Beethoven	Symphony no. 4
Beethoven	Funeral March from *Leonora Prohaska*
Beethoven	Symphony no. 5
Beethoven	Symphony no. 6
Beethoven	Symphony no. 7
Beethoven	Symphony no. 8
Beethoven	Symphony no. 9 (Amanda Halgrimson, Cynthia Clarey, Patrick Power, Robert Holl)
John Adams	*Lollapalooza* (première)
Knussen	*Flourish with Fireworks*
Vaughan Williams	*Serenade to Music*

Beethoven	Symphony no. 9 (Amanda Halgrimson, Cynthia Clarey, Patrick Power, Robert Holl)
Rimsky-Korsakov arr. Green	*Procession of the Nobles* (*Mlada*) (Prince of Wales Brass)
Britten	*Prelude and Fugue* (Birmingham Ensemble)
Colin Matthews	*Hidden Variables* (BCMG)
Beethoven	Symphony no. 9 (Amanda Halgrimson, Cynthia Clarey, Patrick Power, Gilles Cachemaille)
Weir	*Forest* (Feeney Trust commission; première)
Mahler	*Das Lied von der Erde* (John Mitchinson, Thomas Hampson)
Tchaikovsky	Piano Concerto no. 1 (Peter Donohoe)
Tchaikovsky	*The Nutcracker* (Act II complete)
Berlioz	Overture: *Le corsaire*
Sibelius	Violin Concerto (Sarah Chang)
Ravel	Ballet: *Ma mère l'oye*
Ravel	*La valse*

Towards the Millennium: the 1950s

Stravinsky	*Agon*
Messiaen	*Chronochromie*
Stockhausen	*Gruppen* (two performances, with John Carewe and Daniel Harding)

Towards the Millennium: the 1950s

Martinů	*The Epic of Gilgamesh*
Shostakovich	Symphony no. 10
Corelli	Concerto grosso, op. 6 no. 2
Tippett	*Fantasia Concertante on a Theme of Corelli*
Bruckner	Symphony no. 4 (*Romantic*)
Gershwin	*A Cuban Overture*
Gershwin	Piano Concerto in F (Peter Donohoe)
Gershwin	*Walking the Dog*
Gershwin	*Rhapsody in Blue*

Gershwin	*An American in Paris*
Mozart	Overture: *The Marriage of Figaro*
Brahms	Piano Concerto no. 1 (Leif Ove Andsnes)
Dukas	*The Sorcerer's Apprentice*
Fauré	*Pavane*
Ravel	*Boléro*
Berlioz	Overture: *Le corsaire*
Vaughan Williams	*Fantasia on a Theme by Thomas Tallis*
Ravel	Ballet: *Ma mère l'oye*
Beethoven	Piano Concerto no. 5 (*Emperor*) (Christian Blackshaw)
Haydn	Symphony no. 88 in G
Bruckner	Symphony no. 7

SIMON RATTLE You know the line in *Field of Dreams*: 'Build it and they will come.' That was the story with *Towards the Millennium*. We missed Michael Vyner still being around in London in putting it together. The Festival Hall kept faith with it, which was great. I probably couldn't give them enough time, but we had a full house for *Gruppen*. [For Stockhausen's classic of the 1960s, which required three orchestras with three conductors, Rattle was helped out by his teacher, John Carewe, and his protégé, Daniel Harding.] The three performances of that were so completely different. The intimidating one was Vienna, where I knew rather a lot of the audience and I looked out at and saw Friedrich Čerha, Wolfgang Rihm, Pierre Boulez . . . I had to make a little speech and say I realized there were people there who had conducted the first performance! In London it was full of people too old to wear ponytails any more and holes in their jeans but you knew they had done. What an experience – it is the most anti-democratic piece there is, because it is all so precisely notated and exact. It was a sentimental experience that we could do it with John Carewe and Daniel Harding – Daniel exactly as much younger than me as John is older than me.

People said you did Gruppen *the wrong way round in the Festival Hall.*
What? We were doing Messiaen and Stravinsky in the same programme! Putting it into the Festival Hall was very difficult when you had those other pieces to do as well; so, yes, I used the normal podium position. In Birmingham we didn't do it in Symphony Hall but used the largest hall of the centre, which is about the size of a small village in Norfolk! We could set it

up the other way round, and if you look at the television recording we did in Birmingham as a part of *Leaving Home*, then I was facing the audience with the two other orchestras left and right.

The only time I can remember changing Rattle's mind about something was for the BBC Proms programme that summer, when he had suggested Stravinsky's *Agon* with Bruckner 7. After that concert with *Gruppen*, it was clear that the Messiaen would be so much better a companion piece for the Bruckner that I suggested they change it round, which Ed Smith did at enormous inconvenience – I had not realized that there was an entire European tour, as so often at this time in the orchestra's life, based around that programme. Andrew Clements in the *Guardian* got the point:

> Messiaen and Bruckner were both devout Catholics who dedicated their art to a celebration of their faith, and both composed edifices in sound whose articulations seem to imagine some resonating cathedral acoustic in which their music could hang and revolve in a timeless way. The Albert Hall doesn't have quite this sense of space, but it is a close-run thing . . . Simon Rattle and the CBSO gave a triumphantly convincing demonstration of their versatility. Both works received performances pitched at the very highest level, and the result was one of the finest concerts in the season so far.

VI
Beethoven and the Brum Apotheosis

The big event of the season, however, was the CBSO's first Beethoven cycle with Rattle, an event to which he had been building up for some time. There was a lot at stake here; the cycle was eagerly awaited on the Continent, though for the moment the CBSO shrewdly decided to take it to Germany rather than Vienna. In *The Sunday Times* Rattle spoke to Stephen Pettitt, hinting for almost the first time at the thought that he would move on from the CBSO, 'because the players will need to be told different things by different people at some stage'. But not yet: 'We're doing very exciting work at the moment, exciting because it's not easy. The thing to do is to keep setting ourselves new challenges.' Which is exactly what the Beethoven cycle was. 'Obviously it's a huge mountain. The journey from the First to the Ninth is the greatest journey in any musical style, even greater than in Verdi.' Rattle was taking advice from

Alfred Brendel: 'His comments on some of my Beethoven performances –
autopsy might be a better word – have been wonderful, direct. I admit
I've done some dreadful performances of Beethoven. For orchestras, this
is still the hardest of all challenges, the most disciplined. There's a sheer,
desperate physical exertion. Beethoven asks more and more, so that in
the end you almost have to hurt yourself.'

The cycle was a landmark for Rattle and the orchestra; as he put it in
the programme: 'Through long collaboration and trust, we have earned
the right, ingested the vitamins, to take this journey.' It was also a risk
for those with long memories, as there had been performances in the
past, notably of the Third and Fifth, that had really not worked well; as
Rattle said to Paul Griffiths, 'As a younger musician I gave so many
monomaniac performances, each down a different road, to the point
where five or six years ago I had to give up doing [the Third] at all.' The
Eroica in particular had been a crucible for his different interpretational
ideas as the years progressed: at one time Giulini had been an influence,
at another Harnoncourt – impulses difficult to reconcile. There had been
a memorable moment in a televised *South Bank Show* during the Giulini
phase where, conducting the first movement very broadly, Rattle tried to
demonstrate how playing it at Beethoven's much faster metronome mark
really didn't work. But actually it did, that was the most convincing
musical moment in the programme, and from that experience Rattle
developed some of his most exciting rethinkings of Beethoven.

The critics were quick to respond to the freshness of the cycle:

> In choosing to open the CBSO's seventy-fifth anniversary season with the
> complete cycle of Beethoven symphonies, Sir Simon Rattle has accepted the
> ultimate challenge. All the other major cycles he has undertaken – Nielsen,
> Sibelius, Mahler – have their problems, but nothing as daunting as the
> note-by-note familiarity of the Beethoven. Only a very exceptional inter-
> pretation can stimulate a rediscovery where these scores are concerned . . .
> a remarkable cycle. (Gerald Larner, *The Times*)

> This cycle will surely become one of the most significant musical events of
> the current season, as Rattle's rejuvenating process on a well-worn series of
> masterpieces progresses. (Matthew Rye, *Daily Telegraph*)

> From the first instalment of Symphonies 1 and 3 there can be no doubt that
> the time is right. His readings are a strong, coherent synthesis of period
> sensitivity and Grand Tradition. They feel thoroughly absorbed but bril-
> liantly alive, with an exhilarating rhythmic ardour and a crystal clarity of
> sound throughout the orchestra. (Michael White, *Independent on Sunday*)

Rattle's accounts of the Fourth and Fifth were of the highest interest and achievement. His Fourth was more richly toned and more expansive than you often hear . . . As for the Fifth, well, you would have to live a long life to hear a better performance. (Martin Kettle, *Guardian*)

Having said that he was not sure about presenting Beethoven's Sixth and Seventh Symphonies in the same concert, Sir Simon Rattle went on to demonstrate what congenial programme companions they can be . . . An extreme of pressure was applied to celebrating the vertiginous progress of the work and all caution was eventually abandoned. It was one of those performances which, as the reaction of the cheering audience afterwards confirmed, cut right through concert-hall convention. (Gerald Larner, *The Times*)

In November 1995 the seventy-fifth anniversary of the orchestra was celebrated with an open day at Symphony Hall in which all the associated groups of the CBSO took part. After performances and live recordings of Mozart's *Così fan tutte* with the Orchestra of the Age of Enlightenment, Rattle was named Musician of the Year by the *Independent on Sunday*, 'partly because he is incapable of dullness, but specifically for his Beethoven cycle . . . Having held back from this standard rep, he made it anything but standard. It was brilliant, vital, dynamic, and for Rattle himself a rite of passage from *enfant terrible* to established master.'

There was another vital rite of passage, just before his birthday in the new year. On 8 January 1996 he was married to Candace Allen, screenwriter and now a novelist, at the Marylebone Register Office in London. It was the end of the most difficult period in his life, and the beginning of a new period of real happiness for him, during which everyone who knew him would say he became more relaxed and more at ease with himself. Access to his children was still a difficulty to be overcome, but there was a basis for moving forward. There was only a brief flurry in the press: the public face of the remarriage had been of total support from his first wife Elise, now living in San Francisco, but a remark by one of Rattle's friends that it was music that had caused the break-up of the marriage caused a brief rebuttal from Ellie, saying, 'Devotion to music was a bond between us and did not cause the breakdown of our marriage.' With that the matter was, much to Rattle's relief, over.

It seemed aptly symbolic of the sea-changes in his life at this time that it was just a month later, in February 1996, that he finally announced he would not renew his contract with the CBSO beyond the end of the 1997–98 season. The decisive moment had finally come, and Rattle would leave Birmingham with nothing permanent to put in its place. Oddly, the announcement caused less stir than it might have done, because there was every indication that he would continue to have a warm relationship with the orchestra. But, as one somewhat tendentious profile around that time reported, 'Although the stress of his broken marriage has obviously worn very heavy on him, there are plenty of professional reasons why it is time for him to take a break. He has simply been working too hard . . . He appears in many ways to be exhausted.' Anyone who thought that the break with the CBSO would mean less musical adventure for Rattle, and a period of relaxation, had read the signs completely wrongly.

1996–97

Shostakovich	Symphony no. 14
Bruckner	Symphony no. 7
Haydn	*The Seasons* (John Mark Ainsley, Christiane Oelze, David Thomas)
Ravel	*Le tombeau de Couperin*
Szymanowski	Symphony no. 4 (*Sinfonia Concertante* for piano and orchestra) (Leif Ove Andsnes)
Stravinsky	*Four Norwegian Moods*
Borodin	Symphony no. 2
Wagner	Prelude to Act I, and Act III of *Parsifal* (Wolfgang Schöne, Poul Elming, Robert Lloyd)
Elgar	Introduction and Allegro for Strings
Strauss	*Four Last Songs* (Amanda Roocroft)
Mahler	Symphony no. 4
Weir	*Sederunt Principes*
Brahms	Double Concerto for violin and cello (Ida Haendel, Ralph Kirshbaum)
Kurtág	*Grabstein für Stephan*
Beethoven	Symphony no. 5

Towards the Millennium: the 1960s

| Stravinsky | *Requiem Canticles* |
| Henze | *The Raft of the Medusa* (Juliane Banse, David Wilson-Johnson, Franz Mazura) |

Towards the Millennium: the 1960s

Berio	*Sinfonia*
Lutosławski	Cello Concerto (Lynn Harrell)
Messiaen	*Et exspecto resurrectionem mortuorum*

Towards the Millennium: the 1960s

Penderecki	*Threnody to the Victims of Hiroshima*
Britten	*War Requiem* (Andrea Gruber, Robert Tear, Simon Keenlyside)
Brahms	Piano Concerto no. 2 (Emanuel Ax)
Brahms	Symphony no. 4
Delius	*On Hearing the First Cuckoo in Spring*
Schumann	Symphony no. 1 (*Spring*)
Britten	*Spring Symphony* (Joan Rodgers, Catherine Robbin, Ian Bostridge)
Walton	*Anniversary Fanfare*
Turnage	*Four Horned Fandango* (EMI commission; Peter Dyson, Claire Briggs, Peter Currie, Mark Phillips)
Elgar	Violin Concerto (Nigel Kennedy)
Walton	*Belshazzar's Feast* (Simon Keenlyside)
Mozart	Serenade in B♭ for thirteen wind instruments K361
Bruckner	Symphony no. 9
Turnage	*Drowned Out*
Mahler	Symphony no. 5

The 1960s dawned for *Towards the Millennium*, which could easily have been an awkward moment. But once again Rattle had chosen skilfully, and the programmes included a Britten *War Requiem* (which worked in Birmingham but suffered from the Festival Hall acoustic), prefaced by Penderecki's *Threnody for the Victims of Hiroshima*.

Michael White called the Britten 'a triumph over acoustical limitations
... Rattle engineered the performance so expertly that he capitalized on
the particularity a dry sound offers, with incredible finesse of detail in the
chamber sections, and elsewhere fabricated an illusion of spaciousness
from careful measurement of the accumulating climaxes.' The EMI
anniversary concert reunited Rattle and Kennedy in a successful Elgar
Violin Concerto which was recorded, but that relationship soured for
good when Kennedy agreed to take on Gubaidulina's major *Offertorium*
and then cancelled.

At the BBC Proms at the end of this season, Rattle conducted a late-
night Mozart wind serenade, at which he received the first *BBC Music
Magazine* award for Artist of the Year. Then the CBSO gave Mahler's
Fifth, a symphony which Rattle had avoided until this period, with
what Hilary Finch in *The Times* described as 'an incandescent performance of penetrating clarity of vision'.

1997–98

Mozart	Symphony no. 38 (*Prague*)
Mahler	Songs from *Des Knaben Wunderhorn* (Simon Keenlyside)
Brahms	Piano Concerto no. 1 (Leif Ove Andsnes)
Mozart	Symphony no. 38 (*Prague*)
Strauss	*Till Eulenspiegel*
Bartók	*Duke Bluebeard's Castle* (Kristine Ciesinski, John Tomlinson)
Adès	*Asyla* (première)
Mahler	Symphony no. 3 in D minor
[Weir	*Storm* (Youth Chorus commission) conducted by Simon Halsey]
Mahler	Symphony no. 5
Mahler	Symphony no. 7
Rameau	Suite: *Les boréades*
Haydn	Symphony no. 86
Beethoven	Symphony no. 3 (*Eroica*)

Towards the Millennium: the 1970s

Takemitsu	*A Flock Descends into the Pentagonal Garden*
Lutosławski	*Les espaces du sommeil*
Shostakovich	Symphony no. 15

Towards the Millennium: the 1970s

Knussen	Symphony no. 3
Birtwistle	*The Triumph of Time*
Tippett	Symphony no. 4

Ravel	*Le tombeau de Couperin*
Rakhmaninov	Piano Concerto no. 3 (Ilya Itin)
Shostakovich	Symphony no. 15

Towards the Millennium: the 1970s

Boulez	*Rituel in memoriam Bruno Maderna*
Messiaen	*Des canyons aux étoiles*
Szymanowski	*King Roger* (Thomas Hampson, Elzbieta Szmytka, Ryszard Minkiewicz, Robert Gierlach, Jadwiga Rappé, Philip Langridge)

| Beethoven | Symphony no. 1 |
| Beethoven | Symphony no. 3 |

| Beethoven | Symphony no. 6 |
| Beethoven | Symphony no. 8 |

| Beethoven | Symphony no. 2 |
| Beethoven | Symphony no. 5 |

| Beethoven | Symphony no. 4 |
| Beethoven | Symphony no. 7 |

| Beethoven | Symphony no. 6 |
| Beethoven | Symphony no. 5 |

| Birtwistle | *The Triumph of Time* |
| Beethoven | Symphony no. 9 |

| Adès | *Asyla* |
| Mahler | Symphony no. 2 (Hillevi Martinpelto, Anne Sofie von Otter) |

And so, with inevitability but still the shock of surprise after eighteen years, Rattle's final season as music director and principal conductor in Birmingham arrived. An astonishing feat of planning by Ed Smith, it was a remarkable summation of everything Rattle and he had achieved over the years. Not that it was backward-looking: there was a new piece that was a stunning success, Thomas Adès's *Asyla*, coupled with a great Mahler symphony which Rattle was yet to record for the first time, to begin the season. *Asyla* was repeated with Mahler 2, which had marked Rattle's start with the CBSO, so that even the final concert celebrated the new. There were pieces that had become Rattle hallmarks, the Rameau *Boréades* suite, but also Beethoven's *Eroica*, alongside pieces he had only just begun to explore, such as Mahler 5. The complete Beethoven cycle was repeated to international acclaim, with Beethoven 9 brought alongside Birtwistle's *The Triumph of Time* to Salzburg and the BBC Proms, and the complete cycle interleaved with contemporary works with the BCMG in Salzburg.

In the autumn of 1997, the CBSO set off across Europe, taking Mahler 5 to Zurich, Montreux, Basle, Linz, Berne, Geneva and Vienna: a triumphal procession across Europe at the end of a decade that had decisively established Birmingham's orchestra on the world stage. Rattle took off for the Beethoven piano concertos with Brendel in Vienna, managed to squeeze in a charity concert at the Albert Hall with Elton John (Rattle conducted the Royal Philharmonic Orchestra – he must have been in a generous mood), and then undertook major programmes in Boston and again with the Vienna Philharmonic, this time in Salzburg for the annual Mozartwoche in January. That year too matters moved on domestically as the Rattles moved into a larger house, which had once been owned by the composer Richard Rodney Bennett, in a quiet square in Islington.

There followed the CBSO's triumphal tour of the United States, continuing straight on to Japan, taking Mahler 7 and the Beethoven symphonies. It is little wonder if Rattle was feeling exhausted at the end of this unique undertaking. Followed by a television crew in Japan he said, 'I would often like to shut down and close up and hide. I'm very jealous of the private life and that it stays like that . . . This is a stupid profession to have taken up because I'm not that comfortable being in the public eye. But you know it's stupid saying that, isn't it, because there's no way you can't be.' The tension was becoming pretty unbearable as the final concerts approached. Rattle says, 'The CBSO is a very special group of people. One of the things that was most fun for me was seeing the orchestra look after each other on the tour, because I think everybody was dreading a month away. It's very tough, and it's very disorientating. Everybody is on the line.'

Almost incredibly, there was another big project to integrate into this sequence, performances at Salzburg and the Proms of an opera Rattle had felt to be consistently neglected, Szymanowski's *King Roger*. A cast of Rattle's favourite singers, including Thomas Hampson, Philip Langridge and Elzbieta Szmytka, had been assembled, and EMI were doubtless hoping that their success with Rattle's recordings of Szymanowski could be repeated, for the investment in an almost unknown work (which had only once been staged in London) was large.

It is impossible to think how Ed Smith can have achieved the miracle of getting the orchestra in the right hall at the right time, juggling promoters, record companies and festivals, and coming out with a programme that it was possible to perform without burn-out exhaustion. Perhaps it wasn't. It's worth recalling what happened: between the middle and the end of July *King Roger* was rehearsed, performed in Birmingham and at the Proms, and then recorded. Then the Beethoven symphony cycle was rehearsed, and performed complete in Birmingham, while the BCMG prepared the British contemporary works. They gave those in a late-night Prom (see p. 10); the full orchestra gave Beethoven 9 at the Proms, and then all the concerts were repeated in Salzburg during a week in August. Not content with that, *King Roger* was then revived in Salzburg, and the orchestra returned for its two farewell performances with Simon in Symphony Hall on 29 and 30 August.

Between August 1997 and August 1998 the CBSO performed in thirty-nine towns and cities in ten countries across four continents to over a quarter of a million people, giving a hundred and forty concerts, celebrating a phenomenal impact on Europe's music-making and sealing the worldwide recognition of what Rattle had achieved in Birmingham. Ed Smith looked back over the eighteen years of Rattle's conductorship:

ED SMITH When he was about to step down as music director I spent a long time, but a very enjoyable time, doing some statistics. So between 1980 and 1998, during his time as music director, he conducted 934 concerts including 16 world premières; 337 concerts in Birmingham; 339 elsewhere in the UK, including 28 BBC Proms, 46 at the Royal Festival Hall and 39 at the Barbican; and 208 concerts on foreign tours to 25 countries on 4 continents.

The 934 concerts that he did included music by 113 composers, of whom 84 were twentieth century and no fewer than 36 were living when we played their pieces. To accomplish all that Simon rehearsed the orchestra for a staggering – and I use that word advisedly – 5,098 hours. A total of 69 recordings for EMI were made, taking 978 hours in the studio; if you add TV to all that, well it was altogether something like ten thousand hours – an incredible commitment. Is it any wonder that they could play together as such an incredible team?

As the Beethoven cycle came to Birmingham again, emotions were running high, and the press had a field day. Anthony Holden wrote in the *Observer*:

That mane of Renaissance curls may have turned a distinguished grey, but Simon Rattle is still only forty-three – youthful as conductors go and impossibly young to be giving an entire city a collective nervous breakdown by leaving its orchestra after only two decades in charge.

A succession of full houses at Birmingham's Symphony Hall, awed into rapt silence by his farewell Beethoven cycle, proved touchingly reluctant to let their eternal wunderkind go, ovation after ovation expressing disbelief that musical life might somehow go on without him . . . Come his very last hurrah, they will probably block off the ring road and chain him to the podium.

The best summary of Rattle's achievement was by Hugh Canning in *The Sunday Times*:

When the history of music-making during the 1980s and 1990s is evaluated, the name of Simon Rattle will be writ large. What this young conductor, not yet forty-five, has achieved in Birmingham should – but probably won't – serve as a model for running a symphony orchestra and galvanizing a musical public in favour of a wide-ranging and progressive repertory. Above all, he will be for ever revered in Birmingham as the man who inspired the building of Britain's best concert venue, Symphony Hall, and who took a fine municipal orchestra into the international league . . . Rattle gave his final concerts as the CBSO's music director last weekend, well outside the orchestra's normal season, as a sort of triumphant postscript to eighteen years' outstanding work. Two performances of the Mahler *Resurrection* Symphony brought the Rattle era to a resounding close. I attended the first, which I count among my greatest Mahler experiences in the concert hall.

The Rattle era was over. But he would be back, and for those who guided the fortunes of the brilliant young conductor who was taking over, Sakari Oramo, this would be a two-edged sword.

1998–99

Berlioz	Overture: *Les francs-juges*
Falla	*Nights in the Gardens of Spain* (Joaquin Achucarro)
Rakhmaninov	Symphony no. 2

Berlioz	Overture: *Les francs-juges*
Elgar	Cello Concerto (Truls Mørk)
Rakhmaninov	Symphony no. 2

Towards the Millennium: the 1980s

Lutosławski	Symphony no. 3
Takemitsu	*To the Edge of Dream* (John Williams)
Takemitsu	*Vers l'arc-en-ciel, Palma* (Christine Pendrill)
John Adams	*Harmonium*

Towards the Millennium: the 1980s

Nicholas Maw	*Odyssey*

Towards the Millennium: the 1980s

Kurtág	*Grabstein für Stephan*
Gubaidulina	Violin Concerto (*Offertorium*) (Vadim Repin)
Birtwistle	*Earth Dances*

1999–2000

Bach	Brandenburg Concerto no. 1
Haydn	Symphony no. 71
Strauss	*Ein Heldenleben*

Towards the Millennium: the 1990s

Lindberg	*Gran Duo* (première)
Turnage	*Blood on the Floor*

Towards the Millennium: the 1990s

Weir	*We Are Shadows* (première)
Messiaen	*Eclairs sur l'au-delà*

Towards the Millennium: the 1990s

Henze	The Tempest (première)
Ligeti	Violin Concerto (Tasmin Little)
Holt	Sunrise Yellow Noise (première; Lisa Milne)
Tippett	The Rose Lake
Janáček	Overture: The Makropoulos Case
Fauré	Pavane
Brahms	Violin Concerto (Kyung-Wha Chung)
Mussorgsky–	
Ravel	Pictures at an Exhibition

There was still more to be done, and Towards the Millennium to complete. There was at last time to squeeze in a couple of projects that had been previously impossible to schedule: Simon's wife Candace organized a memorable Evening of Banned Music at the Union Chapel in London, where Simon took up the piano again, accompanied Jill Gomez and played in Messiaen's Quartet for the End of Time. His commitment to young people was highlighted by an incredible re-run of 'The World's Largest Orchestra', a project previously mounted in Symphony Hall in order to gain entry to the hallowed pages of the Guinness Book of Records, but which had proved to last just twenty-seven seconds short of the five minutes' tutti playing time required to win the record. There were no errors this time: some 3,503 kids played Malcolm Arnold's Little Suite no. 2 and became part of history.

In the future with the CBSO Rattle will complete some Szymanowski recordings, and is premièring Henze's Tenth Symphony, which was written for him, at Lucerne in 2002. His final recording with the CBSO is planned to be Mahler's giant Eighth Symphony in 2004, something even EMI could not find practical in Berlin.

The Birmingham alliance gradually broke up: Simon Rattle began his freelance years – quite brief as they turned out. Ed Smith eventually left the CBSO for a period of quiet reflection and then moved briefly to Toronto to take over the Toronto Symphony, where he found that a decade of instability had created an organization he would find impossible to repair. Anthony Sargent left the city council for Gateshead to create an exciting new music centre there. Rattle said in a revealing aside in an interview in 1999, 'It's wonderful to have time and space and I realize that I've been chronically exhausted for the last three or four years. I was muddling along, but was it waving or drowning?'

ANTHONY SARGENT I think in the 1980s the arts community thought that anything was possible for the CBSO, but that they were toiling in a rather grim, different vineyard. By the time Simon left there was a much more equally shared sense that Birmingham was a place where you could be brave, take risks, be creative and dream dreams. He gave that sense to the whole arts community. And the thing he gave to audiences generally was this inspiring sense that music isn't exclusive, something to be dressed up for and worshipped. He gave them a sense that music was a palpable life force that surges through people's everyday lives and their bloodstream. He created the sense of a musical event as being something that has the naked energy and excitement that football matches can have. He positioned the notion of culture differently for the whole of Birmingham.

In a strange way I don't feel I knew him any better at the end of that ten years working together than I did at the beginning. He's incredibly warm and involved; I just haven't any clue what mattered to him other than when we were sitting face to face. I think over projects I've done with people, the rewarding people I've worked with, and cherish them. I'm never quite sure he would feel the same way. But the fact that he was in Birmingham for those ten years made it a completely inspirational chapter in my life; in some ways I suspect it was something that will never be surpassed. His generosity and his energy and his open-mindedness made it possible to achieve things that we couldn't have imagined doing at any other time in any other place.

For the CBSO, the eighteen years were the source of a unique vision and achievement, as one of Rattle's closest collaborators, the cellist and founding director of the Birmingham Contemporary Music Group, recalls:

SIMON CLUGSTON I think it gave me the most extraordinary optimism about how an orchestra could be. Whether the funding system in this country will allow that to happen now or happen again is a question mark, but I think that above everything Simon gave back the responsibility for fantastic performance to each individual member of the orchestra. That makes for very exciting music-making. Simon's got very clear ideas but he's never been slow to go and seek advice. He'll talk to William Christie about Rameau, or Harry Birtwistle about *Earth Dances*, and he's created a situation where the orchestra feels it can absorb all those things. The interaction comes about because this is the place where ideas are allowed.

It was so skilfully paced, both the continual development within the orchestra and the sense of audience-building. For instance, Schoenberg had rarely been performed in Birmingham, so he didn't do the *Five Orchestral*

Pieces until he'd done two years of earlier Schoenberg. He had a clear sense
of the orchestra needing to do a particular piece in a particular year because
they were at the right stage. The thinking was: 'Rakhmaninov *Symphonic
Dances* in Year 3 will be a huge challenge, but we can see that far now.' An
awful lot of those markers went past, and in the middle of it all there was
the development plan which for good or ill – I have to say I think mainly
good – attracted another group of musicians that took the orchestra up
another step.

And can it go on now?
I'll have to take a deep breath with this. To be honest, I just don't know. I
think the economic realities are the real problem. The legacy that Simon
has left of a really committed, interested group of musicians, that in itself is
great, and they've chosen an extremely talented conductor. There's every
reason theoretically why that can go on and be a huge success. The problem
everyone worries about is the Arts Council, the level of financial support:
the funding issue is that if you want orchestras at a certain level it costs
money. If they are to be more flexible and creative they need to be larger
not smaller. Someone along the line is going to have to decide whether we
want that or not. It would be a real pity if some of the extraordinary,
radical changes that Simon encouraged – more flexible working patterns
for players and space for personal development – ceased, and you got less
interesting repertory, all that would be distinctly unhealthy. It would be
too simple to get into a downward spiral. But I'm convinced that the more
you invest in special events, major projects and thrilling performances, the
more people will come.

Simon Clugston has now left the BCMG to join Anthony Sargent in
Gateshead. The conundrum of where the CBSO goes from here, in the
post-Rattle era with a new music director, and with increasing pressure
on funding, is one that will have to be solved by Sakari Oramo in partnership with a new chief executive of the orchestra, Stephen Maddock,
who was formerly administrator of the BBC Proms.

STEPHEN MADDOCK When I was appointed, the external perception of
the orchestra was that its future was uncertain, that life without Simon
would be difficult, and that when he was no longer there it would inevitably slip back down on to a lower level. In reality it was very clear that the
orchestra and the organization as a whole were ready to move on. There
was a great deal of confidence internally and a great deal of excitement
about what Sakari could bring. So the important part of Simon's legacy is
not just that he might come back and conduct occasionally, but the physical legacy – the existence of Symphony Hall, the CBSO Centre, the improved

quality of the orchestra, the strength of the choruses, and especially the offshoot activities such as the BCMG and the chamber-music series.

Aren't those activities the things that will be difficult to maintain under financial pressure?
Those are things you cannot turn your back on. We have taken the existence of those things as given in looking at our financial situation, because apart from anything else they provide huge amounts of player motivation. So we need to maintain the range and breadth of what we do while slicing a little off the cost of doing it. It's not really understood that the gradual financial decline happened across the period of Simon's departure: sponsorship, external engagements, audiences and income from touring, all went down; it's a general experience.

Has it proved as difficult to establish Sakari with the audience as it was for Simon to establish himself?
Well, he got there in eighteen years! There was a previous pattern whereby Simon's concerts definitely sold better than anyone else's, and in Sakari's first seasons it was a much more mixed picture. Then I think the audience was impressed rather than warm. It took another year for them to become warm, and now we're getting closer to him, he's becoming a household name in Birmingham. He now has a profile where his concerts do sell better than everyone else's. At the same time the subscription base for the concerts has gradually declined, so we're taking a different approach to programming, and spreading the unfamiliar repertory across the season, so that every single concert has something to attract the audience.

Not having Millennium *concerts entirely of 1980s or 1990s music must help there . . .*
Actually what happened – which is a great tribute to what Simon had done through his time here – was that the audience really responded and the 1990s did brilliantly in Birmingham. It was the 1960s and 1970s that were the problem! Perhaps because the music of all the composers Simon had conducted came back in the final series – Henze, Judith Weir, Ligeti – and the audience felt more comfortable with it because it had been introduced to them in the right way.

Are there differences now in the way the orchestra is regarded by the city?
The city is still incredibly supportive, but one of the big differences between now and the late 1980s is that then culture in Birmingham *was* the CBSO and Simon. Now the Birmingham Royal Ballet is at least as significant in terms of the regard in which it's held by the city, and the Rep is a major producing house, and so on. A number of other organizations have really grown in the last ten years, very much encouraged by the CBSO and

encouraged by city investment. So where we were a big fish in a small pool, we are now a big fish in quite a big pool.

Do you see the CBSO post-Simon as being a very different thing from when he was there?
That's a very difficult question: you'd make a good journalist one day! It's a constant process of change and evolution and it will continue to develop, in ways that would not have been envisaged by him. The things that will continue are the great value placed on the ideas and initiatives that come from within the organization, a great determination to be uncompromising in terms of the repertory being innovative, contemporary, cutting edge. The culture of funding in this country is changing, and this was one of the things that undoubtedly contributed to Simon eventually leaving. The culture of the Simon–Ed era was to dream your dreams and believe that eventually someone would fund them. The culture we now live with is: 'Here's an amount of money; what can you do with it?' And a lot of the problems we are now grappling with are the result of those two approaches being basically incompatible.

By the beginning of 2001 it was clear that the Oramo partnership was working. As Richard Morrison wrote in *The Times* under the headline 'ORCHESTRA STILL ON A ROLL WITHOUT RATTLE':

When Rattle left there were predictions that the band's hard-won world-class reputation and taste for adventure would quickly be diminished. Such fears were understandable, given Rattle's towering stature. But if they have not been dispelled, they were decisively quashed in Madrid this week. The CBSO blazed through two concerts . . . under Rattle's successor. One of these programmes was quite the most testing collection of avant-garde pieces that I have heard any symphony orchestra risk on foreign soil: four virtuoso works, all written in the past ten years. And the impact? Extraordinary. If the CBSO's Madrid triumph belonged to any one individual, it belonged to Oramo . . . His conducting technique is stupendously assured, he has boundless musical curiosity, and he knows the repertory from the inside.

As the orchestra's artistic success under Oramo grew, however, so did its financial problems. It became bogged down in one of the Arts Council's most opaque schemes, stabilization, designed to help organizations create new structures and write off deficits – but only with the promise of radical change. This process has already claimed the head of one excellent orchestral chief executive in Liverpool, whose players had later voted for proposals that would buy out rights and potentially reduce their salary package. In May 2001, ironically just as the Berlin crisis over funding was beginning, the Birmingham players voted by a large majority not to accept new proposals for their contracts. But in July 2001 the problems began to be eased with the award of £3 million from the Arts Council under its stabilization scheme, which gave the orchestra the confidence to build for the future. The CBSO-Oramo relationship continued to develop and mature, and received wide exposure at, for instance, the South Bank Centre's Kurtag Festival in April 2002 where the CBSO provided both the main orchestral concerts. But money continues to be a worry.

Where his successors, who have to depend on funding, have to be careful, Simon Rattle can now afford to be outspoken about the present orchestral debate.

SIMON RATTLE The solution is not to go for the middle way and I know Sakari and Stephen [Maddock] will not do that. When I went to talk to the Arts Council all those years ago I said, 'Promise me one thing: that you will not give us the money for one year and let us set all this up and then leave us high and dry.' No prizes for guessing what they did. They will scream when you write this, and you must. They abandoned us. Thank God for Birmingham city council because otherwise we would have had to sack a lot of musicians. One of the top people in the Arts Council had the nerve to tell me and Ed, 'You are the villains of British orchestral life. You've let people get above themselves having these ideas of doing better, earning more . . .' Now at the Arts Council, there's no one there with any knowledge of music except for Joanna [MacGregor, the pianist], who famously doesn't like orchestras, unless I've got her very wrong. People think you can just have freelance orchestras. It's not true – especially somewhere like Birmingham.

I am stunned at how British orchestral musicians manage to survive and do what they do. Shame on the Arts Council for knowing so little, for being such amateurs, for simply turning up a different group of people every few years with no expertise, no knowledge of history, to whom you have to explain everything, where it came from and why it is there, who don't listen and who don't care. Shame on them.

CHAPTER NINE

'He conducts life, not notes'
Around the World in the 1990s

Rattle rehearsing the period-instrument players of the Orchestra of the Age of
Enlightenment, 2001 (photo Jim Four)

I
Back to the Future

The scene is a small Indian restaurant somewhere on Haverstock Hill,
Hampstead, and as it's only 6 p.m. it's completely deserted, so we have
the place to ourselves. It is summer 1987 and Simon Rattle has slipped
away from rehearsals for his first project with the Orchestra of the Age
of Enlightenment, a pair of concert performances of Mozart's *Idomeneo*,

to get something to eat, and I've lent him a tenner to do just that. The occasion sticks in my mind, not so much because I never got the ten pounds back, but because of the eight words Simon utters as soon as we sit down: 'Do you think this would work at Glyndebourne?'

I was taken aback, because I knew by then how slowly he liked to pace things in unfamiliar areas, and this would be a massive leap into the unknown. It was still only the rehearsal period for what was his very first encounter with period instruments, with an orchestra that had been formed only a year before, in an untried style, without any guarantee of success. And I also knew him well enough to be certain that the fact that he asked the question meant that his mind was already made up. We discussed the awkward pit in the old Glyndebourne theatre, whether you could build it up so the players were more visible, the problems of the dry sound there, but I felt, as so often with Simon, that he was far down the track of a mental process that left you running to catch up.

Sure enough, almost before that first *Idomeneo* had happened in August 1987, he had enthused Glyndebourne with the period-instrument idea. He had persuaded them to overturn what was a long-standing commitment to doing all their operas with the London Philharmonic, so that he could undertake the Mozart–Da Ponte cycle from 1989 with the Orchestra of the Age of Enlightenment. Period instruments and Glyndebourne were not a natural match: the house had had huge success with Raymond Leppard's pioneering but resolutely romantic Monteverdi and Cavalli, full of swooning harps and luscious strings, and Leppard was among those who believed that we needed a revival of period strings as little as we needed a revival of period dentistry. Glyndebourne will maintain that they wanted to do it, that they were bowled over by the quality of the *Idomeneo*, and that they went into the relationship with the Age of Enlightenment gladly. And so they did, in retrospect, but I remember commenting to one now-departed Glyndebourne executive there at the performance of *Idomeneo* with the OAE that this certainly showed the limitations of a modern orchestra in Mozart, and getting a pretty frosty response. It was more likely the case that they recognized that if they wanted to keep Rattle on board at Glyndebourne, this was the only way to do it. They went for it, with results that are now remarkable: the OAE is established at Glyndebourne not only in Mozart – and indeed Mozart has sometimes reverted to modern instruments – but especially in Handel, the success of the 1990s for the house. Stylistically, Glyndebourne is now more up-to-date than any major European opera house, thanks to Rattle's insistence back in 1987.

The period-instrument movement has been one of the most remarkable features of British musical life over the last quarter-century. Although early music began as a revival of forgotten repertories and forgotten instruments, first in the hands of specialists including the Dolmetsch family, and in the popular arena with the tragically short-lived David Munrow, it was the impact of old instruments on conventional repertory that began to make an impression in the 1970s. The first groups of baroque players had come together around 1973, when both Christopher Hogwood's Academy of Ancient Music and Trevor Pinnock's English Concert were founded. There was a great deal of experiment and adventure, and the record companies, particularly at that point Decca L'Oiseau-Lyre, backed the experiments, recording the results arguably some time before they were ready to be recorded. Roger Norrington, at that time conducting his Schütz Choir, started to expand into period-instrument baroque and classical repertory, and already by 1983 was moving into Beethoven on period instruments.

There was a popular buzz around the old-instrument exploration of the classical repertory in the late 1980s, so much so that there were three concurrent old-instrument cycles of the Beethoven symphonies being recorded by 1990. That rapidly outpaced the then old-fashioned classical sounds of the mainstream orchestras, and some of those orchestras abandoned this repertory altogether, with regrettable results. Others tried either to retrench or to adapt, a process in which Simon Rattle became much involved.

In the 1970s and 1980s this was a development that many conventional musicians frowned on, not just because it deprived them of repertory, but because they felt it produced out-of-tune, substandard results – as indeed it sometimes did as players worked to master the techniques of old instruments. But those players were taking considerable risks to learn new techniques and Simon Rattle knew enough of the people involved to take it very seriously. He had been at the Royal Academy with Monica Huggett, one of the pioneer violinists of this school, and knew quite a few players as friends and colleagues for years. The first person he shared a flat with, Cathy Giles, had friends in the early-music area, including the cellist Timothy Mason (who was hugely influential in the first years of the OAE before tragically dying of cancer), and one of Rattle's closest friends at the Academy and after was the harpsichordist and conductor Nicholas Kraemer. Rattle had been at several key events, notably John Eliot Gardiner's historic revival of Rameau's *Les boréades* in 1976, soon after which Gardiner too had taken to period instruments.

It was from the players' own enthusiasms that the Orchestra of the Age of Enlightenment sprang in 1986. Most of the old-instrument bands were dominated and driven by their own directors – Norrington, Gardiner, Hogwood, Pinnock – whose individual taste predominated. The idea of those who formed the OAE was to have a period-instrument orchestra that would be open to many tastes and styles, and be driven by the players themselves. One of the leading lights was the bassoonist Felix Warnock; he and other leading players recalled the genesis of the relationship:

FELIX WARNOCK I think it was in our minds from the very beginning that if we created the right sort of orchestra, not tied to a single conductor or director, Simon would be interested in working with us. He knew quite a few of the people involved. I had known him slightly for years: my mother knew his father; we were in the National Youth Orchestra together; then very on early when he was at the Academy we asked him to Oxford to conduct the Hertford College Orchestra, and I played in that and helped to organize it. Various other people had various other connections, so I think he felt comfortable with that group of people.

He agreed to do *Idomeneo*, but that came within a whisker of not happening for financial reasons. It was a real saga. It was entirely because of him that the OAE went to Glyndebourne, because he said to them that if he was to do what they really wanted him to do, the Mozart–Da Ponte cycle, with *Figaro*, *Così* and *Giovanni* over several years, he would have to it with the OAE. I don't think it was any overwhelming enthusiasm on Glyndebourne's part; it was Simon's insistence that made it happen.

ANTONY PAY I had known Simon going back to his very first professional engagement with the Nash Ensemble doing *Pierrot lunaire*. When he must have been quite young he had been to the John Eliot Gardiner première of *Les boréades*, and I remember that he came to a rehearsal for one of our first OAE concerts, with Roger Norrington at the Queen Elizabeth Hall in 1986. We knew he was fascinated by it all.

ANNETTE ISSERLIS I think there was something in the idealism of people who did early music and contemporary music that appealed to him. There were a lot of people common to both worlds, Jenny Ward Clarke, Tim Mason, and Tony Pay, and the thing that the two worlds had in common was about the composer being very important, that the process was trying to get to the heart of what the composer wanted rather than imposing an interpretation. *Idomeneo* I did not play in but I went to it and it was electrifying. There was obviously a real feeling of trust and excitement between Simon and the band.

Whatever it was that attracted Rattle to the world of period instruments – and it was certainly a mixture of the sounds they made and the people who played them – he was quick to move into action as soon as the Orchestra of the Age of Enlightenment was formed. The *Idomeneo* project took root very quickly, but was still an enormous challenge for the new band. Given the cast that Rattle wanted – Arleen Augér and Philip Langridge among others – it was hugely expensive and came very near to being cancelled. It was thanks to the feisty first manager of the OAE, Judith Hendershott, that it did happen, and her energy was essential in those early times to make the orchestra work. She later fell foul of the very thing the orchestra had been set up to protect, the wishes of the players, and Felix Warnock took over as manager before David Pickard arrived in 1993. He moved to Glyndebourne in 2001.

In spite of the financial problems, *Idomeneo* did happen, and was a stunning success. In rehearsals, far from being uncertain about the potential of the period instruments, Rattle displayed a detailed knowledge of their possibilities and invigorated the players with his quest for higher and higher standards. He demanded far more flexibility in tempo and expressiveness than old-instrument bands usually expect. As a result there were some problems in actually getting the orchestra to play together. But those were quickly overcome, and the two performances in the QEH were amazing experiences: disturbing for some who expected a more purist approach to eighteenth-century style; thrilling for others, who heard the range and accomplishment of period-instrument performance suddenly enlarged.

'Unalloyed pleasure,' wrote David Murray in the *Financial Times*. 'I have not heard a more exciting *Idomeneo*.' 'Rattle clearly relished the pungency and delicacy of sound available,' commented Jan Smaczny in the *Independent*. Rattle displayed what Paul Griffiths in *The Times* called 'a sure, wonderfully revealing sense of the heroic romantic . . . There was nothing half ready in this début.' In the *Telegraph*, Alan Blyth completed the unanimity by comparing it with the previous Glyndebourne performances by Rattle with the LPO: 'an exhilarating evening. Here with original instruments it was all in sharper focus, more pointed in phrasing and refined in texture while not losing that rhythmic bite that is the hallmark of all Rattle interpretations.' In the first edition of this book I guessed: 'It is difficult to imagine, after such a tumultuous success, that this is an orchestra to which Rattle will refuse to return. As ever, new doors are opening, and this one leads in a particularly interesting direction.' In fact, it was a direction that would be crucial to the whole of Rattle's music-making in the 1990s.

The stage was set for the Glyndebourne experience. *Figaro* was planned for 1989, *Così* for 1991 and *Giovanni* for 1993. In the event, *Figaro* wasn't quite the artistic success it should have been. Rattle tried to do everything at once, adding complex ornamentation to the vocal lines (and so disorienting the Glyndebourne faithful) as well as using old instruments, which received little bloom from the old Glyndebourne theatre. In addition there was a new but rather fussy Peter Hall production in decorative sets, a sad falling-off from the magical Hall production of 1973 that so many used as a touchstone for musical, insightful Mozart direction.

As Rattle said to Hugh Canning in *Opera* magazine it was surprising that Glyndebourne should have decided to do Mozart in period style 'when they have been playing Monteverdi like Brahms for all those years. Horrific! But the Mozart there has always been, in its very particular time-warped way, very beautiful. John Pritchard is certainly one of the greatest Mozart conductors I have ever heard. There were some wonderful nights in that theatre and I learned more about Mozart from him than anyone else. I had a message from John saying lots of love, but he was going to picket the theatre the night we did *Figaro* with period instruments!'

Canning's interview was supportive on the question of old instruments, but another article in *The Sunday Times* at the time tried to stir up trouble, with its references to 'Figaro-in-the-raw', and the 'summary displacement' of the LPO, and this certainly helped to create an aura of uneasiness around the production. George Christie leapt to the defence of the OAE, saying that Glyndebourne 'jumped in with both feet and without any shadow of reluctance', but some damage may have been done. The first night of *Figaro* was very uneasy, and it was the only occasion I can ever remember Simon ringing me on the morning the reviews came out, a bit baffled and hurt for his cast and his players, and wondering why it had not gone down better with the critics.

But Rattle learned incredibly quickly, as he always does. The most artificial excesses of the ornamentation were removed, and the next instalment of the cycle was already far better. The Trevor Nunn *Così fan tutte* was lively, but still hampered by the old theatre, and was a somewhat cosmetic production set on a boat. It was when *Così* escaped from the theatre into the concert hall, for concert performances with the OAE in 1995, that the critics really responded:

> What a relief it is to have a concert performance of *Così fan tutte*, superbly cast and winningly acted, without intrusion from any opera director determined to impose his own clever reinterpretation of Mozart and Da Ponte . . . Eat your heart out, Peter Sellars, whom I saw looking pensive in the audience. (Edward Greenfield, *Guardian*)
>
> . . . a glorious account . . . had all the drama one could wish for . . . the Orchestra of the Age of Enlightenment is wonderful; but not all wonderful orchestras make this kind of effort for every conductor. (Philip Hensher, *Daily Telegraph*)
>
> . . . an evening as near to perfection as one could dare to expect, masterminded by Rattle's genius . . . (Michael Kennedy, *Sunday Telegraph*)

The real move forward came when the new Glyndebourne house opened in 1994. The period instruments of the Orchestra of the Age of Enlightenment were liberated by the new acoustics, and the move to the new theatre opened Rattle's collaboration with Deborah Warner. She is one of the most original voices in British theatre, and had directed only one previous opera production (a stunning *Wozzeck* for Opera North). She had been brought to Glyndebourne by Anthony Whitworth-Jones, whose determined attempts to broaden the production style of the house had already produced one controversial Mozart production, the Peter Sellars *Magic Flute*, and was about to produce another. A perennially controversial figure, Deborah Warner had just been banned by the Samuel Beckett estate from ever directing his work again, because she and Fiona Shaw dared to alter the text and stage directions of one of his plays.

The production of *Don Giovanni* in 1994 was Rattle's first encounter with the work, though it had been prepared with some concert performances earlier in the season with the CBSO, as *Figaro* had been. This was a production that caused controversy for all the best reasons. To the *Observer* Rattle confided, 'It's like going down the Niagara Falls in a barrel. It's fantastic, but there's not a lot of time to enjoy the view.' Rattle was glad to acknowledge the influence of John Eliot Gardiner's *Don Giovanni*, which he had heard in concert performance at the Queen Elizabeth Hall. 'There's no feeling of state secrets in the period-instrument world. There's a lot of sharing of ideas and resources between conductors. We avoid the ideas we don't like and often copy those we do.'

The Warner production was felt to be stimulating but in the end not quite thought through. A single tilting platform served for the whole drama, albeit with extremely sophisticated lighting, and a denouement involving Don Giovanni with a statue of the Virgin Mary was sure to cause controversy with the Glyndebourne faithful. The première was roundly booed by some, but the critics were positive. Under the headline 'LUDDITES ARE THE LOSERS', Rodney Milnes got the point:

> It is musically superb. The playing of the Orchestra of the Age of Enlightenment is beautifully blended and balanced ... Simon Rattle has the gift of conveying precisely why he chooses sometimes unconventional tempos – a couple of bars in and you think, 'That's what Mozart really meant.' And without any hint of the didactic, he makes you feel you're hearing the music for the first time ... *pace* an audience baying for blood, an exemplary evening.

In the *Guardian* Andrew Clements noted that

> He matches Warner's detailed stagecraft with lovely instrumental details, and perfectly timed pauses. The recitative prickles with tension – real people talking to each other. But then this is a production about real people, those you might meet every day, even see at the opera. Hence, perhaps, the boos.

The growing relationship between Simon Rattle and the OAE outside Glyndebourne was an important and surprising development, bearing in mind all the other demands on Rattle's touring time. Their manager through much of the 1990s, until his recent appointment at Glyndebourne, was David Pickard.

DAVID PICKARD I arrived in November 1993, and though I could see that there was obviously a great working relationship between Simon and the orchestra, I didn't realize at the time that it was about to take off. Until then it had been entirely confined to opera. The orchestra was planning a major tour for February 1994, which was, incredibly, its first big European tour. So this was a very symbolic moment for them, going into the heart of Berlin, Paris and Vienna with Simon, and it was also crucial for the relationship.

The tour went marvellously, and I think it was at this moment that we realized that there could be a relationship with Simon that went beyond the Mozart operas at Glyndebourne.

He had always been fascinated by the sound world, and that was certainly something he wasn't getting elsewhere. The instruments we use and the possibilities of sound we can get from them, that's one thing that attracts him. The other thing, which is not unique to the OAE but which is very special, is the incredible commitment to the performance and the sort of energy you get from within the orchestra. These players are not doing orchestral work every day of the week; they are doing their chamber music and their teaching in between. Now these things do fit together, because I do think that the sort of person who is reckless enough to try and make a career with period instruments is the sort of person with an enquiring mind, not a person who has become a musician so as to get a nice salaried stable job in a symphony orchestra. A lot of them play contemporary music, for instance.

I think Simon relates to this sort of personality very strongly. You are dealing with strongly motivated people who are not necessarily temperamentally suited to playing in an orchestra at all! Some conductors don't manage to get all that energy going in the same direction, but that is what Simon achieves.

The very interesting thing now as he continues to conduct us in parallel with his other orchestras is what order he does things in. Very often he wants to tackle works first with a modern orchestra and then with a period orchestra, which you wouldn't think of as the natural way round. When he does Bach's *St John Passion* – for the first time! – in 2002, it will be with Birmingham first, then Berlin, and then with the OAE. Only two or three years ago when we said, 'Would you do Bach with us?' he said, 'Oh no, you have people like Leonhardt and Brüggen who do these things much better than I could ever do.' Yet not much later here we are with it planned.

When he stepped into Beethoven and Schubert territory with the OAE he had begun to do Beethoven with the CBSO and was wanting to explore it further with the amazing results that we've all heard. When he did Berlioz recently he said, 'I will never again be able to conduct the *Symphonie fantastique*' – and this is a work he's conducted with great orchestras like the Vienna Philharmonic – 'in the same way again, having conducted this piece with the OAE.' And now Brahms and Schumann are being discussed, which certainly weren't within the realms of possibility in 1994. So things continue to develop. I don't know what plans he has to do Berlioz again with a modern orchestra, but it would be interesting to see how far it might change having done it with us.

What difference will the Berlin appointment make to the OAE?
He said very clearly when he left Birmingham that he would go on being
committed to a very few groups, including the CBSO, Vienna, Berlin and
the OAE, and he's continued to say the same thing after being appointed to
Berlin. We are going through a glorious, golden period at the moment
before he starts in Berlin because he actually has some time! We've had the
massive Berlioz tour with our largest orchestra ever; we've got *Fidelio* at
Glyndebourne; we've a tour of Mozart symphonies next summer, and then
in January 2002 a Châtelet residency with *Fidelio*, and later in May 2002
the *St John Passion*. I suppose everyone was obviously worried that, as
Simon developed, his interests might be diverted away and the relationship
would sort of fizzle out. Exactly the opposite has happened. Every single
time we've worked with him the experience has got better and I don't see
any sign of that commitment wavering. He talks about the orchestra to his
colleagues, and time and again if I'm having a conversation with a new
conductor or a new soloist about the possibility of coming to us, it turns
out they've just been working with Simon Rattle who's been enthusing
about us to them. You cannot ask for more.

ANNETTE ISSERLIS I think he's always horrified how we sound the very
first time, at the first rehearsal. He's used to working with orchestras who
play on the same instruments day in day out and we're not like that. We
play on different instruments according to the repertory. So there's always
this horrible moment when he brings down the first beat and you see his
eyes have a certain sort of glazed expression as if he can't quite believe
what's he's hearing and he doesn't want people to know he's horrified. His
eyes glide away from making any contact! But we're all amazed by how
quick the learning curve is, second time 200 per cent better, third time 400
per cent better.

It was interesting the first time we did Beethoven with him, because he
came along with his own parts from the CBSO, which resulted in some
lively discussions about bowings: our gut strings and earlier bows don't
necessarily respond in the same way. We learned a lot from that in terms of
getting him together with people beforehand. He is actually very suggest-
ible but there are times when it might seem like a weakness for him
to change what he is suggesting. He does think so much about music,
sometimes almost too hard.

Was the first Figaro *an example of that?*
Yes, because he was anxious to do it right and every little corner was
looked at and it became a sequence of orchestral details. He said very
firmly, 'I don't want my Mozart filleted' – which is such a Simon-ish thing to
say; he likes it bones and all. He'll say, 'Just trust me. Watch me. Use me.

Don't look at each other to get things together' – which of course is exactly what we do. The orchestra is made of strong personalities and when the energy is pulling in the same direction, which he achieves, it has an incredibly positive effect. If you haven't got someone like that we can easily break out into little factions.

MARSHALL MARCUS It's a challenge for us, but actually I think when he goes to Berlin the OAE could be more important for him than it has been up to now. It's a group of people he can be part of and relax with. With Berlin, those big orchestras, it's like talking any foreign language, not literally but musically – it's very stimulating but it can be very tiring. The OAE Simon feels at home with; if it went off the boil musically of course that could be a problem, but as long as we continue with that questing, developing OAE attitude it will be fine. And we have improved; I think in the Berlioz series there was a first violin section he could really work with in this repertory, and that hasn't always been the case.

So now he's prepared to look at later music too, as well as going back to Bach for the first time. I wonder what he'd do with Handel; I'm sure that could work. In some repertory – baroque and classical – I feel there are aspects of gesture that are not the way many of us like to do things, but for instance the Haydn symphonies he's done with us have been just marvellous. When we're doing that you just feel there is no one else who could do it better because he understands the language and the grammar but still has this amazing spontaneity.

The other aspect of Simon is that extraordinary charm. He doesn't make an obvious fuss about most of the things he dislikes. You just know not to do it again! And in just that way he has certainly made us feel we have to get better and improve. You know the whole feeling that period-instrument bands just weren't good enough – well, there have been specific instances where he's really implied that we could do better, that he expects better. And that insistence on our need to improve has really helped us to keep believing that we can get better, and it has made us actually get better. I think that discipline has been vital for our development, but the magic of his charm is that it's happened in a way that hasn't compromised our passion, but liberated it.

The status that the orchestra acquired in a very short period was reflected by Martin Hoyle, who followed the OAE for the *Financial Times* on a European tour in 1997 that included the completion of Schubert's Tenth Symphony by Brian Newbould (trust Rattle to pick another piece no one knew), Beethoven 3, the Mozart Clarinet Concerto and Haydn 102:

A decade ago, they were iconoclastic trailblazers in Britain's early-music scene, both in their 'authentic' sound and their decision to choose their own conductors and eschew a permanent figurehead. Today the musicians of the OAE are almost regarded as Old Masters, coolly appreciated by the French, admiringly admitted to the inner circle by the Viennese, and greeted uproariously like old friends by the Spanish . . .

At Vienna airport, sweltering in the high 20s, a welcoming sign from Siemens to a 'conference on semiconductors' occasioned some hilarity in the orchestra . . . To my ears this was the best performance yet, and even the Viennese, especially the young, stamped and shouted . . . Only cynics could be unmoved by a Viennese audience shouting for British musicians playing Beethoven; and only the most sceptical could deny feeling a kind of European-ness that has nothing to do with politics and everything to do with civilization.

Heard back home in the surroundings of the small church of St George's Brandon Hill, in Bristol, where the OAE had developed a successful residency, the impact of the Beethoven was overwhelming. All the results of Rattle's work on the symphony with the CBSO had been fed back into the period sound-picture, creating a unique synthesis.

Another composer that the OAE enabled Rattle to move towards was Rameau. It is only the insights of the period-instrument movement that have enabled the French baroque style to be revived successfully in modern times. The twists and turns and ornaments of the music, you feel, can succeed only on the instruments of the time. Almost perversely, however, Rattle has used Rameau as the touchstone of whether a modern-instrument orchestra is as flexible as he wants it to be. For a full-scale opera, though, it was only the Age of Enlightenment that he would consider using. As a result, thanks to Salzburg's insistence on doing an opera with Rattle (and Rattle's refusal to use the Vienna Philharmonic because they could not guarantee their players), *Les boréades* became a huge project in 1999. One of the directors of the Salzburg Festival was Hans Landesmann, a long-time Rattle admirer who had been involved with the Barbican Centre in London as an adviser, and is a close friend and colleague of Claudio Abbado. He was in charge of the Vienna Konzerthaus when he originally met Rattle:

HANS LANDESMANN My first encounter with Simon was way back in 1980. When I was running the Konzerthaus in Vienna I invited him to conduct the Vienna Symphony Orchestra there. And – this was very typical of him – he said he would not do that until he had made his début in Vienna with the Birmingham orchestra. Well, I didn't have much idea about Birmingham at the time, but I decided to invite them and they came in 1982. I remember it very well because it was a Stravinsky celebration. We created a little Stravinsky festival and they opened it and they had a huge, huge success: a string concerto, the *Symphonies of Wind Instruments* and then, with the full orchestra, *Petrushka*.

That was the beginning of our collaboration and it went on from there with regular visits, until they started this massive *Towards the Millennium* festival which the Konzerthaus began to take regularly, certainly in the later years. He made a very big impact on the public. Of course I can remember that some of the critics said he was a young shooting star and let's wait and see what will happen, but it was on the whole a very positive reception from both the public and the critics.

And did he ever conduct the Vienna Symphony?
Oh no! He was always very clear about what he really wanted. He was extremely clever at choosing his repertory, and extremely forceful. He's probably one of the conductors in my experience to whom I had the least to say about programming. I have to laugh about that. It usually went that he would suggest a programme and talk a lot about it and we would discuss other ideas and then at the end we always came back to the programme he had suggested in the first place! He was very kind and very interesting to talk to, but at the end he said, 'Well, Hans, I think this is what I want to do.'

Can you ever remember him changing his mind about anything?
Absolutely not. I mean, I don't want to overstate it, but he is a very practical person and he knows the limitations of a hall, the limitations of rehearsal time, and he knows exactly what can be achieved. That has helped him a lot.

So when you went to the Salzburg Festival, you wanted to work with him there?
Yes, I immediately invited him with the Birmingham orchestra. In one programme they did Mahler 10, which I absolutely did not want. In Salzburg I felt that one should do the Adagio and not the whole Cooke completion. So this was probably exactly why he wanted to do the whole piece, because it was not really accepted in Salzburg. And of course it took place! And there was a really wonderful Janáček *Glagolitic Mass*, a great success.

And were you trying to persuade him to work with other orchestras there?
Well, it was really only the Vienna Philharmonic, but they made contact with Simon themselves very early and that turned into a great partnership, which then happened at the Festival. From the beginning Gerard Mortier wanted to do a Mozart opera with him, but this was more difficult. At first

it was a question of Glyndebourne because he was so often there in the summer. But then it was the question of the Vienna Philharmonic and the fact that they did not want to guarantee the same players for every performance because then everyone else would have wanted it. So we talked about various operas, including, I remember, *Peter Grimes*, but in the end we agreed on a completely different idea, which was Rameau's *Les boréades*.

Was that similar to Mahler 10 in that he wanted to persuade you to do something you had never done before?
No, it was a completely different idea, and it was no problem at all. He knew the piece because he had heard it when John Eliot Gardiner had dug it up originally, and it was the perfect idea for us. There was hardly any discussion because the first time he mentioned it we said, 'This is exactly what we want too.' And because we used the Age of Enlightenment, Simon was comfortable with those players and that style, and it was a smashing success.

You also brought the CBSO for a Beethoven cycle in 1998, which was a cycle with a difference . . .
Here again I must say that I needed some persuasion to do it because I had just done a cycle with Harnoncourt and the Chamber Orchestra of Europe which was really brilliant. But it was Simon's last year with the orchestra and it was a very big event for them. So we decided to do a compromise and to play the Beethoven but with contemporary scores in the programmes, played by the Birmingham Contemporary Music Group. Now I wanted, of course, to do some Austrian composers, and he wanted to do some British composers. So I sent him loads of scores and we talked in Paris and other places, and he looked at the Austrian scores and said, 'How interesting, how interesting!' And in the end the composers were all British! It was one of those times where I just didn't succeed at all in persuading him. And, to be frank about it, it didn't hit the ceiling as an event. I mean, it was received very well, it was sold out, it was a success, but it wasn't quite a major breakthrough. Some music travels well and other music doesn't.

II
European Journey: Salzburg to Vienna

The relationship between the Salzburg Festival and the Vienna Philharmonic is very close, some would say unhealthily so: the orchestra plays for most of the opera performances at the Festival, under its system (which also operates at home at the Vienna State Opera) whereby a large pool of musicians provides the resources for different groups of players under the orchestra's unique self-governing system. The Vienna Philharmonic (see p. 17) is a law unto itself, an orchestra arguably sometimes of more refinement and flexibility than Berlin, and with a particular ease in the classical repertory. Rattle's first appearance with them took even longer to achieve than with Berlin; he was wary of working with the orchestra at the Salzburg Festival because of its policy on players, and he would certainly not have done opera with them in Vienna for the same reason. But once the principles had been talked through with the orchestra management, it was possible for them to consider Rattle as one of their conductors in their short regular season in Vienna.

The performance of Mahler's Ninth he gave on that first visit in 1993 has passed into legend, and his agent Martin Campbell-White believes it was one of the greatest musical occasions he has attended. As reported in the *Guardian* by journalist Michael Henderson, who has followed Rattle religiously around the world, and wrote his farewell tribute in the CBSO programme, this was the biggest moment of Rattle's career:

> Simon Rattle stormed the imperial city's musical ramparts with two performances of Mahler's Ninth Symphony that defied description. If a single word can convey the impact of his astounding début with the Vienna Philharmonic it is 'unbeatable' . . . On each occasion Rattle was summoned back for a personal ovation after the musicians had departed . . . All round the hall people were speechless . . .

The conservative Vienna press seemed equally smitten, though their headline writing is perhaps not as snappy as ours:

> WORTHY OF THE HIGHEST PRAISE: . . . thanks to the strictest self-control and to his level-headedness, Rattle has never fallen victim to megalomania. The members of the Philharmonic clearly recognized this, and rewarded him by paying 100 per cent attention to his beat, and thereby contributed to the sensational effect of this début. (Edith Jachimowicz, *Die Presse*)

> His interpretation was utterly convincing . . . and since he was able to convince the orchestra, it sounded absolutely right . . . it was shattering. (Franz Endler, *Die Kurier*)

> For one and a half hours we walked with him along a narrow mountain ridge, with vision of the inferno to left and right . . . I look forward to

further co-operation with eager anticipation. (Karlheinz Roschitz, *Neue Kronen Zeitung*)

Fortunately this performance is more than legend as the radio recording by ORF, Austrian Radio, was subsequently issued by EMI, as Peter Alward explained:

PETER ALWARD We'd never intended to record Mahler 9 at the time, but then after the concerts we were all so thrilled by it that we thought we should just see whether there was a chance with the Austrian Broadcasting tape. And we were incredibly lucky because ORF normally records the Saturday concert only as a back-up, then the live broadcast is on Sunday morning, and they throw away the Saturday tape. But in this case they had kept it – thank God, because there was a horn fluff half through the Sunday concert, which would have ruined it as a disc. So David Murray got the tapes of both performances – one of the last things he did for us before he went back to the BBC – and did a splendid job of splicing them together.

We decided to do the Beethoven cycle with Vienna then, but no sooner was that signed, sealed and delivered, than Berlin came along. Of course Berlin promptly made noises about wanting the Beethoven cycle, and wouldn't it be nice if we could take it away from Vienna. Typical Simon: absolutely loyal, decent and honest; he said, 'No, I've made my decision; you guys came too late. If I were to do this to Vienna now, there's no guarantee I wouldn't do exactly the same to you in future years.' I thought, 'Hats off to you.' Though, actually, it does make our lives rather difficult because at the same time as trying to establish Simon in the public mind with Berlin, which Mahler 10 did so well, here comes this great huge Beethoven cycle from Vienna! But that's life.

The President of the Vienna Philharmonic is the violinist and historian of the orchestra Clemens Hellsberg:

CLEMENS HELLSBERG We had a lot of information about him. You talk with promoters and other artists and conductors and then we talk about conductors with our colleagues. I knew from my predecessors, Professor Resel and Professor Blovsky, that he was very promising. I was in hospital at the time of the first Mahler Ninth concert but it was immediately a major success for an enormous majority of colleagues, and we felt we could release the recording of the radio broadcast, which is a document it is marvellous to have. Then the way was clear to invite him for further concerts, and that was Mahler in Vienna, Brussels and Amsterdam and then Bartók and Beethoven in the Salzburg Festival.

Something that characterizes him and the collaboration with us is his care about programmes. When we later did Berlioz and Strauss it was not an obvious combination, but in our discussions he explained that Strauss's *Metamorphosen* is about finding the dark depths of the soul and so is the Berlioz *Fantastique*. Last December we had a tour with Haydn, Berg and Beethoven 5 and during the rehearsals I talked with him to discuss an encore. At first he said it was completely impossible to do one after Beethoven 5, but then he said that it must be something completely contrasted. He came up with the Sibelius *Scene with Cranes* which we had never played before. And the effect of that encore showed how well he had judged the audiences in those cities.

I think that he guarantees unusual ways into the music, and at first it may seem to be illogical, but after all his emphasis and enthusiasm there is suddenly a new understanding of the music. In the Beethoven *Eroica* there were some moments that were unusual but these situations arise less and less frequently. I think the orchestra still sounds like the Vienna Philharmonic, and as long as it sounds like that then there is no problem because what he brings us is an interpretation for today. We are now living today and not sixty years ago and each generation has to find its own way to Beethoven. What Shakespeare or Schiller said to human beings has to be discovered anew by each generation.

We know we have to look for challenges. Harnoncourt and Boulez are both very important to us. They are seventy-two and seventy-six, but both of them are young guys mentally! Simon is physically young and I am sure he will remain young whatever he does. In the past Karajan was always a challenge to us; Bernstein was a challenge, and beside these giants there were the younger men – Mehta, Maazel, Abbado – who were the young conductors of that time and they went the way of a new generation.

You haven't yet succeeded in doing an opera with him . . .
We are used to playing in opera so we are used to being aware of the stage, to reacting immediately and to working with new generations of singers. We are not at the end of that discussion and my feeling is that if something is a question, it is better not to force it. Give it time and it develops by itself.

There was a rumour that at one point you wanted to offer Simon a title with the orchestra . . .
It was not only a rumour and this could have been attractive in some ways. But we cannot change our system and we depend in our work on the fact that all our guest conductors are equal. I know all of them personally very well indeed and I know that they are very close friends of ours, and a special title for a relatively young conductor would disturb this relationship. We had special titles for two conductors as an honour at the end of their careers: in 1967 there was Karl Böhm, who was absolutely the main conductor of the orchestra and conducted the most concerts, and then

Karajan whom we asked to be honorary conductor when he was seventy-five and he accepted when he was eighty, for all his life's work. So there was no question of it.

The Beethoven Ninth concert at the site of the Mauthausen concentration camp sounds to have been unique.
That was one of the milestones in the history of our orchestra. I'm absolutely convinced it was. I'm sure that sometimes you feel *la forza del destino*; it was the ideal thing that we played this concert with Simon, and we tried to keep out of controversy, to ignore what was written in the papers attacking it, and concentrate on the music itself. The idea is much greater than the objections. It was very impressive. The trees were blooming and the birds sang and as everyone lit candles for the end of the symphony; it was very moving in a place of such horror. That brought us all very close that evening, and created a special relationship between Simon and the orchestra.

Following his début with the orchestra, Rattle took them to the large-scale Mahler Festival in Amsterdam, with the symphony he had made a speciality in Birmingham, the Seventh. For Richard Fairman in the *Financial Times*, it was the highlight of the Festival:

By contrast [with the Fifth and Sixth], the emotions flashed past in Simon Rattle's performance of the Seventh Symphony with the Vienna Philharmonic. Suddenly, Mahler seemed a twentieth-century composer . . . pushing the orchestra to its limits with abrupt reversals of tempo and dynamics, colour and feeling . . . Reports of Rattle's debut in Vienna with this symphony [actually no. 9] last year suggested that he had struck up an immediate rapport with the players, and that seemed to be borne out here with their wholehearted commitment to the kind of life-and-death performance that he wanted. It was the most spontaneous of the three concerts and arguably the most Mahlerian.

Having made a big impact with Mahler and Strauss (and being less satisfied with the Viennese response to Bartók), Rattle started the biggest experiment of all, working on classical repertory with the orchestra.

IMOGEN COOPER We played together with the Vienna Philharmonic in the Salzburg Mozartwoche in the 1990s in the big Festspielhaus, which is a heap and really not relevant to the Mozart concertos. Although Simon was really fired up, it was terribly hard for us to have any contact in that huge place. So he just stopped everything and said, 'OK, let's sit differently. Why don't the woodwind sit at the end of the piano at the front?' They rather hummed and said, 'We've never done it this way before.' But then they did it, and there was a real party atmosphere. I sat looking straight at the first oboe, and Simon was actually in front of us on the stage. At one point he turned round and said, 'I don't think I'm going to bother turning round, because there is such a steamy love affair going on between you all that I don't need to be involved!' And that was because he had taken the risk of changing things round, which the orchestra would not have done.

MARTIN CAMPBELL-WHITE He was begged by the Vienna Philharmonic to do some opera with them, and he said, 'If you can guarantee me the same players each night I will.' But they could not do that because it would have changed the whole way they worked and would have caused endless problems with other conductors. He understands why, because they do so much at Salzburg. We got a tiny bit closer there, and I think probably they would have prevailed eventually. In fact he's still got thirty concerts with the Vienna Phil – quite a number. He'll take them to Japan and will give the Beethoven cycle in Berlin and Tokyo in 2001 and in Vienna in 2002, and he is going on a European tour and conducting various other concerts. So he's got more concerts with Vienna than with Berlin in the next couple of years!

The tour Rattle gave in May 1997 with the Vienna Philharmonic Orchestra was one of the most remarkable of his career, and once again it was difficult to find a dissenting voice among the critics when they reached London with Haydn and Berlioz's *Symphonie fantastique*:

The orchestra has visited with a procession of fêted conductors who often seem to have been lured by the siren playing of this remarkable orchestra into giving performances on autopilot. Those that have escaped have either thrown themselves into the luxurious Viennese sound wholeheartedly, or been single-minded in imposing their own ideas. Rattle belongs to this second group . . . a lot of the style came from his work with period instruments . . . if the players felt he was trampling over years of tradition, he did not show it . . . he conducted Berlioz with an unbuttoned freedom we shall be lucky to hear again. The orchestra played like demons. So much praise has been heaped upon Rattle in the UK that critics here risk being accused of partisanship. I thought the concert the most exciting I have heard from the Vienna Philharmonic in recent years and I hope that is not just patriotism speaking. (Richard Fairman, *Financial Times*)

Simon Rattle has conducted the three leading European orchestras, the Royal Concertgebouw in Amsterdam, the Berlin Philharmonic and the Vienna Philharmonic, but it is with the VPO that he has struck up a special rapport . . . Their programme of Haydn, Richard Strauss and Berlioz was one that he might have conducted at any time over the past ten years with his Birmingham orchestra. Haydn symphonies have become a regular part of his music-making, and as a member of the generation that has grown up with period instruments, he has applied the lessons of authenticity to these symphony orchestra performances. Neither work in the first half was any kind of preparation for the overwhelming tumult that he unleashed in the *Fantastic Symphony* . . . It was a performance of titanic proportions . . . a constant source of amazement. Here with a British conductor and an Austrian orchestra, the greatest of all French scores seemed utterly reborn. (Andrew Clements, *Guardian*)

Something like the ultimate in virtuoso conducting . . . downright Mephistophelean in his ability to reveal new colour, move the music at new speeds, and give us a show that was sometimes outrageously intense . . . it was as though the composer himself stood before these players. Rattle found crackling freshness in every phrase . . . this supreme masterpiece of orchestral drama came over as if for the first time, utterly cogent and shockingly avant-garde. (Paul Driver, *The Sunday Times*)

These were the sort of reviews to encourage anyone to bask in early retirement. But it just spurred Rattle on to greater things, and to Stephen Pettitt in *The Sunday Times* he said,

On the face of it, there couldn't be much more difference between their upbringing and mine. But I've never felt at home as much as when I stood in front of the Vienna Philharmonic. I finally found that pair of shoes I'd been wanting to walk in all my life. There was much more flexibility than I'd expected, and an immense open-heartedness, warmth and curiosity. I didn't realize I could have that much of an effect on them. I'd not come across an orchestra that could read me as well, including my own.

Not surprisingly, this led Pettitt to wonder, 'Is this a sign of what lies in store for Rattle when the affair with the CBSO is finally over?' And indeed it might have been in the 1990s if the Vienna orchestra had been prepared to offer him a title. But, as Clemens Hellsberg implies, that was never likely to occur in a situation so essentially traditional and bound by convention.

The orchestra was increasingly showing itself able to depart from the traditions of its past, and the remarkable concert at Mauthausen in 2000 was just such an unconventional event. It was some years earlier that the Vienna Philharmonic had come up with the radical proposal to play Beethoven's Ninth Symphony in the open air, at the quarry of the former concentration camp where more than a hundred thousand people from all over Europe perished during the years in which Austria formed part of the Third Reich. This was a boldly political undertaking, a million miles from the complacency that had tended to mark some of the orchestra's activities. It was clear that they had to come to terms with their past, and this was the only way to do it. There was huge controversy, because by the time the event was actually planned the government in Austria had been joined by Jorg Haider's Freedom Party in a coalition. This for a moment put the whole project in doubt but, as Rattle commented, 'I don't believe these people are Nazis, but I think opportunistic xenophobic bigots are dangerous enough. And a very large part of the country is very aware of that also.' Some journalists came out firmly against the event; Marta Halpert expressed a widespread view when she wrote that 'a slaughterhouse is not a concert hall'.

SIMON RATTLE It was brought to me very much as a collaboration between the orchestra and the Jewish community. And it had obviously been a long time in the thinking. But where we really met was in the idea that musicians can be more eloquent in music than in words, and that possibly the only way that one can now approach that is by music. I know there been quite a lot of dispute about whether this concert was a reasonable idea or not. One has enormous sympathy for that viewpoint, but I think there is also a truth that musicians feel that some goodness can be spread by the act of playing music, and that one should take the risk, and the start of a new century is the time to do it.

Did it work as an event?
No, fortunately it wasn't an event. It worked as a ritual. I thought it was incredibly brave of them to come up with the idea and no one could have known then what the political situation was going to be. They also couldn't have guessed how much of a lightning rod it was going to be for all types of strife and argument and opinion in Austria. Not only did we play in this terrible place for twenty thousand people, including many survivors and children of survivors, who managed to stand with candles in complete silence at the end. It was also broadcast on the major television channel throughout the country. There were big screens in several towns where parents with young children came together. There were loads of police because they thought there might be trouble, but there wasn't. It was an extraordinary, peaceful thing. There were some very hard-hitting speeches saying, 'This is what happened. Remember this.' And it provoked almost by accident a debate in Austria, which I saw from the outside.

There were so many extraordinary things. There was the passive aggression of the government who really didn't want it to happen but who couldn't stop it, so they did everything to make it as difficult as possible. There was the fact of how angry it made those who were on the side of the angels. The article that argued that 'a slaughterhouse is not a concert hall' is completely right. Of course it isn't. From the very first chord we were aware that we were doing something, but our puny efforts simply could not express the real situation. The most you can do is mark it, and play with love and respect and say to people, 'Remember.' You're doomed to fail.

You can't redeem the situation . . .

No, and what I as an outsider had to say to some of the very angry Jewish people is that I know these people, the orchestra, are not asking for absolution or forgiveness. They have their own struggles; some of the orchestra came to talk to me in really anguished terms about their parents and how involved they were . . . And some people were saying, 'You can't play Beethoven, because this was music beloved of the Nazis.' You have to knock that one on the head. There were only two pieces you could have: *Fidelio* or the Ninth. You must not fall into the trap of thinking that what it has been used for is what it is. The idea that music could in some way act as a healing agent is important. For all sorts of people, such as my wife's osteopath's mother, who was not at that camp but at another, but whose father was there: I saw her in the afternoon standing there on the site of all that – 'no swimming or fishing in the lake' is not a joke, because if you put a pole in, you bring up human bones – with tears streaming down her face, and she said, 'I must come because this enables me to come to terms with it in some way.'

III
American Shuttle: LA to Boston?

America remained important to Rattle as the 1990s progressed, and it is at least likely that he might have ended up in the United States had firm offers been made to him before Berlin became a real possibility. New York he continued to refuse; Cleveland he would not return to; and Los Angeles was joined in his affections by two East Coast orchestras, Boston and Philadelphia. He had a lot of fun as guest director of the Ojai Festival in 2000, introducing audiences to some of his favourite new British works, including Turnage's *Kai* and Adès's *Asyla*, as well as conducting two French one-act operas by Ravel and Poulenc. The increased attraction of America was at least partly related to the fact that when he divorced in the mid-1990s, Elise Ross took their two sons to live in San Francisco, and so it would be increasingly difficult for him to maintain as much contact with them as he wanted, unless he were based somewhere in America. (As recently as June 2002, he took the opportunity of being in San Francisco to give a fund-raising concert for the Marin Academy there, playing piano in Mozart's Kegelstatt Trio.)

By 1997 the Philadelphia Orchestra was making a determined bid for Rattle, and the *Philadelphia Enquirer* might not have helped when it headlined a huge Rattle profile:

WANTED: MUSICAL GENIUS
SEX APPEAL A MUST
ENGLAND'S SIMON RATTLE FITS THE BILL
CAN PHILADELPHIA GET HIM?

The idea seemed to be that Rattle could do everything for them and make everything happen. The paper described him as 'the man who may become the orchestra's seventh music director – a maestro with the magnetism to pull up a perilously low 60 per cent season-ticket rate, a civic leader who might finally move the [new] concert hall off the blueprints, a global player who can get the orchestra back on the radio, back into record bins, and back into the consciousness of music lovers everywhere'. So that wasn't too much for starters. As journalist Peter Dobrin admitted, 'The only trouble is, Sir Simon Rattle says he's not coming . . .'

MARTIN CAMPBELL-WHITE Philadelphia was a real possibility, but in the end Simon and Candace decided it wasn't for them. He went there in January 1999, and they were still putting enormous pressure on him. He had a fantastic time, loved the orchestra, and everyone from the mayor downwards was very keen. But he came back and in the end he said, one, he really didn't want to live in Philadelphia and two, he is a European. He loves Vienna; he loves Berlin; he loves London. He does not want to lose that.

If Boston had moved more swiftly, he could now be the music director of the Boston Symphony and Europe's music would be rather different. He had said he was interested in principle but nothing happened at all. Then, as we know, the moment Seiji Ozawa finally said he was leaving was the day before Berlin announced its choice! And to go to Vienna . . .

SIMON RATTLE Philadelphia was very special. They all looked like my father; at that point it was a very elderly orchestra but no one had told them that they were elderly and no one had told them that you don't give lots of energy all the time and they would be ashamed if they came off the stage not perspiring. So they all still play as if it was their probation year!

They haven't got much to prove; they can do it so well, and if anything could ever have seduced me to the States it would have been that group of musicians. They've now turned themselves around in terms of what they feel an orchestra could be, and they're a great orchestra. I hope that is a relationship I can keep.

When I first went to do Mahler 9, just after doing it with the Vienna Phil, some older players said, 'Well, the things you are asking for are what we did in a previous era, in terms of sounds and types of bowing.' I said I didn't have time to fall in love with another orchestra but I'm very hopeful for them. We did the *Boréades* music and that was certainly the most anti-Ormandy half-hour they have ever spent! Was it natural to them? No. American orchestras are – sweeping generalization – basically about the big romantic repertory, and the big modern repertory. I am thrilled they have appointed Christoph [Eschenbach, recently named music director]. A very contemporary man with a very olde-worlde culture. I think they've done better than they know.

In the spring of 2002, Philadelphia planned what would surely have been a triumphant welcome to Rattle had he decided to throw in his lot with the city: in the newly opened Verizon Hall just next to the city's old Academy of Music, there was a three-week festival of concerts devoted to great Viennese music, enabling Rattle to explore his favourite territory in Schubert's Ninth and Bruckner's unfinished Ninth (which will be part of his initial Berlin season). He brought Dawn Upshaw to sing in an orchestral version of Schoenberg's Second String Quartet, and Pinchas Zukerman to play Berg's Violin Concerto, while running in Mahler's Fifth before his Berlin opening in the autumn, and adding for good measure H. K. Gruber's outrageous *Frankenstein!!*, which he had prem-ièred in Liverpool so many years before. In spite of the hall's teething problems (on which Rattle was able to offer sound advice to the acousti-cian, Russell Johnson, who had worked on Birmingham's Symphony Hall a decade earlier), the concerts planned with artistic administrator Simon Woods were tremendous events which increased Philadelphia's sense of loss that Rattle would not be leading them in the future. Still, he will be back, notably for a newly commissioned concerto by Sofia Gubaidulina, part of an adventurous joint American orchestras' com missioning plan. Boston, meanwhile, chose James Levine in succession to Seiji Ozawa, and Rattle does not look likely to return there in the foreseeable future.

IV
Fox Cubs to Holy Grail

Opera for Rattle in the 1990s did not turn out to be quite as important as might originally have been guessed. Two major projects were cancelled in 1995 and 1996, partly because of his divorce, and there was more activity abroad than at home. It seems incredible – and quite shaming to London – that after the success he had in 1990 at Covent Garden, the next time he is working there is over a decade later, at the end of 2001 in *Parsifal*.

He had originally been propositioned by Colin Davis many years ago but, as he recalled, 'He asked me to work on the Mozart cycle with him, but I just didn't think it was going to be a particularly good idea. They were never very serious; they said you could come to do whatever you liked and so on but it always turned out to be the *n*th revival of *Salome*.' So it happened that his opera exposure was far more at Glyndebourne (see earlier in this chapter) and in special projects abroad.

Rattle appeared once at English National Opera conducting Janáček's *Katya Kabanova* in 1985, though this was not a house he returned to, and his Covent Garden début was finally fixed for 1990 with the opera that had been closest to his heart since he was at the Royal Academy, Janáček's *The Cunning Little Vixen*. His son Sacha, then aged six, had a role as a fox cub, and this was predictably the popular story in the press. The first night was planned to coincide with the first night of the Covent Garden Midland Bank Proms, providing an auditorium with the stalls taken out and packed with enthusiasts, providing just the right kind of unstuffy listeners.

Rattle explained to Daniel Snowman in the Royal Opera's magazine: 'It was the piece that made me want to go into opera in the first place. I assisted Steuart Bedford on it as a student at the Royal Academy. I played the celesta and conducted the offstage chorus and fell head over heels in love with the score ... At Glyndebourne Tom [Allen] and I both felt it was a work that gets into your bloodstream and stays there, and we vowed we would do the piece together again one day if we could.' Rattle had seen Bill Bryden's *Mysteries* at the National Theatre and decided this was the director for him. 'It's the orchestra more often than not that tells you what is really going on. The vocal lines are frequently merely speech phrases with the orchestra – as in Mozart – doing all kinds of dangerous, subversive things underneath.'

I couldn't get a ticket so I stood throughout the admittedly short opera. Mentioning this to Rattle in his dressing room afterwards, I got a look of amused disdain: 'The first act of *Götterdämmerung* wouldn't be over yet!' Once again the critics were positive:

> This was generally accounted a big heart-warming success for the Royal Opera, and rightly so: any reservations about the production pale beside the superb orchestral and vocal standards ... Simon Rattle's conducting spoke of his deep knowledge and love of a score he first worked on as a student at the Royal Academy in 1973 – he was the offstage conductor – and later made his Glyndebourne début with in 1977. His reading is at once suffused with late-romantic warmth and subjected to almost neo-classical, twentieth-century discipline. Thanks to an orchestra on top of its current form, textures were pellucid and both internal and external balance perfectly judged. (Rodney Milnes, *Opera*)

The Covent Garden *Vixen* happened, but plans to follow that up with a new production of *Wozzeck* were eventually cancelled. As much as anything it fell victim to the break-up of Rattle's marriage, as it had been planned for his most difficult year, 1995, and Elise Ross had been cast as Marie. Various other ideas were mooted – *Hansel and Gretel* was even considered, but nothing happened through the traumatic years of Covent Garden's redevelopment. The two next major projects were *Parsifal* for December 2001, and the long-awaited world première of Nicholas Maw's *Sophie's Choice* in December 2002. This was originally commissioned by the BBC and planned as a culmination of the *Sounding the Century* project in December 1999, but Maw was happy to wait for Rattle to be available to conduct and for Trevor Nunn to direct, reuniting the team that triumphed with *Porgy and Bess*.

Parsifal, at the end of 2001, turned out to be one of Rattle's most remarkable triumphs; the staging was not admired by many, but that left the critics all the more time to lavish praise on the wholly distinctive sound that Rattle drew from the Royal Opera orchestra. With the experience of conducting *Tristan* by then behind him (see Chapter Ten), Rattle seemed wholly at ease with the textural effects he wanted to create, and there was admiration for his architectural command of the score. Rupert Christiansen in the *Daily Telegraph* wrote of his 'bold and muscular reading, rich in colour and gloriously played ... never one to wallow, Rattle brings the music down to earth'. 'AN UNFORGETTABLE MUSICAL TRIUMPH' was *The Times* heading; Rodney Milnes wrote that 'the buzz suggested a gradual and communal realisation that something quite extraordinary was happening, as indeed it was ... a musical experience never to be forgotten, one for which Simon Rattle deserves praise beyond words'.

Rattle's operatic relationship with Glyndebourne and the Orchestra of the Age of Enlightenment continued with *Fidelio* in 2001 (directed by Deborah Warner). It proved another controversial production, admired by some and strongly disliked by others, but Rattle's re-imagining of the score, heard for the first time on period instruments with the OAE, won all the plaudits. Typical was *The Times*, which headlined its review 'RATTLE BREAKS FREE WITH MASTERLY BEETHOVEN'. Rodney Milnes wrote that 'Simon Rattle and the Orchestra of the Age of Enlightenment made you listen to every bar of it afresh . . .'

Fidelio also travelled to the Châtelet in Paris. The achievement of the Châtelet in giving an international dimension to opera in Paris goes back to 1996, when Stephane Lissner brought the entire CBSO over to realize the Janáček *Jenůfa* that Rattle had talked to various opera houses about doing over the years. Highly praised, it prompted an even more ambitious plan, which was even closer to Rattle's heart: a full-scale *Parsifal* with the CBSO in June 1997. Unfortunately this was cancelled by Lissner, and this was one of the few times that Rattle was so upset by the cancellation of a major project – which, after all, happened extremely rarely – that he complained vigorously.

That cancellation had two consequences. First Rattle went and conducted *Parsifal* for the Netherlands Opera instead as the successor to *Pelléas*, followed in 2001 by the biggest challenge of all, *Tristan und Isolde*. Second, when Lissner went, in the merry-go-round of French artistic appointments, to run the prestigious festival at Aix-en-Provence, he was determined to cement the relationship with Rattle again. So he invited the CBSO once more, this time for Janáček's *The Makropoulos Case*. That was a great success, and opened up the most intriguing possibility of all: that over the last years of this coming decade there might be a Wagner *Ring* cycle in Aix, masterminded by Rattle and Lissner with his artistic consultant Eva Wagner-Pasquier, the most operatically knowledgeable member of the Bayreuth family, as a collaborator. It now looks likely to happen.

Meanwhile, in Amsterdam . . .

CHAPTER TEN

'*What you see is really all there is*'
Rattle 2001

Simon and Candace Rattle, 2001 (photo Maurice Foxall)

February 2001. Amsterdam's Musiktheater, on the Waterlooplein, is the city's gleaming-white state-of-the-art opera house. Between the first and second acts of Wagner's *Tristan und Isolde*, which he is conducting for the first time, on 1 February 2001, Simon Rattle is violently sick. He's been building up to a touch of flu for a few days, the pressure and the fevered intensity of the rehearsal period has been one thing, but this is something else as well. Between the dress rehearsal and the first night, he's seized by gastric flu and has difficulty getting through to the end of the opera. We've arrived very late (thanks to flight delays), but it's clear that there is either something wrong or Rattle is behaving very unusually. He's restrained in the pit, sips water furtively and, as the

Isolde notices, never smiles. For someone as resilient as he is – he hasn't cancelled more than a handful of concerts through ill health in his life – he is laid low. 'I didn't think it could just be nerves!' he says weakly in the dressing room afterwards. 'It must be Wagner.'

The next day, still not well and confined to his apartment by the doctors, he is much more upbeat about it on the phone: 'This being ill was good for me. It meant I didn't charge into the pit like Errol Flynn on the gangplank . . .' I wondered if he had ever really suffered from nerves:

> It comes and goes. Quite interestingly it is related to how big a deal it is, and of course it's also to do with expectations. The first time I went to the Vienna Philharmonic to do Mahler 9 I was sick with nerves. I was as completely incapacitated as I was here, but here it got worse so it must have been real . . . and the first time I went back to Berlin after having been elected, and feeling, 'Oh, they're all going to know it was a big mistake.' But also, you simply must have some fear. If you don't, you are lacking respect; you know you should be frightened doing something like this. So what it's about is everyone saying – this sounds like a travelling psycho-therapy club, but it's so important – everyone saying, 'These are our fears; let's get past them together.'

It's clear that *Tristan* has been an exhilarating, dangerous experience for him, a learning journey into an area of the repertory to which he feels very attracted but which is full of hidden power. It makes me wonder about the question of how you work in an opera house compared to with an orchestra. It relates to Rattle's reluctance to throw in his hand with any operatic institution, however much they have offered him the terms and conditions he has needed.

A day later, Rattle is still in his apartment in his dressing-gown, up the top of three flights of stairs in a typically narrow Amsterdam house, with a magnificently open view sweeping across the canal towards the opera house. The ground is thick with snow; the opera house blends into a seamlessly brilliant white scene broken only by the grey of the canals. While Candace is doing some shopping and stocking up with videos, Simon says through gritted teeth, 'Now I'm going to make you a cup of coffee, because I know that's what I do. I've read the book . . .' (Although I had tried hard not to include personal trivia in the first edition of this book, Simon's coffee-making rituals did slip through. Still, I'd never been quite sure whether he had ever read that bit . . .)

In his Tristan-like state, and still a bit feverish, Rattle is more communicative than ever.

Do you have the same degree of control in an opera house that you have with an orchestra?
Look, this is absolutely not to do with control. It is completely and utterly to do with trust. I know a whole lot more about this now than when we talked before. It is so much better without hierarchy. The person in control could be the director, the diva, the conductor – whoever, as my wife says, has the biggest dick at any moment. But there's a quality of people knowing they have that power or influence and *not* using it that is desperately important. People give their best only if they're supported and encouraged and when there is mutual trust. In Wagner everybody has to go into an unnatural state, and admit immediately what's difficult. Now for me, coming into a work with strong traditional ways of doing it, the difficulty is that the traditional ways aren't necessarily the best ways to navigate this treacherous ocean. You would be a fool to cross the ocean of *Tristan* in a canoe but, equally, a great majestic liner is not the only way to do it.

So how is your approach different musically from the majestic liner?
You miss a lot of the texture, and particularly the personal intimate feeling, the grain of it. These are not large people shouting; there is a chamber music between the personalities. Now, I mean, if I could conduct it like Furtwängler I'd be thrilled. But I can't. It simply doesn't come out of my imagination like that. I am far less twitchy about this than I used to be. The times are not the same and we don't hear it the same. Is there a reason why a composer as theatrical as Wagner would set sentences that take people five breaths to sing? I don't believe it. Now we have some evidence: we know the thing about Wagner saying the *Mastersingers* overture was taken too slowly, which does mean that tempi have broadened over the years. But it is also a matter of flexibility, tension and release, supporting the great structure with different weights and different centres of gravity.

And how does this affect the singers?
Well, it's a question of saying to someone like Gabby [Gabriele Schnaut, the Isolde] – you can ask her anything because she is without inhibition – 'Let's find a way where you don't have to use all the voice all the time.' It took a lot of courage, and there was a point where she said to me, 'My God, you'll have me singing Pamina again!' Don't be a cello with loads of *portamento*, sing it more like an oboe, take it back to the words. I wanted something that sounded like a Rothko painting looked, something with immense depth, throbbing and pulsing but you can't tell where it begins

and ends. This type of art can make people pretty strange. If you dealt only with this music all the time you certainly feel you could do out-of-character things. It's a drug. And not an entirely beneficent drug.

You said Parsifal *was like a giant bird you had to keep aloft. Your* Tristan *sounded more like the ebb and flow of water . . .*
It is completely imbued with the sense of waves in every way. You know at the end when she sings, 'Do I sip it, do I drown in it . . . ' It is perfectly obvious what we are talking about: an ocean made of amniotic fluid! What it does to you physically and emotionally is extraordinary and you are taken to this strange place where you don't know where you are. At the dress rehearsal, after the second act, I felt completely . . . as completely lost as I have ever been. You begin to realize why people have behaved so strangely around this music.

How did you come to Wagner? It doesn't seem central to you.
Oh, don't be so sure. I had my Wagner period, as one does, as a late teenager. I went as an assistant to one of the music camps and did the first and third acts of *Walküre*. I was the number two conductor and many professionals came to play and sing. Norman Bailey was there for instance and a number of the Covent Garden orchestra came to play for fun. When I was a student there was Reggie Goodall at the Coliseum, the *Ring* and *Tristan* later. I listened to him endlessly; then bits of the *Ring* with Alex Gibson when I was in Scotland. There was a lot going on and I heard a lot.

Is the relationship with the director generally difficult for you?
I've been pretty selective in who I've worked with, and very lucky too: Stefan Brauschweig for the Janáčeks in Paris and Aix; the Hermanns who did the Rameau (I'll be doing *Così* with the Hermanns in Salzburg); Deborah Warner at Glyndebourne. You do need someone who realizes the musical implications of what they're doing. This was something Peter Sellars realized early on and even though he drives you crazy he knows what is going on in the music and he once said to me, 'Oh shit! If I change that move, it's going to change the way the viola plays, isn't it!?' – which of course is true. In *Tristan* we really need to know why these characters are doing this, what went on before the opera started, and you want a director to come with that worked out. This time we had to work it out for ourselves, which was not easy. We asked ourselves questions all the time about why people were doing things and we didn't find many answers.

We wanted to know why Tristan comes in on his first entry singing early *Lohengrin* crossed with Italian opera. We know Wagner did set out to write a small-scale opera in the Italian style, which is pretty hilarious but, still, it's the only moment in the piece when there is that sort of music – so what does it mean? Alfred [Kirchner, the director] had no idea and was never able to tell us. What happened with the two of them back then: who is lying; why are Tristan and Isolde both lying to each other in the second act? When you are in love you rewrite things, true, but what exactly are they rewriting? You can find out these things only by going into them in depth; you can't do it by gut instinct alone.

But the design answered a lot of questions for us. We sat and talked about this last year and said, 'Look, the problem of the third act is that we need to create somewhere that is a dream, a dream world that is like the inside of somebody's head. But there is the really practical problem of stamina and balance in this act so can you give us something that helps us to project but expresses difficulty of movement?' So when I went up to the balcony in the second week of January to see this set for the third act and saw this house, which is a slope, a box that would push the voice forward, and with incredible weight . . . I just cried.

It's been rewarding but have there been difficult moments?
At the pre-dress rehearsal the orchestra completely fell to pieces, because, you know, they are a wonderful orchestra with a great conductor who has simply no time to be a music director as he is at the Kirov. Everything is a special occasion for Valery [Gergiev], and it usually is when he conducts, but he won't put anything permanent into the ground, so the orchestra are under pressure and things started falling apart. So I had to stop a couple of times and say, 'What do you think you are doing here? A singer gets faster, slower, and your ensemble gets ninth-rate. We have to start working together.'

A day later, Simon is now feeling well enough to turn up briefly at a conference arranged around *Tristan und Isolde* by the Nexus Institute, on the theme of 'Love and Death'. On a panel with the Wagner scholar Bryan Magee, director Pierre Audi and composer Robin Holloway, Rattle dazzles three hundred assorted philosophers, academics, cultural historians and intense members of the Dutch public with a devastatingly simple explanation of the *Tristan* chord and some further thoughts on the opera:

Wagner said, 'I realize I have gone beyond the limits of the permissible.' When you rehearse this for days you realize that at the end of the day someone's going to get hurt – usually the stage director, I'm glad to say. The puzzle is how did a man who had so little natural talent, because – let's be frank – he did not come into the world with great gifts . . . [*Slight frisson and shuffling in the audience can be heard at this point.*] What he had was genius. Was there another genius in the world of music with so little natural talent? I wonder. He was one of the great magpies. If you know *Walküre* – well, it's a shock to listen to the Liszt *Faust Symphony* and to hear how much Wagner just stole from it. I've just had the luck to be doing Berlioz's *Romeo and Juliet*: Wagner went to three performances and asked for the score and, boy, can you hear it.

What is fascinating is that the other composers felt rather honoured to be stolen from, because they felt Wagner was in another class, rather like golfers feel about Tiger Woods. He was able to take this material and turn it into something extraordinary . . .

Tonality in this piece is the love that dares not speak its name. It is there in the background at the beginning in the famous chord, which does not resolve until four hours later.

Meanwhile the British critics have been critical as ever of the casting of Rattle's operas, but unanimous in their praise of his work with the orchestra. Richard Fairman in the *Financial Times* catches the mood well:

One has to sympathize with monarchs through the ages. Once the heir-in-waiting comes of age, everything he does hogs the limelight until the day he takes possession of the crown himself. The media – today's courtiers – were out in force to witness this event prior to the next coronation in the world of music . . . It seems for ever since Rattle's appointment as chief conductor and artistic director of the Berlin Philharmonic was announced. But there is still another year to go until he takes up the post. In the interim the big question is whether he will be accepted in the all-important German repertory . . . [After *Parsifal*] the warm glow of the orchestral sound was rekindled and this time Rattle showed a firmer grasp of how to pace the long paragraphs that make up a four-hour Wagner opera . . . His command of Wagner is now idiomatic and in its own way thoroughly satisfying.

And Hugh Canning in *The Sunday Times* agreed that 'the musical results are revelatory . . . The music breathes and pulsates with a spellbinding inner tension that is exquisitely pleasurable and simultaneously painful.'

What does a conductor do today? Is conducting in crisis? Some would have us believe so. In January 2001, just as Rattle was preparing *Tristan*, Richard Morrison wrote in *The Times*:

Where have all the monstrous maestros gone? I mean those craggy, charismatic, terrifying conductors who ruled their orchestras like despots and

conjured up performances that struck one like thunderbolts . . . Top orchestras don't want conductors who will frighten the horses, or their blue-rinse
clientele . . . This is like offering Diet Coke to those accustomed to swilling
vintage champagne . . . It is said that the New York Philharmonic, spurned
by one jet-setter, Daniel Barenboim, is now raising a sum adjacent to the
gross national product of Denmark to hire another, the preposterously self-
important Lorin Maazel . . .

Luckily, in Britain our musical institutions are so impoverished that they
are compelled to book conductors who are either too young or too quirky
to interest America. The result is nearly all gain. With Paul Daniel in electrifying form at ENO, the thrusting Tony Pappano expected to hit Covent
Garden like a whirlwind, the twenty-eight-year-old Vladimir Jurowski
about to inject some Russian fizz into Glyndebourne, and free spirits like
Mark Elder, Yan Pascal Tortelier and Sakari Oramo in charge of our
leading regional orchestras, there is a buzz about top-level British
music-making at present which seems quite absent across the Atlantic.

Meanwhile Simon Rattle, the man who revolutionized British orchestral
life, must now attempt to instil the same visionary nerve in the proudest
orchestra of them all, the Berlin Philharmonic. But will such boldness
appeal to German audiences? Or will the iron rule of classical music life –
the higher you rise, the duller you get – stifle even Rattle's spirit?

It would be terrible if it did. He is one of the few world-class conductors
around who puts Miss Jean Brodie's celebrated maxim – 'safety does not
come first' – at the heart of his music-making. If the system forces even him
to compromise, one feels, we really would have to write the obituary of the
symphony orchestra.

What is actually changing is the idea of what a conductor should be. It
is true that Rattle believes that the autocratic idea of a conductor has had
its day. But maybe it was always overstated. In his biography of Herbert
von Karajan, Richard Osborne contradicts cliché by writing of Karajan
as an enabler rather than an autocrat, quoting opinions from the Berlin
Philharmonic that what he was doing essentially was enabling the superb
players of the BPO who understand their tradition to play within that
tradition. This is something Rattle acknowledges (see p. 26). If you
accept the tradition as something that should not be fundamentally
altered, that stance is fine. But if you believe, as Rattle does, that tradition is something that needs to be moved on and challenged, it is not so
easy.

There is a basic contradiction here. Rattle, as he explained in chapter
1, wants musical change by consensus. But the whole idea of a

conductor, it can be argued, is that of one person telling a hundred other people what to do. There are different schools of thought as to whether it's better if you make them *want* to do it, or whether the result is the same whether they want to or not. No contest, surely: we have all seen sullen orchestras, reluctant orchestras, rebellious orchestras, and they are not pretty sights. For someone who wants change as much as Simon Rattle does in the way orchestras play, co-operation is a necessary, basic, given. And he acquires that co-operation through a combination of emotional passion, which inspires complete trust, and a technical ability, which commands complete respect.

> SIMON RATTLE As I get older I'm getting more selfish, and part of selfishness is knowing what you must learn now. This is a time for me to be stretched in every possible direction and for me not to have it too easy. Part of the job is to balance continuity and revolution. But I shall keep on the places where I can do things on the highest level because I am so spoilt: the Age of Enlightenment, the Vienna Philharmonic. If I am to do new music it would be with the Berlin players or the BCMG.
>
> I don't mind a fight now, much less than I did, and I have enough confidence now to say, 'Well, I'm sorry I'm wrong,' or 'Help me . . . '

Rattle will undoubtedly have some of those fights on his hands in Berlin. But at least he and the orchestra are coming at the situation from an attitude where music comes first, even though there will be disagreements. One insider I talked to contrasted the situation in Berlin, where money is short and priorities are stretched, with the situation in Munich, 'where you have x and y and z, all just shovelling the money into their own pockets and not caring what the artistic end result is'. An exaggeration, of course, but it is the inability of some sectors of the classical-music business to see that things are changing radically that leads to problems. The best conductors think it an advantage that fewer records are made. Esa-Pekka Salonen is on record as saying that the crisis in the CD industry was a good thing, because it brought people to their senses and stopped the vanity of conductors recording simply because they wanted to make records.

The point about a conductor, as Rattle says so often, is that he is not the person who does it. The players do it, so it is a challenge to the conductor to bring about change. The conductor must be able to hear more, listen more, perceive more, challenge more. As Gunther Schuller once defined it, 'Conducting a large orchestra is an impressive feat that simultaneously requires the intake of the whole musical *Gestalt* and the analytical decomposition of the orchestral sound into its components.' A report of German research into the effects of auditory attention in conductors, pianists and non-musicians in *Nature* in February 2001 revealed that conductors were able to perceive random sounds across a wider arc of listening than others, because their brains and ears had been highly trained. Or, as the scientists put it, 'Experienced professional conductors develop enhanced auditory localization mechanisms in peripheral space.' The tests were based on those used to show how blind people identify the place where sounds are coming from. The logical conclusion was that training and long experience do enable people to develop different brain mechanisms: 'Improved learning-induced use of spectral cues generated by the head and outer ears and analysed by the auditory cortex might underlie the localization advantage enjoyed by conductors.'

There have been very few serious analyses of the role of a conductor. There is one in Elias Canetti's book *Crowds and Power* which emphasizes the magical, distancing power of the conductor as controller: 'He has the power of life and death over the voices of the instruments; one long silent will speak again at his command. The willingness of the orchestra members to obey him makes it possible for the conductor to transform them into a unit, which he then embodies.' Canetti suggests that if a conductor were to turn round during a performance, that spell would be broken. (When Richard Osborne put this point to Karajan, he said that on the contrary the most popular seats in the Philharmonie in Berlin were those facing the conductor, i.e. him.) It is a somewhat romantic concept: 'His eyes hold the whole orchestra. Every player feels that the conductor sees him personally, and still more hears him. At any given moment he knows precisely what each player should be doing. His attention is everywhere at once . . . he is inside the mind of every player.' That could apply to Karajan or Rattle at their best, for the conductor is first and foremost a communicator and the audience is ineluctably drawn into that communication. But the method of that communication is changing. He does not yearn for control in the same way as Toscanini, who is supposed to have ranted at some brass-players who messed up the end of a symphony for him: 'I hide my head in shame . . . I can live no more. But you . . . you will sleep with your wife tonight as if nothing had happened.'

There are different sorts of conducting, and different ways of relating to the *Zeitgeist*. Beecham is supposed to have said, 'Get the best players, pay them well, and then conducting is not so difficult.' Audiences loved him because he appeared to make music-making spontaneous, fun and easy. A conductor such as Carlos Kleiber can persuade you that his performance is the only possible one for the length of time it takes. It seems to stand outside time, miraculously. A conductor of talent can nudge a performing style one way or the other, and may have a modest influence on how others perform. A real maverick such as Nikolaus Harnoncourt will argue against the taste of the times and may then change it. A conductor of little talent in tune with the temper of the times can pick up the mannerisms and nuances of current fashion and work with them quite effectively, but won't change anything. But a conductor of real genius who is also in tune with the temper of the times can change performing tradition quite decisively – and this is what Simon Rattle is now. His influence is already radical, and can only become more so as he moves to Berlin.

Fifteen years ago Rattle was clear why he was a conductor:

> SIMON RATTLE I could give you any number of untrue answers as to why I conduct, but the real answer is quite simple, I think. It's to do with the fact that I was never happy as a solitary musician, just doing my own thing. That very awful business of being alone with a recalcitrant instrument just wasn't for me. So it had to be with other people, and things like my first blinding experience with Mahler 2 just told me, 'That's what I want to do, to make all that happen.' And also, let's face it, compared with violinists or pianists or whoever, conductors do have some of the best repertory there is.

Fortunately for the power of music, you cannot encapsulate in words what makes Simon Rattle a great conductor. Having observed him at work on and off for what is now a quarter of a century, since he conducted at the Dartington Summer School of Music while I pushed pianos around and put up music stands, I still find it difficult to explain what makes his music-making work at such a high level. Sometimes, more often in the past than now, some things work and some things just misfire. You can observe the sharpness of detail, the attention to both short-term nuance and long-term phrasing, the rhythmic spring and melodic flow ... but on top of all that there is the indefinable quality which makes the listener feel that Rattle has penetrated right to the heart of a piece of music, and the emotional response so many have experienced in a Rattle performance which just makes you feel glad to be alive (as Matthew Rye wrote of his Mozart symphonies with the Orchestra of

the Age of Enlightenment in June 2001, his energy generates 'an
adrenaline-pumping sense of sheer joy . . . an inspirational concert').

The aspect the audience never sees, though it is crucial to his success, is
his total commitment to the whole process behind the performance, not
just what he does on the night. He has a long-term vision of where he,
and the music, and the players are going; he has short-term patience for
all the tiniest details, both musical and logistical. He has inexhaustible
energy and appetite for rehearsal: you will never find him, like some
conductors, skipping rehearsals because he simply can't be bothered and
feels it will be all right on the night. He learns continually, and drives
himself, sometimes too hard, as the *Tristan* experience showed. The rest,
what he regards as the inessentials, he will push aside, and that is where
you can justifiably use the word 'ruthless'. There is not an ounce of
sentimentality in that. He knows that if he is bound by friendship, a
purely musical decision may be more difficult for him. Perhaps this is
why, while he makes acquaintances with complete ease, he does not
make close friends in the profession easily.

He has a profound but constantly developing musical understanding,
picking up new stylistic ideas and learning from other musicians, 'as a
sponge absorbs water', in John Carewe's words. Then, which is even
rarer, he makes those ideas totally his own. One other factor in his success, which it is easy to underestimate, is his instinctive understanding of
planning a good programme. Look through the eighteen years of Rattle's
Birmingham programmes recorded in chapters 5 and 8. He knows how
to make pieces of music add up to more than the sum of their parts, and
that is also true of every performance he gives.

In retrospect, and rationalizing in the way it is too easy for an observer
to do, the trajectory of Rattle's development is very clear:

- an almost chaotic level of activity and growth until 1980, trying
  everything in sight;
- a steadier development with the CBSO through the 1980s, acquiring
  responsibilities;
- a self-exploring new strand of adventures starting from 1987 after the
  débuts with Berlin and the OAE;
- the long-term development of *Towards the Millennium* and the building
  of Symphony Hall;
- a big emotional dip in the mid-1990s, his early mid-life crisis as he
  divorced (it never for a moment affected the professionalism of his
  performances, but it did affect his psyche);

- after 1996 and remarriage, superb tours in 1997 with the Vienna Philharmonic and OAE, and the triumphant climax of the CBSO relationship in 1998;
- a new period of glorious experimentation in 1998–2001, maximizing variety from Rameau to Ellington;
- the big challenge of Berlin 2002 – in musical terms, the second marriage; but now the stakes are even higher.

The handover is now complete. At the traditional private rehearsal during his final Salzburg Easter Festival in 2002, Claudio Abbado spoke briefly but warmly to the audience; as reported by Andrew Clark in the *Financial Times* he said 'I'm glad Simon is taking over and I'm convinced he will usher in a great new era'. In April and May 2002 Abbado conducted his final concerts as music director of the Berlin Philharmonic (at his own request, he will not return in Rattle's first season but will do so later). In Berlin, he gave a quirky programme bringing together Shostakovich's two film scores for *King Lear* with Brahms and Mahler, then in Vienna's Musikverein during May, Mahler songs, Schoenberg, and the following night his farewell Mahler Seventh. At exactly the same time, in Vienna on adjacent days, Rattle was completing his own Beethoven cycle with the Vienna Philharmonic. Rattle's Beethoven Ninth was cheered to the rafters by the Vienna audience; Abbado's farewell to his Berlin orchestra was even more emotional, with repeated calls for the conductor to return alone to a platform strewn with flowers (see p. 20).

So the wheel has turned and Rattle's big challenge begins. How much of a risk is it for him to take on the Berlin Philharmonic? I received several interestingly different answers to that question from some of the people I interviewed for this book:

ELMAR WEINGARTEN I don't know if it's a big risk but it is a risk, because Simon is a really British conductor and the orchestra is really very, very German. I want to stress I value both things highly, but seeing them come together will be fascinating. German musicians generally tend to be ploughing deep into whatever they play, very seriously, and the thing I find about British conductors, whether it's Colin Davis or Roger Norrington, is that they enjoy themselves much more when they make music, and Simon has a wonderful ironic distance in some things he does – when he does Haydn or Rameau the music sparkles with wit. I don't mean he distances himself, but he lets the music dance and enjoys listening to it.

JOHN DRUMMOND Simon is just as used to getting his own way as Claudio. He'll have a honeymoon period, because it's a honeymoon period for the city of Berlin. Then he will have to think really hard about how difficult he wants to be. Ohnesorg will be a great asset; he's a really good man and I think they'll get on very well.

It's a very proud orchestra. It's proud of its tradition, its reputation; it's particularly proud of Berlin's role in German culture, the whole business of the city reviving. It sees itself as absolutely central to the life of Berlin, and in a way that no orchestra in London, or Paris or New York could possibly feel.

HANS LANDESMANN I don't think it's a risk from the artistic point of view. It's always a huge challenge, to take on Berlin or one of the major orchestras. But I think it's a risk whether he can cope with all these political forces, the whole culture of Berlin's situation, the funding problems, the Berlin opera question and all that. It needs somebody very smart and astute like Simon to be above the fray, not get involved in the intrigues and to say, as he does, 'Well, this is what I want: take it or leave it.'

Claudio enlarged his repertory quite a lot in the Berlin years, but Simon can bring a lot of repertory that Claudio never touched. He wasn't a Strauss enthusiast but Simon is. And Claudio did a particular sort of contemporary music: he grew up with the Second Viennese School and everything that followed from that, but Simon has a much wider view from Gershwin to Duke Ellington, which is fine. I could never imagine Claudio doing *Porgy and Bess*! I think there is a lot Simon can bring in. In playing style I don't see them as total opposites: they are both very practical and of course every conductor has his own style but they belong in the same stylistic world. It wouldn't be like Simon taking over from, say, Muti.

The other thing the orchestra must do is to widen their range of conductors and I would think to discontinue some of the work with conductors who don't really fit. The roster of conductors must be changed and modernized, naming no names.

IMOGEN COOPER Whether it's risky I would not say, but I'm sure he will take some risks. Berlin is changing so much, he's going to be working in a city which is not Furtwängler's city any more. The values will be different; for all they're a rich orchestra there will be commercial pressures, and he's an Englishman learning German, which matters there. On the other hand he is an enormously popular appointment with the people who matter, the musicians.

STEPHEN JOHNS The politics in Berlin make the Royal Opera House look like a tea party; the situation is not at all settled. If there's an expectation that Simon will programme standard fare, then there will be many surprises. Simon will have his own agenda for development, and this will undoubtedly be a challenge for an orchestra that has such a life and power and identity of its own. This synthesis of talents is going to make for a musically explosive combination.

JOHN CAREWE The appointment of Simon to the Berlin Philharmonic is the best thing that has happened to the musical profession in fifty years. It's a signal to all young conductors that this is not about ego and not about a million dollars. The Maazels and whoever may still be earning that money, but somehow they've all been swept to the side in terms of what is going on that is interesting and musically worthwhile. I don't think I'm being romantic in believing that it will bring a sea change in music.

I never thought of it as a risk at all. They're lucky. They faced a junction in the road and in my view if they had chosen any other conductor they would have signalled that they were just another good orchestra and that they were content with that. By choosing Simon they are going to be the flagship for performance worldwide for many, many years. Because everything Simon does is a catalyst, wherever he goes things change for the better: the city, musical education, the other arts. This is really powerful. He's forty-six. You go to Berlin for life. They could have thirty-five, forty years! Though he would be the first to recognize if he got beyond the point of no return. He's not the sort of person to hang on in a situation like that.

On 19 June 2002 it was announced that Deutsche Bank would be the sponsors of the Berlin Philharmonic for a three-year period. The establishment of the Stiftung was bearing fruit and Rattle's ambitious plans for a major educational project for the orchestra could begin to be funded. So the story of Rattle in Berlin is beginning, and it is safe to predict that it will turn out to be a vital part of the history of the Symphony Orchestra, as it faces the challenge of the twenty-first century.

Postscript

When Simon Rattle saw his picture on the cover of this book, he suddenly said,

Oh no, that's the other man, isn't it? It's the unreal one. I've felt him more and more over the last year and a half. I utterly don't believe in him. The only way you can sanely cope is to think of it being somebody else, because it has nothing to do with any real person. Not the reputation, not the stories, the rumours, the nothing, neither the good or bad.

In my life as the other guy I see some pretty awful things. I went to the Lucerne Festival and I said, 'I really don't want to play for these people.' They don't know what they are listening to, they don't care, they are just here for the social event. You can't buy tickets for those concerts even on day one of booking because all the tickets have gone to hotels. I want to drive that audience away, I'm sorry. I suppose I've spent a protected life playing in Birmingham, with the Age of Enlightenment, for people who want to listen.

Aren't we protected because our post-war generation was brought up to value the arts?
We grew up in a very enlightened time, didn't we, when everyone believed this activity – the arts, music, education – should be available to all. We'll end up on our Zimmer frames, chanting, 'Jennie Lee, Jennie Lee,' and no one will have a clue what we're talking about. And that has really been under threat now. But the tide will turn again, because in spite of all the Roger Scrutons and people who fulminate in this really snobbish way against the availability of art, the real creative people know there are no boundaries and demarcation lines between different art forms and different types of music – there was no division for Schubert and there is none today for Tom Adès or Ligeti or Yo Yo Ma.

And have we had it too easy? Have we been tested?
We haven't been tested by living through world conflicts, maybe, but life tests people in a big way and you have to come to terms with that. One can't imagine how they did face it. I mean, I was so grateful that in the last year I was able to talk to my father about the wartime. He had really thought he shouldn't say anything about it, he didn't want to, but I thought, 'No, this is impossible. I can see him dying before my eyes, even though I don't want to admit that, and I must find out what happened, just the chronology of it all.' Just to have a vague idea of what he had gone through.

To know Candace's father – he's in his seventies now – to know a black man from Virginia who lived under the constant fear of being lynched, or seeing Candace's birth certificate with 'C' next to her name, just to make sure they knew this was a coloured person . . . But surely we also have to think that the huge global conflicts of the last century were extraordinary occurrences, that they were not the norm, just because our parents and grandparents lived through them. Terrible things happened, and we find it very difficult to bond with that unless someone opens the door personally for us. I'm thinking very personally now, but when Rudi Schwarz was telling me of his experiences [in concentration camp] I simply couldn't take it all in, even though the door was open. It was obviously very important for him to share that, but I realize that, although I don't think I've forgotten a single word he said, it took a very long time for my psyche to accept it.

And what about everything you've been through, personally?
There was an unusually poetic thing Karajan said: 'It's not how the bird sings naturally; it's how the bird keeps singing when life has attacked it.' I'm paraphrasing, but that was the thought. It's how you do it, not when it's easy, but with death and disease and divorce and whatever surrounds you. That is the real test.

So what is the real you about?
I couldn't have said this to you before because, you know, what's a good northern boy like me doing being so pretentious, but what this is about is joy. It's a celebration, and saying that you are not alone. And if I've got anything to bring it's about joy. I know it may be problematical for some people, but that's all I've got to offer.

Maybe people invent this other you, the cliché conductor, because they don't know you . . .
Maybe they don't believe that what they see is all there is! Why do people suppose, just because of course there are great mythic wonderful monsters in this field, that we all have to be like them? I am not a workaholic. I work very hard but I also want to live. At the end of it all, the music is about life, not the other way round, and as time goes on the balance gets better. When I arrived for *Tristan*, Gabby – who I had never met – admitted she was saying to herself, 'Oh God, it's going to be another of these star conductors and terrible bullshit, and I'm going to have to behave like a diva . . . '

I find myself honestly bewildered. I wasn't brought up like that and I don't see any reason why anyone who isn't clinically insane should behave like that, though of course by the very nature of this job some people are and do. And you realize that all around you myths are being created. There is something mythic about people's gifts when some people can do things that other people can't, but that doesn't mean there's something abnormal about them. Cecilia Bartoli: when you come across someone with as many gifts as her, anything could happen, but she's actually completely normal, though a lot of the stuff around her is definitely not . . .

Surely your gifts are not a burden to you because you've made so much of them . . .
It's very hard to do. There is almost no moment when I feel confident. OK, I must be completely honest and say that every now and then you feel, 'Yes, we did as well as we could; it worked as well as we could expect.' But just this business of being sick was so good for me, I'm thinking of staying sick

a bit longer. I thought to myself on that first night, Claudio Abbado, nearly dead, conducted this opera with no stomach, having just had some shot to get him through it . . . You know, come on!

But what I meant about your gifts is . . .
I fucking avoided it again, didn't I?

Yes.
As ever . . .

After that last conversation, I thought of these little-known lines of W. H. Auden, which he drafted for Britten's *Hymn to St Cecilia*, but then in the end didn't use. I'd come across them in a book of essays for Donald Mitchell a few years ago and they had always resonated at the back of my mind.* Perhaps they say something of what Simon Rattle had in mind about joy and not being alone . . .

> Go forth, O Daughter of Song; go towards life.
> O gather the societies together; gather them to the dance.
> For what the heart-beat of a mother promises her
>   unborn child, your rhythm shall repeat: that
>   the otherness of the universe is not against us.
> And your harmony is a re-assurance: that, though
>   we are always solitary, we are never abandoned . . .
>
> O gather the finite creatures into that choir;
>   through whom the Uninhibited rejoices for ever.
> That its determined moment of gladness may possess
>   each tiny resonant structure,
> Its life be echo, and its nature praise . . .

* W. H. Auden, from the first draft of the *Hymn to St Cecilia*, 1940: see Edward Mendelson, 'The Making of Auden's *Hymn for St Cecilia's Day*', in Philip Reed (ed.), *On Mahler and Britten, Essays for Donald Mitchell on his Seventieth Birthday* (The Boydell Press/ Britten–Pears Library, 1995) reprinted with the permission of the Estate of W. H. Auden.

Discography

This list includes all Simon Rattle's commercial recordings, not all of which are currently available. The record numbers are for a recently available issue. The label is EMI except where listed.

Thomas Adès *Asyla, Concerto Conciso, These Premises Are Alarmed, Chamber Symphony*
City of Birmingham Symphony Orchestra, Birmingham Contemporary Music Group, Simon Rattle, Thomas Adès
CDC 556818 2; rec. Symphony Hall, Birmingham, August 1998

John Adams *Harmonielehre, The Chairman Dances, Tromba Lontana, Short Ride in a Fast Machine*
City of Birmingham Symphony Orchestra, Simon Rattle
CDC 555051 2; rec. Symphony Hall, Birmingham, July and September 1993

Bartók Piano Concertos nos. 1, 2 and 3
Peter Donohoe, City of Birmingham Symphony Orchestra, Simon Rattle
CDC 754871 2; rec. Warwick Arts Centre, October 1990 and Symphony Hall, Birmingham, October 1992

Bartók Violin Concerto no. 2
Iona Brown, City of Birmingham Symphony Orchestra, Simon Rattle
Argo ZRG 936; rec. Walthamstow Town Hall, August 1980

Bartók Violin Concerto no. 2, Rhapsodies nos. 1 and 2
Kyung-Wha Chung, City of Birmingham Symphony Orchestra, Simon Rattle
CDC 754211 2; rec. Cheltenham Town Hall, July 1990 and Symphony Hall, Birmingham, May/June 1992

Bartók *Concerto for Orchestra, The Miraculous Mandarin*
City of Birmingham Symphony Orchestra, Simon Rattle
CDC 555094 2; rec. Symphony Hall, Birmingham, October 1992 and April 1993

Bartók Sonata for two pianos and percussion, Concerto for two pianos, percussion and orchestra

Katia and Marielle Labèque, Sylvio Gualda, Jean-Pierre Drouet, City of
Birmingham Symphony Orchestra, Simon Rattle
CDC 747446 2; rec. Warwick Arts Centre, September 1985

Beethoven Piano Concertos nos. 1 and 2
Lars Vogt, City of Birmingham Symphony Orchestra, Simon Rattle
CDC 556179 2; rec. Warwick Arts Centre, October 1995

Beethoven Piano Concertos nos. 1 and 4
Philips 462 782–2
Piano Concertos nos. 2 and 3
Philips 462 783–2
Piano Concerto no. 5
Alfred Brendel, Vienna Philharmonic Orchestra
Philips 468 666–2; rec. Musikverein, Vienna, December 1997 and February/
December 1998

Beethoven Symphony no. 5
Brahms Violin Concerto
Kyung-Wha Chung, Vienna Philharmonic Orchestra
CDC 557165 2; rec. Musikverein, Vienna, December 2000

Berg Suite: *Lulu*
Schoenberg *Five Orchestral Pieces*, op. 16
Webern Six Pieces, op. 6
Arleen Augér, City of Birmingham Symphony Orchestra, Simon Rattle
CDC 749857 2; rec. Warwick Arts Centre, December 1987 and April 1988

Bernstein *Wonderful Town*
Kim Criswell, Audra McDonald, Thomas Hampson, London Voices,
Birmingham Contemporary Music Group, Simon Rattle
CDC 556753 2; rec. EMI Abbey Road Studios, June 1998

Brahms Piano Concerto no. 1, Three Intermezzi, op. 117
Leif Ove Andsnes, City of Birmingham Symphony Orchestra, Simon Rattle
CDC 556583 2; rec. Symphony Hall, Birmingham, September 1997

Brahms/Schoenberg Piano Quartet in G minor
City of Birmingham Symphony Orchestra, Simon Rattle
CDC 74730S 1; rec. Snape Maltings, June 1984

Britten Cello Symphony
Elgar Cello Concerto
Truls Mørk, City of Birmingham Symphony Orchestra, Simon Rattle
Virgin Classics VC 545 356 2; rec. Symphony Hall, Birmingham, March/April
1999

Britten *Diversions* for piano (left hand) and orchestra, *Sinfonia da Requiem,
Ballad of Heroes, Suite on English Folk Tunes, 'A time there was . . . ', Scottish
Ballad, Quatre Chansons Françaises, Canadian Carnival, Young Apollo, Praise
We Great Men, An American Overture, The Building of the House, Occasional
Overture*
Jill Gomez, Robert Tear, Philip Fowke, Peter Donohoe, City of Birmingham
Symphony Chorus and Orchestra, Simon Rattle
British Composers CDS 754270 2 (2CD); rec. Warwick Arts Centre, May 1984
and July 1990; Cheltenham Town Hall, April 1982

Britten *Sinfonia da Requiem*
Shostakovich Symphony no. 10
City of Birmingham Symphony Orchestra, Philharmonia Orchestra, Simon
Rattle
Studio + Plus CDM 764870 2; rec. Warwick Arts Centre, May 1984; EMI Abbey
Road Studios, April 1985

Britten *War Requiem*
Elisabeth Söderström, Robert Tear, Thomas Allen, Boys of Christ Church
Cathedral Oxford, City of Birmingham Symphony Chorus and Orchestra,
Simon Rattle
CDS 747034 8 (2CD); rec. Great Hall, Birmingham University, February and
March 1983

Britten *The Young Person's Guide to the Orchestra*
City of Birmingham Symphony Orchestra, Simon Rattle
CDC 555394 2; rec. Symphony Hall, Birmingham, January 1995

Bruckner Symphony no. 7
City of Birmingham Symphony Orchestra, Simon Rattle
CDC 556425 2; rec. Symphony Hall, Birmingham, September 1996

Debussy *Images, Jeux*, Incidental Music for *King Lear*
City of Birmingham Symphony Orchestra, Simon Rattle
CDC 749947 2; rec. Warwick Arts Centre, February 1989

Patrick Doyle *Henry V*: original soundtrack recording
City of Birmingham Symphony Orchestra, Simon Rattle
CDC 749919 2; rec. CTS Studios, Wembley

Elgar Violin Concerto
Vaughan Williams *The Lark Ascending*
Kennedy, City of Birmingham Symphony Orchestra, Simon Rattle
CDC 556413 2; rec. Symphony Hall, Birmingham, July 1997

Elgar *Enigma Variations, Falstaff, Grania and Diarmid*: Incidental Music and Funeral March
City of Birmingham Symphony Orchestra, Simon Rattle
British Composers CDC 555001 2; rec. Warwick Arts Centre, April 1992 and Symphony Hall, Birmingham, August 1993

Elgar *The Dream of Gerontius*
Janet Baker, John Mitchinson, John Shirley-Quirk, City of Birmingham Symphony Chorus and Orchestra, Simon Rattle
CDS 749549 2 (2CD); rec. Great Hall, Birmingham University, September 1986

Classic Ellington
Duke Ellington arr. Luther Henderson
Lena Horne, Clark Terry, Bobby Watson, Joshua Redman, Joe Lovano, Regina Carter, Geri Allen, Peter Washington, Lewis Nash, City of Birmingham Symphony Orchestra, Simon Rattle
CDC 557014 2; rec. Symphony Hall, Birmingham, November 1999

Falla *El retablo de maese pedro*, *Psyche*, Concerto for harpsichord and five instruments
Jennifer Smith, Alexander Oliver, Peter Knapp, John Constable, London Sinfonietta, Simon Rattle
Argo ZRG 921/Decca 433 908-2; rec. Rosslyn Hill Chapel, London, April 1975

Gershwin Piano Concerto, *Rhapsody in Blue*, Song-Book
Peter Donohoe, City of Birmingham Symphony Orchestra, Simon Rattle
CDC 754280 2; rec. Warwick Arts Centre, October 1990, and CTS Studios, Wembley, December 1986, January 1987

Gershwin *Porgy and Bess*
Willard White, Cynthia Haymon, Damon Evans, Cynthia Clarey, Harolyn Blackwell, Bruce Hubbard, Marietta Simpson, Gregg Baker, The Glyndebourne Chorus, London Philharmonic Orchestra, Simon Rattle
CDS 556220 2 (3CD); rec. EMI Abbey Road Studios, February 1988

Goldschmidt *Ciaconna Sinfonica*, Passacaglia Op 4
City of Birmingham Symphony Orchestra, Simon Rattle
Decca 452 599 2; rec. Symphony Hall, Birmingham, July 1995

In a Nutshell
Grainger *In a Nutshell, The Warriors, Train Music, Pagodes, Country Gardens*, etc.
CDC 556412 2; rec. Symphony Hall, Birmingham, December 1996

Grieg Piano Concerto
Schumann Piano Concerto
Lars Vogt, City of Birmingham Symphony Orchestra, Simon Rattle
CDC 754746 2; rec. Warwick Arts Centre, April 1992

Haydn Symphonies nos. 22 (*The Philosopher*), 86 and 102
City of Birmingham Symphony Orchestra, Simon Rattle
CDC 555509 2; rec. Symphony Hall, Birmingham, July, October and December 1994

Haydn Symphonies nos. 60 (*Il distratto*), 70 and 90
City of Birmingham Symphony Orchestra, Simon Rattle
CDC 754297 2; rec. Warwick Arts Centre, October and December 1990

Haydn *The Creation* (in English)
Arleen Augér, Philip Langridge, David Thomas, City of Birmingham Symphony
Chorus and Orchestra, Simon Rattle
CDS 754159 2 (2CD); rec. Warwick Arts Centre, March/April 1990

Henze Symphony no. 7, *Barcarola per grande orchestra*
City of Birmingham Symphony Orchestra, Simon Rattle
CDC 754762 2; rec. (live) Symphony Hall, Birmingham, May 1992

Holst *The Planets*
Janáček *Sinfonietta*
Philharmonia Orchestra, Simon Rattle
CDM 764740 2; rec. Kingsway Hall, London, December 1980 and November 1982

Janáček *The Cunning Little Vixen* (in English)
Lilian Watson, Diana Montague, Thomas Allen, Gwynne Howell, Robert Tear,
Nicholas Folwell, Chorus and Orchestra of the Royal Opera House Covent
Garden, Simon Rattle
CDS 754212 2 (2CD); rec. EMI Abbey Road Studios, June 1990

Janáček *Glagolitic Mass, Sinfonietta*
Felicity Palmer, Ameral Gunson, John Mitchinson, Malcolm King, Jane Parker-
Smith, City of Birmingham Symphony Chorus and Orchestra, Simon Rattle
CDM 566980 2; rec. Great Hall, Birmingham University, January 1981

Liszt *A Faust Symphony*
Peter Seiffert, Berlin Philharmonic Orchestra, Simon Rattle
CDC 555220 2; rec. (live) Philharmonie, Berlin, April 1994

Lizst Piano Concerto no. 1
Saint-Saens Piano Concerto no. 2
Cécile Ousset, City of Birmingham Symphony Orchestra, Simon Rattle
CDC 747221; rec. Warwick Arts Centre, March 1982

Mahler Symphony no. 1
City of Birmingham Symphony Orchestra, Simon Rattle
CDC 754647; rec. (live) Symphony Hall, Birmingham, December 1991

Mahler Symphony no. 2 (*Resurrection*)
Arleen Augér, Janet Baker, City of Birmingham Symphony Chorus and
Orchestra, Simon Rattle
CDS 747962 8 (2CD); rec. Watford Town Hall, April, May and June 1986

Mahler Symphony no. 3, Eight songs from *Des Knaben Wunderhorn*
Birgit Remmert, Simon Keenlyside, City of Birmingham Youth Chorus, Ladies
of the City of Birmingham Symphony Chorus, City of Birmingham Symphony
Orchestra, Simon Rattle
CDS 556657 2 (2CD); rec. Symphony Hall, Birmingham, September/October
1997

Mahler Symphony no. 4
Amanda Roocroft, City of Birmingham Symphony Chorus and Orchestra,
Simon Rattle
CDC 556563 2; rec. Symphony Hall, Birmingham, May 1997

Mahler Symphony no. 5
Berlin Philharmonic Orchestra, Simon Rattle
rec. (live) Philharmonie, Berlin, September 2002

Mahler Symphony no. 6
City of Birmingham Symphony Orchestra, Simon Rattle
CDS 754047 2 (2CD); rec. Watford Town Hall, December 1989

Mahler Symphony no. 7
City of Birmingham Symphony Orchestra, Simon Rattle
CDC 754344 2; rec. (live) Snape Maltings, June 1991

Mahler Symphony no. 9
Strauss *Metamorphosen*
Vienna Philharmonic Orchestra, Simon Rattle
CDS 556580 2 (2CD); rec. (live) Musikverein, Vienna, December 1993 (Mahler),
April 1997 (Strauss)

Mahler–Cooke Symphony no. 10
Bournemouth Symphony Orchestra, Simon Rattle
CDC 754406 2; rec. Guildhall, Southampton, June 1980

Mahler–Cooke Symphony no. 10
Berlin Philharmonic Orchestra, Simon Rattle
CDC 556972 2; rec. (live) Philharmonie, Berlin, September 1999

Mahler *Das klagende Lied*
Helena Döse, Alfreda Hodgson, Robert Tear, Sean Rae, City of Birmingham
Symphony Orchestra, Simon Rattle
CDM 566406 2; rec. Town Hall, Birmingham, October 1983 and June 1984

Mahler *Das Lied von der Erde*
Thomas Hampson, Peter Seiffert, City of Birmingham Symphony Orchestra,
Simon Rattle
CDC 556200 2; rec. Warwick Arts Centre, December 1995

Nicholas Maw *Odyssey*
City of Birmingham Symphony Orchestra, Simon Rattle
British Composers CDS 754277 2 (2CD); rec. (live) Town Hall, Birmingham,
October 1990

Maxwell Davies Symphony (no. 1)
Philharmonia, Simon Rattle
Decca HEAD 21; rec. Kingsway Hall, London, August 1978

Messiaen *Turangalîla-Symphonie, Quartet for the End of Time*
Peter Donohoe, Tristan Murail, City of Birmingham Symphony Orchestra,
Simon Rattle, Saschko Gawriloff, Heinz Deinzer, Siegfried Palm,
Aloys Kontarsky
CDS 747463 8 (2CD); rec. Warwick Arts Centre, January/February 1986

Mozart *Così fan tutte*
Hillevi Martinpelto, Alison Hagley, Kurt Streit, Gerald Finley,
Ann Murray, Thomas Allen, Orchestra of the Age of Enlightenment,
Simon Rattle
CDS 556170 2 (3 CD); rec. (live) Symphony Hall, Birmingham, December 1995

Nielsen Symphony no. 4 (*The Inextinguishable*), *Pan and Syrinx*
Sibelius Symphony no. 5
City of Birmingham Symphony Orchestra, Philharmonia Orchestra,
Simon Rattle
CDM 764737 2; rec. Warwick Arts Centre, September 1984, and EMI Abbey
Road Studios, October 1981

Prokofiev Symphony no. 5, *Scythian Suite*
City of Birmingham Symphony Orchestra, Simon Rattle
CDC 754577 2; rec. Symphony Hall, Birmingham, January 1992

Prokofiev Piano Concerto no. 1, *Suggestion diabolique*, op. 4 no. 4
Balakirev *Islamey*
Tchaikovsky Piano Concerto no. 1, Theme and Variations, op. 19 no. 6
Andrei Gavrilov, Philharmonia Orchestra, Riccardo Muti, London
Symphony Orchestra, Simon Rattle
Studio + Plus CDM 764329 2; rec. EMI Abbey Road Studios, July 1977

Rakhmaninov Symphony no. 2
Los Angeles Philharmonic Orchestra, Simon Rattle
Red Line CDR 569828 2; rec. Dorothy Chandler Pavilion, Los Angeles,
January 1984

Rakhmaninov Piano Concerto no. 2, *Rhapsody on a Theme of Paganini*
Cécile Ousset, City of Birmingham Symphony Orchestra, Simon Rattle
CDC 747223; rec. Warwick Arts Centre, May 1984

Ravel Piano Concerto in D, *Pavane pour un infante défunte*
Prokofiev Piano Concerto no. 1, *Romeo and Juliet* (extracts)
Andrei Gavrilov, City of Birmingham Symphony Orchestra, Simon Rattle
CDM 769026; rec. EMI Abbey Road Studios, London, July 1977

Ravel *Chansons madécasses*, *Trois poèmes de Mallarmé*
Felicity Palmer, Nash Ensemble, Simon Rattle
Argo ZRG 834; rec. St John's Smith Square, London, May 1975

Ravel Piano Concertos, *Le tombeau de Couperin* (piano solo)
Cécile Ousset, City of Birmingham Symphony Orchestra,
Simon Rattle
CDC 754158 2; rec. Warwick Arts Centre, April 1990

Ravel *Daphnis et Chloë*, *Boléro*
City of Birmingham Symphony Chorus and Orchestra,
Simon Rattle
Red Line CDR 569830 2; rec. Warwick Arts Centre, December 1990

Ravel *Shéhérazade*, *Alborada del gracioso*, *La vallée des cloches*, *Ma mère l'oye*, *La valse*
Maria Ewing, City of Birmingham Symphony Orchestra, Simon Rattle
CDC 754204 2; rec. Warwick Arts Centre, October 1989 and April 1990

Schoenberg Chamber Symphony no. 1, *Erwartung*, op. 17, *Variations*, op. 31
Phyllis Bryn-Julson, Birmingham Contemporary Music Group, City of
Birmingham Symphony Orchestra, Simon Rattle
CDC 555212 2; rec. Symphony Hall, Birmingham, April and September/October
1993

Schoenberg *Pierrot Lunaire*
Webern Concerto for Nine Instruments, op. 24
Jane Manning, Nash Ensemble
Chandos ABR 1046; rec. BBC Maida Vale Studios, February 1977

Schoenberg *Gurrelieder*
Karita Mattila, Anne Sofie von Otter, Thomas Moser, Philip Langridge, Thomas
Quastoff, Berlin Radio Choir, Leipzig Radio Choir, Ernst Senff Choir, Berlin
Philharmonic Orchestra, Simon Rattle
CDS 557303 (2 CD); rec. Philharmonie, Berlin, September 2001

Shostakovich Symphony no. 4
Britten *Russian Funeral*
City of Birmingham Symphony Orchestra, Simon Rattle
CDC 555476 2; rec. Symphony Hall, Birmingham, July and December 1994

Sibelius Symphony no. 1, *The Oceanides*
City of Birmingham Symphony Orchestra, Simon Rattle
CDM 764119 2; rec. Warwick Arts Centre, December 1984

Sibelius Symphonies nos. 2 and 3
City of Birmingham Symphony Orchestra, Simon Rattle
CDM 764120 2; rec. Warwick Arts Centre, June 1984 and October 1985

Sibelius Symphonies nos. 4 and 6
City of Birmingham Symphony Orchestra, Simon Rattle
CDM 764121 2; rec. Warwick Arts Centre, December 1986

Sibelius Symphony no. 5, Violin Concerto
Nigel Kennedy, City of Birmingham Symphony Orchestra, Simon Rattle
CDC 749717 2; rec. Warwick Arts Centre, February 1987

Sibelius Symphonies nos. 5 and 7, *Scene with Cranes (Kuolema)*, *Night Ride
and Sunrise*
City of Birmingham Symphony Orchestra, Philharmonia Orchestra, Simon Rattle
CDM 764122 2; rec. various, August 1977, October 1981, October 1985

Sibelius Symphonies nos. 1 to 7, *The Oceanides, Scene with Cranes (Kuolema), Night Ride and Sunrise*
City of Birmingham Symphony Orchestra, Philharmonia Orchestra, Simon Rattle
CMS 764118 2 (4CD)

Sibelius Violin Concerto
Tchaikovsky Violin Concerto
Nigel Kennedy, City of Birmingham Symphony Orchestra, Simon Rattle.
London Philharmonic Orchestra, Okko Kamu
CDC 754127 2; rec. Warwick Arts Centre, February 1987

Stravinsky *The Rite of Spring*
National Youth Orchestra, Simon Rattle
ASV CDQ 56031; rec. Goldsmith's College, London, April 1977

Stravinsky *Symphonies of Wind Instruments, Three Japanese Lyrics*
Nash Ensemble, Simon Rattle
Chandos ABR 1048; rec. BBC Maida Vale Studios, February 1977

Stravinsky *The Firebird, Quatre Etudes, Scherzo à la russe*
City of Birmingham Symphony Orchestra, Simon Rattle
CDC 749178 2; rec. Warwick Arts Centre, October 1987

Stravinsky *Petrushka* (1947 version), *Symphony in Three Movements*
Peter Donohoe, Elaine Donohoe, Robert Johnstone, City of Birmingham Symphony Orchestra, Simon Rattle
CDC 749053 2; rec. Warwick Arts Centre, October 1986

Stravinsky *Pulcinella*
Weill *The Seven Deadly Sins*
Northern Sinfonia; Elise Ross, Anthony Rolfe Johnson, Ian Caley, Michael Rippon, John Tomlinson, City of Birmingham Symphony Orchestra, Simon Rattle
CDM 764739 2; rec. Newcastle, March 1977 and January 1978, and Town Hall, Birmingham, September 1982

Stravinsky *The Rite of Spring, Apollon musagète*
City of Birmingham Symphony Orchestra, Simon Rattle
CDC 749636 2; rec. Warwick Arts Centre, December 1987, April 1988

Szymanowski Violin Concertos nos. 1 and 2, Three Paganini Caprices
Thomas Zehetmair, Silke Avenhaus, City of Birmingham Symphony Orchestra, Simon Rattle
CDC 555607 2; rec. Symphony Hall, Birmingham, April 1995

Szymanowski *Stabat Mater, Litany to the Virgin Mary*, Symphony no. 3 (*Song of the Night*)
Elzbieta Szmytka, Florence Quivar, Jon Garrison, John Connell, City of Birmingham Symphony Chorus and Orchestra, Simon Rattle
CDC 555121 2; rec. Symphony Hall, Birmingham, April and October 1993

Szymanowski *King Roger*, Symphony no. 4, op. 60 (*Sinfonia concertante*)
Thomas Hampson, Ryszard Minkiewicz, Elzbieta Szmytka, Philip Langridge, Jadwiga Rappé, Robert Gierlach, Leif Ove Andsnes, City of Birmingham Symphony Chorus, Youth Chorus and Orchestra, Simon Rattle
CDS 556823 2 (2 CD); rec. Symphony Hall, Birmingham, October 1996 and July 1998

Mark-Anthony Turnage *Drowned Out, Momentum, Kai, Three Screaming Popes*
Ulrich Heinen, Birmingham Contemporary Music Group, City of Birmingham Symphony Orchestra, Simon Rattle
British Composers CDC 555091 2; rec. Symphony Hall, Birmingham, January 1992, June and August 1993, May 1994

Vaughan Williams *Songs of Travel, On Wenlock Edge*
Elgar Songs with orchestra
Butterworth *Love Blows as the Wind Blows*
Thomas Allen, Robert Tear, City of Birmingham Symphony Orchestra, Simon Rattle, Vernon Handley
British Composers CDM 764731 2; rec. Town Hall, Birmingham, May 1983 and Civic Hall, Bedworth, November 1979

Walton *Belshazzar's Feast*, Symphony no. 1
Cleveland Orchestra Chorus, City of Birmingham Symphony Chorus and Orchestra, Simon Rattle
CDC 556592 2; rec. Symphony Hall, Birmingham, July and October 1997, and Warwick Arts Centre, October 1990

Walton Cello Concerto
Lynn Harrell, City of Birmingham Symphony Orchestra, Simon Rattle
HMV 574320 2; rec. Warwick Arts Centre, December 1991

Julian Bream
Rodrigo *Concierto de Aranjuez*
Takemitsu *To the Edge of a Dream*
Arnold Guitar Concerto
Julian Bream, City of Birmingham Symphony Orchestra, Simon Rattle
CDC 754661 2; rec. EMI Abbey Road Studios, October 1990 and February 1992

Simon Rattle: The Jazz Album – A Tribute to the Jazz Age
Milhaud, Gershwin, Stravinsky, Bernstein and arrangements for the Paul Whiteman Orchestra *Sweet Sue, Makin' Whoopee, My Blue Heaven*, etc.
Peter Donohoe, Michael Collins, Harvey and the Wallbangers, London Sinfonietta, Simon Rattle
CDC 747991 2; rec. CTS Studios, Wembley, December 1986/January 1987

Simon Rattle: Orchestra
(inc.) Britten *The Young Person's Guide to the Orchestra*
City of Birmingham Symphony Orchestra, Simon Rattle
CDROM 491616 2 VIDEO

Britten *The Young Person's Guide to the Orchestra*
City of Birmingham Symphony Orchestra, Simon Rattle
MVC 491616 3

The Gershwins *Porgy and Bess* (production directed by Trevor Nunn)
Willard White, Cynthia Haymon, Gregg Baker, Cynthia Clarey, Marietta Simpson, Damon Evans, The Glyndebourne Chorus, London Philharmonic Orchestra, Simon Rattle
VHS MVB 491131 3

Index

Figures in italics indicate captions. 'SR' indicates Sir Simon Rattle.

Giulini, Carlo Maria 119, 141, 143, 159,
208, 209, 210, 221, 267
Glasgow: Theatre Royal 100
Glasgow Schools Symphony Orchestra 77
The Glory of Music series 175
Glyndebourne 58, 67, 68, 72, 74, 87, 89–90,
102, 158, 160, 172, 195–203, 216, 217,
221, 222, 226, 256, 284–90, 292, 295,
307, 308, 309, 313, 316
Glyndebourne Touring Company 110
Godowsky, Leopold 58
Java Suite 58
Goebbel, Heiner 260
Goehr, Alexander 77
Eve Dreams in Paradise 149
Little Symphony 76, 90, 188
Goehr, Walter 76, 142
Goldschmidt, Berthold 24, 31, 159, 173,
219
Ciaconna sinfonica 24, 143, 155
Gomez, Jill 166, 186, 277
Goodall, Reginald 135, 313
Grade, Michael 181
Graham-Hall, John 235
Grainger, Percy 173
In a Nutshell suite 131
A Lincolnshire Posy 131
Gramophone magazine 151, 165, 172, 173,
174, 257
Gray, Linda Esther 89
Gray, Stephen 71, 87, 101, 103
Grayson, Barrie 116
Greater London Council 123
Greene, Gordon 66, 224
Greenfield, Edward 132, 190, 200, 289
Greevy, Bernadette 152
Grieg, Edvard 58
Piano Concerto 58
Grier, Christopher 122
Griffiths, Paul 132, 133, 141–2, 189, 267,
287
Griller, Sidney 66
Grimley, Terry 147, 196, 262
Grinke, Frederick (Fred) 66
Grove, John 66
Groves, Sir Charles 57, 62, 72, 100, 138
Gruber, Andrea 236, 270
Gruber, H. K. 180
Frankenstein!! 102, 306
Guardian 24, 36, 94, 132, 148, 155, 190,
194, 266, 267, 289, 290, 297, 302
Gubaidulina, Sofia 16, 306
Offertorium (Violin Concerto) 152, 246,
271, 276
Zeitgestalten 258
Guinness Book of Records 277

Gulbenkian 70
Gummer, John Selwyn 256
Gunson, Ameral 120, 124, 149, 193, 235, 245
Gutman, David 173
Guttridge, Kathleen (SR's paternal grand-
mother) 51
Guttridge, Maggie 51
Guttridge family 51

Haas, Pavel 10
Study for Strings 259
Haenchen, Hartmut 46
Haendel, Ida 124, 139, 269
Haider, Jorg 303
Haitink, Bernard 2, 4, 81, 160, 197, 198,
200, 210, 222
Halgrimson, Amanda 251, 263, 264
Hall, Peter 193, 201, 247–8, 288
Hallé Orchestra 113, 147
Halpert, Marta 303
Halsey, Simon 254, 271
Hampson, Thomas 264, 272, 274
Handel, George Frideric 6, 111, 284, 293
Fireworks Music 63
Messiah 111
Handford, Maurice 86
Hannan, Eileen 127
Harding, Daniel 264, 265
Harewood, George 201
Hargan, Alison 119, 139, 155
Harnoncourt, Nikolaus 4, 6, 40, 44, 160,
165, 200, 267, 296, 299, 319
Harold Holt Ltd 71, 72, 86, 256
Harrell, Lynn 119, 127, 149, 236, 270
Harris, Dinah 193
Harris, Roy: Symphony no. 3 251
Harrison, Max 94
Haydn, Franz Joseph 6, 27–8, 35, 40, 81, 91,
93, 99, 172, 206, 221, 223, 293, 299,
301, 321
The Creation 19, 32, 127, 129, 140, 153,
172
La fedeltà premiata 199
The Seasons 262, 269
Sinfonia concertante for violin, cello, oboe
and bassoon 134
Symphony no. 22 90, 124, 258
Symphony no. 60 89, 119, 140
Symphony no. 70 137, 144, 155
Symphony no. 71 276
Symphony no. 86 in D 89, 245, 251, 271
Symphony no. 88 in G 20, 265
Symphony no. 89 134
Symphony no. 90 in C 32, 148, 155
Symphony no. 91 90
Symphony no. 95 89, 124